Arab Civilization to A.D. 1500

D. M. Dunlop

Longman
Librairie du Liban

LONGMAN GROUP LIMITED
London
Associated companies, branches and representatives throughout the world

LIBRAIRIE DU LIBAN
Immeuble Esseily, Place Riad Solh, Beirut

First published 1971

ISBN 0 582 50273 X

Printed in Great Britain by Butler and Tanner Ltd, Frome and London

Arab background series

Editor: N. A. Ziadeh
American University of Beirut

Contents

Editor's preface

The Arab world has, for some time, been attracting the attention of a growing public throughout the world. The strategic position of the Arab countries, the oil they produce, their sudden emancipation and emergence as independent states, their revolutions and *coups d'état*, have been the special concern of statesmen, politicians, businessmen, scholars and journalists and of equal interest to the general public.

An appreciation of the present-day problems of Arab countries and their immediate neighbours demands a certain knowledge of their geographical and social background; and a knowledge of the main trends of their history—political, cultural and religious—is essential for an understanding of current issues. Arabs had existed long before the advent of Islam in the seventh century A.D., but it was with Islam that they became a world power. Arab civilization, which resulted from the contacts the Arabs had with other peoples and cultures, especially after the creation of this world power, and which reached its height in the ninth, tenth and eleventh centuries, was, for a few centuries that followed, the guiding light of a large part of the world. Its rôle cannot, thus, be ignored.

The Arab Background series will provide the English-speaking, educated reader with a series of books which will clarify the historical past of the Arabs, and analyse their present-day problems. The contributors to the series, who come from many parts of the world, are all specialists in their respective fields. This variety of approach and attitude creates for the English-speaking reader a unique picture of the Arab world.

N. A. ZIADEH

Acknowledgements

We are grateful to the following for permission to reproduce copyright material.

Ernest Benn Ltd for an extract from *Ancient Arabian Poetry* by C. J. Lyall; Basil Blackwell and Mott Ltd for an extract from *The Eclipse of the Abbasid Caliphate* translated by D. S. Margoliouth; Cambridge University Press for an extract from *A Literary History of the Arabs* by R. A. Nicholson.

Foreword

By way of comment on the title it may be asked, Why Arab and not Arabic, or Islamic, or Muslim civilization? Any one of these descriptives might perhaps have served, but 'Arab' (like 'Roman') indicates in a special manner the leading group in the great Empire whose cultural achievements we have to attempt to describe, and has been chosen on that account in preference to 'Arabic' which (like 'Latin') is applicable in the first place simply to the language of the Empire. More than one of the literary works to be mentioned was written in Persian. 'Islamic' and 'Muslim' as religious terms seem less appropriate to a work like the present, in which religion is treated only incidentally.

And here we come to a further consideration. Strictly speaking the title might rather be Chapters, or Aspects of Arab Civilization, for it is apparent that such important fields as religion and law, for example, are not treated specifically, or not treated at all. The reason is that having been informed by Professor Ziadeh that in writing the book I had a perfectly free hand, I have taken this very literally and have dealt only with those aspects of Arab civilization about which I thought that I had something fresh to say. The last chapter on famous women in Islam is an exception. Nearly all the information in this chapter is well enough known, and if not, is readily available elsewhere. In adding it, I have followed the example of Ibn Qutayba.[1]

As regards fields not treated here, the student may safely be directed to the works of such masters as Arthur Jeffery (religion), Joseph Schacht (law), K. A. C. Creswell (architecture) and H. G. Farmer (music). Any non-specialist who attempts to write on these and similar subjects is obliged merely to repeat what the experts have said (a task from which the terms of my brief have, I hope, exempted me) or run the risk of falling into serious error.

In making acknowledgements I have in the first place to thank Professor Nicola A. Ziadeh, who invited me several years ago to contribute the present volume to his series and has patiently awaited its completion. A large share of the typing was undertaken by Miss Carlene Richardson of the Middle East Institute, Columbia University, who rendered yeoman service in pointing out discrepancies in the manuscript, and help was also rendered by Miss Martha Hollins and Miss Lois Mergentime. Much of the revision of the text and checking of references was

[1] See pp. 51–2.

done at St Andrews, and my thanks are due to the University Librarian, Mr MacArthur, for permission to use the Library, and to his staff for their unstinted and expert assistance.

It may be of general interest to mention that these studies can now be pursued at St Andrews with greater facility than ever before, thanks largely to the efforts of Professor A. M. Honeyman in adding very extensively to the University Library's holdings of Arabic books and sets of Orientalist periodicals.

August 1970 D. M. DUNLOP

Chapter 1

The Arabs and the Arab world to 1500

1. Western interest in the Arabs in modern times

In the remote days before the First World War the Arabs did not figure at all prominently among the political and cultural preoccupations of the West. They were well enough known as the principal inhabitants of a number of cities and provinces in the Levant and Mesopotamia (the terms then current for the eastern Mediterranean countries and Iraq), in North Africa, and above all in Arabia itself. Some of these regions still belonged to the Ottoman empire, in particular Syria, Palestine, Iraq and part of Arabia. Others had passed into the hands of European powers, notably Britain and France, who between them controlled Egypt and the Sudan and vast territories in North Africa. Yet Western knowledge of the Arabs and the Arab lands was confined within relatively narrow circles of scholars and government officials. In the English-speaking countries what was known to the educated public at large was derived principally from a few remarkable books of travel written in the nineteenth century: Edward William Lane's *Manners and Customs of the Modern Egyptians* (1836); Sir Richard Burton's *Pilgrimage to Al-Madinah and Meccah* (1855); the *Travels in Arabia Deserta* of Charles M. Doughty (1888); perhaps also William Gifford Palgrave's *A Year's Journey through Eastern Arabia, 1862–63*, published in 1865,[1] and of course the *Arabian Nights*, strictly the *Thousand and One Nights* (*Alf Layla wa-Layla*). Already familiar from Galland's French translation and its derivatives, the *Arabian Nights* was translated afresh from Arabic into English three times during the nineteenth century.[2]

In consequence a very incomplete and somewhat romantic view of the Arabs prevailed. The real history even of the heyday of the ʿAbbāsid Caliphs in Baghdad, with which the *Arabian Nights* purported to deal, was obscured, for the *Nights* is but loosely related to facts, being essentially an ever-expanding cycle of folk-tales, of considerably later origin than

> the golden prime
> Of good Haroun Alraschid.

The military prowess of the Arabs which had at one time caused consternation in southern Europe, their governmental achievements (especially under the Umayyad Caliphs, who preceded the ʿAbbāsids) in holding together a vast empire, and the centuries-long development of a rich literary, scientific and artistic culture in the Arab countries—all this was alike forgotten or disregarded.

The Arabs came more prominently before the public during and after the 1914–18 war, in the course of which they cooperated especially with the British against the Turks, and in the peace settlement they secured a measure of independence, under British and French mandates from the League of Nations, in several parts of the Middle East. This was merely the beginning of an upsurge of Arab political nationalism (literary and theoretical nationalism appeared earlier[3]), which after the Second World War had developed so far that the only viable method of securing anything like ordered government in the Middle East was generally recognized to be the according of full independence to the Arabs in the former mandated territories. Transjordan (nowadays usually simply Jordan), Iraq and Syria came into existence as Arab states, with Lebanon. At the cost in some cases of bitter fighting, the kingdoms of Morocco and Libya, the republics of Algeria, Tunisia and the Sudan, and the United Arab Republic (Egypt) became independent. In a separate category were the kingdoms and shaykhdoms of Arabia proper, regions which mainly owing to their comparative remoteness from Europe and from the unsettling effects of the 1939–45 war were less shaken by internal commotions in the postwar period. One further important development has been the progressive utilization of the oil resources of the Middle East. The net result of these changes, and not least the discovery of oil, has been a virtual transformation of the scene and the focusing of far more attention on the Arabs by the general public.

Official interest showed itself notably in stocktaking of the existing facilities for Middle East studies. In Britain the situation was investigated by the Scarbrough Commission, whose findings were published as early as 1947.[4] The whole Middle East, as well as other areas, was envisaged in the Report, and specific recommendations were made for the creation of university teaching posts and postgraduate studentships. The impetus thus given was soon felt at the teaching centres. More students than ever before have come forward to essay the difficult paths of Oriental languages, especially Arabic. Parallel with the official development, which has followed the same course also in the United States, has been a heightened interest in the Middle East beyond merely professional circles. Books and articles in newspapers and magazines have multiplied. The excellent one-volume *History of the Arabs* of Professor Hitti[5] has passed through as many as eight editions, a hitherto unprecedented number for a work of this type. The Arabs have swung back into the thoughts of their contemporaries in a way which certainly could not have been predicted fifty years ago.

2. Early history of the Arabs

It is almost superfluous to say that the history of the Arabs is a long one. The view has frequently been expressed that the Bedouin of the Arabian peninsula, who down to the present century have retained the tribal and nomadic customs of their ancestors, represent a way of life which goes back to prehistoric times. Broadly speaking, this is so (see also below). Exactly how far the Arabs go back, and what their origin may be, appear at present insoluble questions. According to Arab tradition, the Prophet Muḥammad who died in A.D. 632 was twenty-one or twenty-two generations removed from ʿAdnān, ancestor of the North Arabians,[6] and ʿAdnān himself nine generations removed from Ishmael and ten from Abraham, or fewer according to another account.[7] On the other hand, the Yemenite or South Arabian descent reckons thirty-two generations from Qaḥṭān to an-Nuʿmān III, king of al-Ḥīra[8] at the beginning of the seventh century A.D., with five further generations from Qaḥṭān to Noah.[9] These genealogies of North and South Arabians, the great historical divisions of the race, go back in each case to a biblical patriarch placed far too far down in time. The generations above Qaḥṭān are actually the same as in Genesis 10:21–5. (Qaḥṭān is identified by some with Yaqṭān, i.e. Joktan of Genesis, or else he is his brother.)[10] Setting aside the upper part of the genealogies which is presumably an Islamic borrowing[11] and therefore not part of the most ancient tradition, we have not more than thirty-two generations to the earliest beginnings of the race (cf. the statement that Yaʿrub b. Qaḥṭān was 'the first who spoke the Arabic language').[12] On the basis of three generations to a century this is not much more than 1000 years from the seventh century A.D., which is obviously much too short a time. Long before the middle of the fourth century B.C., the earliest date which these genealogies permit us to assume, the Arabs are mentioned by name in foreign sources (see below). For chronology therefore the genealogies are worthless (though not necessarily for other purposes).[13]

Turning to another line of investigation, Arabic belongs most obviously to the great Semitic family of languages. This is easily shown from a few common words in the Semitic languages: 'house, tent', Accadian (i.e. ancient Mesopotamian) *bītu*, Hebrew *bayth*, *bēth*, Arabic *bayt*; 'king', Accadian *maliku*, *malku*, Hebrew *melekh*, Arabic *malik*; 'bread', Ugaritic (i.e. ancient Syrian) *lḥm* (vowels uncertain), Hebrew *leḥem*, Arabic *laḥm* with the meaning 'meat'. Language is notoriously no guide to race, but the similarities evidently bring the Arabs into close relations at some point in the past with other Semitic speakers.

Anthropologically the matter is far from clear. On a popular level, it is difficult especially in the circumstances of today to get an Arab to admit that the Jew is his cousin. No doubt the Arab of the desert, often said to represent the purest surviving form of the Semitic-speaking races, does not resemble the Jew at all closely, yet at several points the affinity is noticeable. Apart from the genealogy of the Arabs, alleged by themselves, as we have seen, to go back to the Hebrew patriarchs, and the similarity of language just noted, it is surely not mere coincidence that the Arabs with the Hebrews have been historically the great carriers of monotheism. Granting the predominant influence of Judaism on Muḥammad at one stage of his career, which seems indisputable,[14] the affinity of the two races much earlier is suggested by, for example, the ancient tale of Eden (Genesis 2:8 ff) with its four rivers, two of which are evidently the Euphrates and the Tigris (Hiddekel, Arabic *Dijla*) and a third apparently in Arabia itself. This is the remarkable *wādī* or watercourse, at present called al-Bāṭin, with steeply sloping banks and a width of from one to four miles in its lower reaches, which forms part of the boundary between Iraq and the state of Kuwayt on the Gulf.[15] As the Wādī ar-Ruma or ar-Rima it is traceable upwards as far as Najd in central Arabia. Though nowadays it contains water only after heavy rains and in places is obliterated by the sands, the *wādī* presents the appearance of having formerly been a great river, though attested as such by no historical sources. The identification with Pison of Genesis 2:8 (Hebrew *Pīshōn*), made by a German scholar more than forty years ago,[16] appears to be confirmed by the existence of a Wādī Fayshān in central Arabia in the Middle Ages.[17] If the system al-Bāṭin–Wādī ar-Ruma is in fact a 'relic of a pluvial period' in Arabia, it is a measure of the extent of our ignorance.

We do not know even whether the earliest Semites, that is Semitic speakers, came out of Arabia into the Fertile Crescent. This may be said to be the prevailing view, and it is often associated with the 'wave theory'—the idea that over a period of millennia Arabia has been a reservoir of manpower which has from time to time spilled over, giving rise in turn to various Semitic civilizations or cultures in the adjoining lands. The principal historical facts adduced have been the eruption from Arabia in the seventh century A.D. after the first preaching of Islam, and as parallel with this the conquest of Canaan (Palestine) by the early Israelites after 'forty years in the wilderness' according to the biblical narrative. Other invasions of the settled country from the Arabian desert seem much less well attested, though of course the creators of the extraordinary monuments of Chaldaea and Assyria in ancient Mesopotamia and of Mari, Ugarit and Byblos in ancient Syria may all in their time have been desert-dwellers. T. E. Lawrence appears to have felt, when he entered Damascus with his Arab force in 1918, that he was part of a movement of the Desert against the Sown, the like of which had taken place many times in the past,[18] and it might be argued that a new period of Semitic predominance in the Middle East was then ushered in. However this may be, for the extreme form of the wave theory, according to which the population of Arabia overflowed in recurrent cycles of about a thousand years, there is no evidence whatever. One may see some remarks of W. F. Albright on the supposed drying up of Arabia as an explanation of periodic migration from the desert.[19]

On the other hand, Arabia may not be the original home of the Semitic speakers, with the Arabs themselves autochthonous there, as seems to be the corollary of this view. It is feasible that at some point the Arabs were extruded into the Peninsula from somewhere else, e.g. Mesopotamia. If the name ʿArab itself is the same as Hebrew *ʿerebh*, evening, and means '(land of) the West', this could plausibly be taken as viewed from Mesopotamia. There is, however, no certainty that ʿArab does mean the West. The present consensus would rather be that it stands for 'desert' or 'people of the desert'.[20]

Most of the above considerations remain speculative. Nor is it possible to draw firm general conclusions from the thousands of South Arabian inscriptions which have survived. Ṭhese inscriptions are called, after successive or contemporaneous kingdoms in what is now the Yemen, Minaean, Sabaean, Qatabānian, etc., or in general Ḥimyarite, from a group of the name Ḥimyar, one of the latest comers to power in this region whose name was remembered in Islamic times. The characteristic script in which they are written, or something very like it, has also been found in North Arabia in the Dedanite, Lihyanite, Thamudic and Safaitic inscriptions, which are not necessarily of later date than the South Arabian inscriptions proper,[21] and it has been generally considered, when so found, to be an importation from the South. The later Arabs easily identified the South Arabian script, which they called *musnad* (meaning uncertain, perhaps 'set up' in the sense of 'straight up and down'), but they were normally unable to read it. The South Arabian inscriptions date according to what is known as the 'long chronology' from *c.* 1300 B.C., or even earlier, to well within the Christian era. This of course makes chronologically possible the visit of the 'queen of Sheba', as reported in 1 Kings 10:1 ff = 2 Chronicles 9;1 ff, to Solomon (*c.* 950–922 B.C.)[21a] at a time when the South Arabian town Saba', presumed = Sheba, was flourishing. According to the 'short chronology' the South Arabian inscriptions date only from about 800 or 700 B.C., and in this case the queen of Sheba may be supposed to have come to the Jerusalem of Solomon from some off-shoot of the South Arabian Sabaeans in the north of the Peninsula. The queen is called in Arab legend Bilqīs, and it has remained a minor problem who she may have been.

Recently an extensive reappraisal of the whole subject has been made by Jacqueline Pirenne, arguing for an even shorter chronology. She considers the Minaean inscriptions not earlier, as has usually been thought, but later than the Sabaean, and has brought grounds for regarding the characteristically elegant form of the South Arabian alphabet (stylistically different from any of the other Semitic alphabets) as due to the influence of Greek (Dorian) lapidary style, i.e. perhaps not older than the beginning of the fifth century B.C.[22] It is at all events certain that South Arabia possessed an important local trade in incense, much in demand in antiquity for use in temples and in the homes of the rich, and was an entrepôt of commerce between the classical world and India. Apart from literary notices, tangible evidence of the presence of South Arabian traders in Greek lands is afforded by the bilingual inscription (Minaean–Greek) dating from the second century B.C. found in Delos,[23] on an altar dedicated to the ancient Arabian deity Wadd. Remarkably enough, this deity is still mentioned in the Qur'ān.[24]

Apart from the inscriptions, the chronology of which cannot be said to be settled, the Arabians are mentioned at an early date in the Bible, in the Joseph story as Ishmaelites (for Ishmael, cf. above) and as *B^e^nē Qedhem* ('Easterners')[25] also in Genesis[26] and rather frequently elsewhere. Apparently much earlier is the list of Arab tribes in Genesis 10, but there are difficulties about the dating.[27] Where the Arabs appear to be mentioned under their own name, for example 1 Kings 10:15 in the time of Solomon (tenth century B.C.), the vocalization of the group of consonants *ʿrb* remains uncertain.[28] Uncertain also is the identification of the *Eremboi* of Homer, mentioned with the Ethiopians, the Sidonians and Libya, as Arabs.[29] The passage is discussed inconclusively by Strabo.[30]

On the other hand, some information comes from the Assyrian records. An account of operations of Shalmaneser III from 853 to 841 B.C. tells of a certain Jindibu' of Arabia (cf. classical Arabic Jundub), who possessed 1000 camels.[31] Texts of the reign of Tiglath-Pileser III between 743 and 732 B.C. refer to the Arabian queens (cf. Bilqīs above) 'Zabibe' and 'Samsi'.[32]

Somewhat later the classical sources on the Arabs begin. Aeschylus seems to speak of the 'flower of Arabia in arms',[33] and there are important notices in Herodotus (fifth century B.C.), and in Strabo (first century B.C.). Strabo was a friend of the Roman general Aelius Gallus, who led a disastrous expedition into Arabia Felix in 24 B.C.[34] Many interesting details on Arabian ports and trading as far as India appear in the anonymous *Periplus of the Erythraean Sea*, usually dated in the first century A.D., but possibly as late as the third century.[35] The classical authorities just cited are exclusively Greek. We should not omit the Roman Pliny (died A.D. 79), who appears to be the earliest author to mention the Saracens.[36]

Civilization among the Arabs, having attained considerable

heights, as the South Arabian monuments clearly indicate, declined sharply after the first centuries of the Christian era. The decline, due probably to a variety of causes, economic and sociological,[37] is ascribed traditionally, by the Arabs in Islamic times, to the bursting of the great dam of Ma'rib in the Yemen, the remains of which still exist. The date *c.* A.D. 450 is sometimes given for its destruction.[38] It is at all events clear that at some point, or successively, the irrigation system of South Arabia was ruined, and there is reason to believe that, as the later Arabic sources tell, large numbers of the inhabitants were then forced to emigrate north. The change of conditions has been described as the 'bedouinization of Arabia',[39] and this would apply to most parts of the Peninsula, south as well as north, where earlier centres of civilization, such as Petra, had already ceased to exist as such. Petra may have recovered after siege and capture by the Romans in A.D. 105 under Trajan. It is scarcely mentioned in Muḥammad's time and later. On the other hand, Palmyra (Tadmur) at least until the third century A.D. and the civilized Ghassānids of Syria, perhaps also the Lakhmids of al-Ḥīra, both in the period immediately before Muḥammad, were exceptions to the general decline.

Both Lakhmids and Ghassānids are frequently mentioned in the pre-Islamic poetry of North Arabia, which was, it seems, the only higher art form and at the same time the principal vehicle of intellectual culture in the oases and among the desert men in the centuries before Muḥammad. This was a real classical poetry with an accepted poetical diction and elaborate rules of scansion. Its origin is obscure, but was apparently in the North (but see below). A good deal has survived, thanks to the interest which it possessed for later times, when it was extensively imitated and commented upon by the Muslim Arabs. The best, by general consent, of classical pre-Islamic poetry was contained in the 'Seven *Muʿallaqāt*', sometimes called *al-Mudhahhabāt* or 'Golden Odes', from the legend that they were written in letters of gold on fine Egyptian linen and suspended (*muʿallaqāt*) in the Kaʿba, the temple of Mecca.[40] As illustrating this ancient poetry the following piece of a dozen lines from the close of the *Muʿallaqa* of Imru' al-Qays in the translation of Sir Charles Lyall may be given.[41] (Imru' al-Qays, the earliest author of one of the *Muʿallaqāt*, was of the royal house of Kinda and spent a wandering life seeking his lost inheritance. He died about A.D. 540 on the way back from a visit to the court of Justinian.[42])

O Friend—see the lightning there! it flickered, and
now is gone,
as though flashed a pair of hands in the pillar of
crownèd cloud,
Nay, was it its blaze, or the lamps of a hermit that
dwells alone,
and pours o'er the twisted wicks the oil from his
slender cruse?
We sat there, my fellows and I, twixt Ḍārij and
al-ʿUdhaib,
and gazed at the distance gloomed, and waited its
oncoming.
The right of its mighty rain advanced over Qaṭan's ridge:
the left of its trailing skirt swept Yadhbul and
as-Sitār;
Then over Kutaifah's steep the flood of its onset drave,
and headlong before its storm the tall trees were borne
to ground;
And the drift of its waters passed o'er the crags of
al-Qanān,
and drave forth the white-legged deer from the refuge
they sought therein.
And Taimā—it left not there the stem of a palm aloft,
nor ever a tower, save one firm built on the living rock.
And when first its misty shroud bore down upon Mount Thabīr,
he stood like an ancient man in a grey-streaked
mantle wrapt.
The clouds cast their burden down on the broad plain of
al-Ghabīṭ,
as a trader from al-Yaman unfolds from the bales his
store;
And the topmost crest on the morrow of al-Mujaimir's cairn
was heaped with the flood-borne wrack like wool on a
distaff wound.
At earliest dawn on the morrow the birds were chirping
blithe,
as though they had drunken draughts of riot in fiery wine;
And at even the drowned beasts lay where the torrent had
borne them, dead,
high up on the valley sides, like earth-stained roots of
squills.

It is of some interest to note that Imru' al-Qays was a Qaḥṭānī or South Arabian (cf. above), and that traditionally the first man to compose a classical *qaṣīda* or ode was Muhalhil b. Rabīʿa, who, though a North Arabian (of Taghlib), was the uncle of Imru' al-Qays.[43] It is therefore not impossible that the classical poetry of the Arabs, still in vogue today alongside of modern forms, is derived in the long run from a literary art once practised in South Arabia, by the same men as produced the inscriptions mentioned above.

The metre of the original of the above passage is the *Ṭawīl* or 'Long' measure:

⏑ – ⏓ | ⏑ – ⏓ – | ⏑ – ⏓ | ⏑ – ⏓ –

(repeated),

which Lyall has imitated in his rendering as far as possible. In the following translation by R. A. Nicholson of some lines from a *qasīda* in the *Dīwān* of a later poet, an-Nābigha,[44] the end-rhyme of the original reappears in English, but its metre, which is the *Ṭawīl* as before, had not been retained, and the effect is quite different. The poet is praising the Ghassānids, who were Christians.

> Theirs is a liberal nature that God gave
> To no men else; their virtues never fail.
> Their home the Holy Land: their faith upright:
> They hope to prosper if good deeds avail.
> Zoned in fair wise and delicately shod,
> They keep the Feast of Palms, when maidens pale,
> Whose scarlet silken robes on trestles hang,
> Greet them with odorous boughs and bid them hail.
> Long lapped in ease tho' bred to war, their limbs
> Green-shouldered vestments, white-sleeved, richly veil.[45]

3. Muḥammad and the promulgation of Islam

It is at all events against a background predominantly Bedouin that the work of the Prophet Muḥammad, the greatest of the Arabs, was carried out. He himself spent most of his life in towns. Born towards A.D. 570 in Mecca, a station on the long desert route between the Yemen and Syria, prosperous enough by contemporary standards but doubtless much less splendid than Maʾrib, Maʿīn and other South Arabian capitals of former times, Muḥammad was the son of ʿAbd Allāh, an inconspicuous member of the Meccan clan of Quraysh, who had died young. Muḥammad's nearest relatives on his father's side were among the leading men in the town and, more important perhaps for his future development, through his family connection he had a special interest in the religious centre of Mecca. This was the famous Kaʿba already mentioned, a shrine of pagan worship not excelled for sanctity by any in Arabia, and possessing a history going back certainly for several centuries. The early ventures of Muḥammad in trade, which took him at least once as far as Syria,[46] his marriage with Khadīja, a respectable widow much older than himself, his early religious struggles and final attainment of certainty, his preaching, the growing opposition at Mecca which ended in the severing of all relations with Muḥammad and his little band of followers, his flight in 622 to Yathrib, henceforward to be known as al-Madīna[47] —all these are matters of history. It is from the Flight or Hijra of 622 that the Muslim era begins, though not fixed at the time. After his arrival in Medina Muḥammad went from strength to strength, and was able to defeat all attempts on the part of the Quraysh of Mecca to destroy him (battles of Badr, 624; Uḥud, 625; al-Khandaq, or siege of Medina, 627). In A.H. 8/A.D. 630 at the head of, it is said, 10,000 of his adherents, the Muslims, he took the unbelieving town of Mecca, and defeated his remaining enemies at the battle of Ḥunyan. Henceforward Muḥammad was for a brief time, until his death in Rabīʿ I, A.H. 11/June 632, the undisputed lord of Arabia.

If it is difficult to account satisfactorily for the extraordinary success of his propaganda, one thing is clear, that Muḥammad was no impostor. Whether the preaching of Islam was for the permanent good of mankind is another matter, but like other successful propagators of a revolutionary creed, Muḥammad undoubtedly believed in what he professed. He had a message for his time and place, derived in part from contact with Judaism and/or Christianity (see above), in part from the traditions of his race and family, in part too from his own religious endowment. Recognized as something higher than most of them had known, but not drawn out too fine for the Arabs with whom he had principally to do, the religion of Muḥammad resolved conflicts and mitigated problems which had hitherto remained insoluble, in what we have to regard as the deteriorating condition of Arabia at this time. Islam was no doubt accepted at first by the finer natures and the simple-hearted among his hearers, then by a process of growth, the exact character of which remains obscure but which was certainly not unconnected with Muḥammad's growing militancy, proved irresistible, so that the most independent of the tribal chiefs[48] and the most hard-headed of the merchants in general found it necessary to give at least formal assent to the astonishing claims of Muḥammad as Messenger of the Lord of the Worlds and accept the new rules of conduct which he enjoined.

Muḥammad showed himself a sharp critic of the pagan poets (see above) on the ground of their worldliness. He himself was capable of a kind of inspired eloquence which acted even more powerfully on the minds of his hearers than the most famous productions of the poets, before or after him. This is to be seen in the Qur'ān, a work which was already in existence, in the form in which we know it, some time between A.H. 30 and 35, in the Caliphate[49] of his third successor ʿUthmān (23/644–35/656). It was originally delivered by Muḥammad before and after his Hijra to Medina in 622, and since then until the present day has influenced the lives of countless millions of mankind to an incalculable extent. The delivery of the Qur'ān by Muḥammad was accompanied by signs of physical stress. He himself seems usually, after the first two or three deliverances in which he spoke of visionary appearances, to have considered that the words of the Qur'ān were somehow conveyed to him from a heavenly prototype, which he simply read off. Thus he thought, at least sometimes, on the occasion of the delivery of a particular portion, that he knew where it fitted into the whole, that is, the *sūra* (chapter) in which it should be placed.[50] Apparently his secretaries and private persons took the Qur'ān down in writing, when it was delivered, but no attempt was made to collect it in its entirety during his lifetime. As examples of the poetic style of the Qur'ān (as distinct from the prosaic, legislative style, of which there is plenty, especially from the later period of his life, at Medina) the following may be cited (the reader should consult for them any good translation of the Qur'ān[51]): *Sūra* 1 (The Opening), 1–7; *Sūra* 2 (The Cow), 255/256; *Sūra* 24 (Light), 35;[52] *Sūra* 97 (Power), 1–5. It cannot be doubted that in some of these verses, especially perhaps the celebrated Throne-verse (2, 255/256), the style borders upon sublimity.

The results of Muḥammad's religious activity and the *élan* thereby—we cannot doubt it—imparted to the Arabs were momentous. The idea of the *jihād fī sabīl Allāh*,[53] 'striving in the way of the Lord', in effect, fighting for the faith, was inculcated in the days when the Muslim community at Medina was struggling for its life against powerful enemies within Arabia. Brought into hostile contact almost casually, it would seem,[54] first with the Byzantines, then with the Sāsānid Persians, the Muslims almost invariably won resounding victories, culminating in the battles of the Yarmūk (Jordan) in 636 and al-Qādisiyya (Iraq) in 637, and the capture of al-Madā'in (Seleucia-Ctesiphon in Iraq) in 638,[55] after which neither the former Greek rulers nor the Persians were able for long to hold their ground. The reasons for their discomfiture and defeat, total in the case of the Persians, are not far to seek. At the time of the Arab invasions, militarily, both Byzantines and Sāsānids were exhausted by recent exertions against each other. In addition, the subject peoples of the Fertile Crescent, also of Egypt, where the Muslims made rapid progress from 640,[56] were many of them Semitic-speaking and in any case had little interest or inclination to support régimes which, though of old standing, were yet felt to be alien, when a chance came to be rid of them. Of the favouring circumstances the Muslims under the prudent direction of the second Caliph, ʿUmar b. al-Khaṭṭāb (who succeeded Abū Bakr in 634), took full advantage. The Byzantines evacuated Alexandria and virtually the whole of Egypt in 642.

The work of consolidating the newly gained provinces necessitated or was facilitated by new Muslim foundations, at first military camps, later teeming cities. Such were Basra, founded perhaps in 14/635–6,[57] and Kufa a few years afterwards, both in Iraq, and al-Fusṭāṭ,[58] now the oldest part of Cairo, founded in 641 or 642, followed a generation later by al-Qayrawān (or Kairouan—the word is the same as our 'caravan') founded A.D. 670 in what had hitherto been Byzantine Africa, by which time the whole of the Iranian possessions of the Sāsānids were securely in Muslim hands. The rate of expansion slackened owing to a series of civil wars among the Arabs themselves, but the Muslim advance was not permanently held up. There was fighting between ʿAlī, cousin and son-in-law of Muḥammad, and Ṭalḥa and az-Zubayr, old Companions of the Prophet, supported by ʿĀ'isha the Prophet's widow, who were dissatisfied with ʿAlī's conduct when ʿUthmān, his predecessor in the Caliphate, was murdered by insurgents (battle of the Camel, 656). In the next year war broke out between ʿAlī and Muʿāwiya, the ambitious governor of Syria and later founder of the Umayyad dynasty (from 41/661) (Battle of Ṣiffīn, 657). A third war and the most costly in blood saw opposed to each other the Umayyads Yazīd I (Caliph 680–3) and ʿAbd al-Malik (Caliph 685–705), on the one hand, and ʿAbd Allāh, son of az-Zubayr already mentioned, on the other. ʿAbd Allāh represented conservative Muslim opinion, especially in opposition to the new dynastic principle. At one time he was acknowledged as Caliph by most of the Muslim world,[59] but his strength, as events proved, lay in the Ḥijāz, and it was here and in Iraq that some of the bitterest fighting took place (destruction of the Kaʿba, 683; fall of Mecca, 692). All this offered to the religious the unedifying spectacle of Muslims fighting not against the unbelieving 'polytheists' (*mushrikūn*)[60] but against their Muslim brothers, and indeed the central provinces of the empire were convulsed at various times. The Umayyads made good their hold upon the Caliphate, but the seeds of the Shīʿa (ʿAlid) movement which has divided the Muslim world until the present were sown when the descendants of ʿAlī were set aside from the succession, and above all by the violent death of ʿAlī's younger son al-Ḥusayn in tragic circumstances at Kerbela (Karbalāʾ) in Iraq (10 Muḥarram, 61/10 October, 680).

Even so, the flood of Muslim conquest in foreign lands continued to run, northwards from Syria across the Amanus range (the frontier for a time) to the Taurus mountains, eastwards through Armenia and Albania (Arrān) to the Caucasus, and yet further east, skirting the Caspian and the deserts of Khwārizm (Chorasmia) to the remotest lands of the Sāsānids, then on across the Oxus, called by the Arabs at first simply 'the River' or 'the River of Balkh' (Greek, Bactra), later the Jayḥūn, to Turkestan, and as far as the Indus valley. In the West the conquests were on the same tremendous scale. North Africa was subdued some time after the foundation of al-Qayrawān (see above), and in 710 the first Muslims set foot in Spain, Arabic, al-Andalus, 'the (country of the) Vandals'.[61] A great battle on the river Barbate in the south of Spain broke for ever the power of the ruling Visigoths (Ramaḍān, 92/July, 711), and a campaign or two sufficed to give the Muslims control of by far the greater part of the Peninsula. Only in the extreme north-west, in the wild mountains of the Asturias, a handful of Visigothic resisters, men and women, held out under the chief Pelayo, traditionally in the cave of Covadonga, presumably the locality called by Muslim writers aṣ-Ṣakhra, 'the Rock'.[62] From their descendants came the royal lines of the later Spanish kingdoms, destined after the lapse of centuries to reconquer the Peninsula for Christianity. In the west the Pyrenees set the limits of Muslim and Arab conquest as effectively as did the Caucasus in the east. This does not mean that Muslim armies did not penetrate into the lands of the Franks, as into the Khazar country beyond the Caucasus.[63] Narbonne, an important crossroads giving access west and north as well as south, was taken and held for many years.[64] It had belonged earlier to the Visigoths of Spain.[65] There is no doubt about the fact that Narbonne was once Muslim, only about the length of time during which it remained so. It is mentioned in a short article by Yāqūt[66] who gives the distance of 1000 miles between Narbonne and Cordova. An Arabic author quoted by Maqqarī[67] says that Spain 'in length' from Narbonne to Lisbon is sixty days journey for a fast horseman. The late (seventeenth century) writer Maqqarī takes his authority to task for saying that Narbonne is in Spain. Narbonne was lost by the Muslims about 133/751, according to others in 759.

In 114/732 a great battle was fought in central France which at least from the times of Gibbon and Sir E. Creasy has often been considered decisive for the fate of western Europe.[68] In that year the Arab governor of Spain ʿAbd ar-Raḥmān b. ʿAbd Allāh al-Ghāfiqī attacked Bordeaux (Arabic, Burdīl), scattered the forces opposed to him, and was apparently on his way from Poitiers to the cathedral town of Tours, when he was met by Charles Martel and his Franks and suffered defeat and death (battle of Tours or Poitiers, Ramaḍān, 114/October, 732). There is no doubt that the Arabs found incursions into what they called the 'Great Land' (*al-arḍ al-kabīra*, in this context Europe north of the Pyrenees), congenial perhaps, but certainly dangerous. Before ʿAbd ar-Raḥmān met his death at Tours, two Arab governors of al-Andalus had already been killed while on military expeditions into France, as-Samḥ b. Mālik al-Khawlānī in Dhū'l-Ḥijja, A.H. 102/June A.D. 721 at Toulouse,[69] and ʿAnbasa b. Suḥaym al-Kalbī in Shaʿbān, 107/January 726, returning after the capture of Qarqashūna (Carcassonne), on a raid in which he subdued the country as far as Nîmes (between Montpellier and Avignon[69a]) and seems to have reached Autun and perhaps Luxeuil.[70] If so, the latter would be the furthest point attained by an Arab army in France.[71] It is consonant with the difficult military situation in the North that the Caliph ʿUmar II (ʿUmar b. ʿAbd al-ʿAzīz), whose letters, we are told, reached Narbonne,[72] was credited with the intention of removing the Muslims from Spain because of their remoteness, and would that he had lived long enough to do so, added the tenth century historian who reported this, for their dealings with the unbelievers are leading to destruction![73]

On the other hand, at least some of the Muslims clearly intended to settle in France. This appears not only from a passage of Ibn al-Athīr referring to the campaign of ʿAnbasa in 107/725–6 analysed by Codera,[74] in which the terms granted to Carcassonne are set out, but also from a characterization of the governorship of ʿUqba b. al-Ḥajjāj as-Salūlī (from Ramaḍān 116/734) in Maqqarī:[75] 'He continued five years as governor, praised for his conduct, fighting the *jihād* (see above) and successful, till the habitation (*suknā*) of the Muslims reached Narbonne, and their posting (*ribāt*) came to be along the river Rūduna (Rhone).' This, it will be noted, is after the battle of Tours already mentioned. The Rhone infrequently appears in the Arabic sources. It occurs again with the 'rock of Avignon' and the 'fortress of Lyons' in another passage of Maqqarī.[76] It is quite certain that the later Arabs were themselves badly informed about these expeditions. Thus we read that the poet Abū Dhu'ayb 'raided Ifranja, France, in the time of ʿUthmān'.[77] This from the context is evidently a mistake for Ifrīqiya, Africa, and the same error may be the explanation of a statement in Ibn Bashkuwāl, quite a good Spanish historian of the sixth/twelfth century—the name means 'son of Pascual'—that ʿUthmān (Caliph 644–56) sent an expedition from al-Qayrawān to Spain, which Maqqarī himself denied vigorously.[78]

Britain appears definitely to have been within the purview of the Arabs of Spain. Thus, according to the tenth-century chronographer Aḥmad ar-Rāzī, one of the angles of the Peninsula (Cape Finisterre, or possibly Cape Ortegal) 'looks over to the country of Britain'.[79] The same thing is said by Ibn ʿAbd al-Ḥakam an-Naẓẓām.[80] Maqqarī, who cites both these authors, also mentions the 'Circumambient Ocean (Atlantic) in the direction of the island of Britain' as the source of a valuable fur which is brought to Saraqusṭa (Saragossa) and manufactured there.[81] In another passage he mentions the same fur (*sammūr*), which should be sable (sometimes also beaver), as manufactured at Cordova.[82] Its origin, he here says, is uncertain. It may be vegetable (*nabāt*), but it is likely to be from an animal which lives in the sea and comes up on dry land. This is an odd description for sableskin, which in any case was well enough known to the medieval Arabs, and apparently rather sealskin is meant. If both passages refer to an import of sealskin into Muslim Spain, they may be taken with others which indicate a knowledge of whales and whaling in the northern seas.[83] On the other hand, there is no evidence of Arabs in Britain in these centuries.[84]

At about the same time as Spain was being overrun, we find the Arabs pressing for a decisive advantage against the Byzantines in Asia Minor. Though the country had repeatedly been invaded, as far as Constantinople (attacked several times in the seventh century and again in 717–18 under Maslama, brother of the Caliph Sulaymān), no prospect of a Muslim conquest was in sight.[85] On the other hand, all was over with the once great empire of the Sāsānids. Iran lay subjugated, and indeed to a large extent had been so even before the death of the last Sāsānid ruler Yazdagird in 651. The Caucasus line had been reached and crossed, and the Muslim armies had passed the Oxus. The situation on the Caucasus, as already mentioned, somewhat resembled that on the line of the Pyrenees. The Khazars, a Turkic people, settled in towns or nomadizing behind the great mountain barrier, in their prolonged and successful resistance to the Muslims (first Arab–Khazar war, 642–52; second Arab–Khazar war, 722–37) played a role similar to that of the Franks in the West. The Transcaucasian lands were repeatedly invaded under some of the best Umayyad generals, including Maslama above-mentioned, but the outcome of much bitter fighting was that the Caucasus remained the effective frontier of the Caliphate in this direction.[86]

Further east Qutayba b. Muslim campaigned in Turkestan and Muḥammad b. al-Qāsim ath-Thaqafī in Sind. About 92/710 al-Ḥajjāj b. Yūsuf, the celebrated Umayyad viceroy of Iraq, promised the governorship of China to whichever of these two generals should first reach it.[87] Nothing came of the proposal, but the Arabs defeated the Chinese in a great battle north of the Jaxartes (Sayḥūn, Syr Darya) in Dhū'l-Ḥijja, 133/July 751.[88] Previous to this, just before the death of al-Walīd in 715, a body of troops under Qutayba's command is said to have reached Kāshghar in Chinese Turkestan,[89] and there is a romantic but not necessarily legendary account of a visit of Arab envoys to the T'ang court about the same time.[90]

4. Outline of the history of the Arabs to A.D. 1500

We cannot but wonder at these extraordinary conquests, which carried the Arab fighting men in the same years across the Pyrenees and the Caucasus and round the Pamirs. We have seen the rise of an Arab empire, effective in regions so far apart as Spain, even France, in the west, and Turkestan and India, even China, in the east, and this not without the development of naval power, first demonstrated in the struggle with Byzantium in the eastern Mediterranean.[91] The Arabs have become a world state, the greatest of that age, in size comparable with or rather superior to the Roman empire at its greatest extent.[92] How is this astonishing expansion of the Desert to be accounted for? Looking back in later times, the Arabic historians had no doubt that it was God who had opened the lands to the Muslims. Certainly the part played by religion cannot be disregarded. It was as the carriers of a new faith that the Muslim armies swept over large tracts of three continents. In political and sociological terms, it is patent that the victories of Islam were the result of a mass movement affecting great bodies of men in the Middle East in somewhat the same way, though on an even larger scale, as the French Revolution of 1789 and the subsequent expansion of the revolutionary idea through Europe, which made possible the victories of Napoleon. We have to think of a great unleashing of the energies of ordinary men, and the development of a feeling of community among the Muslims, of a kind which may be described as socialistic. (It is perhaps on this ground, in part, that the setting aside of ʿAlī, the cousin and son-in-law of Muḥammad, from the Caliphate during many years has to be explained. If privilege has ceased among the Muslims, rank must depend on other considerations than the mere chance of birth.) The ferment died down after the defeat and death of Napoleon, though not before the old Europe had been permanently changed. Something of the same kind happened in the East, and it is notable that after the downfall of the Umayyad dynasty and the advent of the ʿAbbāsids (in 132/750) there were no great new military conquests. In all the fighting of the early decades (and much later) the old opposition between North and South Arabians was liable to make itself felt, in ways sometimes dangerous to the general welfare of the Muslims. But the map of the world had been effectually changed. From those times until the present, wide regions where formerly Greek and Latin were the principal languages have remained Arabic-speaking, and oriental rather than European ways of life have prevailed.

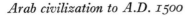

This fact of the replacement of the Roman by the Arab empire, involving the substitution of Arabic for classical culture over much of the former Roman territory, appears to be the element of truth in the thesis of Henri Pirenne, which has caused so much stir among historians since it was first promulgated. Pirenne considered that the end of classical antiquity and the beginning of the Middle Ages of Europe came about as the result, not of the Germanic invasions, but of the break-up of Mediterranean unity through the advance of the Arabs. He pointed out that the northern barbarians had no objection to adopting the language and religion of Rome (Christian nominally since the reign of Constantine I in the fourth century) and respected the *status quo*.[93] The Arab invaders, on the other hand, possessing Islam and the Qur'ān, enough for their needs, certainly, at this time, felt no interest in the culture and religion of the conquered peoples, but only in their subjection to the authority of God, whether as Muslim brothers or as tributaries making apparently no great difference. (Here, we may say, is the main ground of the frequently remarked toleration of the early Muslims.) On the other hand, and by the same token, no possibility of assimilation to unbelievers, principally Christians, remained open.[94]

Pirenne's thesis, though attractive and stimulating, has not won universal assent, principally because it has been felt that by the time the Arabs arrived in force in the civilized lands the ancient world had already to all intents and purposes disappeared. However willing the Germans may have been to become Romanized and Christianized, they had done their work of destruction. The Western empire long before the seventh century had ceased to exist,[95] and the Germanic invaders had been succeeded by other barbarians in the East, for example the Bulgars, who were by no means disposed to become assimilated to the Eastern (Byzantine) empire. In the Mediterranean the power of Byzantium was a shadow of what Rome had been. While Byzantine arms had regained North Africa from the Vandals, neither in Spain nor in Gaul (France) nor in Italy was the situation any longer like that of classical antiquity. There at all events the Middle Ages had already begun.

The invaders from Arabia who settled in the conquered territory were at first with few exceptions rough and unsophisticated. But they did not remain so. Ibn Khaldūn speaks as if the civilizing process had already begun by the reign of the Umayyad Caliph ʿAbd al-Malik (65/685–86/705).[96] The beginnings of Arabic literature, apart from the traditional poetry and the Qur'ān, about which something has already been said, are perhaps to be seen in a book published a little later, the translation into Arabic, probably from Syriac, by one Māsarjawayh of a compendium of medicine.[97]

Under the Umayyad Caliphs Arabic literature with the other appurtenances of civilized life slowly developed, but it is in ʿAbbāsid times, corresponding with a new turn given to the still rising civilization by a dynasty which felt itself as much, or more, dependent on the class of *mawlās*, i.e. foreign converts to Islam, as on Arabs of the original stocks, that the characteristic life of the Muslim Middle Ages begins. Now the rich merchant, who travels far by land and sea in pursuit of gain, and the *qāḍī* (judge) or *faqīh* (canon lawyer) skilled in the religious sciences, holding high office in the state or communicating his knowledge by teaching, become the ideal type, rather than the *ghāzī* (raider) of the early days or the *mujāhid* (fighter for the faith, cf. *jihād*). Works appeared in Arabic in ever increasing numbers on law and devotion, history, belles lettres and poetry, the sciences and the useful arts. The fine arts remained, as they have continued, as regards both theory and practice, under something of a ban, varying in rigour at different times and in different places, though there is quite an extensive Arabic musical literature.[98] We may indeed place music with architecture as perhaps the most highly developed of the Islamic arts. The prejudice against the representational arts, painting and sculpture, derived from religion: to represent a living object was thought of as an infringement of the prerogative of God as Creator. A contributory reason may have been originally antipathy to the characteristic works of the Greeks.

One early translation into Arabic has already been mentioned. The great period of translation in Islam was under the earlier ʿAbbāsids, at least one of whom, al-Ma'mūn (Caliph 198/813–218/833), seems to have been personally interested. Greek works on philosophy and the sciences, translated directly, or indirectly from Syriac, may be said to have formed the staple of the translation activity, but Persian (Pahlavi) and Indian books were also rendered, and of course the Bible, for the benefit of Arabic-speaking Christians and Jews, numerous throughout the Arab empire. It is remarkable that Greek literature, as distinct from science and philosophy, did not pass into Arabic, no doubt as being too remote from the interests and mentality of that age. Passages in Greek in which poetry is cited or reference is made to public institutions often caused the Arabic translators grave difficulties.[99] Translation from Latin into Arabic in medieval Islam is barely represented by one or two works, notably the *Histories* of the Spaniard Orosius (fifth century A.D.), which appeared in

Arabic in Spain in the tenth century, and was made use of by Ibn Khaldūn.[100]

Arabic literature now rose to its highest point of development. Typical of the varied production are the works of famous poets such as al-Buḥturī (died 284/897) and al-Mutanabbi' (d. 354/965)—to name only two of many—the *Annals* of aṭ-Ṭabarī (d. 310/923), the *Kitāb al-Aghānī* (Book of Songs) of Abū'l-Faraj al-Iṣfahānī (d.356/967), the philosophical writings of al-Fārābī (d. 339/950) and Ibn Sīnā (Avicenna) (died 428/1037), the *History of India* and *Chronology of Ancient Nations* of al-Bīrūnī (d. 440/1048), the belletristic *Maqāmāt* of al-Ḥarīrī (d. 516/1122) and the great *Geography* ('Book of Roger', so-called after its patron, Roger II of Sicily) of ash-Sharīf[101] al-Idrīsī (d. *c.* 1162).

At the same time the political fortunes of the Arabs declined ever more steeply. Gradually excluded from political place and influence, they saw the ʿAbbāsid Caliphate, which still remained in name the central authority of the empire founded by the Arabs, shorn progressively of its outlying provinces in east and west and overshadowed at home in Baghdad and Sāmarrā by other powers. At first Iranian then Turkish influences prevailed. From 945 the Buwayhid dynasty, originally from Daylam,[102] dominated over the Caliphs. Later still, with the advent of the Saljūq Turks in 1055, a new functionary, the Sulṭān,[103] was military and administrative chief and the real head of affairs. Spain had been lost to the ʿAbbāsids almost from the beginning of the dynasty, when the Umayyad ʿAbd ar-Raḥmān (ʿAbd ar-Raḥmān I), a grandson of the Caliph Hishām, succeeded in establishing himself there in 756, even before the founding of Baghdad (762). North Africa fell to lesser dynasties, mostly shortlived. The same thing happened in the east, where the Sāmānids (from 874) were succeeded by the Ghaznawids (from 962). By 800 everything west of Egypt had passed out of ʿAbbāsid control. In 358/969 Egypt, which for a century had been virtually independent, first under the Ṭūlūnids (from 868), then the Ikhshīdids (from 935), was invaded successfully by the Fāṭimids from Ifrīqiya (modern Tunisia), who built Cairo (Arabic al-Qāhira, 'the Victorious') as a new quarter of al-Fusṭāṭ (see above), and founded the famous al-Azhar mosque, to this day a seat of learning. The Shīʿite Fāṭimids from the beginning of the dynasty (297/909) had claimed the Caliphate by virtue of their descent, real or alleged, from Fāṭima, daughter of Muḥammad. It was therefore as Caliphs that they ruled in Cairo with varying fortune till 567/1171. In 316/929 the Spanish Umayyad ʿAbd ar-Raḥmān III asserted his right to the Caliphate. At this time the Islamic world was thus distracted by three claimants of its highest title and office. The reality of unity had long disappeared, and the ʿAbbāsid Caliph of Baghdad, the unfortunate al-Muqtadir (295/908–320/932), as a ruler enjoyed incomparably less power than his Fāṭimid or Umayyad rival. Henceforward the unity of the empire, like the authority of the ʿAbbāsid Caliphs after ar-Rāḍī (322/934–329/940), [104] was not even in semblance, but the shadow of a shade.

In Egypt the Fāṭimids were succeeded by the Ayyūbids, the dynasty founded by Ṣalāḥ ad-Dīn b. Ayyūb (Saladin, the famous opponent of the Crusaders). The main crusading movement lasted from 1096 (First Crusade) to 1291 (fall of Acre) and made a great commotion at the time, but the strength of both sides, so far as it was brought into play, was too evenly balanced for either of them to gain permanent advantage over the other. Iraq, still in some sense the heartland of the Muslim empire, was not reached by the Crusaders, and the forces of the ʿAbbāsid Caliphate, reduced as they were, were scarcely involved.

More terrible antagonists than the Christian knights and squires from Europe were the pagan Mongols, who first made their appearance in the Muslim East in 1216 under the redoubtable Chingiz Khān, and carried all before them. Baghdad itself was not called upon to face the brunt of Mongol attack till 1258, when Hūlāgū, grandson of Chingiz Khān, took and sacked the ʿAbbāsid capital and put to death al-Mustaʿṣim, the last of the Caliphs of Baghdad. This was the end of a long chapter of history, going back for five hundred years to al-Manṣūr (Caliph 136/754–158/775), the real founder of the ʿAbbāsid dynasty, who had built Baghdad *de novo* in 762 and to his brother before him Abū'l-ʿAbbās as-Saffaḥ ('the Shedder of Blood') (Caliph 132/750–136/754), who in his time had shown no more compunction for the defeated Umayyads than the Mongol now had for his last successor. A puppet ʿAbbāsid Caliphate was created in Egypt by the Mamluk Baibars[105] (659/1261) and remained till the Ottoman conquest of Egypt in 1517 (see below). It is in any case to be noted that the ʿAbbāsids outlasted their rivals for the Caliphate. The fall of the Fāṭimids (1171) was not delayed for long after the advent of Saladin (cf. above). In Spain, after many victories gained over the Christians in the north by ʿAbd ar-Raḥmān III (died 350/961) and the dictator Ibn abī

ʿĀmir, called al-Manṣūr (Almanzor) (died 392/1002), the Umayyad Caliphate foundered owing to factional strife amid grim scenes of confusion and bloodshed, and was finally suppressed in 1032.

There followed in Spain the century of the so-called Party Kings (*Mulūk aṭ-Ṭawā'if, Reyes de Taifas*)—ʿAbbādids in Seville and Cordova, Dhūnnūnids in Toledo, Zīrids in Granada, and others—who though they often gave considerable impetus to culture at the rivalling petty courts, lacked all cohesion and fell piecemeal to the Berbers from Africa. The latter in the course of the fifth/eleventh century had been called in as defenders of Islam against the Spanish Christians, but turned their arms against their allies and came to rule Muslim Spain in their place (Almoravids from 1090, Almohads from 1145). Originally hardy desert fighters, the Berbers submitted to the enervating influences—unaccustomed luxury, soft climate, urban living—of their new home. By 1258, the year which saw the end of the ʿAbbāsid Caliphate of Baghdad (see above), Muslim Spain was ready to succumb to the mounting offensive of the Spanish Christians. But it is to be noted that the movement called by the Spaniards the *Reconquista* lasted for centuries. Not until 1492, by the fall of Granada, the last possession of Islam in Spain, was the verdict of 711 (see above, Muslim conquest of Spain) reversed. Before this final disaster overtook them, the Muslims of Spain had made notable contributions to Arab civilization, of which the works of the philosopher Ibn Rushd (Averroes), who lived under the Almohads and died in 1198, and the marvellous Alhambra (Arabic al-Ḥamrā', the Red Palace) of the Naṣrids at Granada are conspicuous examples.

By contrast with Spain, Muslim North Africa early fell apart as a unit (cf. above), and we find the modern divisions of the region taking shape long before the eclipse of the ʿAbbāsid Caliphate, Morocco as early as 172/788, when a descendant of ʿAlī founded the Idrīsid dynasty. The history of North Africa, which cannot be gone into here, is full of commotion, owing in part to the presence of a vigorous native race, the Berbers, who have maintained their identity until the present time, in part to the character of the country, broken by mountain ranges along much of the coast and with a desert hinterland in the Sahara. It seems that the Arabs were at first unable or unwilling to maintain the material culture of Graeco-Roman Africa, to a greater extent than elsewhere, and that subsequently the initial decline was never made up. Probably in consequence, Muslim Africa, though always fertile in vigorous individuals and groups who played prominent political roles, often outside their native country, as we have seen them in Spain, never possessed the basis for the kind of compact and developed Muslim culture which appeared elsewhere, though at centres such as Fez and al-Qayrawān a tradition of civilization has been continuous for many centuries. For long the North African coastal towns were the home ports of the redoubted Barbary pirates, called by the Europeans corsairs or rovers, and this continued beyond the Ottoman conquest of the lands of Islam, the next great event with which we have to deal.

Prior to the Ottoman conquest the situation in the lands of the former Caliphate for the most part worsened still more. Under various dynasties, usually Turkish or Mongol in the East, Arab in the West, the inhabitants over much of the area suffered the disadvantages of weak and violent rule. Conditions were perhaps at their best, paradoxically, in Egypt, where political power was in the hands of slaves, the celebrated Mamlūks, who defeated the Mongols in the open field more than once, notably at ʿAyn Jālūt (Goliath's Spring) in Palestine (Ramaḍān, 658/September 1260),[106] and saved their adopted country from a Mongol invasion.[107] Two 'dynasties' of Turkish and Circassian slaves, respectively called the Baḥrī and the Burjī, ruled in Egypt from about 1250 until 1517. There was no regular hereditary succession, the likeliest Mamlūk in the military establishment assuming control on the death of his predecessor. The assassinations and fighting which frequently occurred involved principally the military caste, not the general population. Under the aegis of the Mamlūks, Egyptian Arabs of respectable family held the principal legal offices and occupied themselves with religion and learning, or with commerce. *Mutatis mutandis*, the situation was not greatly different in the Cairo of Lane's time, though the power of Mamlūks had long passed away.[108] In general, however, the Arab world was in sore case when the Ottoman Turks early in the sixteenth century took Egypt and Syria, with Mecca and Medina, from the Mamlūks (1516–17).

The Ottoman Turks, coming into the more settled lands from central Asia, built up a state in Asia Minor at the expense of their predecessors, the Saljūqs, and the dwindling Byzantine empire. In 1453 they took Constantinople. The fall of age-old Byzantium, which had successfully resisted the forces of the Arab Caliphate at the height of its aggressive strength, was an epoch-making event with repercussions in both East and West. Modern European history is often said to begin in 1453, and if the capture of Constantinople marks the close of the Middle Ages in Europe, the same holds good for the East. The establishment of the Ottoman Turks as the dominant power in the lands of the former Arab empire, which was secured within the next few decades, did not result in any immediate transformation of the scene, but the Arab Middle Ages are now in effect over, and at least the stage is set for the future. Continuity in appearance was secured by the transference to the Ottoman Sultan, perhaps as is often said, from the puppet ʿAbbāsid in Cairo at the time of the conquest of Egypt, perhaps gradually,[109] of the ancient titles and privileges of the Caliphate.[110] The complex and eventful history of the Ottoman empire in Europe and Asia does not concern us here, but it was against this background and in direct contact with Ottoman as well as European influences that Arab nationalism in the modern sense of the term arose, especially in Egypt. With Arab nationalism we are back at our starting point.

Chapter 2

Arabic literature

1. Early poetry in Arabic

Classical Arabic literature begins with the pre-Islamic poetry, composed and recited within the tribe or at some general concourse of the Arabs, such as the fair of ʿUkāẓ, near Mecca, seldom written down but carried in the memories of men, especially the class of reciters (*rāwī*, *rāwiya*, plural *ruwāt*) who were often poets themselves. Of this literature the first great representative is Imruʾ al-Qays, of the royal house of Kinda, whose dates fall in the late fifth and early sixth centuries A.D. Though not regarded as the inventor of the typical verse form of classical Arabic poetry, the *qaṣīda* or ode (that honour being reserved, as already mentioned, for his uncle, Muhalhil b. Rabīʿa of the tribe of Taghlib), Imruʾ al-Qays is considered to have been the author of the earliest of the Seven *Muʿallaqāt*, the 'Suspended Poems' (see above, p. 8). Imruʾ al-Qays, the poet's *laqab* (nickname)—his real name Ḥunduj b. Ḥujr was less euphonious and doubtless less romantic—possessed a high antiquity, even in his days. For Imruʾ al-Qays b. ʿAmr, 'king of all the Arabs, who subdued Asad, Nizār and their kings', appears in the proto-Arabic inscription of an-Namāra in the eastern Ḥawrān (Syria) dated 223 in the era of Bostra (Buṣrā), i.e. A.D. 328, and seems to have been one of the Lakhmid kings of al-Ḥīra in Iraq.[1] No doubt there is some connection here with Imruʾ al-Qays, the poet of the sixth century, whose grandfather al-Ḥārith was for a time king of al-Ḥīra. His father Ḥujr b. al-Ḥārith maintained a precarious ascendancy in central Arabia, till he was killed by the same Banū Asad as are mentioned in the inscription. Thereafter Imruʾ al-Qays devoted himself to avenge his father's death and recover his kingdom. His life was spent in an exile's wandering, which eventually took him as far as Constantinople. He failed to secure help from Justinian I, who was then ruling, and died, it is said, from the effects of a poisoned dress on the road back to Arabia, about the year A.D. 540.

If he did not originate it (there is some doubt about the matter), Imru' al-Qays set the fashion, long maintained in Arabic poetry, of beginning a *qaṣīda* with what was called, later at least, the *nasīb*, or sentimental introduction addressed to some girl. The first lines of his *Muʿallaqa*, beginning:

> Stay, both of you! Let us weep over the memory of
> a love and a lodging,[2]
> At the fall of the sandhills between ad-Dakhūl
> and Ḥawmal!

are among the most famous in the Arabic language, evoking in the simplest words the desert journeys of the race from time immemorial. The setting also is of the simplest. The poet and his two companions have come upon the traces of an old encampment. The somewhat commonplace sight, realistically described, induces a mood of tender melancholy, which soon gives place to thoughts of action, in this case hunting in the desert, in other poems tribal politics or war. The mode at all events persisted, whatever the subject of the poem, and although yet another Imru' al-Qays (ibn Humām, or ibn Khidhām) may have anticipated him in setting the scene of his *Muʿallaqa* at a former camping-ground and in choosing lost love as the introductory theme, there is no doubt that *al-Malik aḍ-Ḍillīl*, the Vagabond Prince, was a real innovator, as well as a romantic figure, in the impulse which he gave towards the creation of a national poetry. His *Dīwān* (collected poems) also exists, besides the *Muʿallaqa*. Though in recent times doubt has been cast on the authenticity of the poems attributed to him, principally on the ground of the unreliability of some of the *rāwīs*, for which there is plenty of evidence dating from early times, the figure of Imru' al-Qays remains in the beginnings of Arabic literature, shadowy but real. The arguments of critics like D. S. Margoliouth[3] and Ṭaha Ḥusayn[4] amount to little more than a *caveat* before taking all that has been attributed to him and the other pre-Islamic poets as authentic without investigation. Of the existence of Imru' al-Qays in the sixth century there is no reasonable doubt, nor of the fact that in what survives under his name we have the main lines of a very considerable poetic achievement.

One of the most outstanding of the early poems, dating from a time later than Imru' al-Qays, perhaps a hundred years before Muḥammad, perhaps less, is the famous *Lāmiyyat al-ʿArab*, 'Poem-rhyming-in-*lām* (the letter 'l') of the Arabs', in contradistinction to the much later *Lāmiyyat al-ʿAjam*, 'Poem-rhyming-in-*lām* of the non-Arabs (Persians)', composed by the vizier aṭ-Ṭughrā'ī in 505/1111. The *Lāmiyyat al-ʿArab* is ascribed to ash-Shanfarā of the tribe of Azd, whose story is given in the *Kitāb al-Aghānī* (Book of Songs), the great tenth century repository of the lore of the pre-Islamic Arabs. Disappointed at his treatment by a girl of the Banū Salāmān and rebuffed by her father, he swore to avenge the insult by killing a hundred men of the offending tribe. Hence his murderous raids on foot across the desert, where he could baffle pursuit by such stratagems as the concealment of water in ostrich eggs at points known only to himself and later resume his attacks. It is said that in his lifetime he thus slew ninety-nine men of the Banū Salāmān and that afterwards a splinter from his skull caused the death of another, so that his oath was fulfilled.

W. G. Palgrave gave a sympathetic account of the brigand in his essay on Ta'abbaṭa Sharran,[5] 'He that carried mischief[6] under his arm,' ash-Shanfarā's fellow outlaw, who sometimes accompanied him on his raids. The piece, which is among Palgrave's best, evidently caught the attention of Sir Richard Burton, since in speaking of ash-Shanfarā he adopted several of Palgrave's descriptive phrases, 'indomitable self-reliance' and 'the absolute individualism of a mind defying its age and all around it',[7] as applied to the author of the *Lāmīyat al-ʿArab*.

It would seem that, compared with most pre-Islamic poems, there is as much or more ground for concluding against the authenticity of this work, apparently so redolent of Arab antiquity and the dark times of the Jāhilīya or Age of Ignorance before Muḥammad. It has been attributed to Abū Muḥriz Khalaf al-Aḥmar ('the Red') of al-Baṣra (born *c.* 115/733), who himself a freedman of non-Arab stock—he was by origin from Farghāna in the Syr Darya basin—became an authority on the ancient Arabic poetry. This attribution appears first, it seems, in the *Kītāb al-Amālī* (Dictations), of Abū ʿAlī al-Qālī, who had it from the philologist Ibn Durayd (223/837–321/933).[8] It may be correct. Ibn Durayd was separated by two generations at most from Khalaf al-Aḥmar (d. *c.* 800). Abū ʿAlī al-Qālī came to Baghdad in 303/915, and may easily have heard Ibn Durayd, as he said he did, especially after the latter's removal from al-Baṣra to Baghdad in 308/920.

The idea of Krenkow was that Khalaf al-Aḥmar took the famous fragment in the *Ḥamāsa* of Abū Tammām beginning

> Bury me not! Truly my burial is forbidden
> Unto you, but rejoice at the good news, O hyena!

in regard to which there is no doubt that it is by ash-Shanfarā (facing his enemies at the time of his death), and built it up into the picture of the outlaw as presented in the *Lāmiyyat al-ʿArab.*[9] The authenticity is not without its defenders, notably the German scholars G. Jacob and Brockelmann, and of those who contest it Rêgis Blachère, one of the most recent, admits that Khalaf's authorship as asserted by the medieval philologist is not demonstrable.[10] It is a good deal less than this if, as appears from what has already been said, it depends on al-Qālī's recollection of what was said by one aged man (Ibn Durayd), together with the argument from silence (no mention of the *Lāmiyyat al-ʿArab* in the long notice on ash-Shanfarā in the *Kitāb al-Aghānī*[11] or the *Kitāb ash-Shiʿr waʾsh-Shuʿarāʾ* (Book of Poetry and Poets), of Ibn Qutayba). Psychologically it is difficult to think of such a poem having been produced by a scholar like Khalaf al-Aḥmar, but if he was in fact the author, he would appear to deserve a much more solid fame than is usually conceded to him, for in that case, as Nicholson said, his own poetical endowments must have been of the highest order.[12] It would be strange if this escaped the notice of his own countrymen. The matter could perhaps be settled if Palgrave had given the source of his statement that the Caliph ʿUmar b. al-Khaṭṭāb (d. 644) expressly recommended the study of the *Lāmiyyat al-ʿArab* to the youth of his time as a lesson of genuine manliness.[13] If ʿUmar b. al-Khaṭṭāb actually said this, then of course there is no question of a later fabrication.

The poem at all events finds the author at the point of departure from his people. It is night with a clear moon, and the camels are girthed and ready. Somewhere, the poet hopes, he will find a country where he will be free from insults, even if it means separation from all human companions and consorting with the wild beasts of the desert. He proceeds to the self-glorification (*fakhr*), which is an admissible, indeed favourite, theme of early Arabic poetry. He speaks of his personal qualities of generosity and resourcefulness, and describes his heroic conduct in previous desert journeys. The hunting of the *qaṭā* (sandgrouse) is then described, next his deeds in war. It is especially at night or under the burning heat of the Dog-star (*ash-Shiʿrā*, Sirius) that he piques himself on his valour. Night or day, alone and on foot, he presses to his goal across the immensity of the Desert, all the while bringing to the sights or sounds of the wilderness the sensibility of a true poet, and, come what may, prepared to meet it, not as the hunted man and common criminal which he seems through his hard fortune to be, but as a noble of Azd.

The theme, we notice, is somewhat similar to what we find in Imruʾ al-Qays, that is to say, not simply man against nature, though this motif and that of rebellion against organized society also appear, but the individual against the world. Undoubtedly this was congenial to the Arab consciousness, as the acclaim which these poems have always met with may be taken to prove. Titanism has been considered to be a trait of the Celtic race, and perhaps is so. It is curious to think that in this, as perhaps also in other matters, there is an affinity between such discrete groupings as the Celts and the Arabs.

We may now leave the oldest stratum of Arabic literature, the Jāhilīya poetry, and coming somewhat nearer to our own time, approach the age of Muḥammad. The great literary monument of this age was of course the Qurʾān, which is spoken of elsewhere (Chapter 1). The earlier part of the seventh century, which saw the successful culmination of Muḥammad's preaching in the establishment of the new monotheistic community of Islam, inevitably saw also many changes in the life of Arabia. One aspect of life did not change, or did not change greatly, in spite of the hostility of the new religion, namely the addiction of the Arabs to poetry. In a fairly early (Meccan) *sūra* of the Qurʾān we read: 'Shall I tell you on whom the Satans descend? They descend on every lying, wicked person. They report what they have heard, but most of them are liars. It is the poets whom the erring follow. Hast thou not seen how they wander distraught in every *wādī*, and how they say that which they do not?'[14] In spite of this, poetry continued to be composed during the age of Muḥammad and later, and indeed its indispensability seems to be shown by the presence of Ḥassān b. Thābit, a respectable but perhaps not very outstanding performer, as a kind of court poet at al-Madīna in the Prophet's lifetime. His principal business was apparently to reply to poetical addresses brought by deputations from the tribes, when making their submission. A more notable poet in some ways was Kaʿb b. Zuhayr, whose father was the Zuhayr celebrated as author of one of the *Muʿallaqāt*. Kaʿb at first exercised his talent in verses deriding Muḥammad, and had been requited by a sentence of outlawry or death. He made timely submission, which was accepted, and in gratitude composed in praise of the Prophet a poem famous as the 'Mantle Ode' (*Qaṣīdat al-Burda*),[15] either because Muḥammad covered him with his mantle (*burda*) as he recited it, in token of protection accorded, or bestowed the garment as a reward. The *nasīb*, now customary in these poetical pieces (see above), began

> *bānat Suʿādu fa-qalbī ʾl-yauma matbulū* . . .
> (Suʿād has departed and my heart today is love-sick),

whence the piece is sometimes referred to, from the first words, as *Bānat Suʿād*. The poet goes on to describe his beloved, her eyes, her neck, her cheeks, her movement, his despair of attaining her since he is pursued for his life. This leads on naturally enough to Muḥammad, also at one time a fugitive, praise of whom is the real purpose of the poem. Muḥammad is described. When Kaʿb recited the fiftieth (or fifty-first) line of the *qasīda*:

> Truly the Apostle is a sword who spreads light,
> An Indian blade, of the swords of Allāh, drawn from its scabbard,[16]

Muḥammad, who had hitherto shown indifference, appeared moved and made a sign to the company to listen, while the poet brought his recitation to an end by celebrating the high qualities of the Emigrants:

> Among a company of Quraysh, whose spokesman said
> In the valley of Mecca when they embraced Islam: Set forth!
> They set forth, no weaklings, no unarmed ones
> In combat, none sitting ill on the saddle and helpless—
> Haughty heroes, clad on the day of battle
> In coats of mail of King David's workmanship,
> Glittering, ample, the links thereof struck
> Like the interlacing of the *qafʿāʾ* tree, compact.
> They break not out in joy when their spears smite
> An enemy, nor are they filled with lamentation when smitten.
> They march forward like white camels, and blows
> Defend them when the short, black men draw back.
> No spear-thrust falls but in their breasts
> Nor do they shrink from the cisterns of death.

Such is the famous Mantle Ode, for which according to the most probable account the poet received a hundred camels and the yet more valuable award (as it proved in later days[17]) of the *burda* of the Prophet.

A tone of a different kind pervades the verses of the next poet whom we shall consider. Hunting and war, tribal rivalry and politics, have no place in the poetry of ʿUmar b. Abī Rabīʿa, though he is said to have ended his life in a sea-battle (see p. 35). His full name was ʿUmar b. ʿAbd Allāh b. Abī Rabiʿa, though the shorter form with mention of his grandfather instead of his father is nearly always used, and he lived under ʿUthmān, ʿAlī and the early Umayyad Caliphs, two generations after Muḥammad. It was a stirring time for the Arabs, of war and conquest on an unprecedented scale, but ʿUmar b. Abī Rabīʿa belonged to the family of Makhzūm and his father ʿAbd Allāh was one of the richest merchants of Mecca. There was consequently no economic necessity to take the boy to the frontiers in the armies of Islam, and apparently he had no ambition to distinguish himself as a soldier, in the way that most of his contemporaries were doing. There may have been other reasons, but what they may have been we can only conjecture. His grandfather Abū Rabīʿa, to judge from his nickname Dhū'r-Rumḥayn, 'He of the two spears', was a fighting man.[18] The father ʿAbd Allāh was a half-brother of Abū Jahl b. Hishām, the Prophet's personal enemy, but he was employed by Muḥammad in an important government post in the Yemen, and was killed in Sijistān (eastern Iran) probably on some expedition. At all events, ʿUmar b. Abī Rabīʿa as he grew up showed no inclination to be anything but a poet, and a poet of a new style. His biographers attach some importance to the fact that his mother was originally a slave-girl from Ḥaḍramaut or Ḥimyar, in any case from South Arabia, from whom he might have derived his gift for love-poetry (*ghazal*), this being considered as characteristic of South Arabia as flirtation (*dall*) was characteristic of the Ḥijāz,[19] and of course ʿUmar b. Abī Rabīʿa had both strains in his inheritance. That such an opinion could be held at all, points of course to a period of poetical development in both regions about which we know little or nothing. It may be remarked in general that the importance of South Arabia for the rise of the classical Arabic poetry may be greater than is usually supposed. While the latter is commonly regarded as a product of North Arabia, three of the four poets whom we have hitherto considered (Imru' al-Qays, ash-Shanfarā and ʿUmar b. Abī Rabīʿa) appear to have been in whole or in part of South Arabian extraction (see pp. 9–10 above).

There may be a link here with a forgotten poetical art of South Arabia, the remains of the civilization of which survive indeed to our own times, but in stone (inscriptions and architecture).[20]

ʿUmar b. Abī Rabīʿa wrote much in praise of a girl called ath-Thurayyā. Ath-Thurayyā like himself belonged to the richer class of Meccans and was a granddaughter of that Qutayla who, after the battle of Badr in the year 2 of the Hijra, recited verses to Muḥammad, reproaching him with the death of an-Naḍr b. al-Ḥārith, her father or her brother, killed at his orders by ʿAlī or another Companion.[21] ʿUmar b. Abī Rabīʿa's girl was in any case a beauty and high-spirited, and the love-affair did not always go satisfactorily. There were quarrels followed by reconciliations, and on one occasion we are told that ath-Thurayyā, feeling herself insulted, struck her lover with her hand, loaded with rings—on all five fingers, the custom of the women in those days, as the author of the *Kitāb al-Aghānī* (tenth century) tells us,[22] so sharply that the blow loosened two front teeth. The poet at once betook himself to al-Baṣra for treatment. The teeth were saved but remained black for the rest of his career. Eventually ath-Thurayyā married one Suhayl b. ʿAbd ar-Raḥmān. The poet was evidently less than well pleased and, punning on their names, composed the verses:

> O you who join in marriage ath-Thurayyā and Suhayl,
> Allāh preserve you! how are they to meet?
> She (ath-Thurayyā, the Pleiades) rises in the Syrian (northern) sky,
> And Suhayl (Canopus) rises in the sky of the Yemen (the south)![23]

In spite of all ʿUmar b. Abī Rabīʿa remained fondly attached to ath-Thurayyā, another of whose exploits along with her sister ʿĀ'isha was to set free their slave al-Gharīḍ, the friend of Maʿbad, both of whom came to be reckoned among the most famous singers of Islam. After her marriage ʿUmar followed her to Syria, and spent a long night of sentimental conversation until dawn in her company, parting with tears on both sides.

Then he rose up, and mounted his horse, and watched them as they saddled the camels. Then he followed them with his eyes till they passed out of sight, and he recited:

> O my two friends! Stay, let us ask the traces of the encampment
> Concerning the one who halted there yesterday, what she has done!

and so on, to the end of the *qaṣīda*.[24] It was probably to another girl that the fragment which pleased Ibn Khallikān was written:

> Greet a vision of a sweetheart come to visit
> After sleep prostrated the night-conversers,
> Appearing in a dream under the darkness of night—
> Grudging that she should visit by day!
> I said, 'Why should I have been treated cruelly, and
> Before that I was the ears and the eyes?'
> She replied, 'I am as you once knew me, but
> The necklace occupies the wearer too much for it to be lent!'[25]

It is verses like these that have gained for ʿUmar b. Abī Rabīʿa in the West a conventional reputation as the Ovid of the Arabs. Whether the comparison is an apt one is perhaps open to doubt, since the Arab poet's feeling appears fresher and less artificial than Ovid's. He certainly did not write nearly so much, to judge by the rather short *Dīwān* of his collected works which we possess.[26] In one respect the Arab and the Roman were alike—the disfavour with which they were regarded by those in authority. Although he was personally well known to the Umayyads, Caliphs and others, as a prominent member of a distinguished Arab family, and indeed their distant kinsman, his preoccupation with love and poetry, and the occasional scandal which this unavoidably led to, but perhaps most of all the poet's insouciance in regard to what were considered serious subjects, earned him dislike in the highest quarters, which at least on one occasion almost brought him to ruin, if it did not actually do so indirectly.

He was sent for to Damascus along with his fellow-poet al-Aḥwaṣ (almost as prominent in the *Kitāb al-Aghānī* as ʿUmar himself, but less famous in later times), and orders were given by the Caliph, then ʿUmar II b. ʿAbd al-ʿAzīz, a man known for his austerity, that the two poets should make the journey in fetters.[27] Arrived at Damascus the offenders were interviewed by the Caliph, who turned first to ʿUmar b. Abī Rabīʿa and quoted some verses of his from a fragment beginning: 'And how many a one is slain (sc. by love) whose death is unavenged'—verses quite characteristic of the poet, in which he seems to say that there are some people, himself included, for whom the annual Pilgrimage is principally an opportunity for admiring pretty women. 'If you were really concerned with your pilgrimage,' said the Caliph sternly, 'you would have no eyes for anything but yourself.' He then gave orders for his banishment. 'Or better than that, O

Commander of the Faithful,' said the poet. 'I swear by Allāh that I will never again make such poetry, or mention women, and I repent anew at your hands.' 'But will you?' said the Caliph. 'Yes,' said ʿUmar, and having taken a solemn oath of repentance, the Caliph let him go. His companion al-Aḥwaṣ was less fortunate, and was banished to Dahlak, an island in the Red Sea off Eritrea, which, as Yāqūt tells us, was a regular place of banishment under the Umayyads.[28]

It has been pointed out that, as ʿUmar b. Abī Rabīʿa by now was over seventy, it was probably not very difficult for him to keep his oath. The note of his age at the time (ʿUmar II was Caliph 99/717–101/720) seems right, if there is any truth in the statement that the poet was born on the day on which another ʿUmar, the Caliph ʿUmar I b. al-Khaṭṭāb, was murdered (in Dhū'l-Ḥijja, 23/October–November 644). We can assume at least that his birth was about this time. But it is also stated that he died at the age of seventy in a sea-fight, when the ship he was on was burned.[29] The date for this occurrence is said to have been A.H. 93/A.D. 712. This cannot be reconciled as it stands with the other story, but if true, it is surely remarkable that the poet of pleasure in his old age took part in a naval expedition of a regular kind (as we are to understand from the text) which most probably must have been against the Byzantines. The fact, if fact it is, would have to be explained. A plausible explanation would be that he was ordered to do so as a punishment. Clearly, however, if we are to accept this, it was not ʿUmar b. ʿAbd al-ʿAzīz but one of his predecessors who took the poet to task for his conduct, and the interview in Damascus did not pass off so favourably for him as in the other account.

Though there was normally in this period little love lost between Umayyad Damascus and the Hijāz, it is a remarkable fact that the famous poets of the capital had a high regard for ʿUmar b. Abī Rabīʿa. Jarīr, his contemporary (died 110/728), had a special liking for the fragment beginning:

> Ask the spring-encampment in al-Bulayy and say:
> Long will last the emotion you bring this morning![30]

Jarīr said: 'That is what we try to do and fail, but this man of Quraysh gets it right!' He meant the sentimental effect of the *nasīb*, which here closely follows the original pattern of Imru' al-Qays (see p. 27). Al-Farazdaq, on the other hand, who made fun of the deserted camping-ground, heard ʿUmar b. Abī Rabīʿa reciting another of his poems, where he again spoke of the ceremonies of the Pilgrimage and the opportunities which they afforded to the sentimentally inclined. It begins:

> A well-wisher carried me news of her affection for me,
> And the Day of the Stoning at Minā nearly brought me to my death!

The poem was by no means of the conventional pattern, and al-Farazdaq interrupted the recital to exclaim, 'This, by Allāh! is what the poets want to achieve, but they fall short and weep over abandoned camping-grounds!'[31] Another time the two poets met at al-Madīna, in the company of two humorists who a short while before had introduced themselves to al-Farazdaq as 'Pharaoh' and 'Haman'—both characters, naturally enough, ill-seen in the Qur'ān[32]—and again, when ʿUmar b. Abī Rabīʿa had recited a pleasant little piece in which the poet meets with his girl of the moment and her friends, and they urge her to stay with him, while she is reluctant, before he ended al-Farazdaq cried, 'By Allāh, you are the most skilful of men in making love-poetry! The poets cannot make the *nasīb* like this, or charm hearts as you!'[33]

Jarīr and al-Farazdaq were no doubt good judges of poetry and, in the opinion of their fellow-countrymen, excellent poets themselves. We shall not here pause to give examples of their work, nor of that of al-Akhṭal, another poet closely associated with the Umayyad court, who was somewhat older than either of them. The impression which one gains especially of al-Farazdaq is not very pleasant. Jarīr and al-Farazdaq became engaged in a rivalry of merit. This became a bitter feud, in which al-Akhṭal joined on the side of the latter, and a great deal of their energy was taken up with mutual abuse, in which no insults were neglected. To this we may add that aṭ-Ṭabarī has a story[34] of how with other courtiers of the Caliph Sulaymān (ruled 96/715–99/717) Jarīr and al-Farazdaq helped to strike off the heads of a group of Byzantine prisoners who had just arrived at al-Madīna. An ʿAlid was invited by Sulaymān to behead the chief of the group, a *patrikios* (*biṭrīq*) who according to one account was in chains, and did so with a clean stroke which won the commendation of the Caliph. Jarīr did the same with another victim. Al-Farazdaq, when his turn came, had, like the other executioners, no sword of his own and, receiving a blunt, heavy weapon, missed his blow several times. The Caliph and the people laughed at him, and he threw away the sword, at once improvising verses excusing his failure, with nauseating flattery of Sulaymān. The scene is a painful one, and we forbear comment.

In contrast, we have the scene where the orthodox Ibn ʿAbbās (who died in 68/687–88) interrupts an interview with another theologian to listen to a long *qasīda* about a girl called Nuʿm,[35] recited to him by the youthful ʿUmar b. Abī Rabīʿa, with whom he is evidently on the best of terms. At the conclusion of the poem, which the narrator of the story says contained eighty verses, the other man expostulated that he had come a long way to consult Ibn ʿAbbās on a matter of religion, but he seemed to prefer to listen to nonsense. 'It was no nonsense,' said Ibn ʿAbbās, and in the sequel repeated the whole from the beginning, never having heard it before.[36] The tale is told, no doubt, principally to show the contempt of Ibn ʿAbbās for his interlocutor, the Khārijite heretic Ibn al-Azraq, perhaps also to illustrate his wonderful memory, but it also presents ʿUmar b. Abī Rabīʿa in a very favourable light. Later in life the attention of religious men like Ibn ʿAbbas was usually directed to him in a strictly unfriendly fashion. If we inquire what his work amounted to, beyond the pleasure which it brought to many hearers and readers in later times, it is most obviously in the extension of the *nasīb*, which originally served simply as the introduction to a poem, into an independent *genre*, love poetry as such. This was a notable achievement. Love poetry had an important development in later Arabic literature.[37]

2. Arabic prose and the beginnings of a written literature

As yet we have said nothing in this chapter about prose writing in Arabic, and nothing about books as such, apart from a brief mention of the Qurʾān, for the *Dīwāns* of the poets, if they existed, appear to have been written down only later. To take the first point first, prose or at all events literary prose among the Arabs as among many, perhaps most, other peoples, developed subsequently to poetry, and in this case after a long interval. There is no evidence for a classical Arabic prose contemporary with and comparable to the pre-Islamic poetry. We can be fairly certain that the age-old custom, amounting almost to an institution, of the *samar*, or night-conversation, in the tents of the desert, and similar meetings in the towns, gave rise to story-telling about the deeds of past and present chiefs in fight or foray, or in times of peace. The most interesting of these prose tales would be remembered and repeated, and we know in fact not only of accounts of the *ayyām al-ʿArab*, 'days of the Arabs' (famous battles among the tribes), but also of incidents from the Persian heroic saga, as rehearsed before Arab audiences in early times. Further, we have to take into consideration rhetorical displays in old Arabia, of which a well-known example are the sermons of Quss b. Sāʿida al-Iyādī, bishop (or a presbyter) of Najrān. One of these discourses, delivered at the fair of ʿUkāẓ, had a powerful effect on the youthful Muḥammad, who long afterwards expressed admiration for the speaker.[38] The material for a prose literature in Arabic thus existed, but we have no reason to think that anything was written down, or at least published, till Umayyad times, when we hear of books on the history of South Arabia by ʿAbīd[39] b. Sharya, who was patronized by Muʿāwiya (Caliph 41/661–60/680) and died at a great age under ʿAbd al-Malik (65/685–86/705), and Wahb b. Munabbih (died as *qāḍī* of Ṣanʿāʾ in 114/732. The *Kitāb al-Mulūk wa-Akhbār al-Māḍīn* (or *Akhbār ʿAbid b. Sharya al-Jurhumī fī Akhbār al-Yaman wa-Ashʿārihā wa-Ansābihā*) of the former and the *Kitāb at-Tījān fī Mulūk Ḥimyar ʿan Wahb b. Munabbih* of the latter, both apparently authentic, actually exist and have been published, though in both the hands of later editors seem to have been busy.[40]

We have on the other hand a notice in the Spanish author Ibn Juljul, whose *Ṭabaqāt al-Aṭibbāʾ waʾl-Ḥukamāʾ* (Classes of the Doctors and the Sages) was written in 377/987–88, that the Jew Māsarjawayh undertook under Marwān (Caliph, 64/683–65/685) the translation into Arabic of 'the book of Ahrūn al-Qass (Aaron the Priest, of Alexandria)', who as we know from other sources was the author of a *Kunnāsh* or collection of notes on medicine.[41] No doubt this is the work intended here. It was originally composed in thirty discourses, to which Māsarjawayh added two more. The language from which the translation was made appears to be nowhere stated, but may have been Syriac, less probably Greek. A successor of Marwān's, the pious Caliph ʿUmar II b. ʿAbd al-ʿAzīz, found the translated work in the collections of books belonging to the Umayyads—so we must translate the expression *khazāʾin al-kutub* of the text[42]—and ordered it to be brought out and placed in his oratory. There on forty days in succession he sought divine enlightenment on the question of whether or not to make it available to the Muslims, and finally decided to do so.

A tenth-century author is not very good authority for an event which is said to have happened in the seventh or eighth century, and Ibn Juljul expressly tells us that he got his story, not from any eastern source but in a mosque in Spain,[42a] from his contemporary, the Spanish historian Ibn al-Qūṭīiyya, whose very name ('son of the Gothic woman') indicates how far away we are from the Muslim East. On the other hand, both Ibn Juljul and Ibn al-Qūṭīiyya are careful writers, and Ibn Juljul thought the account which he had heard important enough to be recorded. What exactly does he intend should be understood by his notice? Hardly that this was the first book in Islam after the Qur'ān. There is reason to think, as we have seen, that some other books already existed, and, to take Ibn Juljul at the foot of the letter, there was already a library, presumably in the residence of the Caliphs in Damascus called al-Khaḍrā', 'the Green Palace', of which all traces have now disappeared. What he means perhaps is that this was the first non-Muslim work to appear in Arabic, in other words that this was the first Arabic translation—a significant development, in view of the importance which the translation literature came to assume, as Ibn Juljul himself was well aware. Whether it is strictly the case that Māsarjawayh's was the first translation is another question, which we need not go into here. There is some evidence that part of the New Testament was translated into Arabic in the first half of the seventh century.[43] Or Ibn Juljul may mean—and this is somewhat more likely in view of his interests as a doctor—that now for the first time a scientific book in Arabic made its appearance. If this is what is meant, it is no doubt right. In any case, his notice fits quite well into the facts as we know them.

We can account easily for the presence of the book in the library of the Umayyads, if not for the library itself, by the preoccupation of the Umayyad prince Khālid b. Yazīd with intellectual matters, which is well-attested,[44] though Khālid b. Yazīd seems to have resided not at al-Khaḍrā', but at another palace in Damascus called Dār al-Ḥijāra.[45] Not only so, but it seems likely that it was Khālid, the contemporary of Marwān, who gave the impulse to the translation in the first place. The *Fihrist* states that he ordered philosophers living in the 'city of Egypt', apparently Alexandria, to translate the books on alchemy from Greek and Coptic into Arabic. The author of the *Fihrist* says that these were Greek philosophers, and adds that they knew Arabic well.[46] This is consistent with a commission to Māsarjawayh to translate the medical work of Aaron the Priest, and the notice of the translation in Ibn

Juljul, though late, is no doubt to be accepted. Arabic work on medicine and science in general had of course a long way to go, as will be mentioned in its place (see Chapter 6). Here we are concerned with the beginnings of a literature in prose, and from what has been said it will appear that the source of Arabic prose was not solely romantic legend and saga, native or foreign, though it was both of these, nor exclusively the Qur'ān and the marvellous amplification of religious and legal literature based on the Qur'ān which rapidly came into existence, but also, at a different level, the scientific literature of other nations, especially the Greeks (of whom the Syrians, Copts, even the Indians, from whose writings translations were often directly made, were in some sense the pupils). This meant that Arabic possessed a plain style as well as a literary style, and this has always remained so. While at times men of letters among the Arabs have adopted fashions with which the euphuism on sixteenth-century England pales in comparison, a simpler, more rational prose has continued to be available for scientific enquiries in the broadest sense, and was used by all who wished to retail facts, not fancies or mere verbiage. This has been of great importance in the survival of Arabic, amid great vicissitudes, to the present day, and accounts also for the readiness with which the language has been able to adapt itself to modern needs and requirements. It is safe to say that if Arabic had developed solely along the lines of poetry and artificial prose, it would now be obsolete or obsolescent.

3. Great poets and prose writers: Abū Tammām, al-Mutanabbi', Ibn al-Muqaffa', al-Jāḥiẓ

For a long time it was generally considered that al-Farazdaq, Jarīr and al-Akhṭal were the greatest of the poets of Islam. This is stated more than once in the *Kitāb al-Aghānī* (fourth/tenth century),[47] and in so saying the author of the *Aghānī* re-echoes the opinion of the *Jamharat Ash'ār al-'Arab* (Collection of the Poetry of the Arabs), there given as follows.

All men agree that the most poetical of the people of Islam were al-Farazdaq, Jarīr and al-Akhṭal, and the reason is their poetical endowment which was given to no one else in Islam. They praised people, and exalted them. They censured people, and abased them. Some satirised them, whom they refuted and dumbfounded. Others did so, whom they disdained to reply to and left to be forgotten. These are the poets of the people of Islam.[48]

The reputed collector of the *Jamharat Ashʿār al-ʿArab*, Abū Zayd al-Qurashī,[49] cites for this Abū ʿUbayda, a well-known philologist of al-Baṣra (110/728–*c.* 210/825). If the collection was really brought together about A.D. 1000, as has been said,[50] it is somewhat striking that no mention is made in it of any poet more recent than the famous trio. This alone would not be good ground for placing it earlier, but there are other considerations suggesting a third/ninth century or even a second/eighth century date.[51] In any case, there were a number of excellent poets in early ʿAbbāsid times, as we should expect, and to some at least of these we must now direct attention.

One of the most outstanding was Abū Tammām, whose *Dīwān* and *Ḥamāsa* are still extensively read. The latter is an anthology of poetry from pagan and early Islamic times, divided into ten books of unequal length according to subject matter, which includes all the main themes of ancient Arabic poetry, the first, 'Courage' (*ḥamāsa*), giving its name to the collection. It has been much esteemed by subsequent ages, and the frequently quoted remark of at-Tibrīzī, an eleventh-century commentator: *Abū Tammām fī Ḥamāsatihi ashʿaru minhu fī shiʿrihi* (Abū Tammām in his *Ḥamāsa* is more poetical than in his poetry) implies perhaps appreciation rather than disparagement. Other anthologies compiled by Abū Tammām are mentioned by Ibn Khallikān,[52] the *Fuḥūl ash-Shuʿarāʾ* (The Stallions among the Poets) and the *Kitāb al-Ikhtiyārāt min Shiʿr ash-Shuʿarāʾ* (Book of Selections from the Poetry of the Poets). If different from the present *Ḥamāsa*, these have not survived, though possibly some material from the other anthologies is included in its later books.

Abū Tammām is regularly called Ḥabīb b. Aws aṭ-Ṭāʾī, i.e. of the Bedouin tribe of Ṭayy, with a long genealogy going back to Qaḥṭān, the eponym of the South Arabians in a remote antiquity. On the other hand, his father is said to have been Taddūs, or Thaddūs (the name perhaps from Theodorus, cf. Thaddaeus), a Christian perfumer (*ʿaṭṭār*) or wine-seller (*khammār*) of the village of Jāsim, south of Damascus. It appears more likely that the poet, after conversion to Islam, adopted Aws as his father's name with the rest of the genealogy, or had this attributed to him, than that the Christian origin was invented by ill-disposed persons, as one biographer has suggested.[53] The urge to identify with the dominant race is a well-marked social phenomenon in early Islam, not least among the poets, as the cases of Ḥammād ar-Rāwiya (a Daylamite),

Dīk al-Jinn (originally from Mu'ta,[54] in former Byzantine territory) and Ibn ar-Rūmī show. Most converts to Islam became clients (*mawlās*) of an Arab tribe. It would therefore not be surprising, though this is expressly denied by the author of the *Kitāb al-Aghānī*,[55] if Abū Tammām were a *mawlā* of Ṭayy, not a tribesman.

Jāsim, where the poet was born (the likeliest date is 188/804) belonged to the district of al-Jaydūr (Ituraea), and was important enough to be named in the classical sources (Gasimea). It was evidently an old centre with a sedentary population, to which Abū Tammām's family may have belonged. Perhaps we have to think of the sedentaries of Jāsim as claiming kinship with Ṭayy, among whom at this time or a little earlier Christianity is a well-established fact.[56] Abū Tammām, whose humble origin is obvious enough, might therefore have had grounds for regarding himself and being regarded as of Ṭayy, and at the same time have been the son of Taddūs, a Christian wine-seller or perfumer. There was certainly no reason to stress this, in relating the life of one who became a great Muslim poet and the panegyrist of Caliphs.

Abū Tammām grew up apparently in Damascus,[57] and then, after some time spent in Ḥimṣ, where he met and was influenced by the older poet Dīk al-Jinn already mentioned, passed to Egypt. His gifts had already made themselves known, but he was obliged to occupy the menial position of a water-carrier in the mosque, apparently that of ʿAmr in al-Fusṭāṭ. His poems during this period of his life, which lasted for several years, not unnaturally reflect discontent with his impoverished condition and homesickness for Syria. Yet he was making his way as a poet, for we hear of him as engaged in a contest of satirizing (*hijā'*) with some Egyptian authors, and as writing an elegy (*marthiya*) on a governor of Egypt who was killed in 214/829.[58] Shortly after this he returned to Syria, at the age of about twenty-six. It was in Syria apparently that he made the acquaintance of the Caliph al-Ma'mūn and praised him in a *qaṣīda*, al-Ma'mūn at that time being intermittently engaged in wars against the Byzantines which necessitated his presence there. The two men, however, were not in agreement on religious questions, for Abū Tammām had developed strong ʿAlid views, and it seems that there was never any prospect of his becoming a poet of al-Ma'mūn's court. Perhaps realizing this, Abū Tammām went on his travels again. We find him in north Syria, al-Mawṣil (Mosul), al-Baṣra, even Armenia, but he was rarely, if at all, in Baghdad, the capital of the empire, till after the death of al-Ma'mūn in 218/833. Now, as a poet already famous, he was induced to visit Baghdad, where he met al-Muʿtaṣim, the brother and successor of al-Ma'mūn, and from this time till his death in 232/846 he enjoyed the highest reputation and the society of some of the leading men in Islam. It was on a journey to Khurāsān where he visited the governor ʿAbd Allāh b. Ṭāhir that he compiled the *Ḥamāsa* already mentioned, while detained at Hamadhān owing to snow, in the house of a friend who conveniently had a large library.[59]

The name of Abū Tammām is specially linked with that of al-Muʿtaṣim for whom, after the capture of the Byzantine town of ʿAmmūriya (Amorium) in Asia Minor, he wrote what is perhaps the most celebrated of his *qaṣīdas*, beginning:

> The sword is truer than what is told in books:
> In its edge is the separation between truth and falsehood,[60]

an ominous verse, followed by others in the same sense:

> In the white sword-blades, not the black pages of texts
> Is found the clarification of doubt and uncertainty,
> And knowledge is in bright spears flashing
> Between the armies, not in the Seven Shining Ones [the planets]

with special reference, we are told, to the predictions of the Byzantine astrologers, who had falsely promised victory to their own side. The whole poem is animated in the extreme and breathes inveterate hatred against the enemy.

Ibn Khallikān reports a story to the effect that Abū Tammām praised one of the Caliphs—his name is not given[61]—in his *qaṣīda* rhyming in *sīn* (=s) and when he came to the line:

> The daring of ʿAmr with the generosity of Ḥātim,
> The forbearance of Aḥnaf and the acumen of Iyās,

the vizier interrupted him, and said, 'Do you compare the Commander of the Faithful to the rude Bedouin?', which is no doubt what the heroes mentioned were or could be represented to be. Abū Tammām was silent for a time, then raised his head and recited:

> Do not object to my likening him to inferiors
> Who are currently proverbial for liberality and courage.
> Allāh has before this compared the least thing to His light—
> Taking the comparison from the niche and the lamp.

The reference here is to a famous verse of the Qur'ān: 'Allāh is the light of the heavens and the earth. His light is like a niche in which is a lamp, the lamp in glass and the glass like a brilliant star, lit from a blessed tree, an olive neither of the East nor of the West whose oil would almost give light even though no fire did touch it . . .'[62] The vizier was satisfied, and said to the Caliph: 'Whatever he asks, give him. He will not live more than forty days, for blood has appeared in his eyes from intensity of thought, and he of whom this is true lives no longer.' On the Caliph's inviting him to name his reward, Abū Tammām is said to have requested al-Mawṣil (Mosul), the town or province, presumably as a governorship, and to have received it, but to have lived no more than the forty days mentioned.

Ibn Khallikān decisively rejects the story as it stands, and quotes another version from Abū Bakr aṣ-Ṣūlī,[63] according to which the verses already cited were spoken by Abū Tammām before Aḥmad b. al-Muʿtaṣim, a prince who was never Caliph. A third interlocutor in the story, the anonymous vizier, is now named and turns out to be the celebrated philosopher al-Kindī, who of course as a *ḥakīm* (wise man, doctor) is well able to diagnose the poet's state of health. This version omits any mention of Abū Tammām receiving Mosul as a reward for his verses, and gains something in credibility since Aḥmad b. al-Muʿtaṣim is otherwise known as an associate of al-Kindī and probably his pupil. It records the interesting fact that a poet might apparently *read* his *qaṣīda* to the person praised, or at least that Abū Tammām had a written copy by him on this occasion, as can scarcely have been the practice in earlier times. We are told that when the *qaṣīda* was taken from his hand, the two additional verses quoted above were not found[64] and those present were astonished at his talent of quick improvization. Ibn Khallikān mentions that he had made a check and had found no record of Abū Tammām as governor of Mosul, but that he had been in charge of the government post (*barīd*) there for some two years before his death. Whatever the exact facts may be, the case of the poet of Ṭayy (Abū Tammām) who received Mosul as a reward was cited long afterwards in the time of the ʿAbbāsid Caliph al-Mustarshid (512/1118–529/1135) by that remarkable exponent of Arab antiquity the poet Abū'l-Fawāris al-Hīṣ Bīṣ,[65] when he advanced the comparatively modest claim for the town or large village of Baʿqūbā.[66]

Abū Tammām died amid general regret probably in 232/846,

in his early forties, at Mosul, where his tomb was afterwards known to the common people as that of 'Tammām the poet', and is at present marked by a handsome monument.[67]

Among the poets contemporary with Abū Tammām or later in the ninth century the names of al-Buḥturī, Ibn ar-Rūmī and Ibn al-Muʿtazz stand out, and their work may be characterized very briefly. Al-Buḥturī (205/820–284/897) was by way of being a protégé of Abū Tammām, was like him a Syrian (from Manbij, north-east of Aleppo) and stood in much the same relationship to al-Mutawakkil as Abū Tammām had stood to al-Muʿtaṣim earlier. Also like Abū Tammām he compiled a *Ḥamāsa*. The work has survived, but enjoys a less high esteem than the other. Ibn ar-Rūmī (221/836–283 or 284/896 or 897), born in Baghdad, was a more troubled spirit than al-Buḥturī, but in modern times, perhaps for that very reason, has been given the preference over him.[68] Ibn al-Muʿtazz, son of a Caliph and for a single day in December 908 Caliph himself, was the author of an interesting *Dīwān*, in which the themes which might be expected to attract a prince of the ruling house are treated in a 'modern' style, yet with a feeling for the past. Ibn al-Muʿtazz also signalized himself by the composition of prose works on literary criticism, of which the most important is the *Kitāb al-Badīʿ*,[69] the first systematic treatment in Arabic of poetical style and rhetoric.

With al-Mutanabbiʾ (303/915–354/965) we come to one who in the past has been valued less highly than Abū Tammām, but at the present day would probably be considered the greatest of Arabic poets, at all events by his own countrymen. In the West, as al-Mutanabbiʾ has become known, there has been a certain reservation of admiration, perhaps because of the very force of his utterance in praise and blame, love or hate, where the expression of a violent nature seems on occasion to transgress the rules of art and even the limits of self-control. Yet he has a splendid rhetoric, which runs the gamut of all the emotions, and some wonderful lines, for example:

> Night and the horses and the Desert know me,
> Also the sword and the guest and paper and the pen.

This verse is said to have been the cause of the poet's death, for when he was returning from a visit to the Buwayhid ʿAḍud ad-Dawla in Fārs (south-west Persia) and had reached a point near an-Nuʿmāniyya between Wāsiṭ and Baghdad, he and his company were attacked by marauders, in much the same way as had happened to the philosopher al-Fārābī in Syria, a few years previously, and with equally fatal results. Al-Mutanabbi' had a chance of escaping by flight, but when his servant reminded him of what would be said when people heard that the author of 'Night and the horses, etc.' had fled, he turned back, and was killed. Al-Mutanabbi' was associated with the Hamdānids of Aleppo, especially Sayf ad-Daula.

Another less well known but still respectable poet of the Hamdānids was Abū Firās, a cousin of Sayf ad-Dawla, whose verses to his mother, written in a Byzantine prison, are deservedly praised.[70]

Turning now to consider prose works written in Arabic during the early ʿAbbāsid period, we come first to the well-known name of Ibn al-Muqaffaʿ, author of a famous work, *Kalīla wa-Dimna*, an Arabic translation of the Pahlavi (Middle Persian) *Fables of Bidpai*, which in turn was a version of the Indian Mirror of Princes *Panchatantra*[70a]. The Kalīla and Dimna of the title are jackals, and their relations to the lion and other animals, are set forth in a series of amusing episodes, in which the political life of these times (under autocratic rule, not varying greatly from country to country, or from century to century) is allegorically represented with verve and ingenuity. The Arabic style of *Kalīla wa-Dimna* is much admired, and altogether it is not surprising that the work has retained its popularity down to the present day.

Ibn al-Muqaffaʿ translated other Middle Persian books, notably the *Khudāy-nāma*, a moralizing history of the Persian kings. Both Ibn al-Muqaffaʿ's Arabic translation and the Pahlavi original are lost, but the material which the work contained was very influential in Arabic and modern Persian literature, to judge by the numerous important authors who appear to have utilized it.[71] Further Ibn al-Muqaffaʿ is said to have translated into Arabic from Pahlavi the *Categories*, *De Interpretatione* and *Analytics* of Aristotle, of which only the first had hitherto been translated,[72] and he wrote several original works, among them a *Kitab al-Adab al-Kabīr* on ethics and correct behaviour, which has been several times printed in recent times. Another work of the same nature attributed to Ibn al-Muqaffaʿ is the *Risālat al-Adab al-Wajīz li'l-Walad aṣ-Ṣaghīr*, which was translated into modern Persian by Naṣīr ad-Dīn aṭ-Ṭūsī (thirteenth century A.D.) and has appeared in the original Arabic.[73] As the title signifies, it contains instruction for a little boy, who is the author's son. A work entitled *Kitāb al-Adab aṣ-Ṣaghīr*, evidently in contrast with the *Kitāb al-Adab al-Kabīr* already mentioned, by or at least attributed to Ibn al-Muqaffaʿ also exists and has been published, but doubts have been cast upon its authenticity in several quarters.[74] It is perhaps worth mentioning that al-Jāḥiẓ, the great master of early Arabic prose, complained that he was unable to win attention with good books put out under his own name, while inferior and less useful works of his, if published under the name of Ibn al-Muqaffaʿ or another of his predecessors, were eagerly read and transcribed.[75] It is in any case to al-Jāḥiẓ—an unflattering nickname meaning 'goggle-eyed' (he was actually Abū ʿUthmān ʿAmr b. Baḥr al-Baṣrī)—that we opportunely come.

Al-Jāḥiẓ was born about 160/776 in al-Baṣra, one of the great new cities of the Islamic dispensation.[76] His most important writings were the product of his advanced years. (He lived to be upwards of ninety.) These are the *Kitāb al-Bayān wa't-Tabyīn*, a somewhat unsystematic work on rhetoric which has been printed in several volumes more than once in modern times;[77] the *Kitāb al-Ḥayawān* (Book of Animals), printed in Cairo in seven volumes, a work of *adab* (here *belles lettres*) rather than zoology;[78] and the *Kitāb al-Bukhalā'* (Book of Misers), a discursive account, sometimes amusing, sometimes to modern taste rather tedious, of outstanding examples of meanness, among which figure various well-known people including apparently the philosopher al-Kindī,[79] as well as others, unknown or imaginary.

An interesting group of works of al-Jāḥiẓ was edited by the Dutch Orientalist Van Vloten, viz. *Risāla ilā 'l-Fatḥ b. Khāqān fī Manāqib at-Turk wa-ʿĀmmat Jund al-Khilāfa* (Epistle to al-Fatḥ b. Khāqān on the Good Qualities of the Turks and the Common Soldiers of the Caliphate), which deals with the formation of the Turkish guard;[80] *Kitāb Fakhr as-Sūdān ʿalā 'l-Bīḍān* (Book of the Boasting of the Blacks over the Whites), having a special interest because al-Jāḥiẓ himself was partially black, 'probably of Abyssinian origin';[81] and a work with the strange title *Kitāb at-Tarbīʿ wa't-Tadwīr* (Book of Squareness and Roundness).[82] This was directed against one Aḥmad b. ʿAbd al-Wahhāb who somehow had been so unfortunate as to annoy al-Jāḥiẓ. He 'claimed all kinds of knowledge according to the measure of his ignorance of them' and 'listed the names of books without understanding their contents'. 'I decided to uncover his veil and show his true colours to townsman and nomad and the dwellers in every frontier and capital, by asking him 100 questions in which I make fun of him and let people know the measure of his ignorance.'[83] Al-Jāḥiẓ proceeds to address him with mock solemnity in a lengthy preamble, in which *inter alia* the meaning of the title of the work appears.

Aḥmad b. ʿAbd al-Wahhāb has been described as a short, thick-set man of commonplace appearance, anything but tall and good-looking. He has developed a theory, which al-Jāḥiẓ clearly gives us to understand is absurd, that the poets in describing handsome persons of either sex choose their metaphors from natural objects which are round and broad, that the celestial spheres and heavenly bodies, the earth and its contents such as leaves, dates, grain and fruit, are round, and that roundness is prior in nature to squareness, which exists only in what is artificial and composite, whereas roundness exists in what is left in its natural state. What is the reason for such views? Obviously, al-Jāḥiẓ suggests, because you yourself are a round, tubby man (whatever you suppose you are) and have a natural prejudice in favour of rotundity.[84]

All this is not very serious, and the burlesque tone continues. You are undoubtedly a great genius, and possess the wisdom of the ages, so much so that you must have been contemporary with all past events, like the vulture of Luqmān.[85] Tell me then, what like was the Flood, and when was the bursting of the dam of Ma'rib? How long since the death of Og,[86] and when were the tongues confused at Babel? What detained Noah's raven, and how long were you in the Ark (you must of course have been there)? Is Hermes the same as Idrīs? Is Jeremiah one with al-Khiḍr? Is John, son of Zechariah, Elias? Is Dhū'l-Qarnayn Alexander? Who were his father and his mother? Inform me about the Seven Seas and the mountain of Qāf, and how long it is since mankind were one people and their languages the same, and after how many generations the Negro became black and the Slavonian white.[87] Inform me if the giraffe is the offspring of a female camel and a hyena, and what bird is the phoenix (*ʿanqāʾ mughrib*).[88] Al-Jāḥiẓ overwhelms his opponent with these and similar questions, drawn as is evident from a variety of sources and reflecting more than one national culture and religious tradition. The net result, as intended, was no doubt the discomfiture and discrediting of Aḥmad b. ʿAbd al-Wahhāb, but it is brought about in a genial manner. There is no doubt of al-Jāḥiẓ' sense of humour.[89]

Charles Pellat, who since the time of Van Vloten has done most towards the understanding of al-Jāḥiẓ, writing in the new *Encyclopaedia of Islam*, article *al-Djāḥiẓ*, points out that we have no information about any official post held by him or about any regular employment which he may have taken up, while on the other hand, at least for a time, he received an allowance from the Baghdad government, and suggests that some of his works may have been inspired by the authorities. The suggestion seems helpful. Two such works could easily have been the *Kitāb al-ʿUthmāniyya*, in which al-Jāḥiẓ 'asserts the legitimacy of the first three Caliphs, attacks the claims of the S̲h̲īʿa and thereby justifies the accession of the ʿAbbāsids to power',[90] and the *Kitāb ar-Radd ʿalā 'n-Naṣārā* (Book of Confutation of the Christians)[91] where he addresses himself to a given situation, in which young and inexperienced Muslims of a particular locality, not specified, have been led to confusion (*labs*) by the questions of the Christians about certain statements in the Qur'ān, and it is feared that their replies have not been sufficient.[92] Al-Jāḥiẓ says that he will answer all the difficulties, several of which have been cited, e.g. that of Jesus speaking in the cradle (*Sūr*. 3, 41/46; 5, 109), a fact unknown to the Christians, according to them, and equally unknown to the Jews (except where they have heard it from the Muslims), Magians, Ṣābians and Buddhists, not to mention the (pagan) Turks and Khazars.[93] But first he will point out that the Christians are more popular with the common people than either the Magians or the Jews, the reasons for which he explains at some length. Yet in spite of this popularity the Muslim nation is more tried by the Christians than by any others. Unfortunately, every Muslim considers himself a theologian (*mutakallim*), thinking that no one is more entitled than anyone else to argue with deviators (*mulḥidūn*).[94] The half-serious touch is characteristic, and tells us something that we might not have gathered about the life of the time.

Ibn Qutayba glances at the first of these two books and mentions the other by name in a passage where he speaks of al-Jāḥiẓ as a leader of religio-political thought and a defender of Islam against the Christians.

We now come to al-Jāḥiẓ, the last of the *mutakallimūn* and the assailant of the ancients, the best stirrer up of argument, the most articulate in raising the small and depreciating the great, who succeeds in doing both the thing and its opposite. He argues for the superiority of the blacks over the whites. You find him at one time bringing proofs for the

ʿUthmāniyya [who held the views mentioned above as in the book of al-Jāḥiẓ of the same name] against the Rāfiḍa [extreme Shīʿites], and at another for the Zaydiyya [Shīʿites] against the ʿUthmāniyya and the people of the Sunna. . . . He is the author of a book in which he mentions the arguments of the Christians against the Muslims, and when he proceeds to refute them, he does less than he should (*tajawazza*) in the proof, as if he merely wishes to instruct them concerning what they do not know and to cause doubt to the weak of the Muslims. You find him aiming in his books at jokes and jesting, wishing thereby to conciliate the young and the drinkers of *nabīdh* [intoxicating liquor]. He derides the *Ḥadīth* [tradition of Muḥammad] in a way which is easily discernible to the learned. . . . He is at the same time among the most untruthful of the nation and the most disposed to falsify *Ḥadīth*.[95]

This is a severe judgment, and Ibn Qutayba is somewhat unfair to al-Jāḥiẓ, whose intention was certainly not to mislead the Muslims in the *Kitāb ar-Radd ʿalā ʾn-Naṣarā* or anywhere else, though he no doubt found it difficult to resist a joke even when speaking upon serious subjects. Another judgment of a very different kind is worth recording, made by ʿAbd Allāh b. Hammūd az-Zubaydī al-Andalusī, a great admirer of al-Jāḥiẓ. Az-Zubaydī said: 'I should be content in Paradise with the books of al-Jāḥiẓ, in exchange for its bliss.[96]

4. Ibn Qutayba and other exponents of *adab*

Ibn Qutayba himself deserves consideration as a prolific writer of books on various subjects, a number of which have survived down to our own time. He was a learned scholar of a conservative cast, considerably younger than al-Jāḥiẓ, having been born in 213/828. He died in 276/889. The difference between the two is illustrated by their attitude to the translations into Arabic from the Greek, which were being made in ever growing numbers during the third/ninth century (see pp. 20, 173–4). Al-Jāḥiẓ gives a list of these, including the 'Logic' (*Kitāb al-Manṭiq*), that is, some or all of the *Organon*, *De Generatione et Corruptione* (*al-Kawn waʾl-Fasād*), *Meteora* (*Kitāb al-ʿAlawī*, more usually called in Arabic *al-Āthār al-ʿAlawiyyah*) and 'other works' of Aristotle, the *Almagest* of Ptolemy, the 'Book of Euclid', the 'Book of Medicine' of Galen, the 'Books' of Democritus, Hippocrates, Plato, 'and so on, and so on', in quite an appreciative tone, and without expressing any opinion, for or against them, adding that the Byzantine Greeks of today, who possess no philosophy, do not deserve the credit, which is commonly accorded to them, of having written such works.[97] Ibn Qutayba in the preface to his *Kitāb Adab al-Kātib* (Literary Composition for the Secretary) speaks very differently. He first criticizes the modern *kātib* who is content if he can write a fair hand and turn a poem in praise of a singing-girl or in description of a wine glass, and prides himself on knowing enough astrology to cast a horoscope and a little logic.[98] This kind of man, he continues, finds it tedious to examine the science of the Qur'ān and the accounts of the Prophet, and equally the sciences of the Arabs (such as genealogy) and their language and literature. He is the sworn enemy of all such studies, and turns away from them to a science of which there exist purveyors to him and his like and but few opponents, which has an interpretation with appeal but without meaning, and an impressive name but no body. When the inexperienced and the young and heedless hear him speaking of 'generation and corruption' (*al-kawn wa'l-fasād*),[99] 'physical auscultation' (*samʿ al-kiyān*),[100] 'singular terms' (*al-asmā' al-mufrada*), 'quality' (*al-kayfiyya*) and 'quantity' (*al-kamiyya*), 'time' (*az-zamān*), 'demonstration' (*ad-dalīl*), and 'composite propositions' (*al-akhbār al-mu'allafa*), they think that what they have heard is wonderful and imagine that under these expressions are all kinds of profit and all kinds of subtle meaning, but when they study them, they derive no advantage from them.[101] Aristotle himself, or rather Porphyry, is not spared.

> If the author of the 'Definition of Logic' had reached our time and been able to hear the fine points of speculative theology (*al-kalām fi'd-dīn*), law (*fiqh*), obligations (*farā'iḍ*), and grammar (*naḥw*), he would account himself dumb, or if he had been able to hear the doctrine of the Prophet and his Companions, he would be certain that wisdom and the decision between truth and falsehood belonged to the Arabs.[102]

The same note of antipathy to Greek philosophy is struck elsewhere in Arabic literature, sometimes in quarters where we should expect it less than in Ibn Qutayba,[103] but for him it is quite characteristic.

The *Kitāb Adab al-Kātib* is a philological work, and, from the nature of the case, throughout fairly technical. It probably finds fewer readers than others of Ibn Qutayba's extant writings, for example the *ʿUyūn al-Akhbār* (Sources of Narratives),[104] which Brockelmann considered to be his masterpiece. The latter is divided into ten books, dealing respectively with (1) the Sulṭān, (2) war, (3) aristocracy, (4) moral qualities, (5) eloquence, (6) asceticism, (7) friendship, (8) requests, (9) table manners, and (10) women. The work is full of interest, and brings authentic information on the various subjects of which it treats, from Islamic and pre-Islamic times. Book 6, on asceticism, was for a long time set as a prescribed text in the Cambridge Oriental Tripos, and proved a very suitable selection, not too difficult for beginners and affording an insight into *adab* literature (*belles lettres*) in Arabic, as good as or better than could be obtained in such short compass elsewhere.

Other notable works of Ibn Qutayba are his *Kitab ash-Shiʿr wa'sh-Shuʿarā*,[105] containing excerpts from the classical Arabic poets with criticism of the same, and the *Kitāb al-Maʿārif*, a handbook of genealogical and biographical information, which proved useful for a long time in the edition of F. Wüstenfeld, published at Göttingen in 1850. An elaborate new edition with over 150 pages of indices compared with 35 pages in Wüstenfeld's edition was published in 1960 in Cairo.[106] Ibn Qutayba is one of several Arabic authors, knowledge of whom has been greatly extended by the French Orientalists within recent years. The measure of the advance in Ibn Qutayba's case is illustrated by comparison between an older book, *The Life and Works of Ibn Qutayba* by Isḥāq Mūsa Ḥuseini (Beirut, 1950), and G. Lecomte's *Ibn Qutayba, l'Homme, son Oeuvre, ses Idées* (Damascus, 1965), where most of the questions hitherto raised concerning this author are dealt with at length.

One outstanding puzzle has been whether the *Kitāb al-Imāma wa's-Siyāsa* (Book of the Imamate and Political Authority) treating the history of Islam under the Orthodox Caliphs (Abū Bakr to ʿAlī) and the Umayyads in considerable detail, with some observations on the ʿAbbāsids, is authentic or not, and if not, who the author may be. M. Lecomte makes a slip here, for he seems to think that he is recurring to the view held by R. Dozy and J. Ribera, when he says that the author of the *Kitāb al-Imāma wa's-Siyāsa* was not Ibn Qutayba but Ibn al-Qūṭiyya, the Spanish author of the fourth/tenth century.[107] This appears to be M. Lecomte's own idea. Certainly it is not affirmed by Dozy or Ribera in the passages to which he refers.[108] We must therefore allow that the authorship of the *Kitāb al-Imāma wa's-Siyāsa* is still *sub judice*, and while most people would probably be prepared to judge it away from Ibn Qutayba, its authenticity as a work of the latter is still defended.[109]

Even without it, Ibn Qutayba's contribution to Arabic letters was evidently highly important. Another of his works, the *Kitāb Ta'wīl Mukhtalif al-Ḥadīth* (Book of the Interpretation of Divergent Tradition) shows him active and authoritative in a different department, that of the Tradition of Muḥammad (*Ḥadīth*). A translation of this work has recently been made in French, also by M. Lecomte,[110] and from it the non-Arabist can readily gain an impression of Ibn Qutayba as the defendant of the *Ḥadīth* against *Kalām* (speculative theology), on the one hand, and *Ra'y* (individual opinion), on the other. We have already cited from this book Ibn Qutayba's sharp appreciation of al-Jāḥiẓ.[111]

Ibn Qutayba was primarily an exponent of *adab*, that is, as previously mentioned, *belles lettres*, polite literature. Another contemporary of similar interests was Abū'l-ʿAbbās Muḥammad b. Yazīd al-Azdī (*c.* 210/826–285/898), universally known as al-Mubarrad, which was apparently the nickname given him by the grammarians of al-Kūfa, perhaps equivalent to 'the Frigid'. Al-Mubarrad was the most important in his day of the grammarians of al-Baṣra, and is famous for his *adab* book *al-Kāmil*, 'the Perfect'. It can still be read with pleasure. The subject matter, as usual, consists of stories of the Arab past, written in an admirable style and interspersed with verses. Al-Mubarrad's principal rival at the time was Thaʿlab, 'Fox', properly Abū'l-ʿAbbās Aḥmad b. Yaḥyā, a *mawlā* (freedman) of the Arab tribe Shaybān. The *Majālis* of Thaʿlab, also called *Mujālasāt* and *Amālī* with the same general significance of 'Conferences' or 'Dictations', have recently been published (2nd edition, Cairo, 1960) in the series *Dhakhā'ir al-ʿArab*, 'Treasures of the Arabs', of the Dār al-Maʿārif.[112] The editor, ʿAbd as-Salām Muḥammad Hārūn, characterizes the work as follows.

The *Majālis* of Thaʿlab contains different kinds of sciences of classical Arabic. It includes in its contents a great many grammatical questions according to the school of the Kūfans, and we can say that the work is among the most important scientific documents in explanation of the school of the people of al-Kūfa. It is worth mentioning also that Thaʿlab in the *Majālis* often pays attention to some of the views of the people of al-Baṣra. He equally gives an account of a good deal of the Qur'ān and the *Ḥadīth*, and mentions the opinions of the learned doctors (*ʿulamā'*) and the grammarians thereon, contesting their opinions and also giving his own opinion in interpretation and commentary, with discussion of the inflection and the exegesis. In all this Thaʿlab is the trustworthy, reliable man, who fills the mind of the reader with confidence in the soundness of the true tradition which he finds in him. Abū'l-ʿAbbās (i.e. Thaʿlab) was scholar of marvellous taste, and with respect to what he chose of the poetry, *rajaz*-works[113] and narratives of the Arabs the reader perceives the good selection and excellent choice, the cultivated spirit and scholarly precision.[114]

Contemporary with Ibn Qutayba, al-Mubarrad and Thaʿlab, and, at least in the opinion of some,[115] as notable as al-Jāhiz himself was Abū Ḥanīfa al-Dīnawarī, who died in or about 282/895. His principal surviving work, the *Kitāb al-Akhbār aṭ-Ṭiwāl* (Long Narratives)[116] is historical, and has some perspectives drawn from Persian sources. But Abū Ḥanīfa wrote on a variety of subjects, including botany (*Kitāb an-Nabāt*: Book of Plants) and astronomy (*Kitāb al-Anwāʾ*: Book of the Settings and Risings of Stars) and is not usually classed as a historian, which is why we take him here. The two books last mentioned are said to have been his most popular works,[117] but appear not to have survived in their entirety. It has been supposed from a remark in the *Murūj adh-Dhahab* (Meadows of Gold) of al-Masʿūdī that Ibn Qutayba plagiarized Abū Ḥanīfa's *Kitāb al-Anwāʾ* in a work of his own of the same name,[118] and indeed al-Masʿūdī's charge of plagiarism against Ibn Qutayba is conceived quite generally,[119] but as yet it has not been clearly made out.[120]

To Abū Ḥanīfa is attributed at least one book on a literary subject, *Kitāb ash-Shiʿr waʾsh-Shuʿarāʾ* (Book of Poetry and Poets)—the title is the same as that of Ibn Qutayba's work—but he wrote also on theology and jurisprudence, philology, mathematics, including algebra, and astronomy, and was as much man of science as man of letters. In this he differs from the other prose writers of his time who have been mentioned, and we have probably to regard him as an early example of the type of man who takes all knowledge for his province, the encyclopedist, who later is a not uncommon phenomenon in Arabic literature.

Coming down more than a century in time, and turning further east to the lands of Iran, with which indeed some of the writers we have already mentioned had close connections, we arrive at ath-Thaʿālibī, Abū Manṣūr ʿAbd al-Malik b. Muḥammad, of Nīsābūr in Khurāsān, who enjoyed an extraordinary reputation among his contemporaries, and may be considered typical of the enthusiasm with which Arabic was cultivated in Iran at this period.[121] Ath-Thaʿālibī lived from 250/961 to 429/1038. His name refers to the trade, somewhat specialized one would think, of stitching the skins of foxes (*thaʿālib*, plural of *thaʿlab*). Ibn Khallikān, who gives us this information, adds that he was a furrier (*farrāʾ*).[122] He is to be distinguished of course from Thaʿlab already mentioned, and also from ath-Thaʿlabī or ath-Thaʿālibī, Abū Isḥāq Aḥmad b. Muḥammad, described by Ibn Khallikān as the famous Qurʾān commentator,[123] with whom confusion is the readier since he was not only a contemporary of ath-Thaʿālibī, author of the poetical anthology to be mentioned immediately, but like him came from Nīsābūr.

The most celebrated work of ath-Thaʿālibī is the *Yatīmat ad-Dahr fī Maḥāsin Ahl al-ʿAṣr* (The Unique Pearl of the Age in the Beauties of the People of the Time, or, as the four-volume Damascus edition, dated 1302/1884–5, has for the second part of the title, 'in the Poets of the People of the Time', *fī Shuʿarāʾ Ahl al-Aṣr*). This is self-explanatory. The poets are divided according to countries, and, as we should expect, the Muslim East is well represented (volumes 3 and 4 of the Damascus edition, i.e. half the work). Volume 2, which deals with Baghdad and the Arabian Iraq (the rest of the Muslim world, i.e. Syria, Egypt, the Maghrib, etc. is included in volume 1), begins as follows.

I start, after praise of Allāh Who is exalted and blessings on Muḥammad the Chosen and his Family, with a section (*bāb*) restricted to the kings of the Buwayhids who composed poetry and whose poems have been transmitted. . . .

ʿAḍud ad-Dawla Abū Shujāʿ Fannā Khusrū b. Rukn ad-Dawla, in spite of what had been made possible for him in the earth and in spite of having been granted the reins of power, to stretch forth and to withhold, and having been singled out for high estate and having had a wide realm conferred upon him, found time for polite literature and occupied himself with books, preferring discussion with the literary men to drinking with the generals. He spoke much poetry, producing the neat expressions and strokes of wit which are the condition for inclusion here. I know not how many striking passages and brilliant descriptions I have read by aṣ-Sāhib describing (poetry of) ʿAḍud ad-Dawla. For example, 'As for our lord's *qaṣīda* (ode), it comes having the glory of sovereignty, bearing upon it the freshness of sincerity and the stamp of learning, with the tongue of magniloquence and irresistible truth.' Again he says, 'No wonder, when the sea of knowledge has overflowed the tongue of poetry, that there should be opened up the like of what "eye has not seen nor ear heard".' Again, 'If any poetry merited to serve the sweetness of its sources and the majesty of him who speaks it, it would be his *qaṣīda*, but, since this is impossible, I take it as the mark (*qibla*) to which I direct the blessings of honour and I pause upon it with the circumambulation (*ṭawāf*) of respect and reverence.'[124] And again, 'Poetry, which has devoted its service to his thought and is disposed as he wishes at his command. It is he who writes in the blaze on the forefront of the age and crushes the foreheads of the sun and the full moon.' Then, if anyone wishes to examine the history of ʿAḍud ad-Dawla and to be informed of his meritorious deeds, let him study *al-Kitāb at Tājī*,[125] the composition of Abū Isḥāq aṣ-Ṣābiʾ, where he will find united, together with a comprehensive account of them, the eloquence of one who finds their rough places smooth, their difficult texts easy and their sources under his control.

Abū Bakr al-Khwarizmī[126] related to me that a certain literary man and wit was the boon-companion of ʿAḍud ad-Dawla and was responding with descriptions and similes as they occurred to him.[127] Whenever food and drink and the apparatus of either, and other things were presented he recited pleasing poetry thereon, by himself or another. One day while he was with him at table and reciting to him, as his custom was, the rice dish called *bahaṭṭa* was served.[128] ʿAḍud ad-Dawla looked as if he was ordering him to describe it, but the boon-companion was at a loss, and overcome by silence and confusion. Thereupon ʿAḍud ad-Dawla improvised:

> *Bahaṭṭa*—you cannot describe it,
> O claimer of descriptions falsely!
> It is as if it were in the cup bright
> Pearls in water of camphor.

And Muḥammad b. ʿUmar, the ascetic, recited to me a poem he had heard from Abū'l-Qāsim ʿAbd al-ʿAzīz b. Yūsuf,[129] who said, ʿAḍud ad-Dawla recited to me a poem of his own on Abū Taghlib,[130] when he made his excuses to him for Bakhtiyār's[131] frequenting him and requested a pardon in writing from him, which included the verses:

> Has he come to his senses when I have set my foot on
> his neck?
> He now desires a pardon but before this a sharp sword!
> Yes, I shall take a resolution, worthy of ʿAḍud,[132]
> Worthy of Tāj,[132] which will abase them in the dust![133]

An important work of ath-Thaʿālibī is the *Fiqh al-Lugha wa-Sirr al-ʿArabiyya* (Law of the Language and Secret of Arabic), composed later than the *Yatīmat ad-Dahr*, which is referred to in the preface. This preface to the *Fiqh al-Lugha* is interesting as indicating ath-Thaʿālibī's enthusiasm for Arabic and at the same time the difficulty of maintaining the language in Iran. Arabic constantly risks decline, were it not for men like his patron, Abū Faḍl ʿUbayd Allāh b. Aḥmad al-Mīkālī, a Buwayhid *amīr*, whom with somewhat outrageous flattery ath-Thaʿālibī pretends to have inherited the eloquence of both Abū Isḥāq aṣ-Ṣābiʾ and aṣ-Ṣāhib Ibn ʿAbbād.[134] Al-Mikālī certainly did not deserve such a compliment, but he was no doubt a gifted man, and ath-Thaʿālibī recalls with pleasure some months spent in his company at Fīrūzābād, near Shīrāz, and mentions literary gatherings and the conversation of the *amīr*.[135] The *Fiqh al-Lugha* is intended as a lexicographical work and is so, a kind of Roget's *Thesaurus* for Arabic writers. But at the same time some of its thirty sections (*abwāb*) provide information also on *realia*, for example Section 16 on diseases, Section 17 on different kinds of animals, and Sections 23, 24 and 25 on dress and arms, food and drink, and meteorology respectively. The work has been edited a number of times but perhaps not yet studied as it deserves.

One of this author's best known works is the *Laṭāʾif al-Maʿārif* (Pleasant Sorts of Knowledge), a typical *adab* book, which was edited by De Jong a century ago.[136] It contains legend, improbable or impossible, e.g. that the biblical David invented the well-known formula at the head of letters, etc., called *faṣl al-khiṭāb*, 'Now, to proceed' (*ammā baʿd*), as well as breastplates (*dirʿ*), and that Qārūn (biblical Korah) was the first man who lengthened his garments and drew them along, and the first man who practised alchemy![137] The list of 'firsts' (*awāʾil*)—a type of classification which was very popular and is said to have been invented by Ibn Qutayba[138]—includes in some cases information which may be authentic: the first Arab to cross the Oxus was Saʿīd, a son of the Caliph ʿUthmān; the first hospital in Islam was built by Walīd I b. ʿAbd al-Malik;[139] the first *qāḍī* executed was Abū 'l-Muthannā Aḥmad b. Yaʿqūb under al-Muqtadir;[140] al-Manṣūr was the first ʿAbbāsid to give donatives of one million *dirhams* or over (Muʿāwiya and his son Yazīd had previously done so), but such large gifts were not made after the time of the minister al-Ḥasan b. Sahl (*c.* 210/826).[141]

Ath-Thaʿālibī is interested in points of language and usage. In Samarqand the people said instead of *khātūn*, Turkish for a great lady, *khudhayn*.[142] There were several great families known to him in which three generations bore the same name. Al-Jāḥiẓ had mentioned two or three cases. Ath-Thaʿālibī, having visited Khwārizm, can add that its ruler Maʾmūn b. Maʾ-mūn had a son of the same name.[143] While in Khwārizm ath-Thaʿālibī was impressed by the freezing of the Jayḥūn (Oxus, Amu Darya) in winter, when, as he tells us, elephants, caravans, and whole armies passed over it, and it remained frozen for from forty to sixty days. He recounts the pilgrimage of Jamīla, a Ḥamdānid princess, sister of Abū Taghlib already mentioned, to Mecca in the year 366/976, which eclipsed the splendour even of Zubayda's (see pp. 257–8), and the sad reversal of her fortune, through the enmity of ʿAḍud ad-Dawla. Stripped of all she possessed and humiliated beyond endurance, she at last drowned herself in the Tigris.[144] These circumstances are not alluded to in Miskawayh's detailed history of the period, *Tajārib al-Umam* (The Experiences of the Nations), and as the record of a Muslim woman who committed suicide, the account is perhaps unique. (At all times suicide in Islam has been comparatively rare, and the number of prominent people reported to have taken their own lives is very small.) The story told by ath-Thaʿālibī is far from pleasant, contrary to what we should expect from the title of his book. No more so is his notice of those in Islam who killed more than a million men, four in all (Al-Ḥajjāj b. Yūsuf, Abū Muslim al-Khurāsānī, Bābak and 'al-Burquʿī').[145] The last-named is probably the man called by aṭ-Ṭabarī Abū Ḥarb al-Mubarqaʿ,[146] who rebelled in 227/842 in Palestine, possibly al-Muqannaʿ, the 'Veiled Prophet of Khurāsān', a rebel against the authority of al-Mahdī earlier.[147] Of ath-Thaʿālibī's list, Bābak was also a rebel, the other two agents of government.[148]

The *Laṭāʾif al-Maʿārif* is interspersed with quaint or amusing observations, as that the steel mirrors of the Chinese were sometimes sold for double or several times their weight in silver,[149] that the Caliph Marwān II was fair-haired and blue-eyed—a defect, or at least a peculiarity,[150] and that the ʿAbbāsid al-Wāthiq possessed a terrible eye—play is made with this in William Beckford's novel *Vathek*—which affected others even on his death-bed.[151] It is all typical *adab*, the kind of information which a well-educated person should know, or might know, and which would be useful in conversation. Ath-Thaʿālibī in reproducing it is not strictly writing as a historian, though often he is concerned with historical facts, nor as a stylist in prose, but partly as entertainer, because these stories and pieces of information are meant to be interesting in themselves, and partly as professor.[152] A number of passages of the *Laṭāʾif al-Maʿārif* are to be found also in another work of his, the *Thimār al-Qulūb fī 'l-Muḍāf wa 'l-Mansūb* (The Fruits of the Hearts in What is Annexed and Related) (ed. Cairo, 1326/1908) which, though it deals formally with a grammatical subject (genitive connections), is to a great extent another *adab* book. Thus the seventy *Abdāl*, those saints by whose existence the world is maintained in being and whose number is constantly kept up, are to be looked for in Jabal al-Lukkām or Black Mountain (the Amanus), according to both the *Laṭā'if al-Maʿārif* and the *Thimār al-Qulūb*, using nearly the same language. But in the former book this information comes under the heading *Dhikr ash-Shām* (Account of Syria),[153] and in the latter it is given to illustrate the fact that the genitive annexation and relation sometimes indicate a place![154] Similarly there is a short reference in the same terms to the important battle of Talas (Ṭarāz) or Aṭlakh (July 751) in both works,[155] and a number of other coincidences.[156]

Ath-Thaʿālibī was a voluminous writer, but of his numerous other works we can mention only one more, the *Kitāb Ghurar Akhbār al-Mulūk wa-Siyarihim* (Book of the Highlights of the History and Lives of Kings), otherwise *Kitāb Ghurar as-Siyar* (Book of the Highlights of the Lives), which does not survive in its entirety, but of which the part dealing with the kings of Persia was published with a French translation by Zotenberg in 1900.[157] This is of interest for the subject matter, which is the legendary history of Persia, drawn from the same kind of sources as were used by Firdawsī in his great national epic of Iran, the *Shāh Nāma*. The book of ath-Thaʿālibī appears to have been completed between 408/1017 and 412/1021, shortly after Firdawsī brought the *Shāh Nāma* to an end after forty years of labour, as we are told, in 401/1010.[158] In any elaboration of the heroic legends of Persia, if not for the actual history, this part of the *Kitāb Ghurar Akhbār al-Mulūk* would have to be taken into account. It is also of interest because of the debate which has arisen, since Zotenberg's publication, as to ath-Thaʿālibī's authorship. Brockelmann repeatedly claimed an otherwise unknown Abū Manṣūr al-Ḥusayn b. Muḥammad al-Marghanī ath-Thaʿālibī as author, both in his *Geschichte der arabischen Litteratur* and in the *Encyclopaedia of Islam*.[159] The arguments pro and con cannot be gone into here, but parallel passages in the *Ghurar Akhbār al-Mulūk* and in undoubted works of ath-Thaʿālibī, first pointed out by Zotenberg, seem to confirm his authorship, and at present this is the general opinion.

The later literary development

It is a striking fact that in Arabic literature, until modern times, nothing like the stage play has ever developed, with the exceptions which we shall have to mention. No Greek tragedy or comedy ever passed into Arabic, and *a fortiori* no work by a Latin playwright, nor was any of the dramatic poetry of the Hindus translated, at the time when there was much translation from foreign literatures (eighth to tenth centuries A.D.). R. A. Nicholson said rightly enough that the dramatic style has never been cultivated by the Semites,[160] though he might have made passing reference to the *Book of Job* in the Old Testament, and there are adumbrations of the drama earlier in Accadian literature. So far as the Arabs are concerned, the structure of social life, at first patriarchal and tribal, later under the ʿAbbāsid Caliphate pyramidal, with a small ruling class of bureaucrats and generals headed by an autocratic chief, all, nominally at least, the servants of a well-defined religious law, precluded the development of institutions which flourished in other civilizations. Popular assemblies, apart from meetings in the mosque, which, however absorbing for participants or momentous for the political future, as sometimes happened, remained invariably of a strictly local rather than representative character, were practically unknown in Islam, and it is evident that references to the public institutions of the Greeks, the theatre, for example, as these occur in Greek philosophical works, were imperfectly understood, even by highly intelligent translators.[161]

But the feeling for dramatic representation at one time characteristic of the Hellenized Middle East[162] survived, though it might be only in the humble form of the shadow play. At least once, in the hands of the Egyptian Ibn Dāniyāl[163] (died 710/1310), the shadow play came to life, and we have the three titles *Ṭayf al-Khayāl* (Apparition of the Ghost, the ridiculous personal name of the brother of the principal character, the *amīr* Wiṣāl), *ʿAjīb wa-Gharīb* (Wonderful and Strange) and *al-Mutayyam* (The Enthralled by Love). The comic character of these plays is sufficiently clear from the titles, and indeed their humour is of the broadest. This has not prevented Georg Jacob who did pioneer work on Ibn Dāniyāl[164] from describing him as the most witty and amusing poet in the Arabic language,[165] but at the same time he calls Ibn Daniyāl the most difficult of Arabic authors. Several longish passages from the plays have been translated into English by the late Professor Paul Kahle.[166]

But, earlier than Ibn Dāniyāl, we have the appearance of a specific literary form, more important and better known than the shadow play, which also represents the dramatic tendency so far as it comes to expression in Arabic. This is the *maqāma* (plural *maqāmāt*, usually translated 'assemblies' or 'seances'), essentially a conversation piece. Abū Bakr al-Khwārizmī already mentioned (see p. 56) seems to have written *maqāmāt*, in which figures a certain ʿĪsā b. Hishām,[167] and the same ʿĪsā b. Hishām is the narrator in the *Maqāmāt* of al-Hamadhānī, called Badīʿ az-Zamān, the 'Wonder of the Time' (358/969–398/1007). The *Maqāmāt* of Badīʿ az-Zamān were regularly written in rhymed prose (*sajʿ*),[168] usually, but not always, interspersed with verses, and among them we have such titles as the *Maqāma of al-Baṣra*, the *Maqāma of Baghdad*, the *Maqāma of Fazāra* (the Bedouin tribe of that name), the *Maqāma of the Māristān* (the Hospital, in this case at al-Baṣra), the *Maqāma of the Khazars*,[169] and so on, that is, it is customary for the author to call the *maqāma* after the locality where it is supposed to have taken place. Everywhere he goes ʿĪsā b. Hishām is sure to meet under surprising circumstances his slightly discreditable acquaintance Abū'l Fatḥ al-Iskandarī, and the *maqāma* recounts what happened and what was said. These pieces were intended to be read, publicly or privately, not acted, but in so far as they have a definite local setting and present a vivid dialogue between recognizable persons, they have something of a dramatic character, and there is no doubt that, especially in the hands of a later writer, al-Ḥarīrī (446/1054–516/1122), the *maqāma* form was brilliantly successful.

Al-Ḥarīrī changed the names of the principal personages, who are now al-Ḥārith b. Hammām (narrator) and Abū Zayd of Sarūj[170] (the vagabond hero). In other respects the essentials remain the same (rhymed prose for the main narrative, plenty of poetry, the *maqāmāt* named individually after the locality where the encounter takes place). There are also differences. Al-Ḥarīrī was from Iraq not Iran, and this is perhaps reflected in his choice of milieux. Also he seems to have taken the composition of his *Maqāmāt* more seriously than Badīʿ az-Zamān (also a stylist). At all events, their superiority as works of art to the *Maqāmāt* of Badīʿ az-Zamān is not contested, and al-Ḥarīrī has long been considered a classic among Arabic authors. Ibn Khallikān, though he speaks of Badīʿ az-Zamān's originality in the matter of the composition of *Maqāmāt* (as indeed was freely admitted by al-Ḥarīrī himself in very modest language in the preface to his own work), merely states the fact, and goes on to discuss his letters (*Rasā'il*) and verses[171] On the other hand, when he comes to the biography of al-Ḥarīrī, Ibn Khallikān has much to say about his *Maqāmāt*, and indeed most of the notice which he gives of him is taken up with this subject.[172]

He cites the son of al-Ḥarīrī for the occasion of the writing of the original *Maqāma* (the forty-eighth in the present collection, called 'the Ḥarāmiyya'). The elder al-Ḥarīrī was sitting, according to his son Abū'l-Qāsim ʿAbd Allāh,[173] in his mosque in the Banū Ḥarām district of al-Baṣra when an elderly man (*shaykh*) appeared, in tattered garments, having apparently just completed a long journey. In spite of his general appearance of dilapidation, he impressed the group then present in the mosque by his manner of speech and they asked where he came from, and what was his name. He replied that he was from Sarūj, apparently the classical Batnae, at this time a sizeable town in north Mesopotamia, and that his *kunya* was Abū Zayd. The sequel (not here mentioned by Ibn Khallikān) was surprising. There happened to be present in the mosque of the Banū Ḥarām that day a certain *qāḍī* from a neighbouring town, who, having been addicted to drunkenness, was now moved to repentance, and requested any member of the company to indicate to him a suitable atonement for his fault. Hereupon Abū Zayd came forward and recited his story. While he was living at Sarūj, which was near the frontier, the Greeks had occupied the country, confiscated his goods, and, worse than all, seized his daughter, whom they were holding to ransom. No penance, said he, could be more appropriate for the *qāḍī* than that he should pay the sum necessary to set the young girl at liberty. The *qāḍī* in his new mood, touched by the story, at once handed over a considerable amount of money, which Abū Zayd pocketed and departed. He was afterwards discovered to have spent it on wine in a neighbouring tavern.[174] This is substantially the story as given in the forty-eighth *Maqāma*, the first to be composed, as already mentioned. The series, at the request of Anūshirwān b. Khālid, *wazīr* of the Caliph al-Mustarshid (512/1118–529/1135), was afterwards made up to fifty. It is usually supposed that Anūshirwān b. Khālid was the unnamed person mentioned in al-Ḥarīrī's preface to the *Maqāmāt* as having encouraged him to write them.[175]

There is no reason to doubt what may be called the official version of the genesis of this famous book, though Ibn Khallikān makes or quotes a number of discrepant statements. He had himself seen a copy of the *Maqāmāt* written by al-Ḥarīrī himself with a note on the outside in the author's hand that he had composed them for another vizier of al-Mustarshid. This as a precise statement Ibn Khallikān preferred to the other, but it was probably an alternative dedication, such as is found in manuscripts of Ibn Khaldūn's History.[176] Not much weight need be attached to Ibn Khallikān's story that al-Ḥarīrī first composed forty *maqāmāt*, which he took with him from al-Baṣra to Baghdad, that his literary ability was there tested by a *wazīr*, that al-Ḥarīrī failed to pass the test (literary composition on a set theme), and that he was ignominiously returned to al-Baṣra, where he wrote the remaining ten *maqāmāt*. Certainly the suggestion, made at this time by some littérateurs of Baghdad, that the initial forty were not al-Ḥarīrī's but appropriated by him from the papers of an eloquent Maghribī who had died at al-Baṣra, seems absurd.[177] More significant perhaps is the suggestion, also reported by Ibn Khallikān, that the original of Abū Zayd as-Sarūjī was a certain Muṭahhar b. Sallām, a grammarian of al-Baṣra. It would be perfectly natural to suppose that some well-defined personality suggested the main traits of Abū Zayd of Sarūj to al-Ḥarīrī, in the same way as Dr Joseph Bell, the Edinburgh surgeon, is said to have been the original of Sherlock Holmes. But we learn that al-Muṭahhar b. Sallām of al-Baṣra was a younger man than al-Ḥarīrī, and indeed his pupil, who later transmitted one of his teacher's works, the *Mulḥat al-Iʿrāb*, presently to be mentioned.[178] It is not *a priori* likely that the pupil was taken as a model for the elderly and universally experienced Abū Zayd, as the latter is represented as having been. Further, of course, the type for the hero of the *maqāma* literature was already fixed in the person of Badīʿ az-Zamān's Abū'l-Fatḥ al-Iskandarī long before al-Ḥarīrī's day, and was retained by the Spanish Jewish author al-Ḥarīzī, who *c.* A.D. 1200 translated al-Ḥarīrī's *Maqāmāt* from Arabic into Hebrew[179] and later composed his own *maqāmat* under the title *Tahkemoni* (taken from 2 *Samuel* 23:8), where 'Heber the Kenite' (*Judges* 4:11) is represented as the same kind of man. If al-Muṭahhar b. Sallām was the original, then not only was there no such person as Abū Zayd of Sarūj under that or any other name, which would not be difficult to admit, but the scene at the mosque of the Banū Ḥarām is pure fiction also, not to mention the narrative of al-Panjadīhī.[180] Yet according to al-Ḥarīrī's son, the same apparently who transmitted the *Maqāmāt*, what there took place gave the incentive to the composition of the work, and this is consonant with al-Ḥarīrī's own remarks in his preface. In face of all this, the suggestion that the Baṣran student of grammar was the original of Abū Zayd appears to be insufficiently founded and can safely be dispensed with.

Some of the manuscripts of the *Maqāmāt* of al-Ḥarīrī, as befitted a classic, were exceptionally finely produced. This was illustrated rather oddly by a beautiful little coloured print, recently acquired by me at an art shop in New York, of a medieval Oriental scene showing horsemen bearing standards and trumpets, with the title '*Wasiti. Célébration de la fin du Ramadan*', the significance of which was to me at first quite unknown. The work in refinement somewhat resembled a Persian miniature, but was clearly not Persian. A couple of lines of Arabic above the picture turned out to be from al-Ḥarīrī's seventh *Maqāma*, that of Barqaʿīd (a town in north Mesopotamia between Mosul and Naṣībīn), in which the action of the *maqāma* begins just before the *ʿĪd al-Fiṭr*, the 'Feast of the Breaking of the Fast' on 1st Shawwāl after Ramaḍān. Wasiti (Wāsiṭī) remained mysterious, while the Arabic words beginning *wa-tanshudu mudrajahā fa-lammā dānatnī qarantu biʾr-ruqʿa dirhaman wa-qiṭʿatan*,[181] ('and she was looking for her roll of paper, and when she approached me, I put in the paper a *dirham* and a bit'), had no particular reference to the scene portrayed. That is to say this was evidently not a picture in the ordinary sense illustrating a scene from al-Ḥarīrī by an otherwise unknown artist Wāsiṭī. The indication was rather that it might be an illustration in some manuscript. This proved to be the case, for after a little investigation, further facts emerged. As appears from *Persian Miniature Painting* (London 1933) by Laurence Binyon and J. V. S. Wilkinson where mention is made (p. 21), of the famous 'Schefer' Ḥarīrī of the Bibliothèque Nationale, and E. Blochet's *Les Enluminures des Manuscrits orientaux de la Bibliothèque Nationale* (Paris, 1926, 56 ff),[182] the manuscript in question is no. 5847, of the Arabic collection of the Bibliothèque Nationale, a manuscript of al-Ḥarīrī's *Maqāmāt* formerly in the Schefer collection, described by Blochet as 'de tres grande luxe' and as 'le plus beau livre illustré dans les états du khalife abbasside que l'on connaisse'. It was copied, says M. Blochet, probably at Baghdad, by a calligrapher who was at the same time an able illuminator and meritorious painter, Yaḥyā b. Maḥmūd b. Yaḥyā b. Abīʾl-Ḥasan b. Kuwwariha (?)[183] al-Wāsiṭī, who completed his work in May 1237, and belonged perhaps to a family of Aramaean origin. Blochet reproduces in black and white several of the illuminations of the Schefer manuscript, including the little picture we have been discussing, the subject of which he describes as 'le peloton des étendards de la garde du khalife (colour-party of the Caliph's guard)'.[184] It is 'l'œuvre la plus remarquable et la plus originale de toutes celles qui sont nées dans les écoles mesopotamiennes', and a reproduction in black and white now adorns the cover of this book. The same design has been used for postage stamps recently issued by the Republic of Iraq. We may take it with the other illuminations of al-Wāsiṭī in the same manuscript as fine examples of the height reached by Muslim art under the ʿAbbāsid Caliphate shortly before its collapse in A.D. 1258. The reigning Caliph when this work was executed was al-Mustanṣir (623/1226–640/1242), the last but one of the dynasty.

Other works written by al-Ḥarīrī exist and have been edited, but since their subjects are philological, not literary, they need not detain us. One of these is the *Kitāb Durrat al-Ghawwāṣ fī Awhām al-Khawāṣṣ* (Book of the Pearl of the Diver on the False Ideas of People of Distinction), which aims at safeguarding members of the educated classes from errors in speaking and writing Arabic commonly made by the uneducated. It was edited by H. Thorbecke (Leipzig, 1871). There are several more recent Oriental editions. Another grammatical work of al-Ḥarīrī, the *Mulḥat al-I'rāb* already mentioned, the title perhaps to be rendered 'Delight of Inflection', is a poem of some 375 lines, where the rules of Arabic grammar are given in as lively a manner as the subject permits.[185]

From Muslim Spain, earlier than al-Ḥarīrī, we have the celebrated Ibn Ḥazm, in full Abū Muḥammad ʿAlī b. Aḥmad b. Ḥazm al-Andalusī (383/993–456/1064), who, having spent the earlier part of his career as a courtier of the Spanish Umayyads, now in decline, later withdrew to a life of study on his estate near Niebla in south-west Spain, and wrote voluminously, mostly on religious subjects.[186] To his earlier period belongs a little book, *Ṭawq al-Ḥamāma fī'l-Ulfa wa'l-Ullāf* (The Necklace of the Dove, on Love and Lovers), which has attracted much attention since it was first published in 1914 by Professor D. K. Petrov of the University of St Petersburg, from the only known manuscript in the Leiden University Library. It has since been translated into the principal European languages,[187] and is most conveniently to be found perhaps in Léon Bercher's French version of 1949, with the Arabic text opposite.[188] The *Ṭawq al-Ḥamāma* takes up again a subject which had been treated in Arabic prose earlier, for example in the *Risāla fī'l-ʿIshq wa'n Nisā'* Letter, or Treatise, on Love and Women) of al-Jāḥiẓ, and in some pages in the *Murūj adh-Dhahab* (Meadows of Gold) of al-Masʿūdī.[189] It is partly autobiographical, and presents a striking picture of one aspect of life in upper-class circles in Cordova at the time. The treatment is sentimental with philosophical and psychological developments. The general impression which we get is of a milieu of great refinement, with considerable laxity of morals, which is perhaps brought into more prominence by contrast with Ibn Ḥazm's sermonizing at the end of the book, in his last two chapters. The *Ṭawq al-Ḥamāma* contains enough of Ibn Ḥazm's poetry to justify its being characterized by the late Professor E. Lévi-Provençal as in some sort his *Dīwān*.[190] Lévi-Provençal was prepared to judge these verses of Ibn Ḥazm rather critically: 'dont l'impeccable facture ne suffit pas toujours à faire accepter la fadeur ou la platitude', as compared with their setting, sometimes, if not always, 'du périodes de belle venue, dans une prose limpide et dépouillée'.[191] If the *Ṭawq al-Ḥamāma* falls somewhat short of the masterpiece which since its rediscovery it has sometimes been hailed as being, it is full of interest, and apart from its literary value, it is an important historical document. Here is not the place to stress the latter aspect, but we may mention the remark of Ibn Ḥazm about the Umayyads of Cordova that they were all, or nearly all, blonde, notably ʿAbd ar-Raḥmān III an-Nāṣir, his son al-Ḥakam II and their posterity—a surprising fact, nowhere else apparently recorded in so many words.[192] He tells us also that there were statues, certainly ancient,[193] in the baths at Cordova.[194] Ibn Ḥazm himself was perhaps of a Gothic or Celto-Roman family.[195]

We have to pass over perforce a number of well-known Arabic poets—Abū'l-ʿAtāhiya (130/748–213/828), Abū Nuwās (*c.* 139/756–*c.* 198/813),[196] Abū Firās al-Ḥamdānī (320/932–357/968), Abū'l-ʿAlā' al-Maʿarrī (363/973–449/1057), and the Spaniards Ibn Hāni' al-Andalusī, 'the Mutanabbi' of the West' (died 362/973), Ibn Darrāj al-Qasṭallī, also compared to al-Mutanabbi' (347/958–421/1030), and Ibn ʿAbdūn (died 529/1134, or according to others 520/1126)—some of whom were almost as famous as those who have been mentioned. Less well known, on the other hand, is Ibn ʿUnayn (Sharaf ad-Dīn Abū'l-Maḥāsin Muḥammad al-Anṣārī ad-Dimashqī), about whom a few words may be said. He was born in Damascus in 549/1154 and died there in 630/1233. Ibn ʿUnayn's *Dīwān* was published by the late Khalīl Mardam Bey, of the Arab Academy of Damascus, in 1365/1946 with an introduction and valuable notes, which enable us to appreciate this excellent poet almost for the first time. Ibn Khallikān devoted an article to Ibn ʿUnayn, and mentions him also incidentally as a learned authority to whom questions on the older poetry might be referred. Asked about the relative merit of *qaṣīdas* of Abū Nuwās and al-ʿAkawwak, both poets who lived at the end of the eighth century A.D. and the beginning of the ninth, Ibn ʿUnayn is reported to have refused to pass judgment, on the ground that only someone in the same class (*daraja*) as they should decide between them, and of course by this he meant a poet of equal genius, not a contemporary of the same *ṭabaqa*, 'class', in a different sense.[197] His interest in the poetical past is also illustrated by a line from his own deservedly famous poem addressed to an Ayyūbid prince of Damascus, a relative of the great Ṣalāḥ ad-Dīn (Saladin), which begins:

> Do its towers from highest point of Damascus cause you longing,
> And the boys and fair girls in the meadows of the Two Valleys?[198]

The verse in question is:

> May God give water to the great trees of the two Ghūṭas[199] and not
> Be watered of droughty Mosul anything but its tombs!

When this caused perplexity to a *shaykh* of al-Mauṣil, the grammarian ʿAfīf ad-Dīn Abū'l-Ḥasan ʿAlī b. ʿAdlān, he asked the author its meaning. Why an imprecation on Mosul, with the exception of its tombs? For the sake of Abū Tammām, was the reply.[200] The great poet of a previous age, as we saw, had been buried there.

The continued interest shown by Ibn ʿUnayn in the older poets is worth emphasizing, for it is typical not only of the seventh/thirteenth century in which he lived but of later times, down to the present. The classics of the Arabs, unlike our own, are in their own language. While an English poet, Tennyson, for example, is steeped in Virgil, an Arab poet goes back to the writers of his own race and nation and takes from them not only the thought but the words and the form. No doubt this often leads to flatness and triteness as in Shihāb ad-Dīn al-Ḥuwayzī, a poet of al-Baṣra, who lived in the eleventh/seventeenth century under the Persian Ṣafawids and wrote a *Dīwān*, which was very popular and has frequently been printed.[201] It is not perhaps great poetry, but its inspiration comes from the same national source as the greater poets of the past. In another hand the tradition, even today, is capable of coming alive again. It is interesting to note in some of the later poets, with the retention of the traditional form of expression, increasing perception, both aesthetic and moral. This can be illustrated from a poem of Ibn ʿUnayn, where he writes of an incident of trifling character which happened either in Khwārizm (Khiva) or in Herat,[202] and which he witnessed and registered permanently in verses. The well-known Fakhr ad-Dīn ar-Rāzī, one of the great scholars of the age, was being received by the local ruler at a splendid gathering, when a dove pursued by a hawk appeared, and, passing between two lines of guardsmen, who were present to honour the *shaykh*, darted from its pursuer into the folds of the dress of Fakhr ad-Dīn, who took it in his hand. The lines which Ibn ʿUnayn extemporized on the incident are pleasing:

> She came in her anxiety to the Solomon of the time,
> When death was signalled from the wings of a bird of prey.
> Who made known to the dove that where you are
> Is a refuge, and that you are a place of recourse to the fearful?[203]

What one notices particularly is the elevation of sentiment in the poet, who not only sees the dramatic situation and has the wit to express it, but also marks and sympathizes with the action of the *shaykh*. Wit was unquestionably not lacking to the early Arabic poets, but not all of them had the moral insight which here seems to correspond to a higher degree of civilization.

A younger contemporary of Ibn ʿUnayn, the Egyptian Bahāʾ ad-Dīn Zuhayr (581/1186–656/1258), developed in a different way, and while Ibn ʿUnayn still, in the seventh/thirteenth century, is very much of a classical poet, Bahāʾ ad-Dīn by comparison appears quite modern. His work seems at all times to have been popular, especially in Egypt, and it has been noted that of all the older poets he is the one who most appeals to educated Egyptians of the modern age. The *qaṣīda* of traditional type is still employed by Bahāʾ ad-Dīn, but is restricted perhaps, as Brockelmann says, to poems in praise of the Sultan (for him as for Ibn ʿUnayn an Ayyūbid, though they do not seem at any time to have served the same person) and the great men of the Sultan's court.[204] A typical example is the *qaṣīda* congratulating al-Mālik al-Kāmil on the capture of Damietta from the Franks in 618/1221.[205] Bahā' ad-Dīn's characteristic form of expression was, however, not the *qaṣīda*, but shorter poems of various types, more adapted to his eager lyricism. His own countrymen speak of the simplicity of his style, and one of them applies to it the phrase *as-sahl al-mumtaniʿ* (easy but impossible, sc. to imitate).[206] The same critic describes the following poem of Bahā' ad-Dīn as sheer magic, *siḥr ḥalāl*, literally 'allowable magic',[207] and we subjoin it in the translation of E. H. Palmer, now nearly a century old, in order that the reader may test the judgment for himself, making due allowance for Palmer's Victorian style. The original seems much less old-fashioned.

DESPAIR

May'st thou live and long remain,
I am he whom Love has slain!
Light of my eyes, I pray that thou
May'st never feel what I feel now!
Ah well! my past is past and gone:
None lasteth good but God alone.
Between my death and loss of thee,
No difference at all I see.
Thou freest of mankind from care,
How long must I despair?
I've heard things of thee;—Lord! I pray
There be no truth in what they say.
Our compact thou wouldst never break,
When such firm hold on thee I take!
In thee I never used to find
Aught but the kindest of mankind.
Oh, master! gently now with me!
Oh, master! treat me courteously!
Long life to thee, and as for me
I die of love, undoubtedly!
There's little now of me that's left,
And I of that shall be bereft.'[208]

The fact is of course that Bahā' ad-Dīn expresses age-old sentiments in a light and agreeable fashion, which is nearly always welcome. He is not really a modern man, but a cultivated Egyptian of his time. If there were any doubt of this, we need only recall that he was also reputed as one of the best calligraphers of the age.[209]

Chapter 3

History and historians

1. Early chroniclers and historians: *Maghāzī*, *Futūḥ*, etc.

The beginnings of history among the Arabs go back to the time of Muḥammad and earlier, when famous storytellers or authorities on Arab tradition flourished and left their names at least, if not their works, to subsequent generations. Such were an-Naḍr b. al-Ḥārith, who knew the heroic sagas of the Persians and was killed after the battle of Badr (A.H. 2), Makhrama b. Nawfal az-Zuhrī, who with ʿAqīl b. Abī Ṭālib, the elder brother of ʿAlī, was commissioned by the Caliph ʿUmar to make lists and a register of the Arab tribes, and Daghfal an-Nassāba ('the Genealogist') in the time of Muʿāwiya.[1] No sharp break with the past is indicated here. Men of similar information and gifts may be supposed to have existed in previous ages. Somewhat different is the case with two South Arabians already referred to, ʿUbayd or ʿAbīd b. Sharya al-Jurhumī and Wahb b. Munabbih, both of whom were not only knowledgeable, but wrote works whose titles are known and which in some form have survived to the present time. The book of ʿUbayd b. Sharya, printed at Haidarabad in 1347/1928, dealt with the history of the kings of the Yaman and biblical legends, in the form of answers to the questions of Muʿāwiya, who is said to have summoned the author to his court at Damascus.[2] What may be a specimen, though the matter is not historical, can be seen in the *Kitāb al-Muʿammarīn* (Book of Longlived Persons) of Abū Ḥātim as-Sijistānī.[3] Here ʿUbayd b. Sharya philosophizes about the passage of time and answers such questions as, What is the best wealth you ever saw? (Answer, A gurgling well in soft ground, or, as next best, A horse (mare) bearing a horse (unborn foal) followed by a horse with a horse fastened to it).[4] From questions and answers such as these we readily see that the level of accounts of the pre-Islamic *ayyām al-ʿArab* has scarcely been passed.

Wahb b. Munabbih, on the other hand, sometimes said to have been of Persian descent, is given as the author of several works and appears to have tapped a new and fertile source—the history and legends of the Jews. The book already mentioned briefly (p. 38), *Kitāb at-Tījān fī Mulūk Ḥimyar* (Book of the Crowns on the Kings of Ḥimyar, i.e. South Arabia or part thereof), may not really be his but rather, as it stands, the composition of another author who will shortly meet us, the very well-known Ibn Hishām, but in this case it is undoubtedly based on the *Kitāb al-Isrā'īliyyāt* (Book of Israelitish History) of Wahb. In the latter work we have, as well as a new theme, a more sophisticated treatment than in ʿUbayd b. Sharya, as may be seen from excerpts in the *ʿUyūn al-Akhbār* of Ibn Qutayba. The claim recorded of Wahb b. Munabbih that he had read seventy-two divine books (*kutub Allāh*) possibly indicates that he had some knowledge of the Septuagint version of the Bible.[5] As to the Hebrew original, which would be quite natural for Wahb b. Munabbih to have known, if he was a Jew, as some have thought, we shall have to discount a description of man's creation from the four elements, here earth, water, soul (*nafs*) and spirit (*rūh*), cited in several places,[6] and said to have been found by Wahb in the Torah (Old Testament). More promising is a passage in the *Iḥyā' ʿUlūm ad-Dīn* (Revival of the Religious Sciences) of al-Ghazālī, who refers elsewhere by name to the *Isrā'īliyyāt*. This passage quotes Wahb to the effect that he found on the margin of the Torah twenty-two *letters* (*ḥarf*), which the pious men of the Israelites assembled to read and study, e.g. 'No treasure is more beneficial than knowledge', 'No wealth is more profitable than forbearance (*ḥilm*)', etc.[7] This seems to say that these wise sayings, numbered or denoted in some way according to the twenty-two letters of the Hebrew alphabet, were read by Wahb in the marginal *Massorah* (notes and commentary) of a Hebrew manuscript of the Bible, and if this actually was done, the chances of his having been a Jew are great enough to amount to practical certainty. The stories quoted by al-Ghazālī, as it happens, are edifying rather than historical (a pious man contends with Satan,[8] a 'king of Death' legend),[9] and the same applies to the excerpts in Ibn Qutayba's *ʿUyūn al-Akhbār*.[10] It seems likely, however, that a good deal of biblical history reached the Arabs through Wahb's *Isrā'īliyyāt*, and this name came to be given to a special *genre* of writing with at least a historical basis, which continued down to the sixth/twelfth century though by that time no longer everywhere appreciated.[11] It is certainly somewhat striking that account has to be taken of the two South Arabian authors, ʿUbayd b. Sharya and Wahb b. Munabbih, in the beginning of the development of Arabic history, suggesting perhaps a remnant of literary culture in this part of the Arabian Peninsula superior to that which was to be found elsewhere.[12]

Wahb is said to have died at Ṣanʿāʾ in 110/728 or 114/732.[13] A younger contemporary, Mūsā b. ʿUqba al-Asadī, a freedman (*mawlā*) of the family of a well-known Companion of Muḥammad, az-Zubayr b. al-ʿAwwām, inaugurated a series of important early works on the history of Muḥammad. He was known as *Imām al-Maghāzī*, that is, apparently, the 'expert on the early Muslim expeditions', which began in Muḥammad's lifetime and eventually led to the great Muslim conquests and the establishment of the Arab empire. A fragment of his *Kitāb al-Maghāzī* was edited by Edward Sachau from a Berlin manuscript,[14] and he is quoted by later writers, including aṭ-Ṭabarī. He died in 141/758.[14a]

Much better known is Muḥammad b. Isḥāq (d. 151/768), whose work of the same title, *Kitāb al-Maghāzī*, is the earliest biography of Muḥammad. This was composed for the second ʿAbbāsid Caliph, Abū Jaʿfar al-Mansūr, whom Ibn Isḥāq met in al-Ḥīra, and was worked up by Ibn Hishām (d. 218/833). The original has perished, but Ibn Hishām's work *Sīrat Muḥammād Rasūl Allāh* is one of our best existing authorities on the life of the Prophet. The Arabic text was published at Göttingen in three volumes by F. Wüstenfeld, 1858–60, and a German translation by G. Weil, the historian of the Caliphate, appeared at Stuttgart in 1864, since when the work has been generally known in the West. It is now conveniently read in the English translation of the late Professor A. Guillaume.[15] Of the relation between Ibn Isḥāq and Ibn Hishām, W. Montgomery Watt says:

> (Ibn Isḥāq's) contribution to the biography of Muḥammad is the most considerable and has been the most influential. Ibn Isḥāq collected nearly all the available information, including old poems, and so ordered and selected his material that he produced a coherent story. Frequently he gives references to his sources in the usual Islamic manner. Ibn Hishām added a few explanatory notes. Some passages that are missing in his edition are found elsewhere, but it is not clear whether he is responsible for the omissions.[16]

Professor Watt adds, 'Aṭ-Ṭabarī also quotes Ibn Isḥāq, but not nearly so fully as Ibn Hishām.' On the same subject Sir W. Muir had already written:

> There is reason to suspect that Ibn Hishām was not quite so trustworthy as his great authority Ibn Isḥāḳ. Certainly there is one instance which throws suspicion upon him as a witness disinclined at least to tell the *whole* truth. We find in Aṭ-Ṭabarī a quotation from *Ibn Isḥāk*,[17] in which is described the temporary lapse of Muḥammad into idolatry; and the same incidents are given by Al-Wāḳidi from other original sources.[18] But no notice whatever of the fact appears in the biography of Ibn Hishām, though it is professedly based upon the work of Ibn Isḥāḳ. His having thus studiously omitted all reference to so important an incident, for no other reason apparently than because he fancied it to be discreditable to the Prophet, cannot but lessen our confidence generally in this book. Still, it is evident from a comparison of his text with the quotations made by Aṭ-Ṭabarī from the same passages of Ibn Isḥāḳ (the two ordinarily tallying word for word with each other) that whatever he did excerpt from his author was faithfully and accurately quoted.[19]

It is plain that in Ibn Hishām's work we have material which, when taken with the Qur'ān itself and with authors, like aṭ-Ṭabarī, who make use of Ibn Isḥāq, affords, to say the least, a reasonably adequate account of the life of Muḥammad. But this is not the extent of the historical sources for the *sīra* or biography of the Prophet, since, apart from the voluminous *Ḥadīth* literature or traditions of Muḥammad,[20] we have in the work of al-Wāqidī (died 207/823) and especially that of his pupil Ibn Saʿd (died 230/845) another tradition of the momentous events which transpired in Mecca and Medina in the early days of Islam and before its promulgation, in the personal story of Muḥammad. Abū ʿAbd Allāh Muḥammad b. ʿUmar b. Wāqid al-Wāqidī, a freedman of Medina, was a corn-merchant who after sustaining heavy losses in business left his native city and removed to Baghdad, where he eventually became Qāḍī of ʿAskar al-Mahdī, the later Rusāfa, on the east bank of the Tigris, i.e. the opposite side from the Round City of al-Manṣūr. He died in office at an advanced age in the Caliphate of al-Ma'mūn, having been born in 130/747.

A great figure in his time—*wa-kāna lahu ri'āsa wa-jalāla*, says adh-Dhahabī[21]—he left a number of books, of which the *Kitāb al-Maghāzī* (Book of the Raids) has survived and has been edited by A. von Kremer,[22] more recently by Marsden Jones,[23] and translated into German by Wellhausen.[24] This book offers an account of the military expeditions of Muḥammad, which as already mentioned is different from Ibn Isḥāq-Ibn Hishām, and since it is early, is of great interest. Many ancient critics indeed considered al-Wāqidī an unreliable authority, speaking of his 'weakness' (*ḍaʿfuhu*) and asserting that he forged traditions. Aḥmad b. Ḥanbal went so far as to call him a liar.[25] Adh-Dhahabī, who mentions this opinion, elsewhere says that he is no longer cited.[26] This seems to have been the attitude of later times when the practice of the traditionists had come to be determined by hard-and-fast rules, and can be illustrated by the *Mishkāt al-Maṣābīḥ* (Niche of the Lamps) of al-Khaṭīb at-Tibrīzī, a work of great popularity composed in 737/1336, which does not so much as mention the name of al-Wāqidī.[27] On the other hand, earlier writers like Ibn Qutayba in the *Kitāb al-Maʿārif* speak of him respectfully.[28] Ibn Qutayba cites him as an authority in many places.[29] Al-Masʿūdī a generation or two later says roundly that Ibn Isḥāq and al-Wāqidī are the two principal authorities on the raids and military expeditions (*siyar*, cf. Lane, s.v.)[30] and indeed a similar expression was used by adh-Dhahabī in spite of his critical view of al-Wāqidī already mentioned.[31] According to Ibn Khallikān, who may or may not have had positive information, already in his lifetime al-Wāqidī was criticized as a weak authority,[32] and it has repeatedly been suggested that this view of him, which is shared even by al-Masʿūdī,[33] was owing to his Shīʿite (ʿAlid) tendency. This may be doubted for several reasons. Al-Masʿūdī who appears to have been a member of the Imāmiyya sect, a Shīʿite grouping characterized by ash-Shahrastānī as extreme,[34] qualifies al-Wāqidī as weak (*ḍaʿufa*) on other grounds, it seems, than his Shīʿism. Al-Wāqidī, on the other hand, omits to mention the famous incident of Ghaḍīr Khumm (the Pond of Khumm) in A.H. 6, when Muḥammad on his withdrawal from al-Ḥudaybiyya after he had been prevented by the as yet pagan Meccans from making his pilgrimage, declared, 'Whoever has me for master (*mawlā*), has ʿAlī for master.'[35] This tradition, which appears in Sunnī collections of Ḥadīth, but is given no special importance by the orthodox (Sunnite) doctors, is a main basis of the Shīʿite claims that the Caliphate, of right, belonged to ʿAlī and his descendants, and it is surprising that it should have been omitted by al-Wāqidī, who gives a somewhat detailed account of incidents which took place on the march back from al-Ḥudaybiyya, if he was himself a Shīʿite. But of the ancient authorities apparently only Ibn an-Nadīm in the *Fihrist* affirms this.[36]

It may well be that to account for the differing estimates of al-Wāqidī found in the Arabic writers, we should, following an indication of Wüstenfeld,[37] distinguish between his authoritative views on history, especially the raids and military expeditions of Muḥammad and his less authoritative transmission of tradition in regard to religious matters, in which he was presumably less expert. In any case, it is to be noted that modern authors have differed sharply on his value, without drawing this distinction. Von Kremer claimed him as the 'Father of Arabic history', on the grounds of being contemporary with Ibn Isḥāq, whose work is lost, and anterior to Ibn Hishām and Ibn Saʿd, dismissed by Von Kremer as 'mere compilers'.[38] Muir also, as is evident from the passage quoted above, had a high opinion of him. Wellhausen, on the other hand, who mentions that Muir and Sprenger[39] preferred al-Wāqidī to Ibn Isḥāq, strongly dissents, and while admitting that al-Wāqidī is probably earlier than Ibn Hishām (the point apparently not being capable of demonstration one way or the other), so that his *Kitāb al-Maghāzī* is in a sense (Ibn Isḥāq being lost) the oldest historical work in Arabic literature, he seeks to show that, in by far the greater number of cases where there are divergences between al-Wāqidī and Ibn Isḥāq in Ibn Hishām, Ibn Isḥāq is better and more original.[40] For practical purposes, in determining the facts about the career of Muḥammad, it seems that we should use both. No special caveats in regard to al-Wāqidī, either in the *Kitāb al-Maghāzī* or the numerous extracts from him which his pupil, Ibn Saʿd, included in his *Ṭabaqāt*, are suggested by Dr Muḥammad Ḥamīdullāh or by Professor Montgomery Watt, two of the most recent authors of books on Muḥammad.[41] The latter indeed says:

> *The Campaigns* (i.e. the *Kitāb al-Maghāzī*) of al-Wāqidī are a valuable check on Ibn Isḥāq, since they come from an independent line of authorities, and they are usually fuller, but they refer only to the Medinan period. His secretary, Ibn Saʿd, gives variants on many points, but he admits much material of little historical value, and it is only occasionally that he is the sole source for anything of importance.[42]

Al-Wāqidī was the author of other works besides the *Kitāb al-Maghāzī*, of which the *Kitāb ar-Ridda wa'd-Dār*,[43] or shortly *Kitāb ar-Ridda*[44] (Book of the Apostasy) deserves special mention. This dealt with what was usually represented as the falling away from Islam of the tribes of the Arabian peninsula, after the death of Muḥammad in A.H. 11/A.D. 632, and their coercion by the Muslims, principally of al-Madīna, which is evidently the Dār, or 'dwelling' mentioned in the longer title of al-Wāqidi's book.[45] In strictness, it would seem to cover also the bringing in to the Islamic fold of groups which had not as yet accepted the Prophet's religion with all its obligations, notably the payment of taxes to the central authority at al-Madīna. The *Kitāb ar-Ridda* dealt in particular with the wars against claimants to prophecy who had arisen in various parts of Arabia, Ṭulayḥa b. Khuwaylid al-Azdī in Najd, al-Aswad al-ʿAnsī in the Yaman and Musaylima al-Kadhdhāb ('the Liar') in al-Yamāma.[46] It appears to have been the first of a series of works of similar title, so that we can speak of a *Ridda* literature descriptive of the days after the raids of Muḥammad which meet us in the various *Maghāzī* books and before the epoch of the foreign conquests dealt with in the *Futūḥ books*,[47] where again al-Wāqidī appears to have been an innovator (see below) and of which the best example is the *Futūḥ al-Buldān* of al-Balādhurī which will be considered hereafter. It would seem that the term *siyar* noted above as covering part of the expertise of al-Wāqidī refers particularly to the *Kitāb ar-Ridda*. On the other hand, the Spanish historian Ibn Ḥubaysh (504/1110–584/1188) wrote a work *Kitāb al-Maghāzī*, whose full title was *Kitāb (Dhikr) al-Ghazawāt aḍ-Ḍāmina al-Kāfila wa'l-Futūḥ al-Jāmiʿa al-Ḥāfila al-Kā'ina fī Ayyām al-Khulafā' al-Ulā ath-Thalāthāt*, something like 'Book (Mention) of the Endorsing, Guaranteeing Expeditions and the Comprehensive, Superabundant Conquests which Were in the Days of the First Three Caliphs', included the *Ridda* wars as well as the foreign conquests, and appears to have made use of al-Wāqidi's book,[48] to an extent which can be known for certain only when the *Kitāb al-Maghāzī* of Ibn Ḥubaysh is published, or at least compared in detail with an existing copy of what is thought to be al-Wāqidī's *Kitāb ar-Ridda* in the Bankipore library.[49]

The *Fihrist* gives twenty-eight titles of books by al-Wāqidī including a *Futūḥ ash-Sha'm* (Conquests in Syria) and *Futūḥ al-ʿIrāq* (Conquests in ʿIraq),[50] but does not mention other titles of existing works, or parts of works, attributed to al-Wāqidī, some of which have been published: a *Futūḥ Miṣr* (Conquests in Egypt), a 'History of the Conquest of Mesopotamia and Armenia',[51] which may be the same as the *Futūḥ al-ʿIrāq* already mentioned, a *Futūḥ al-Bahnasā'* (in Egypt, al-Bahnasā' being the Arabic name of the ancient Oxyrhynchus) and a *Futūḥ Ifrīqiya* (Conquests in Africa, i.e. the former Roman province of that name). Of these it is of interest to note that the translation of the 'History of the Conquest of Mesopotamia and Armenia' was a youthful work of the famous Roman historian B. G. Niebuhr (1776–1831), son of the Arabian traveller Carsten Niebuhr, published posthumously in 1847.[52] The younger Niebuhr's Arabic studies appear not to be generally known. It may also be noted that the *Futūḥ al-Bahnasā'*—the town was bravely defended by its Byzantine garrison, and was a famous place both before and after the Muslim conquest, though now no more than a heap of ruins—appears as part of the *Futūḥ ash-Sha'm* in the Cairo edition of 1335/1916 (ii, 132 ff). These *Futūḥ* works attributed to al-Wāqidī which we possess are not certainly his. De Goeje, a long time ago, produced evidence to show that as they stand they are later than al-Wāqidī's time, and he considered that they probably date from the epoch of the Crusades, having been intended to encourage the Muslims against the Franks.[53] The question has not been investigated again more recently, but we are perhaps justified in supposing that they contain a substratum of what al-Wāqidī wrote in the early ninth century A.D.

As an example of the style of these works, the following passage from the *Futūḥ ash-Sha'm* may be cited.

Al-Wāqidī said: The chance-comers (*as-sāqiṭa*)[54] were halting at al-Madīna in the Days of the Ignorance (*al-Jāhiliyya*) and in Islam, bringing wheat, barley, olive-oil, cloth and the products of Syria. Some of them came to al-Madīna when Abū Bakr was sending forth the armies, and they heard the words of Abū Bakr to ʿAmr b. al-ʿAṣ, when he said, Be off to Palestine and Īliyā' (Jerusalem, called *Aelia* Capitolina by the Romans). He continued: And they brought word to the king Heraclius. And when he heard it, he assembled the chief men of his empire and his patricians and told them the report which had come, and said, O sons of al-Aṣfar (literally, the Yellow, supposed ancestor of the Greeks),[55] this is what I warned you of long ago, and (said) that the companions of this prophet must rule what is beneath my throne. The promised time is now near. The successor (*khalīfa*) of Muḥammad has sent the armies against you, and it is as if they were here, and had come to you and reached you. Beware for yourselves, and fight for your religion and your dearest possessions (or 'wives', *ḥarīmukum*). If you disdain, the Arabs will rule over your land and your goods. He continued: And the people wept. And he said to them, Leave your weeping. Then his vizier said to him, O king, we desire that you summon one of those who brought you this news. So Heraclius ordered one of his chamberlains to bring a man of the Christianized Arabs (*al-mutanaṣṣira*) who had brought him the news. So a man was brought, and the king said to him, How old is your news? Twenty-five days, was the reply. The king went on, Who is their ruler? He was told, A man called Abū Bakr aṣ-Ṣiddīq has sent his armies to your land. Have you seen Abū Bakr? asked the king. Yes, said the other, He bought a cloak from me for four *dirhams*, and put it on his back. He is like one of them, going about wearing two garments and passing through the streets and circulating among the people, securing the rights of the weak against the strong. Heraclius said, Describe him to me. He is a brown-complexioned man with a light beard, said the other. Then Heraclius said, By the truth of my religion, it is the Companion of Aḥmad who we found in our books would manage the affair after him. We found in our books also that after this man there would be another tall man, like a raging lion, at whose hands would be destruction and desolation. He continued, And the Christian Arab groaned at the words of Heraclius and said, The man whom you described (sc. ʿUmar) I have seen with him, never leaving him. Said Heraclius, This thing is true, by God! I have called the Greeks to right conduct and justice, and they have refused to obey me. My kingdom will be destroyed. Then he fastened to a spear a jewelled cross and gave it to Rūbīs,[56] the commander of his armies, and said to him, I appoint you over the armies. Go, and prevent the Arabs from Palestine, for it is a rich land, abundant in good, and it is our honour, our glory and our crown. And Rūbīs took the cross and went immediately to Ajnadayn, and the army of the Greeks followed him.

Al-Wāqidī said: It has reached me that ʿAmr b. al-Āṣ proceeded to Īliyāʾ (Jerusalem, as above) till he reached the land of Palestine, he and his men. He continued: When the Muslims were encamped in Palestine, ʿAmr assembled the Muslims, the Emigrants and the Helpers, and asked their advice on the situation. While they were in council, there arrived ʿAdī b. ʿĀmir, who was one of the best of the Muslims. He had been often to Syria, and had trodden their land, and knew the places to lodge in and the routes to travel by. When he came in sight of the Muslims, they brought him and set him before ʿAmr b. al-ʿĀṣ. And ʿAmr b. al-ʿĀṣ, said, What is the news, O Ibn ʿĀmir? He said, The news is the Christian Arabs and their armies, like ants.[57]

This is a fair sample of the *Futūḥ ash-Shaʾm* going under the name of al-Wāqidī. Is it authentic? In the short compass of less than a page of text there are one or two difficulties, but this is quite normal in any passage of medieval Arabic. It is not formally in contradiction with a story given by aṭ-Ṭabarī at some length of a visit paid by Abū Sufyān, father of the later Caliph Muʿāwiya, in the year A.H. 6 to Syria, before the submission of the pagan Meccans, in which he is summoned from Ghazza (Gaza) by

Heraclius and tells him what he knows about Muḥammad.[58] This may be a genuine specimen of the *kutub al-futūḥ* which the poet Abū Tammām mentions as in extensive circulation, in his time, i.e. a little later than al-Wāqidī.[59] On the other hand, doubts remain, if not in regard to this or that passage, yet in general when al-Wāqidī is quoted. Take, for example, the question of the first Muslim attack on Constantinople. Though sometimes disregarded by modern historians the advance under Yazīd b. Muʿāwiya in or about 49/669[60] as far as Chalcedon on the opposite side of the Bosphorus from Constantinople is sufficiently authenticated by Greek sources for Professor Hitti to speak of Yazīd's men as the first Arab army to set eyes on Byzantium.[61] But while there is a good deal of evidence for Yazīd's attack on Constantinople, borne witness to by aṭ-Ṭabarī, al-Masʿūdi, adh-Dhahabī and other writers, it is somewhat embarrassing to find that according to al-Wāqidī this was not the first attack of the Muslims on the capital and that aṭ-Ṭabarī, who reports this information from al-Wāqidī evidently doubted it. For *sub anno* 43/663–4 aṭ-Ṭabarī says that in this year took place the winter expedition of Busr b. Abī Arṭāt in which he reached Constantinople, *according to the assertion of al-Wāqidī* (*fīmā zaʿama al-W.*), adding that a number of historians, not mentioned by name, denied this and said that Busr b. abī Arṭāt at no time wintered in the territory of the Byzantine empire.[62] Again the implication is plain. Al-Wāqidī's statements have to be treated with care, even though we do not reject them altogether.

It is natural to consider with al-Wāqidī his pupil and secretary Ibn Saʿd, who as already remarked often quotes him. Ibn Saʿd's main work, the *Kitāb aṭ-Ṭabaqāt al-Kabīr* (Great Book of Classes), depends on his predecessors and is a compilation, as Von Kremer long ago noted (cf. p. 75), but an extremely useful compilation, and we have it in an excellent edition by E. Sachau and others (Leiden, 9 vols, 1904–28). It contains convenient biographies of Muḥammad, his Companions and the later bearers of Islam, arranged in the classes (*ṭabaqāt*) which give the book its name. Ibn Saʿd died in Baghdad in 230/845. With his work ends the series of early, or at least comparatively early, native Arabic texts on which, for the most part, we depend for the life of Muḥammad and the emergence of Islam.[63]

Within the same period other kinds of historical writing developed. It was natural that the origins of the Arabs in their peninsula should not be forgotten, even during the momentous events connected with the foundation of the new Muslim empire. In all matters of Arab antiquity and particularly genealogy the name of Hishām al-Kalbī stood high as that of a great authority. His *Kitāb an-Nasab al-Kabīr* (Great Book of Genealogy), otherwise *Jamhara fī'n-Nasab* (Collection on Genealogy),[64] dealt with the whole subject extensively, and pointed the way to later works, such as the *Kitāb Ansāb al-Ashrāf* (Book of the Genealogies of the Nobles) of al-Balādhurī,[65] better known at the present time than its predecessor which has survived only in fragments. As a specimen of Hishām al-Kalbī's work on the Arab past, we may take his *Kitāb Aswāq al-ʿArab*, i.e. on the *sūqs*, or markets, of the Arabs, which can conveniently be read in a French translation by Dr M. Hamidullah in his biography of Muḥammad.[66] We may also consider al-Kalbī's *Kitāb al-Aṣnām* (Book of Idols), much of which passed into the great geographical compilation of Yāqūt, *Muʿjam al-Buldān* (see p. 171). These passages were translated by J. Wellhausen in his *Reste arabischen Heidentums*.[67] Since Wellhausen's time, the work has become known in a single manuscript belonging to the late Aḥmad Zakī Pasha, and was edited by him in the original Arabic.[68] Another edition with a translation and commentary by Rosa Klinke-Rosenberger appeared at Leipzig in 1941.[69] The work is informative on its subject (the idols of the pre-Islamic Arabs), but makes somewhat dry reading, though short (forty pages of Arabic text), being factual in the extreme. Another of al-Kalbī's works, now lost, like most of those listed in the *Fihrist* (95–8), is the *Kitāb al-Fityān al-Arbaʿa* (Book of the Four Heroes, or Complete Men), perhaps concerned with the first four Caliphs.[70] With Hishām al-Kalbī we may mention another writer of similar interests, al-Haytham b. ʿAdī.[71]

The history of towns also began to be written at the same time, probably the earliest example of what became afterwards a favourite type of work being the *Akhbār Makka al-Musharrafa* (Chronicles of Mecca the Glorious) by al-Azraqī, who died *c.* 219/834.[72] A generation or two later there appeared the *Taʾrīkh Baghdād* (History of Baghdad) of Ibn Abī Ṭāhir Ṭayfūr, a voluminous writer (204/819–280/893), most of whose works are lost. Book 6 of the History of Baghdad, dealing with a part of the Caliphate of al-Maʾmūn, was edited and translated into German by H. Keller (Leipzig, 2 vols, 1908) and translated into English by Kate Chambers Seelye (Columbia University Oriental Series, xvi, 1920). The *Fihrist* (146) gives an amusing account of Ibn Abī Ṭāhir Ṭayfūr, from which we can gather that he was not highly estimated by all his contemporaries including the poet al-Buḥturī, who spoke of his barbarous Arabic and plagiarism. This criticism applied especially to the poetical compositions of which he was also the author, and is no doubt to be accounted for by his having been from Khurāsān, of a distinguished family there, it is said. On the other hand, he enjoyed a great popular reputation, and if that part of his History of Baghdad which survives (204/819–218/833) lacks perfect arrangement and is weak on chronology,[73] it is at all events the work of one who was alive, though very young, during the happenings which he describes.

The earliest work which we possess of distinctively Shīʿa history is the *Kitāb Ṣiffīn*, otherwise *Waqʿat Ṣiffīn*,[74] an account of the battle of Ṣiffīn in 37/657 between Muʿāwiya, then governor of Syria, and ʿAlī, who is referred to in what may be the original title of the book, *Kitāb Ṣiffīn fī Sharḥ Ghazāt Amīr al-Muʾminīn* (Book of Ṣiffīn in Explanation of the Expedition of the Commander of the Faithful). It is understandable that the importance of this battle, which in the long run gave Muʿāwiya the Caliphate, should have been appreciated by the Muslims of his time and later, yet we cannot fail to note with some surprise that this extensive work of several hundred pages was written by a contemporary of Ibn Isḥāq. Its author, Naṣr b. Muzāḥim al-Minqarī, an Arab of Tamīm, lived *c.* 120/738–212/827. He was a native of al-Kūfa, settled in Baghdad, where he studied under the well-known teacher Sufyān ath-Thawrī. A perfumer by profession, he wrote several books, of which alone the *Kitāb Ṣiffīn* has survived.[75] The work was not the first which had been written on the subject. Naṣr b. Muzāḥim was anticipated with a *Kitāb Ṣiffīn* of Abū Miḥnaf Lūṭ b. Yaḥyā al-Azdī,[76] and al-Wāqidī later wrote a work of the same title,[77] so that the merit of absolute originality cannot be claimed for the Shīʿite author.

Naṣr b. Muzāḥim is scarcely used by aṭ-Ṭabarī and not at all for the events of 37/657. For Ṣiffīn he in fact frequently cites Abū Miḥnaf, presumably from the latter's work already mentioned. The famous incident of the raising of copies of the Qurʾān on the lances of the Syrian troops is thus introduced by aṭ-Ṭabarī.

When ʿAmr b. al-ʿĀṣ saw that the ʿIrāqīs (i.e. ʿAlī's troops) had the upper hand and feared destruction on that account, he said to Muʿāwiya, Will you listen to a matter which I shall show you, which will increase our cohesion and increase only their confusion? Yes, said Muʿāwiya.

Let us raise copies of the Qur'ān, said the other, and shout, 'They contain a judgment between us and you.' If some of them refuse to accept them, you will find among them others who say, Certainly, we must accept what is in them, so that confusion will occur among them. And if they say, Certainly we accept what is in them, we shall remove this battle from us and this war for ever, or for a space. So they raised the Qur'āns on the spears and said, 'This—the Book of God Who is great and glorious—is between us and you! Who will be for the frontiers of the Syrians after the Syrians? and who for the frontiers of the people of Iraq after the people of Iraq? And when the people saw the Qur'āns raised upon the spears, they said, We assent to the Book of God, Who is great and glorious, and repent towards Him.[78]

This is given explicitly as the tradition of Abū Miḥnaf.

Naṣr b. Muzāḥim has a description of the fighting at Ṣiffīn.

On the main day Muʿāwiya's companions said, By Allāh, we shall not quit the field today till Allāh gives us the victory, or we die. So they hastened out to fight in the early morning of one of the days of the Dog-star, long and extremely hot. Both sides shot till their arrows were exhausted. Then they thrust at each other till their spears were broken. Then both sides dismounted from their horses, and went on foot against one another with their swords till the scabbards were broken, and the horsemen rose up in their stirrups. Then they fought confusedly with swords and iron maces, and no sound was heard except the shouts of the combatants, the crash of iron on men's heads and the confusion of voices. The sun was darkened as the dust swirled up. The banners and standards were lost in the confusion. Four times the hour of prayer passed when the sole sign of God's worship was the *takbīr*. In these scenes of carnage (previously the writer had mentioned that in this 'Day of Clangour' and the night that followed during which fighting was continuous, 70,000 fell on both sides) the *shaykhs* called aloud, You men of the Arabs, remember Allāh for your women, both wives and daughters! And Abū Jaʿfar (i.e. the narrator) wept while he was reciting to us this tradition.[79]

The account of Naṣr b. Muzāḥim goes on to give a speech of al-Ashʿath b. Qays al-Kindī, one of the chiefs of the party, in which he said that if the two armies engaged again next day, it would mean the end of the Arabs of ʿAlī, and that he feared especially for the dependants of the slain, the women and children. Naṣr continues, giving the words of Ṣaʿṣaʿa b. Ṣūḥan, an authority often used (but not here) by aṭ-Ṭabarī[80] and approved of by adh-Dhahabī:[81]

The spies of Muʿāwiya brought him the speech of al-Ashʿath, and he said, He is right, by the Lord of the Kaʿba! If we meet tomorrow, the

Greeks will turn upon our children and women, and the Persians will turn upon the women and children of the people of ʿIraq. Only people of discernment and intelligence see this. Bind the Qurʾāns on the ends of the lances![82]

This account, it will be noticed, is remarkable for assigning the reason for the move, which was to prove so advantageous for Muʿāwiya and his party, not to the suggestion of ʿAmr b. al-ʿĀs but to Muʿāwiya's own initiative, and, at least in part, to his fear of the Greeks. This may have been an authentic motive, since it is at least hinted at also in aṭ-Ṭabarī's account, already given. One is apt to suppose from the rapid conquests in Syria and elsewhere that the Muslims had nothing to be afraid of from the Byzantines whom they had repeatedly faced and defeated. But there are indications that this was by no means so. Before Muʿāwiya succeeded to the Caliphate, when after Ṣiffīn he remained in confrontation with ʿAlī, he secured himself on his northern border by a truce with Byzantium, by the terms of which he agreed to pay what was in effect tribute to the Emperor Constans II, and in 678 towards the end of his Caliphate, after the failure of the great Arab assault on Constantinople in the so-called Seven Years' War and an attack by the Mardaites on his northern frontier, Muʿāwiya again paid tribute to the Emperor, now Constantine IV.[83] At a later date Byzantine armies invaded Syria and retook Antioch and Aleppo.[84]

In any case, the book of Naṣr b. Muzāḥim on the battle of Ṣiffīn affords insights which are not to be neglected. Isolated details are of interest. The tradition of Ṣaʿṣaʿa continues:

The people of Syria were in commotion and called in the darkness of night, O people of Iraq, who will be for our children if you slay us? and who will be for your children if we slay you? Allāh, Allāh, for the remnant! And when morning came the people of Syria had already raised the Qurʾāns on the heads of the spears and hung them from the horses' necks. And the people according to their companies desired what they called to, and the great Qurʾān-copy of Damascus which took ten men to carry was raised on the heads of the spears. And they cried, O people of Iraq, the Book of Allāh is between us and you! And Abūʾl-Aʿwar as-Sulamī went forward on a white hack and placed a copy of the Qurʾān on his head, calling, O people of ʿIrāq! the Book of Allāh is between us and you![85]

Naṣr b. Muzāḥim's book[86] gives events leading up to the battle of Ṣiffīn, mentions individual exploits, and offers speeches and poetry. Like other Shīʿa authors he is very differently judged, being praised by some and disparaged by others. He is not very partial, for while mentioning the faults of Muʿāwiya, he does not omit criticism of ʿAlī. Some of his authorities, like the Abū Jaʿfar mentioned above (in full, Abū Jaʿfar Muḥammad b. ʿAlī ash-Shaʿbī) and ʿUmar b. Saʿd al-Asadī, are obscure or 'weak', at least in the eyes of later authorities.[87] But the work *Waqʿat Ṣiffīn* is of considerable importance, not only as offering independent traditions on the battle, but also as indicating, what we perhaps could not have gathered from more familiar books, the considerable progress which the idea of history had already made by this time. Both Naṣr b. Muzāḥim and his son al-Ḥusayn are occasionally quoted by aṭ-Ṭabarī.

Little more than a name, in spite of upwards of 200 works attributed to him in the *Fihrist* (100–4), is al-Madā'inī, so called because of his connection with al-Madā'in ('the Cities'), the Arabic for the ancient Persian capital, Seleucia-Ctesiphon. He appears to have invented or popularized the historical tale.[88] His dates are given as 135/753–215/830, but the year of his death is very uncertain.

With al-Balādhurī (died 279/892 at an advanced age) we come to an important historian of early Islam, witness al-Masʿūdī who says 'We know no better book on the conquests of the lands (*futūḥ al-buldān*)', i.e. than al-Balādhurī's work of the same title (*Kitāb Futūḥ al-Buldān*).[89] Al-Balādhuri's name, according to a somewhat ridiculous story first mentioned in the *Fihrist* (113), was due to the fact that either he or his grandfather died insane as a result of having inadvertently taken an overdose of anacardia (*balādhur*), considered beneficial to the memory. The work has often been printed, most recently in a useful edition by Dr Ṣalāḥ ad-Dīn al-Munajjid (Cairo, 3 vols, 1956–7). It is often read in the West in the English translation, *The Origins of the Islamic State* by P. K. Hitti and F. C. Murgotten.[90]

The *Kitāb Futūḥ al-Buldān*, though not particularly well adapted for consecutive reading, is indispensable for the conquests of the Arabs. The work begins with Arabia in the time of Muḥammad and is arranged not chronologically, in the first instance, but geographically. After Arabia come Syria, Mesopotamia, Armenia, Egypt and North Africa, Spain, certain Mediterranean islands (Sicily, Rhodes and Crete), Nubia, Iraq and Persia, etc. Within the chapters the arrangement is of course chronological. Al-Balādhurī gives information which in general can be relied upon (gathered sometimes from personal inquiry of local authorities who might be expected to know something about what had happened in times not so far distant),[91] and this information is often such as cannot readily be found elsewhere, e.g. in aṭ-Ṭabarī. On the other hand, it not uncommonly happens that Balʿamī, the Sāmānid vizier who rendered aṭ-Ṭabarī's history into Persian, and both abbreviated and added to it in the process,[92] has material which is found also in al-Balādhurī.[93] If there is thus a relation between al-Balādhurī and Balʿamī, we may perhaps speak of Ibn Aʿtham al-Kūfī as forming a group with the other two, since the close correspondence between the last-named and Balʿamī has already been noted.[94]

Though al-Balādhurī, as mentioned above, has a section on the conquest of North Africa and a short section on the conquest of Spain (al-Andalus), it is quite natural to find, given his Iranian origin, that he is more interested in and knowledgeable about the Muslim East than the West. He is definitely not one of our better authorities for the Maghrib, but on the other hand, he provides us with some interesting information concerning the Muslim occupation of Bari in south Italy (Apulia). The passage may be cited as a sample of his style, which allows him sometimes to dispense with authorities, as here.[95]

In the Maghrib [i.e. the Muslim West, not specified more closely] is the land known as *al-Arḍ al-Kabīra* [the 'Great Land'] [96] distant fifteen days from Barqa [Barca], or slightly less or more. There on the shore of the sea is a city called Bāra (Bari), whose people were Christians but not Greeks. Ḥabla, the freedman of al-Aghlab, raided it and failed. Then Khalfūn the Berber raided it (he is said to have been a freedman of Rabīʿa, sc. the Arab tribe of that name), and he conquered it in the beginning of the Caliphate of al-Mutawakkil ʿalā Allāh.[97] There arose after him a man called al-Mufarraj b. Sallām who conquered twenty-four fortresses and took possession of them. He wrote to the controller of the post in Egypt informing him and saying that he saw no prospect of public prayer for himself and the Muslims who were with him, unless the Imām (i.e. the Caliph) should confirm him over his territory and make him its ruler, so that he would no longer be a usurper. He built a cathedral mosque. Then his followers revolted against him and killed him. There arose after him, Sawdān, who sent his messenger to the Commander of the Faithful al-Mutawakkil ʿalā Allāh asking him for a contract (*ʿaqd*) and letter of investiture. But he died before his messenger to Sawdān departed. Al-Muntaṣir biʾllāh died, his Caliphate having been for six months, and there arose al-Mustaʿīn biʾllāh Aḥmad b. Muḥammad b. al-Muʿtaṣim biʾllāh. He ordered his agent (*ʿāmil*) for the Maghrib,[98] Ūtāmish, freedman of the Commander of the Faithful, to confirm

Sawdān over his territory. But his messenger had not left Sāmarrā until Ūtāmish was slain. Waṣīf, freedman of the Commander of the Faithful, was given charge of the territory. He granted confirmation and transmitted it.

This passage gives information of a period of twenty or thirty years in the history of the Apulian city about which we might otherwise know nothing. The account in Ibn al-Athīr follows al-Balādhurī.[99] Al-Aghlab is evidently the third son of Ibrāhīm b. al-Aghlab, founder of the Aghlabid dynasty, who eventually succeeded his elder brothers and reigned from 223/837 till 226/840. Ūtāmish is the Turkish vizier of al-Mustaʿīn, killed in an *émeute* in Sāmarrā in 249/863. It is interesting to find this Turkish soldier of fortune in charge of the affairs of the Muslim West (*ʿāmil ʿalāʾl-Maghrib*).[100]

In addition to his work on the Muslim conquests al-Balādhurī is also mentioned in the *Fihrist* as an active translator from Persian, and we know the title of at least one of his translations, the *Testament of Ardashīr* which he wrote in verse form.[101]

But undoubtedly al-Balādhurī's reputation among his own people depended not on his translations but on his historical writings, and on one of these in particular, perhaps even more than the *Futūḥ al-Buldān*. This was the *Kitāb Ansāb al-Ashrāf* (Book of the Genealogies of the Nobles), a work in at least a dozen volumes, which rapidly became rare.[102] Al-Balādhurī began his book with the biography of Muḥammad and the lives of the Companions of Muḥammad. He then went on to the ʿAlids, followed by the other Hāshimids. After the Hāshimids came the descendants of ʿAbd Shams, with special attention to the Umayyads, then the rest of Quraysh and the other divisions of Muḍar. The last part of the book is occupied with Qays, there being particular mention of Thaqīf, and a long biography of al-Ḥajjāj b. Yūsuf, the most celebrated Thaqafī.[103] A table of matters contained in the *Kitāb Ansāb al-Ashrāf* by M. Hamidullah was published in 1954.[104] The work covers the first two centuries of Islam and is arranged by generations. The first part to be published deals with the reign of ʿAbd al-Malik.[105] After a long lull publication was resumed by the Hebrew University of Jerusalem, subsequently to the discovery of a complete MS in the ʿAshīr Effendi Library at Istanbul:[106] vol. 4b (Yazīd I and Muʿāwiya II) by M. Schloessinger in 1938; vol. 5 (ʿUthmān, Marwān I and ʿAbd Allāh b. az-Zubayr) by S. D. Goitein in 1936. Vol. 1 (Noah to Muḥammad) by M. Hamidullah was published in another series[107] in 1958. The section on ʿAlī was translated into Italian by G. Levi della Vida in 1914,[108] and that on Muʿāwiya by O. Pinto and Levi della Vida in 1938.[109] We thus have a substantial amount of material on what must no doubt be regarded as al-Balādhurī's greatest work, which is gradually being studied and appropriated. His life also is better known than formerly, e.g. Ṣalāḥ ad-Dīn al-Munajjid has pointed out that De Goeje, whose early edition of the *Kitāb Futūḥ al-Buldān*[110] is still valuable, was mistaken in regarding al-Balādhurī as one of the masters of Muḥammad b. Isḥāq an-Nadīm, the author of the *Fihrist*.[111]

What used to be thought of, before the *Kitāb Ṣiffīn* (see pp. 81 ff above) was known, as the only ancient historical work by a Shīʿite author is the anonymous[112] *Taʾrīkh* (History) of al-Yaʿqūbī, the third/ninth century writer who meets us again in Chapter 4 (p. 163). It was edited by Houtsma at Leiden in 1883 from the single manuscript then known, in the Cambridge University Library, and has been reprinted in the East within recent years (Beirut, 2 vols, 1379/1960). Its interest is considerable. A re-edition is a desideratum and since other manuscripts are not known would probably prove not too difficult an undertaking. The *Tar'īkh* is divided into two Books, the first of which gives an account of the biblical patriarchs beginning with Adam (according to Houtsma this is based on a Syriac work, the *Meʿārath Gazzē* or Cave of Treasures),[113] followed by the history of Christ and the Apostles, the rulers of Syria, Assyria and Babylon, the Indians, Greeks and Romans, the Persians, the northern nations, the Chinese, Egyptians, Berbers, Abyssinians and Negroes, and finally the pre-Islamic Arabs. The second Book, which is twice the size of the first, treats of the history of Islam with a discernible Shīʿite tendency. It has, however, been criticized less for this than for its neglect to name sources and for the scantiness of the notices of actual history.[114] The sections on biblical history have attracted attention,[115] and would have to be investigated again closely in any re-examination of the question of early Arabic versions of Scripture, for al-Yaqʿūbī gives numerous quotations from the Old and New Testaments. He also has an important section of more than fifty pages where he canvasses the scientific and philosophical works of famous Greeks, Hippocrates, Dioscorides, Galen, Socrates, Pythagoras, Plato, Euclid, Nicomachus, Aratus, Aristotle and Ptolemy.[116] This list represents evidently what was known to al-Yaqʿūbī of Greek science and philosophy, and we may estimate, if we will, from the amount of space which he devotes to them, the relative importance of these authors in the view of the time: Hippocrates (22 pages), Ptolemy (11 pages), Aristotle (6 pages), etc. Al-Yaʿqūbi's account of the northern nations, derived from some unknown source, also repays attention.[117] He has got hold of information, e.g. on the nomenclature of the Khazar kings,[118] which is found nowhere else. Altogether his *Taʾrīkh* is an important work, to be used with other good sources, e.g. aṭ-Ṭabarī, for reconstructing the history of the Caliphate.

Ibn Qutayba (213/828–276/889) has been treated in Chapter 2, but his *Kitāb al-Maʿārif* or 'Handbook of History' as it was entitled by its nineteenth-century editor, deserves passing mention again here, though it is hardly the oldest surviving purely historical work of the Arabs, as Wüstenfeld thought.[119] It deals with the pre-Islamic as well as Islamic history of the Arabs, and is still useful as a reference book, for genealogical and biographical matters especially. It is also of interest as showing what a widely esteemed and highly orthodox author of the time considered to be matters of importance in the historical field, and we can learn from what the comparatively short book (330 pages of Arabic text in Wüstenfeld's edition) omits as well as from what it contains.

Abū Ḥanīfa ad-Dīnawarī also has already been mentioned (p. 54). As a historian he is well known for his *Kitāb al-Akhbār aṭ-Ṭiwāl* (Book of Long Narratives), which deals in principle, as the title suggests, with selected episodes which interested the author, chiefly from Islamic history, but the pre-Islamic period is not completely disregarded and he gives us accounts of Alexander the Great and the Sāsānid kings in some detail down to Yazdagird, the last of the Sāsānids. His account of the Muslim conquest of Iraq is picturesque, and includes many interesting and apparently reliable details, notably for the battle of al-Qādisiyya.[120] Another interesting section recounts the later days of Umayyad rule in Khurāsān and the defeat and death of Marwān II, the last Umayyad Caliph.[121] The narrative is brought down to the death of al-Muʿtaṣim in 227/842, i.e. it continues to the author's own times.

2. Ṭabarī and others

According to Ibn Khallikān, the general History of aṭ-Ṭabarī, the work which Europeans usually refer to as the *Annals* and of which the original title was *Ta'rīkh ar-Rusul wa'l-Mulūk* (History of the Apostles—in the Muslim sense, very nearly Prophets—and Kings), was the soundest and most reliable work of its kind.[122] This is an opinion with which most moderns would agree. For the history of Islam the *Annals* is no doubt the best single native work which we possess, for its scope (fifteen volumes in the Leiden edition of De Goeje and others),[123] for the efforts which the author has made to report only reliable information, and also, it may be said, for the nearness at which he stands to the events related.

Abū Jaʿfar Muḥammad b. Jarīr aṭ-Ṭabarī was born at Āmul, lying north of the great Elburz range in the coastal lowlands of the Caspian then called Ṭabaristān (hence his generic name or *nisba*), in 224/839. He died in Baghdad in 310/923. His principal authorities for the history are not, in general, any of the books which we have mentioned, at all events not *qua*[124] books, but chains of tradition going back wherever possible to eye-witnesses of the various occurrences. This was the method already employed in aṭ-Ṭabarī's time by the experts in the science of *Ḥadīth*, in principle tradition of Muḥammad. The method was applied with rigour by the best of these experts (*muḥaddithūn*), who had criteria for estimating the value of the different traditions, with which aṭ-Ṭabarī as a distinguished student of the religious sciences was perfectly familiar (his *Tafsīr* or Qur'ān Commentary[125] has been as highly regarded by his fellow-countrymen as his History, and he had an extensive work *Tahdhīb al-Athār*—actually on *Ḥadith*).[126] The application of the method on the widest scale might seem to give an almost irrefragable guarantee of truth to a historical narrative, and this was no doubt a main reason for its adoption by aṭ-Ṭabarī. Unfortunately, while there was no lack of material, it was inevitably not always reliable. This is evident in cases where alternative accounts of the same event existed. Here aṭ-Ṭabarī's procedure was to give the alternatives without comment, leaving it to the reader to decide which to accept. In general, he omits discussion of the information contained in the notice (called the *matan* or text) offered to his readers on the authority of the chain of narrators (*isnād*), and is perhaps open to criticism because of this. On the other hand, it can be pointed out[127] that competent scholars like aṭ-Ṭabarī himself were well aware of the authority which individual reporters bore in regard to competence and veracity, and readers of this kind might be expected to judge pretty accurately of the reliability or otherwise of particular pieces of information.

There is in fact general agreement among the Muslims of all periods best able to judge that aṭ-Ṭabarī is reliable. Such evaluation of the men (*rijāl*) who transmitted information became progressively more difficult as the chains of authorities became longer with the passage of time, and it is at this point that aṭ-Ṭabarī's comparatively early date was an advantage. In later times the *isnāds* came to be regarded as no longer providing authentication for what had happened in the past, especially when it was realized that traditions were sometimes deliberately forged in the interest of a particular point of view, or even from motives of vanity or simple mischief. Consequently we find that later historians usually abandoned them. But down to the time of aṭ-Ṭabarī the system on the whole seems justified as providing at least the material from which a discriminating student could obtain authenticated information, reaching back to the early days of Islam. The chief criticism for his *Annals* is not then its method, though this makes for tedium on occasion and can only be fully appreciated by those who have some skill in the branch of *Ḥadīth* called *ʿilm ar-rijāl* (evaluation of authorities) but rather the fact that the work, which ends in the year 302/915, we cannot say is too short, in view of its very substantial size, but breaks off too soon for our liking. There is no doubt that most students of the Muslim Caliphate would have been glad of aṭ-Ṭabarī's company, if that had been possible, much later than the seventh year of al-Muqtadir.

The author of the *Annals* died in Baghdad in 310/923. As one would expect, attempts were made to continue his great History. One of the best known is by ʿArīb b. Saʿd of Cordova, part of which, dealing with Iraq, was printed as a separate volume in the Leiden edition of the *Annals*, under the title of *Ṣilat Taʾrīkh aṭ-Ṭabarī*. This was originally written between 363/973 and 366/976 as part of a *mukhtaṣar* (abridgement) of the *Annals*, which included additions and improvements, notably on the history of Spain, and brought the main narrative down to 320/932.[128] Another, the *Takmilat Taʾrīkh aṭ-Ṭabarī* (Completion of the History of aṭ-Ṭabarī), was written by Muḥammad b. ʿAbd al-Malik al-Hamadhānī, who died as late as 521/1127. The first part of this work, down to 367/977, edited by Albert Yūsuf Kanʿān, was published by the Catholic Press, Beirut, in 1961.

A book of possibly greater interest than either of these is Balʿamī's Persian translation of Ṭabarī, as it is usually called, the work of Muḥammad b. Muḥammad Balʿamī, *wazīr* of the Sāmānid ruler Manṣūr b. Nūḥ. It was produced about the year 352/963, i.e. shortly after the accession of Manṣūr b. Nūḥ to the throne of Transoxiana and Khurāsān in 350/961. The general plan of the work was to give the *Annals* in Persian, suppressing the chains of authorities and selecting a single relation where aṭ-Ṭabarī offers more than one. Apart from this, the work appears much reduced in size (four volumes in Zotenberg's French translation[129] compared with aṭ-Ṭabarī's thirteen volumes of text) not merely because of the omission of the *isnāds* and duplicate accounts just referred to, but also because of a tendency to suppress what was not of interest in Persia and beyond the Oxus. Thus the developments in aṭ-Ṭabarī on Spain and the Muslim West in general are greatly curtailed. About the West of Islam Balʿamī and his friends evidently knew and cared little. Al-Andalus (Muslim Spain) appears in these pages as a town occupied by the Dīvs,[130] i.e. devils of Iranian lore, or else as a fabulous country in Egypt.[131] On the other hand, Balʿamī does not simply excerpt aṭ-Ṭabarī. Sometimes he supplements him to a notable extent on the history of the Muslim East, and what is particularly striking is that occasionally other authors, al-Balādhurī, al-Yaʿqūbī, whom we have already met, and Ibn al-Athīr, yet to be mentioned, likewise give Balʿamī's additional material.[132] It is principally on the strength of these additions that Professor Zeki Validi Togan considered the 'so-called Persian Ṭabarī' to be an independent work.[133] For the History of Thābit b. Sinān, which also continuated at-Ṭabarī, see pp. 123, 290 n., 176.

As organized in the Leiden edition, the *Annals* of aṭ-Ṭabarī are divided into three series. The first (vols. i–vi) contains successively the biblical history, history of the rulers of Persia, history of Muḥammad (chiefly in vols iii–iv), and history of the so-called Orthodox Caliphs, Abū Bakr, ʿUmar, ʿUthmān and ʿAlī, to the assassination of ʿAlī in 40/661. The second (vols i–iii) covers the history of the Umayyads to the successful ʿAbbāsid revolution of the year 130/747–8. The third (vols. i–iv) describes the events which led to the death of Marwān II, the last of the Umayyad Caliphs of the East, the succession of Abū'l-ʿAbbās and the history of the ʿAbbāsids to 302/915, as already mentioned. An Appendix of 250 pages contains various lists of deaths in successive years, Companions who related traditions of Muḥammad, etc., but these strictly do not form part of the work. Even without the Appendix it is sufficiently long: Series I, 3476 pages; Series II,

2017 pages; and Series III, 2294 pages, in all 7787 pages of Arabic text.

It is beyond the scope of our present purpose to point to the high-lights in the *Annals*, but the narratives of the war between the Arabs and the Khazars (22/642–32/652) in Series I,[134] of operations on the Chinese frontier (96/714–15) in Series II,[135] and of the struggle lasting nearly fifteen years (255/869–270/883) against the Zanj or Blacks of Iraq in Series III[136] are full of stirring incidents, and aṭ-Ṭabarī has perhaps been conscious of this in selecting the authorities to which, here as elsewhere, he is bound by his method. An element of legend no doubt enters into some of the accounts, especially of the early days of Islam. Yet the main characteristic of the *Annals* is undoubtedly the effort which has been made to attain to historical truth. This is patent to the most casual reader, for, apart from his method, already described, aṭ-Ṭabarī inserts original documents of various kinds, particularly speeches[137] and letters,[138] and also of course contemporary poetry, the latter sometimes with what strikes a modern as unnecessary profusion. The lists in the Appendix to the *Annals* have already been mentioned. Various other lists appear in different parts of the work.[139] Aṭ-Ṭabarī's work is made available to the non-Arabist by the synopses in Latin at the beginning of each volume of the Leiden edition. On the whole, with the possible exception of Ibn al-Athīr, yet to be characterized, whose great history *al-Kāmil* (the Perfect) has also never been translated in its entirety into any western language, the *Taʾrīkh ar-Rusul waʾl-Mulūk* or Annals of aṭ-Ṭabarī is the best work in Arabic for affording information about the historical development of Islam and the Arab Caliphate, the most characteristic institution to which the new religion gave rise and which marks the zenith in world history of the Arab race. At the present time the attempt is being made, with the help of Unesco, to produce a complete English translation of aṭ-Ṭabarī. If the attempt is successful, it should immediately place at the disposal of historians and others a much-needed instrument for raising our knowledge of the Arab Caliphate during the first and more interesting half of its existence,[140] to something like the level of what already is known about the medieval Papacy, the system among all others, probably, to which the Caliphate most nearly corresponds.

Aṣ-Ṣūlī (Abū Bakr Muḥammad b. Yaḥyā), descendant or at least great-nephew of a Turkish prince, Ṣūl Tigīn of Jurjān, and a skilled chess-player, is a figure of some importance, as the author of a literary history, *Kitāb al-Awrāq fī Akhbār Āl al-ʿAbbās wa-Ashʿārihim* (Book of Pages on the History of the ʿAbbāsids and their Poetry). He was a courtier of the Caliphs al-Muktafī and al-Muqtadir, and enjoyed court favour later. The date of his death is given as 335/946 or 356.[141] His *Kitāb al-Awrāq* appears to have been divided originally into five or six parts, of which four have survived. J. Heyworth Dunne edited the last of these in 1934 under the title *Kitāb al-Awrāḳ, Section on Contemporary Poets*,[142] and an edition of the whole work was planned and has perhaps been carried out in Haidarabad. Another portion of his work was edited by Heyworth Dunne, the *Akhbār ar-Raḍī wa'l-Muttaqī bi'llāh* (History of the Caliphs ar-Rāḍī and al-Muttaqī),[143] and later translated by M. Canard.[144] The general opinion is that aṣ-Ṣūlī's interest is too closely centred on the court and the capital (like some of the Byzantines) for him to rank high as a historian, and his forte no doubt, as Canard indicates, is politico-literary biography.[145]

A Shīʿite historian of considerable interest at present is Ibn Aʿtham al-Kūfī, who wrote an extensive *Kitāb al-Futūḥ* (History of the Conquests, i.e. in the early days of Islam) and is said to have died about 314/926.[146] This work is perhaps best known in a Persian translation, which has several times been reprinted, made as late as 596/1199 by Muḥammad b. Aḥmad Mustawfī al-Harawī (i.e. of Herat).[147] The Arabic original in an Istanbul manuscript (Serai 2956) has been signalized by Professor Zeki Validi Togan and utilized by him in several of his works.[148] The additions made by Balʿamī to aṭ-Ṭabarī have already been mentioned. These are nowhere more conspicuous than in Balʿamī's account of the wars between the Arabs and the Khazars. Here, as has already been pointed out, the additional information given by Ibn Aʿtham al-Kūfī is in places yet more extensive than Balʿamī's, including a long development concerning a large-scale Muslim attack in 119/737 on the Khazar Khaqan made across the 'river of the Saqāliba (*sic*)' or Slavonians, which should be the Don[149] but the Volga is intended.[150] The crossing of the Don or Volga by the Arabs is not elsewhere attested (except perhaps by adh-Dhahabī who mentions an exploit of Marwān in which he once crossed the 'river of the Greeks' when raiding the Ṣaqāliba)[151] at this or any other time, and the passage has therefore been the subject of some discussion,[152] though it obviously should not be made the single test-case for the reliability of Ibn Aʿtham al-Kūfī. This will have to be decided when the Arabic original of the *Kitāb al-Futūh*, the text of which is at present engaging the attention of Dr A. Shaʿban and Mr G. M. Hinds of Cambridge, becomes available *in extenso*. Meantime the work labours under the adverse opinion of Brockelmann, based no doubt on such portions of the Persian version as were known to him.[153] Bockelmann calls it 'a romancing history' (*romanhafte Geschichte*), which it may well be, somewhat on the lines of the *Futūḥ* works attributed to al-Wāqidī of which mention has already been made.[154]

In connection with the crossing of the northern river by the troops of Marwān b. Muḥammad in 119/737, there is mention of 'a brave man of Syria called al-Kawthar b. al-Aswad al-ʿAnbarī' who is at the head of the first detachment to make the attempt, having been specially designated by Marwān for the task.[155] Somewhat remarkably al-Kawthar b. al-Aswad is named by al-Masʿūdī as one of two men of Qays, i.e. of the North Arabians,[156] who accompanied Marwān some years later when as Caliph (Marwān II) he fled from the ʿAbbāsids, to meet his death in Egypt (132/750). The texts of al-Masʿūdī give the officer's *nisba* (generic name) as al-Ghanawī (?), but he appears to be the same man.[157] It does not of course follow that because we seem to have al-Kawthar b. al-Aswad as a trusted and loyal subordinate of Marwān in 132/750, he led an Arab army across the Volga (or the Don) in 119/737, but no doubt the narrative of Ibn Aʿtham al-Kūfī which contains this statement gains somewhat in credibility, when we see that the name at all events was not mere invention.

One might have expected a little more light on the matter from the account of Marwān's flight and death in the *Taʾrīkh al-Islām* (History of Islam) of adh-Dhahabī.[158] Here as elsewhere, adh-Dhahabī cites Yaʿqūb al-Fasawī, an elusive figure, author of a *Kitāb Maʿrifat at-Taʾrīkh* (Book of the Knowledge of History) some time before 277/890–1, the year of his death. We know little about this work, which though short contains an important account of the battle of Ṭarāz (Talas), fought in Turkestan between the Arabs and the Chinese in 133/751,[159] but its author as a native of Fasā in Fārs (Iran) may probably like Balʿamī have been knowledgeable about the East of the empire, and if so, his history, if it had survived, might have filled some of the gaps in our knowledge of this region.

Another author, nearly contemporary with Ibn Aʿtham al-Kūfī and al-Fasawī, was Muḥammad b. ʿAbdūs al-Jahshiyārī, author of a *Kitāb al-Wuzarāʾ waʾl-Kuttāb* (Book of the Viziers and Secretaries), who died in 331/942. The *Kitāb al-Wuzarāʾ waʾl-Kuttāb* was an extensive work which began in pre-Islamic times, and gave an account of the secretaries of the Prophet and the secretaries of his successors down to the end of the Umayyad Caliphate, the narrative becoming fuller as it approached more modern times and constituting something like a history of the administration of the Arab empire until the advent of the ʿAbbāsids. With the latter the wazīrate made its appearance, the first ʿAbbāsid *wazīr* having been Abū Salama Ḥafs b. Sulaymān al-Khallāl, the '*wazīr* of the Family of Muḥammad' (*wazīr Al Muḥammad*), already under Abū'l-ʿAbbās as-Saffāḥ, the first ʿAbbāsid Caliph.[160] The *Kitāb al-Wuzarāʾ waʾl-Kuttāb*, retaining its character as an anecdotal history of Muslim administration, originally ended with an account of Abū Aḥmad al-ʿAbbās b. al-Ḥasan, the vizier of al-Muktafī and al-Muqtadir, who lost his life in a palace conspiracy in 296/908. What survives of the work, estimated at about one-third, comes down only to the wazīrate of al-Faḍl b. Sahl at the beginning of the Caliphate of al-Maʾmūn, the seventh ʿAbbāsid Caliph, who began to reign in 198/813. Al-Faḍl b. Sahl was assassinated in a bath in 202/818, so that for a period of nearly a hundred years, during the whole of the Caliphates of ten of al-Maʾmūn's successors and part of the Caliphate of the eleventh, al-Muqtadir, the surviving part has nothing to tell us, and furthermore is contained in a single manuscript, no. 916, in the Nationalbibliothek, Vienna. It may seem surprising in the circumstances that much attention has been paid in recent times to al-Jahshiyārī's work, which came to light too late to be taken notice of by Wüstenfeld and is noticed only briefly in the standard *Geschichte der arabischen Litteratur* of Brockelmann.

The importance of the *Kitāb al-Wuzarāʾ waʾl-Kuttāb* was first shown, as was appropriate and natural, by an Austrian Orientalist, A. von Kremer in his paper *Ueber das Budget der Einnahmen unter der Regierung des Harun alrašid*, contributed to the proceedings of the 7th International Congress of Orientalists.[161] This is less well known than von Kremer's other paper on a similar subject, *Ueber das Einnahmebudget des Abbasiden-Reiches vom Jahre 306 H (918–919)*,[162] referring to one of the years of the Caliphate of al-Muqtadir, taken from another source,[163] but it can still be read with profit for a view of the finances of the ʿAbbāsids in Hārūn's time.

The Jahshiyārī manuscript was used by the Austrian papyrologist Grohmann,[164] and was published in facsimile by H. von Mzik in 1926, as the first volume of an interesting series *Bibliothek Arabischer Historiker und Geografen*, for which von Mzik was responsible. It was edited in the East (1938) by a group of scholars,[165] and since then its value has been recognized by D. Sourdel in his historical work on the wazīrate in ʿAbbāsid times.[166] Most recently Michael Awad of Baghdad has published a useful little work, *Lost Fragments of Kitāb al-Wuzarāʾ waʾl-Kuttāb* (Beirut, 1965), compiled from manuscripts and printed sources. Though quite short (118 pages), this publication of the ʿIraqi scholar forms a useful supplement to the editions.

Al-Jahshiyārī, though he never attained the highest offices in the state, served as chamberlain to ʿAlī b. ʿIsā, the 'Good Vizier', whose long life extended from 245/859 to 334/946. He was evidently in a favourable situation to get news of what was going on at court, and seems to have had his own sources of information. Thus the account which he gives of the division of authority over the Muslim East and West between al-Faḍl and Jaʿfar, the sons of Yaḥyā the Barmecide, and the subsequent appointment of an obscure secretary to Egypt, events so extraordinary as to have been called in question as belonging to folklore rather than history,[167] but apparently sufficiently authenticated, is developed by al-Jahshiyārī more precisely than by aṭ-Ṭabarī, who seems indeed to have had access to the same original account.[168] Aṭ-Ṭabarī, however, has the narrative of the mission to Egypt of the secretary, ʿUmar b. Mihrān, in the third person, while al-Jahshiyārī lets him speak for himself. The incident recalls the takeover of power in Kufa, almost single-handed, by al-Ḥajjāj b. Yūsuf in 75/694 or 695.[169] The exploit of ʿUmar b. Mihrān is much less well known, but is vivid and arresting.[170] Although it cannot be quoted here as an example of al-Jahshiyārī's style, which it apparently is not, ʿUmar b. Mihrān's account is well worth reading, and indicates at least that al-Jahshiyārī had the faculty of choosing good material. While aṭ-Ṭabarī simply informs us that in 176/792–3 ar-Rashīd appointed Jaʿfar the Barmecide governor of Egypt and he appointed ʿUmar b. Mihrān,[171] al-Jahshiyārī gives specifically that Jaʿfar's western territory extended from al-Anbār on the Euphrates (Furāṭ) to Ifrīqiya (the former Roman province of Africa, modern Tunisia), while al-Faḍl's sphere was from an-Nahrawān, east of the Tigris on the Khurāsān road, as far as 'the furthest lands of the Turks' (*aqṣā bilād at-Turk*).[172] The division of the world, as we may call it, on the scale of Roman times, between the brothers evidently did not last for long, but it is no doubt al-Jahshiyārī's merit that he recalls an arrangement which was apparently more than adumbrated.[173]

The *Kitāb al-Wuzarā' wa'l-Kuttāb* of al-Jahshiyārī, originally ending as we have seen in the year 296/908, came down approximately as far as aṭ-Ṭabarī's great history (to 302/915). It was continued by the work on the same subject, *Tuḥfat al-Umarā' fī Ta'rīkh al-Wuzarā'* (Gift for the Amīrs on the History of the Wazirs) of Hilāl aṣ-Ṣābi' (359/969–448/1056) which began with the period of the resumed Caliphate of al-Muqtadir.[174] Part of this was published by Amedroz at Leiden in 1904,[175] and some fragments were assembled by Michael Awad in 1948. A new edition appeared in Cairo in 1958.[175a] Of at least equal interest is another book by the same author, the *Ta'rīkh* (History), which began in 363/973–4 or a little earlier, and came down to 447/1055. But the *Ta'rikh* of Hilāl aṣ-Ṣābi' is unfortunately lost, except for a fragment from 389/999 to 393/1003 published also by Amedroz in his work above mentioned.[176]

Fortunately not all the works of Hilāl aṣ-Ṣābi are lost. We have now an excellent edition of a short book of his on the etiquette, protocol and diplomacy of the ʿAbbāsid Court, with the title *Rusūm Dār al-Khilāfa* (Forms of the House of the Caliphate).[177] The work dates from the reign of the Caliph al-Qā'im (422/1031–467/1075, to whom it was dedicated.[178] The unique existing manuscript was copied from the author's original in A.H. 455, i.e. seven years after his death.[179] The work may therefore have been written any time between 422/1031 and 448/1056 (death of Hilāl aṣ-Ṣābi'), and these limits could no doubt be narrowed by investigation.[180] A great number of interesting matters are treated, of which we give only a selection: the disturbances in Baghdad up to the time of writing have greatly reduced the size of the palace (*dār al-khilāfa, ad-dār al-ʿazīza*) (p. 7), Bardas Sclerus (here called Ward) was seen by Hilāl aṣ-Ṣābi' in 375 or 376/985 or 986 when he arrived in Baghdad with his brother and son, having fled from Basil II[181] (pp. 14–17); the post from the Hijāz formerly (*qadīman*) arrived in Baghdad in four days, and from the Egyptian capital in eleven days (p. 17); asparagus was brought to al-Muʿtaṣim (Caliph 218/833–227/842) from Damascus in special lead containers within six days (p. 18); decline of the population of Baghdad even since the days of al-Muʿtaḍid (died 289/902) (pp. 18–21); figure for the budget of 306/918–19 and details of expenditure (pp. 21–7);[182] the revenue for 179/795–6 under Hārūn ar-Rashīd (pp. 28–9);[183] comparative wealth of ar-Rashīd and al-Manṣūr (p. 300); gradual introduction of the custom of kissing the earth before the Caliph and exemption of the common people from this (pp. 31–2); Ibrahīm b. al-Mahdī offends al-Muʿtaṣim by excessive use of perfume (pp. 34–5); a financial investigation goes on continuously for two days and nights (p. 40); al-Ma'mūn's adviser is represented by an enemy as a crypto-Christian (p. 44); zoo-men under al-Muʿtaḍid (p. 48); al-Muʿtaḍid shows his skill in dealing with horses (p. 49); the Caliph's mistakes in speech or writing may not be corrected except tacitly (p. 52); ʿAlī b. ʿĪsā greeting ar-Rāḍī unceremoniously and annoying the Caliph (p. 61); Hishām b. ʿAbd al-Malik has a poet executed for an ill-judged reference (p. 62); al-Manṣūr defends his action in dealing with Abū Muslim (p. 65); al-Wāthiq threatens to kill Muḥammad b. ʿAbd al-Malik az-Zayyāt (Ibn az-Zayyāt) who produces inkhorn (*dawāt*) and scroll (*darj*) from his boot (*khuff*), writes a statement on the death of al-Muʿtaṣim and succession of al-Wāthiq, which is approved, and is reappointed vizier (pp. 66–7); water is not asked for nor given in the Palace as a general rule (p. 68); the Roman Calends (*qalandās*) are still known[184] as the New Year's Day festival of the Christians, when the Palace servants (*farrāshūn*) receive a donative (p. 24); and food is prepared with musk as a luxury (p. 27).

As it happens, we possess a work in Greek, the *Syntagma* (Collection) or as it is usually called the *De Cerimoniis Aulae Byzantinae* (On the Ceremonies of Byzantine Court) by the Greek Emperor Constantine VII Porphyrogenitus,[185] composed between A.D. 952 and 959[186] and inviting comparison by reason of its subject with the *Rusūm Dār al-Khilāfa* of Hilāl aṣ-Ṣābi'. The eleventh-century Arabic work is slighter than its Greek counterpart written a century earlier, and its scope is restricted to those matters which came within the purview of members of the class of persons, viz. secretaries, to which Hilāl aṣ-Ṣābi' himself belonged. There is nothing in the *Rusūm Dār al-Khilāfa* corresponding to the inventory of the fleet of the admiral Himerius, defeated by the Muslims off Chios in 912, or the list of the forces employed against Crete in 949, which the imperial author incorporated in his book.[187] On the other hand, Hilāl aṣ-Ṣābi' is very readable, whereas the *De Cerimoniis* finds its principal use as a work to be consulted, and for the most part, in spite of the examples quoted, within the strict terms of reference in matters of court ceremonial. On the question, obviously of great interest, of the comparative wealth of the two courts, the book of Constantine Porphyrogenitus throws no special light, having nothing like the fiscal information of Hilāl aṣ-Ṣābi, and both here and in regard to the related question of the degree of civilization achieved in Byzantium and Baghdad the information which he does provide contributes only indirectly.

3. Al-Masʿūdī

We now come to al-Masʿūdī, Abū'l-Ḥusayn ʿAli b. al-Ḥusayn, a prolific author of works on historical subjects, and in Brockelmann's opinion probably the most important and many-sided writer of his period.[188] This is high praise indeed, though other opinions have been passed, e.g. by J. Marquart, for whom al-Masʿūdī's whole character makes him merely a forerunner of modern reporters and globetrotters.[189] His date of birth is unknown, but he seems to have been native to Baghdad (not, as Ibn an-Nadīm supposed, North Africa)[190] and born probably between 277/890 and 282/895, of a family descended from ʿAbd Allāh b. Masʿūd, a famous Companion of Muḥammad.

For reasons unknown, it appears that al-Masʿūdī did not pass through the usual stages of a learned education, nor do we hear of him in later life as holding any official post. Part of the regular preliminaries to a successful career as a member of the learned class in medieval Islam was a *Lehrreise*, a journey for the purposes of study to some of the principal centres of instruction in Syria, Egypt and the Hijāz as well as Iraq and Iran, which might be almost indefinitely prolonged. In al-Masʿūdī's case, travel seems to have been a principal part of his life and a substitute for regular study under masters, probably from an early age. Details of this are given in his own works, e.g. he was at Iṣṭakhr (ancient Persepolis) in 303/915–16 'in a noble Persian family',[191] in what capacity he does not say. This is perhaps, the earliest reference of the kind which we have.[192] Elsewhere he says that he has 'traversed Sind and the country of the Zanj (East Africa), aṣ-Ṣanaf (South Annam or Vietnam), az-Zābaj (Indonesia), and penetrated East and West, now in farthest Khurāsān, now in the centre of Armenia,

Adharbayjan, Arrān and al-Baylaqān, and again in Iran and Syria'.[193] He also visited ʿUmān on his way to Zanzibar from Sarandīb (Ceylon), was in Egypt more than once and died in al-Fusṭāṭ in 345/956 or 346. Al-Masʿūdī was thus acquainted with the Muslim East in its widest sense (of the West he appears to have had no firsthand knowledge, and it is not clear that he had seen the interior of Arabia). It is not, however, in the first place as a geographer or traveller that he has claims on the interest of posterity, but as a historian. Nor is this due to the chance that only two of his numerous works have been preserved, the *Murūj adh-Dhahab* (Meadows of Gold) and the *Tanbīh* (Admonition). The point is quite clear from the list of his works,[194] in which no specifically geographical title appears.

Al-Masʿūdī more than once speaks of certain of his books on history as forming a sequence, to which he seems to attach special importance. The first of these was the *Kitāb Akhbār az-Zamān*, completed in 332/943,[195] which appears to have survived only fragmentarily. This al-Masʿūdī himself speaks of as his greatest work,[196] and from it he made the *Kitāb al-Awsaṭ*, or Middle Book, described as a chronological sketch of world history.[197] Al-Masʿūdī says that the latter was a history of events from the Creation down to the point at which his major work (*kitābunā al-aʿẓam*, i.e. the *Kitāb Akhbār az-Zamān*) terminated,[198] i.e. in 332/943, when he was in Antioch.[199] He then decided to give an abridgement of the material in these two books, with additional information which he had not previously treated, in another work, the *Kitāb Murūj adh-Dhahab wa-Maʿādin al-Jawhar fī Tuḥaf al-Ashrāf min al-Mulūk wa-Ahl ad-Dirāyāt* (Book of the Meadows of Gold and Mines of Jewels in Presents to the Noble of the Kings and the Learned), to which in due course succeeded the *Kitāb Funūn al-Maʿārif wa-Mā Jarā fī 'd-Duhūr as-Sawālif* (Book of the Different Kinds of Knowledge on What Happened in Past Ages, the *Kitāb Dhakhā'ir al-ʿUlūm wa-Mā Kāna fī Sālif ad-Duhūr* (Book of the Treasures of the Sciences and What Was in Past Ages) and the *Kitāb al-Istidhkār li-Mā Jarā fī Sālif al-Aʿṣār* (Book of the Recollection of What Happened in Past Epochs), in that order. All three are lost. The *Kitāb Funūn al-Maʿārif* dealt with the embassies of Muḥammad and later embassies of Caliphs and kings down to the year 345/956,[200] also with the expedition of Muḥammad to Tabūk[201] in 9 A.H./A.D. 630, in detail, with the divergent opinions.[202] The *Kitāb al-Istidhkār* is referred to for an account of the genealogy of Muḥammad according to different systems,[203] for the reason of Muḥammad's leaving ʿAlī behind (greatly to his chagrin) in charge of Medina, for the first time, when he himself marched with the army to Tabūk,[204] and for the attempt made against Muḥammad during this expedition by the Munāfiqūn (Hypocrites), with a list of their names.[205] The *Kitāb at-Tanbīh*, which still survives, refers rather frequently to the *Kitāb Funūn al-Maʿārif* and the *Kitāb al-Istidhkār* (not so to the *Kitāb Dhakhāʾir al-ʿUlūm*), [206] and al-Masʿūdī tells us in several places that the *Kitāb at-Tanbīh* follows and is based on the *Kitāb al-Istidhkār*. The *Tanbīh* is expressly said to be the seventh of the series.[207]

It is quite clear that this is a series of a special character. Al-Masʿūdī mentions towards the end of the *Murūj adh-Dhahab* that he has the intention of following it with a miscellaneous work without any particular order, to be called *Waṣl al Majālis bi-Jawāmiʿ al-Akhbār wa-Mukhtalaṭ al-Āthār* (Union of Assemblies with Collections of Facts and Miscellaneous Information), which is to serve as a continuation to his previous books.[208] This work was actually written, and is cited in the *Tanbīh* for 'the governors (*wulāt*) of al-Andalus (Muslim Spain), their policy and their wars with the neighbouring Galicians, Gascons (?), Basques, Germans (?), Goths, and others of the Frankish land (?), by land and sea'.[209] Yet it is not referred to in any of the three passages where al-Masʿūdī speaks of his series of seven historical works,[210] any more than is the *Akhbār al-Masʿūdiyyāt* (Masʿūdian Traditions), also cited in the *Tanbīh* for the governors of Al-Andalus as above. The *Akhbār al-Masʿūdiyyāt* is cited again in the *Tanbīh*,[211] not apparently in the *Murūj adh-Dhahab*, and may have been written after the latter work. De Goeje's idea that the 'Masʿūdian Traditions' were those of Ibn Masʿūd, the contemporary of the Prophet, ancestor of al-Masʿūdī[212] is not borne out by their including a notice of the 'Franks' (i.e. Europeans) bordering on Muslim Spain, as we have just seen, and possibly it is an alternate title for the *Akhbār az-Zamān*.

The general impression which we get from what al-Masʿūdī himself says is that his writings were not very systematic. The reason for the existence of what we may call his historical series seems to be that he found himself from time to time in possession of fresh material which he preferred as a rule, but not in every case (see below), to bring out in the form of a new title, rather than attempt to incorporate it in a revision of his main work, the *Akhbār az-Zamān*.

Of all his output, which appears to have been very extensive, not to say immense, there survive as already mentioned the *Murūj adh-Dhahab* and the *Tanbīh*. The first edition of the *Murūj adh-Dhahab*, which is that which we have in the printed texts, is stated to have been completed in Jumādā I, 336, corresponding to November–December 947.[213] One of the lists comes down to the end of 335, corresponding to June 947.[214] According to the *Tanbīh*, however, the original edition of the *Murūj adh-Dhahab* was composed in 332/943–4.[215] This date appears to be due to some oversight since, as al-Masʿūdī tells us elsewhere, it was in that year that the *Murūj* was *begun*.[216] Al-Masʿūdī makes much of the last edition or copy (*an-nuskha al-akhīra*) of the *Murūj adh-Dhahab* which had just been established at the time of the appearance of the *Tanbīh* in 345/956.[217] This contained numerous additions and changes in regard to both substance and form, so that its size now amounted to double that of the first edition (*an-nuskha al-ūlā*). Al-Masʿūdī notes that the first edition was widely disseminated and in the hands of many persons, and it is doubtless due to these circumstances that the existing printed texts represent the original and not the revised edition, which may never have been published and in any case seems to have disappeared. On the other hand, the *Tanbīh* as we know it is a revised edition of a work of half the size, which had appeared in the previous year (344/955).[218]

Briefly expressed, the *Murūj adh-Dhahab* abbreviated al-Masʿūdī's major work, the lost *Akhbār az-Zamān*, while the *Kitāb at-Tanbīh* abbreviated his whole historical series on a much smaller scale. Both these existing works include at once a cosmography and a history from the earliest times, taking account of biblical history and of the history of the Arabs before Muḥammad, which were commonly linked. Both give more or less attention to the past of other nations, Persians, Greeks, Indians, etc., with notices of remarkable customs and other matters of interest about them, and some geographical information. Both culminate in a history of the Islamic world since the appearance of the Prophet, the last occupying about half of the *Murūj adh-Dhahab* (part of volume iv and volumes v–ix in the Paris edition), and rather less than half of the *Tanbīh*.

This scheme which is more or less that of the Islamic historians in general, and may have been influenced in particular by the plan of al-Yaʿqūbī's History,[219] scarcely indicates al-Masʿūdī's originality and independence of mind, which we must suppose to be due, at the same time as his diffuseness and lack of system, to his not having passed through a rigorous and prolonged academic training. For there is no doubt that into a framework used by others before him he has introduced, in addition to material which may or may not have been recorded elsewhere, information which none of his predecessors or successors knew about, or if they knew it, were concerned to record. Typical is his chapter on the Caucasus and the adjacent peoples, Alans, Avars, Khazars, Bulghars, etc., with episodes in the history of the Khazars and the Rūs which are found nowhere else. Marquart formed the opinion that much of this was borrowed by al-Masʿūdī from the lost part of the *Kitāb al-Buldān* of al-Yaʿqūbī dealing with the North.[220] This remains a possibility for some of his information, but even if al-Yaʿqūbī's death was later than 284/897 as is usually given[221] (his *Kitāb al-Buldan* was written in 278/891), al-Masʿūdī has other dates, e.g. 'some time after 300/912–13' for a great Russian raid down the Volga with Khazar connivance to the Caspian,[222] and 'after 320/932 or in that year' for a raid by Turkish nomads on Walandar (? Adrianople),[223] which are surely too late for al-Yaʿqūbī.

Al-Masʿūdī certainly used written sources, and he gives a long list of authors of historical works at the beginning of the *Murūj*,[224] all of whom, he tells us, were well known, not mere traditionists. Well known to him perhaps, but not so in many cases to us. A study of this list readily conveys the abundance of Arabic historiography down to the fourth/tenth century, and at the same time gives an impression of the losses caused by the accidents of the thousand years which have passed since al-Masʿūdī's day. Sometimes he gives an appreciation or criticism of an author whom we still possess, as when he makes the remark quoted above that he knows no better book on the early Muslim conquests than the *Kitāb Futūḥ al-Buldān* of al-Balādhurī,[225] or describes the History (Annals) of aṭ-Ṭabarī as towering above other works and exceeding them all,[226] or gives an estimate of the merits of Ibn Khurradādhbih.[227] Sometimes he names the author he is quoting, but often not, for example when he repeats the information found also in the *Akhbār aṣ-Ṣīn waʾl-Hind* (Account of China and India) of a 'fish called *uwāl*' found in the Indian Ocean.[228] *Uwāl* is apparently a name for the whale borrowed from some northern source.

Al-Masʿūdī, perhaps alone among medieval Arabic authors, is interested in the capital of the Franks (*dār mamlakatihim*), which by a slight modification of the text appears as Barīza,[229] Paris, the seat of government from the time of Clovis.

It may often happen that al-Masʿūdī cites information from some author, lost or unknown, whom he has got into his notes, or simply remembers to have read. (We can take it for certain that either his commonplace books or his memory was capacious—perhaps both.) When this is so, we have no means of knowing. Sometimes, on the other hand, we see the process by which he arrives at his facts, as in the case of his catalogue of the kings of the Franks, which he obtained in al-Fusṭāṭ in 366/947–8 in a work composed a few years previously by Godmar, Bishop of Gerona in Catalonia.[230] To be precise, it had been written by Godmar in 328/939–40 for al-Ḥakam, son of ʿAbd ar-Raḥmān III, who succeeded his father as Caliph of Cordova ten years later. Al-Ḥakam's enthusiasm for learning is well known,[231] and it is natural enough that such a work should reach him from Gerona, though more than a century had passed since Catalonia was under Muslim rule. (If written originally by the bishop in Latin, there were churchmen in Cordova who could translate it into Arabic for the Umayyad prince.) Al-Masʿūdī certainly saw the catalogue of the kings of the Franks in Arabic, and it is proof of his catholic interest that he included it in his book. Other outstanding examples of this will be cited later when we are speaking in more detail of the *Kitāb at-Tanbīh*.

Before leaving the *Murūj adh-Dhahab*, it is of interest to notice the attention paid by Ibn Khaldūn—often from a sharply critical point of view—to this work of al-Masʿūdī. At the beginning of the *Muqaddima* Ibn Khaldūn avers, in the words of Professor Franz Rosenthal's translation, that it is 'well known to competent persons and reliable experts' that the works of al-Masʿūdī[232] are 'suspect and objectionable in certain respects,'[233] and he follows this up a little later by taking him to task for reporting the figure for the armies of Israel as numbered by Moses at 600,000 men or more.[234] Ibn Khaldūn here forestalled modern criticism, but he did not realize that this was the traditional figure in the Hebrew record,[235] and al-Masʿūdī was no doubt excusable in quoting it, in common with other Arabic writers, including aṭ-Ṭabarī.[236] Again, Ibn Khaldūn complains that al-Masʿūdī when he 'undertook to investigate the reason for the levity, excitability and emotionalism in Negroes and attempted to explain it', did no more than quote Jālīnūs (Galen) and Yaʿqūb b. Isḥāq al-Kindī to the effect that this is due to the weakness of their brains and the resulting weakness of their intelligences, which, says Ibn Khaldūn, is 'an inconclusive and unproven statement'.[237] Yet again, al-Masʿūdī, according to Ibn Khaldūn, has discussed divination, but has not found the true explanation. It appears from the man's words that he was far from being grounded in the necessary knowledge and he simply quotes what he heard from experts and non-experts.[238] On the subject of the wedding of al-Ma'mūn to Būrān (see pp. 259 ff), daughter of the extremely wealthy al-Ḥasan b. Sahl, the account given by al-Masʿūdī fills Ibn Khaldūn with astonishment, yet he accepts it.[239] Sometimes he quotes him without comment as a recognized authority, as, for example, on the number (30,000) of the descendants of al-ʿAbbās b. ʿAbd al-Muṭṭalib, uncle of Muḥammad and eponym of the ʿAbbāsids, by the time of the Caliphate of al-Ma'mūn,[240] or for the wealth of leading men in the Hijaz and elsewhere in the days of ʿUthmān, during the early conquests.[241] In one place he gives a very fair summary of the contents of the *Murūj adh-Dhahab*,[242] the work of al-Masʿūdī which he principally uses. Critical though Ibn Khaldūn is of al-Masʿūdī's work, he frequently returns to him, and evidently finds him indispensable.

It is the more striking that in the *Muqaddima*, with one apparent exception, the *Murūj adh-Dhahab* alone of al-Masʿūdī's works is quoted. The *Tanbīh* is not, I think, mentioned by name, though it appears to have been drawn upon.[243] The *Tanbīh*, however, is a somewhat remarkable book, and is much more than a reduced version of the *Murūj*, in spite of the similarity of plan of the two works. Among the matters treated at length in the *Tanbīh* are the history and geography of the former Graeco-Roman now the Byzantine empire, on a much more extensive scale than in the *Murūj*. This can easily be seen by comparing what he has to say in the two works on the subject of Constantine the Great (reigned A.D. 306–37). The respective passages[244] are too long to quote *in extenso*, but it is evident that the treatment in the *Murūj adh-Dhahab* is slighter as well as shorter. It is largely taken up with the accession of Constantine, the transference of the capital to Byzantium, the visit of his mother Helena to Syro-Palestine with the finding of the True Cross and the building of churches, notably that of Emesa (Ḥimṣ),[245] the Council of Nicaea and five other

Councils or synods, the legend of Constantine's conversion to Christianity, followed by a somewhat imprecise description of the 'gulf of Constantinople' (the Propontis, Sea of Marmora), a description of Constantinople itself, and a statement concerning the decline of the sciences which accompanied the change of religion.

In the *Tanbīh* some of the statements previously made are rectified. Constantine is now said to have professed Christianity after reigning for more than twenty years.[246] In the *Murūj* he is said to have done so after one year, if the text is sound, a statement later contradicted by the remark that his conversion was the occasion of the calling of the Council of Nicaea, which we have just been told was held in the seventeenth year of his reign.[247] Again, in the *Tanbīh* al-Masʿūdī says that Constantinople is surrounded on three sides by sea, according to others only on the east and north.[248] The latter is his own opinion in the *Murūj adh-Dhahab*,[249] or perhaps we should say that al-Masʿūdī when he was writing his account of Constantine in the *Murūj adh-Dhahab* depended at least to a certain extent on one Abū ʿUmayir ʿAdī b. Aḥmad b. ʿAbd al-Bāqī al-Adhanī[250] (i.e. of Adana), whom he had met while on the Syrian frontier and who had made the journey by sea to Constantinople,[251] and such an observation may have been made by him and picked up by al-Masʿūdī, as easily as from some book. Abū ʿUmayir Ibn ʿAbd al-Bāqī is mentioned again in the *Tanbīh* as having taken part more than once in official ransoming of Muslim prisoners of war taken by the Byzantines,[252] but not as an authority on the Greek empire. It appears that by the time when he wrote the latter work al-Masʿūdī had found other sources.

The notice of Constantine in the *Tanbīh* is, however, principally a recapitulation of earlier works, among which al-Masʿūdī enumerates the *Akhbār az-Zamān*, the *Kitāb al-Awsaṭ* (both prior to the *Murūj adh-Dhahab*), the *Murūj* itself (cited only in the last edition) (cf. p. 102), the *Funūn al-Maʿārif* and the *Istidhkār* (referred to more than once). It is apparently from the last-named that he cites the differing accounts of pagans and Christians on Constantine's conversion (two versions mention leprosy, which appears also in the Latin legend of Pope Sylvester).[253] The motive of Constantine's vision is connected with a war against the Burjān (Bulgars), also mentioned in the *Murūj*.[254] The building of Constantinople is placed in the fourth year of his reign, and al-Masʿūdī notes that the Greeks of his time call it 'the City' (*būlin*, Greek *polin*) 'and when they wish to express that it is the capital of the

Empire because of its greatness they say Istan Būlin. They do not call it Constantinople. It is only the Arabs who so designate it.'[255] This early occurrence of a name like modern Istanbul, and its explanation by al-Masʿūdī are noteworthy. He goes on in the *Tanbīh* to give a somewhat detailed account of the site of Constantinople and the Propontis, followed by an exact description of the six points on the latter sea (the Marmora, sc.) from which the crossing between Europe and Asia can be made, with interesting historical notices of some of these, the whole much superior to the similar passage in the *Murūj*. Speaking of Abidū (Abydos), he mentions a strong point on the present day Dardanelles used as a defence against 'the ships of the Kūdhkāna and other Russian tribes'. This name has given rise to much discussion, but there is a measure of agreement that the Vikings or Northmen are intended.[256] Al-Masʿūdī also observes in the same connection that in former times it was by this route that Constantinople was attacked 'when the Muslims possessed a fleet and raided the Byzantines from the Syrian frontier, and from Syria itself and Egypt'. Now, as he had written a few years previously,[257] the situation is reversed, and it is the Byzantine fleet that attacks the lands of Islam.

After another glance at Constantinople and the Bulgars, who are said to live 'beyond the gulf',[258] al-Masʿūdī goes on to speak of the Council of Nicaea, but this time, instead of a bare listing of this Council and its five successors, he gives details of the proceedings and personalities. The Council, he knows, was directed against Arius. He goes on to speak of the activity of Helena, the mother of Constantine, who built the Church of the Resurrection at Jerusalem, where is to be seen the spectacle of the Easter fire, still a great occasion today,[259] as well as the Church of Constantine and numerous monasteries and convents on the Mount of Olives, the Church of Emesa,[260] and the Church of ar-Ruhā (Edessa), her native place, which is one of the wonders of the world.[261]

This account is at once fuller than that in the *Murūj* and written with greater care. The geographical description of the Propontis is specially well done, and is to be compared with his account, a little later in the book, of the provinces, here called *bunūd*,[262] of the Byzantine empire in ten pages of Arabic text,[263] to which there is nothing corresponding in the *Murūj*. In the *Tanbīh* he mentions several works on the general subject of the Christians and their history written by authors belonging to different churches: the Maronite Qays, author of a history, which dealt *inter alia* with the *mulūk ar-Rūm*, i.e. the Roman or Byzantine Emperors; the Melkites Maḥbūb b. Qusṭanṭīn of Manbij (Agapius of Mabbug), the celebrated Saʿīd b. al-Baṭrīq (Eutychius, d. 328/940) and Athenaeus, an Egyptian monk; the Nestorian Yaʿqūb b. Zakariyyāʾ al-Kaskarī; and the Jacobite Abū Zakariyyāʾ Dankhā, who treated the philosophy as well as the history of the Greeks.[264] Some of these authors al-Masʿūdī had certainly used before,[265] but they scarcely figure among his authorities in the *Murūj adh-Dhahab*.

Another man from whom he might have learned about the Byzantine empire and its rulers was John Anthypatos Patrikios Mystikos,[266] who came to Damascus in Dhūʾl-Ḥijja, 334, corresponding to July 946, having been sent by the Greek Emperor Constantine VII to arrange an exchange of prisoners between Christians and Muslims. Such exchanges took place from time to time, usually at the river Lāmis in Cilicia (classical Lamus), the boundary at this period between the two empires, and al-Masʿūdī gives a list of twelve ransomings, during nearly a century and a half, from 189/805 until 335/946.[267] According to Theophanes Continuatus, the principal envoy from Byzantium on this occasion was John Curcuas,[268] a famous soldier and former Domesticus (commander-in-chief) who had fallen from power in 944.[269] It was indeed considerably before this date that John Mystikos (his designations in al-Masʿūdī are titles, Anthypatos equivalent to *proconsularis* and Mystikos meaning in the context simply secretary) was removed from the Byzantine court,[270] but he may have returned. In any case al-Masʿūdī was in Damascus at the time of which he speaks, and presumably met the Greek envoy and knew his name perfectly well. He describes him as an ecclesiastic, which would fit the case of John Mystikos,[271] a man of judgment and understanding in the history of the kings of the Greeks and the Romans (*mulūk al-Yunāniyyīn waʾr-Rūm*) and an expert in the classical philosophy.[272] Since the envoy came to Damascus in the company of al-Masʿūdī's acquaintance Abū ʿUmayr ibn ʿAbd al-Bāqī, it is quite possible that they met and talked. Yet another possible source of information, not an informant in the ordinary sense, since his date is too early, was Muslim b. Abī Muslim al-Jarmī, who was in Byzantine captivity and gained his freedom at the ransoming of 231/845. He is briefly mentioned in Chapter 4 (p. 167).

Another work which al-Masʿūdī refers to occasionally is the

Qānūn or *Zīj* of Theon of Alexandria (fourth century A.D.), cited for the 'kings of the Greeks' between Philip, father of Alexander the Great, and Cleopatra, and for the 'kings of the Romans' between Augustus and Constantine the Great.[273] What appears to be intended is the *Royal Canon* of Ptolemy, a catalogue of Assyrian, Persian, Greek and Roman sovereigns, with the length of their reigns, which is said to have been continuated by Theon to his own time and then carried down further to include the rulers of Byzantium,[274] a circumstance which indicates the value which was attached to the earlier part of the list. But if al-Masʿūdī had access to this, aware as he certainly was of the importance of Ptolemy and also of Theon, whom he had already referred to in his previous work,[275] he explicitly rejects Theon's listing of the pagan emperors, which of course he may have seen only in a defective form, and prefers other authority.[276]

We cannot in fact determine with any precision al-Masʿūdī's sources on the Graeco-Roman empire and its history, but it is plain that his notices on the subject, especially in the *Tanbīh*, contain interesting information.[277] What we can say is that the proportionate amount of space devoted to the Greeks and Romans in the *Tanbīh* as compared with the pre-Islamic Persians is much greater (some seventy pages of text as against twenty-three)[278] than in the *Murūj adh-Dhahab* (fifty pages of text each, approximately),[279] and of course the *Tanbīh* is much the shorter book. This would indicate that the Graeco-Roman empire in al-Masʿūdī's scheme of things came to bulk larger as time passed and his knowledge and appreciation grew. But it was certainly not his only interest among foreign peoples, as we have already seen, and as could easily be illustrated further by some very interesting and original remarks about the Jews.[280] We must pass on, however, and can here only draw attention to an extract quoted by al-Masʿūdī giving the area of a number of regions on the earth's surface, including the lands of the Caliphate and the Byzantine empire, from the astronomer al-Fazārī.[281] This presents difficulties and, in any case, if it were to be cited, it belongs properly to the chapter on geography. Yet this is a passage typical of al-Masʿūdī—in this case not original, his source most loosely indicated, but of great interest in itself, since comparative figures on this subject are by no means easily obtained. The date too is early, al-Fazārī having flourished in the eighth century A.D. (see p. 215). Here we shall cite only the figures given for some northern peoples, since the comparison seems of special interest. According to al-Fazārī, as quoted by al-Masʿūdī:

The territory (*ʿamal*) of the Toghuzghuz among the Turks, 1000 parasangs by 500 parasangs; the territory of the Turks belonging to the Khaqan, 700 parasangs by 500 parasangs; the territory of the Khazars and the Alans, 700 parasangs by 500 parasangs; the territory of the Burjān (Bulgars), 1500 parasangs by 300 parasangs; the territory of the Ṣaqāliba (Slavonians), 3500 parasangs by 700 [ed. Cairo, ii, 234, has 420] parasangs.

The passage is briefly referred to by Nallino,[282] who deduces from the names of the rulers mentioned elsewhere in the long extract, that it belongs to the epoch of the Caliph Hārūn ar-Rashīd, shortly after 170/786 when Hārūn came to the throne. So far as I have been able to ascertain, the notice about these northern peoples has not as yet been adduced for what light it may throw on the early history of the Turks, and its preservation seems due entirely to al-Masʿūdī's irrepressible curiosity concerning the world—one would hesitate to speak of encyclopaedic knowledge, which suggests more system than he ever cared to apply—and his unchartered wanderings, intellectually as well as physically, far beyond the common run of Muslim scholars.

One other work, sometimes attributed to him, is the little *Kitāb Akhbār az-Zamān wa-ʿAjāʾib al-Buldān* (History of Past Time and Wonders of the Lands), otherwise called *Mukhtaṣar al-ʿAjāʾib waʾl-Gharāʾib*, neatly rendered by the French translator as *L'Abrégé des Merveilles*.[283] This undoubtedly contains some of the material of al-Masʿūdī's lost *Kitāb Akhbār az-Zamān wa-Man Abādahu al-Ḥidthān* (see above), but it has been manipulated by another hand, and has suffered in transmission. The centre of interest is Egypt, and the greater part of the work (pp. 101 to the close at p. 252 of the edition) reproduces information from the 'books of the Copts'[284] on the history of ancient Egypt before and after the Flood. A somewhat prominent place is given to the activities of 'Aflīmūn' (? Polemon), represented as the chief priest or soothsayer of Ushmūn (Hermopolis) in Upper Egypt in antediluvian times.[285] It is plain that we have here to do with *Märchen*, not real Coptic tradition, but at least some of this material appears to have come from al-Masʿūdī. The book contains also quite an interesting ethnographical account of Yājūj and Mājūj, the Ṣaqāliba, Greeks, Chinese, Lombards, Franks, al-Andalus, al-Burjān (Bulgars), Turks, the Byzantine and Persian empires and Khurāsān.[286] This section stands close to the corresponding part of a little work by the Spanish traditionist Ibn ʿAbd al-Barr (d. 463/1071), the *Kitāb al-Qaṣd waʾl Amam ilā Ansāb al-ʿArab waʾl-ʿAjam*, which, as this title implies, deals with genealogies. Here again the book is not original.[287] The whole section may be compared with some chapters in the *Murūj adh-Dhahab* of similar import.[288]

It is usually said that the author of the *Kitāb Akhbār az-Zamān wa-ʿAjāʾib al-Buldān* is Ibrāhīm b. Waṣīf Shāh, an Egyptian author who lived perhaps in the sixth/twelfth century,[289] and he certainly is quoted in several places by al-Maqrīzī in the well-known book, *al-Khiṭaṭ* (concerning which and its author see pp. 131 f) for passages which occur in the *Kitāb Akhbār az-Zamān wa-ʿAjāʾib al-Buldān*, for example, on the tyrannical giant ʿAdīm (or ʿUdaym) who 'cut through the rocks to build a pyramid, as the first men had done' (where Ibrāhīm b. Waṣīf Shāh is styled al-Ustādh, 'the Professor'),[290] on the king who sent Hermes south to the Nile source in the Mountains of the Moon,[291] and again on the good king 'Nadārus'.[292] These three passages correspond verbally to the text of the other book. Al-Maqrīzī also cites 'Abūʾl-Ḥasan al-Masʿūdī in the *Kitāb Akhbār az-Zamān*' for the arrival of the Adamites in flight from the sons of Qābīl (the biblical Cain) on the Nile and their subsequent settlement there,[293] and this passage too is found in the *Kitāb Akhbār az-Zamān wa-ʿAjāʾib al-Buldān* verbally corresponding.[294] That this is not mere inadvertence and that here al-Maqrīzī does not intend Ibn Waṣīf Shāh when he says al-Masʿūdī, seems proved from other passages where the latter is named. We may note especially one passage where he cites al-Masʿūdī for a mythical queen of Egypt, Dalūka, an enchantress and builder of temples,[295] clearly belonging to the same cycle of *Märchen* as we have found in the work attributed to Ibn Waṣīf Shāh and mentioned in the *Murūj adh-Dhahab* and elsewhere,[296] but not apparently, in this case, the *Kitāb Akhbār az-Zamān wa-ʿAjāʾib al-Buldān*. We may therefore conclude provisionally that when al-Maqrīzī quotes al-Masʿūdī in the *Akhbār az-Zamān* he is not referring to the work attributed to Ibn Waṣīf Shāh. Pursuing the matter, we find that al-Maqrīzī actually quotes al-Masʿūdī in the *Kitāb Akhbār az-Zamān wa-Man Abādahu al-Ḥidthān*, his large book already mentioned, for al-Maʾmūn's visit to Egypt, which is well known and took place in the year 216/831.[297] This too appears in the *Kitāb Akhbār az-Zamān wa-ʿAjāʾib al-Buldān*,[298] and the passage concerns an attempt to demolish one of the pyramids, inspired by the Caliph himself. It is as follows.

Abū'l-Ḥasan al-Masʿūdī has mentioned in his *Kitāb Akhbār az-Zamān wa-Man Abādahu al-Ḥidthān* that the Caliph ʿAbd Allāh al-Maʾmūn b. Hārūn ar-Rashīd, when he arrived in Egypt and came upon the pyramids, wanted to pull down one of them, in order to know what was in it. He was told that he could not do so, but insisted that some part of it must be excavated. The breach which is still open at the present day was accordingly begun after the application of fire and vinegar, by workmen using pickaxes, till he had spent a huge sum on the work. They found the width of the wall nearly twenty cubits, and when they reached the end, they found behind the excavation a green basin containing 1000 pieces of minted gold, the weight of each coin being one ounce (*ūqiyya*). Al-Maʾmūn showed astonishment at the gold and its fineness. He ordered a reckoning of the total amount expended on the excavation, and it was found that the gold found exactly covered the expense, neither more nor less. He was amazed at these people's knowledge of what had been expended and at their leaving the corresponding amount in that place. It is said that the basin in which the gold was found was of chrysolite (*zabarjad*). Al-Maʾmūn ordered it to be taken to his treasury. This was the last to be done of the marvels of Egypt.[299]

The people continued for years to go there and descend the ramp in the interior. Some survived, and some were killed. Twenty young men made an agreement to enter. They prepared what was necessary —food and drink, ropes, candles, and the like, and descending the ramp, saw bats large as eagles, which struck their faces. Then they let down one of their number by means of the ropes, and the cavity closed over him. They attempted to draw him up, but were unable to do so. Then they heard a terrifying sound, and lost consciousness. Eventually they recovered and emerged from the pyramid. While they were sitting in astonishment at what had befallen them, the earth brought forth their companion alive before them, speaking unknown words, and then he fell dead. They lifted him and brought him away with them. The guards (*khufarāʾ*) took them to the governor, to whom they told their tale. Having asked about the words which their companion had spoken before his death, they were told that the meaning was, 'This is the punishment of him who seeks for what is not his own." The man who explained the meaning to them was one of the people of Upper Egypt.[300]

In the *Kitāb az-Zamān wa-ʿAjāʾib al-Buldān* the Caliph who interested himself in the pyramids when on a visit to Egypt is said to be Hārūn ar-Rashīd,[301] and there are other slight differences, but there can be no doubt that the narrative goes back to the original *Kitāb Akhbār az-Zamān wa-Man Abādahu al-Ḥidthān* of al-Masʿūdī.

The solution of the imbroglio appears to be that al-Maqrīzī in the eighth/fourteenth century had in front of him both the *Kitāb Akhbār az-Zamān wa-ʿAjāʾib al-Buldān*, a compilation made by Ibrāhīm b. Waṣīf Shāh from the original *Akhbār az-Zamān wa-Man Abādahu al-Ḥidthān*, and also a copy of the latter work, from which he extracted passages not to be found in Ibn Waṣīf Shāh's compilation. Al-Maqrīzī therefore, on this view, can be used with the *Kitāb Akhbār az-Zamān wa-ʿAjāʾib al-Buldān* to get back quite substantial portions of al-Masʿūdī's original *Akhbār az-Zamān*. But one caveat is necessary. Al-Maqrīzī in citing al-Masʿūdī simply, without mentioning a specific work, does not normally intend his *Akhbār az-Zamān*, but the *Murūj adh-Dhahab*, which he evidently also used. Thus the passage referring to 'Queen Dalūka' mentioned above, unless it occurred verbally also in the *Akhbār az-Zamān wa-Man Abādahu al-Ḥidthān*, which cannot be proven and does not seem particularly likely, is taken from the *Murūj*.[302] This can be said with certainty of another quotation in al-Maqrīzī beginning 'Al-Masʿūdī says', which gives some general remarks on the treasures and monuments of Egypt, and ends in a style familiar to anyone who has ever read al-Masʿūdī, 'but we have dealt with all this in our previous works'.[303] This is evidently from al-Masʿūdī's *Murūj adh-Dhahab*,[306] not the *Akhbār az-Zamān wa-Man Abādahu al-Ḥidthān*, which as we saw was not preceded by earlier books but was the first of his historical series to which the rest were all in some measure either supplements or abbreviations, or rather both at once. And there are other similar quotations in al-Maqrīzī from the *Murūj adh-Dhahab*.[305]

We have had much to say about al-Masʿūdī's extant works, something about his sources and something about his *Akhbār az-Zamān*, at present presumed lost. Our justification for the seemingly disproportionate length of treatment is of course the interest of this writer. We must pass on without finally resolving the difference of opinion in regard to him mentioned earlier, and may perhaps be fairly taxed not only with omitting this but with failing to attempt an estimate of his importance as a historian, evidently a matter connected with the other, which we can less easily dispense with. Summarily we should perhaps say that while al-Masʿūdī is to be carefully used and checked, wherever possible, with other more academic writers (such as aṭ-Ṭabarī) for his version of the main facts, he appears often to be very valuable for incidental observations and comments and for fresh information which is not found elsewhere. Illustrations of this need not be given at this point, for they can be gathered from what has already been said. Nor is it necessary to insist that he is specially valuable for what lies on the periphery of Islam, either physically (i.e. geographically) or in the realm of ideas. Al-Masʿūdī's originality is not to be questioned, but it is no doubt also true that he owes something to the readability of his two existing works, which have been preserved to the present time, while so many other Arabic books have been lost,[306] probably for that reason. No doubt the *Murūj adh-Dhahab* and the *Tanbīh* are to be considered masterpieces of Arabic historical writing. There is no evidence that the same should be said of his other works.

4. Continued development of historical writing; Biography and autobiography; The Muslim West

Not a historical masterpiece but rather a textbook for practical use is the *Annals* of Ḥamza al-Iṣfahānī (284/897–356/967), of which the Arabic title sufficiently indicates its scope: *Taʾrīkh Sinī Mulūk al-Arḍ waʾl-Anbiyāʾ* (Chronology of the Kings of the Earth and the Prophets).[307] In the introduction the author identifies the Aryans (al-Aryān) with the Persians,[308] and mentions the view that in the most ancient times, before the appearance of the religious laws (*ash-sharāʾiʿ ad-dīniyya*) of Judaism, Christianity and Islam, mankind was of one kind—he means apparently pagan—but distinguished by the names Samīniyyūn (more usually Samaniyya, Buddhists) and Kaldāniyyūn (Chaldeans) in East and West respectively.[309] The remnant of the Samīniyyūn are at present, he tells us, in the region of the Indians, China and Khurāsān, while the remaining Kaldāniyyūn have changed their name, since the time of al-Maʾmūn, to Ṣābians and are now to be found in the cities of Ḥarrān and ar-Ruhāʾ (Edessa). The Ṣābians of Ḥarrān in particular are well known for the literary and scientific men they produced, and no doubt the strange-sounding story is perfectly true that they were a pagan group which simply adopted the name of Ṣābian in comparatively late times in order to enjoy the advantages of the People of the Book (*Ahl al-Kitāb*), or Scripturaries, of which the Ṣābians according to the Qurʾān were a class.[310] Who the original Ṣābians of the Qurʾān were is a disputed point.[311] The idea that at one time the Samaniyya or Buddhists were much further west than historical tradition would otherwise indicate is found in al-Bīrūnī, who mentions as Buddhist not only the territory up to the frontier of Syria (? the Eastern empire of Alexander and his successors), but even Mosul.[312]

The work of Ḥamza is divided into ten chapters or books (*abwāb*, plural of *bāb*), dealing respectively with the chronology of the Persians, Romans, Greeks, Egyptians, Israelites, Lakhmids of Iraq (al-Ḥīra), Ghassānids of Syria, the *Tubbaʿs* or Himyarite kings of al-Yaman, Kinda, and Quraysh. Under the last heading he conveniently groups together the rulers of the Arab empire from the time of Muḥammad: Muḥammad himself, the Orthodox Caliphs, the Umayyads and the ʿAbbāsids, bringing the record down to 350/961.

Ḥamza was of course a Persian, and something of a Persian nationalist, perhaps indeed, as Goldziher thought,[313] a typical representative of the Shuʿūbiyya literary movement, which was sharply anti-Arab. The *Taʾrīkh*, however, devotes fewer than sixty pages in Gottwaldt's text to the history of the Persian kings, and approximately 150 to the Arabs when the Lakhmids, Ghassānids, etc. are added to the Caliphs. This does not appear to show any overwhelming predilection in favour of Persia, and has to be taken with the fact that Rome, Greece, Egypt and the Israelites together occupy a bare twenty-five pages. On the basis of this simple enumeration, it would certainly appear that the great fact of history for Ḥamza as for his colleagues, the other historians whom we have been considering, was Islam or at least the rise of the Arab empire, by comparison with which even the glories of ancient Iran bulked small.

Ḥamza was careful about his sources, and when he began to treat of the Persian chronology he had eight codices (*nusakh*) before him, which he enumerates.[314] One of these, and the first mentioned, was the *Siyar Mulūk al-Furs* (Lives of the Persian Kings) in the version of Ibn al-Muqaffaʿ, i.e. his Arabic translation of the *Khudāy-nāma* to which we have already referred (p. 46). Others of his eight codices were differing versions of the same original. He mentions two commentaries (*sharḥ*) of the *Khudāy-nāma* which he has consulted (probably included in the eight), those of Mūsā b. ʿĪsā al-Kisrawī[315] and Bahrām b. Mardān Shāh, *mawbadh* (Zoroastrian high priest) of the *kūra* (province) of Shābūr in Fārs.[316] The last named is quoted as saying that he had consulted more than twenty copies of the *Khudāy-nāma* for his work.

This gives an impression of the great efforts made by Ḥamza's authorities, and also by himself, to get at the chronological facts. In regard to the Graeco-Roman Emperors from Alexander the Great to Heraclius, he relied at first, he tells us, on two Greek prisoners, father and son, especially the father (his name is not given) who was an attendant (*farrāsh*) of Aḥmad b. ʿAzīz b. Dulaf, one of the Dulafid dynasty,[317] and knew Greek well, but could speak Arabic only with difficulty. 'His son', says Ḥamza, 'was in the army of the Sultan and was a competent astrologer. His name was Yumn ("Prosperity").[318] He acted on my behalf as translator for his father, who dictated the dates from a Greek book which he possessed.'[319] It is not clear where this took place, perhaps at al-Karaj[320] in the Jibāl (Media), where for a long time the Dulafids were independent.

Afterwards Ḥamza found in a book by a Qāḍī of Baghdad, Wakīʿ, a chapter on the emperors from Constantine to 301/913–4, which Wakīʿ stated that he had taken from the letter (? or book, *kitāb*) of one of the emperors which had been rendered from Greek into Arabic by a certain translator.[321] Ḥamza gives both versions of the chronology *in extenso*, and then, noting that there is considerable discrepancy, declares that he prefers to rely on what he heard verbally from the Greek, since the translator of the version followed by Wakīʿ could easily have made a mistake in reading.[322] Several works of the Qāḍī Wakī (Muḥammad b. Khalaf) are mentioned in the *Fihrist*, including the *Kitab Akhbār al-Quḍāt wa-Taʾrīkhihim wa-Ahkāmihim* (Accounts of the *Qādīs*, their Chronology and their Judgments), which appears to have survived.[322a] Another of the authorities of Ḥamza for the Greek history was a book said to have been translated by Ḥabīb b. Bahrīz, Metropolitan of al-Mawṣil (Mosul),[323] while for the history of the Jews he had in 308/920–1 consulted in Baghdad a learned Jew, Zedekiah, who appears to have had most of the Hebrew Bible by heart.[324]

We have already said something about the beginnings of the local history, dealing with a particular city or town (see p. 80). Sometimes a whole region was taken as the subject. An early example of this was the *Futūḥ Miṣr wa'l-Maghrib*, otherwise *Futūh Miṣr wa-Akhbāruhā* (Conquest of Egypt and the Maghrib, Conquest of Egypt and the Accounts thereof) in seven books by Ibn ʿAbd al-Ḥakam (*c.* 187/803–257/871), where the interest in the detail of the Muslim conquests crossed with the local interest of a somewhat later period.[325] Ibn ʿAbd al-Ḥakam's Book I dealt with the 'excellencies of Egypt' (*faḍā'il Miṣr*) and the ancient history of the country, Book II with the Muslim conquest under ʿAmr b. al-ʿĀṣ, and especially the question of whether Egypt was captured peacefully or by force, Book III with the *khiṭaṭ* or settlements of the Muslims in al-Fusṭāṭ and al-Jīza (Gizeh), and the holdings in Alexandria and the district of Old Cairo called al-Qaṭā'iʿ, etc., Book IV with various measures of ʿAmr b. al-ʿĀṣ in the Nile valley, the conquest of the oasis of al-Fayyūm, Barqa and Tripoli, the temporary loss and subsequent retaking of Alexandria, the recall and death of ʿAmr b. al-ʿĀṣ, the Muslim expansion into Ifrīqiya (the Roman province of Africa), and the fighting with the Nubians in the south, etc., Book V with the conquest of North Africa and Spain, Book VI with the *qāḍīs* of Egypt down to 246/860–1, and Book VII with various specifically Egyptian traditions.

A little later other Egyptian historians appeared, Saʿīd b. al-Biṭrīq better known perhaps as Eutychius, who became Melkite Patriarch of Alexandria in 321/933 and wrote a well-known book on the history of Egypt entitled *Naẓm al-Jawhar*,[326] translated by Edward Pococke under the title *Contextio Gemmarum* as long ago as 1658–9; Ibn ad-Dāya (died 340/951), author of the *Sīrat Aḥmad b. Ṭūlūn wa'bnihi Khumārawayh*, a biography of the first Ṭūlūnid rulers of Egypt[327] and other works; and the historian al-Kindī (283/895–350/961), whose *Kitāb al-Quḍāti 'lladhīna Walū Qaḍā' Miṣr*, or History of the Egyptian Qāḍīs, based on Ibn ʿAbd al-Ḥakam's Book VI, was edited by Richard J. H. Gottheil (Rome and Paris, 1908), and his *Tasmiyat Wulāt Miṣr* or *Umarā' Miṣr* (Account of the Governors of Egypt) by Nicholas A. Koenig (New York, 1908), and again by Rhuvon Guest (Gibb Memorial Series, 1912).

In Spain the beginning of a long development of historical writing was made with the works of Ibn Ḥabīb (died in Cordova 239/854), Yaḥyā al-Ghazāl (author of an *urjūza*, i.e. a poem in the *rajaz* metre, on the Muslim conquest of Spain, who died at an advanced age in 250/864),[328] Ibn Muzayn (died 259/872–73),[329] Tamīm b. ʿĀmir b. ʿAlqama (died 283/896, author of an *urjūza* on Spanish Muslim history down to the end of the reign of ʿAbd ar-Raḥmān II, i.e. 238/852) and, most important of all, Aḥmad b. Muḥammad ar-Rāzī called at-Ta'rīkhī[330] (274/887–

344/955),[331] member of a family of historians, whose works included an extensive *Akhbār Mulūk al-Andalus wa-Khadamatihim wa-Ghazawātihim wa-Nakabātihim*[332] (Accounts of the Kings of Spain, their Servitors, their Wars and Misadventures), and a *Ṣifat Qurṭuba wa-Khiṭaṭihā wa-Manāzil al-ʿUẓamāʾ bihā* (Description of Cordova and its Settlements and the Houses of the Great therein), which is said to have been modelled on the *History of Baghdad* of Ibn abī Ṭāhir already mentioned (p. 80). For further information about these early Spanish historical works, which for the most part are lost or if they survive do so only fragmentarily,[333] the *Ensayo Bio-bibliográfico sobre los Historiadores y Geógrafos Arábigo-Españoles* of Francisco Pons Boigues[334] should be consulted.

On the other hand, we still have *al-ʿIqd al-Farīd* (The Precious Necklace) of Ibn ʿAbd Rabbihi[335] (born in Cordova in 246/860, died 328/940), which included among the multifarious matters of its numerous books (each named after a precious stone, and thought of as the jewels which form the 'Necklace'), a history of the Umayyads of Spain, culminating with a *rajaz* poem on the military expeditions under ʿAbd ar-Raḥmān III an-Nāṣir. Ibn ʿAbd Rabbihi, whose forte was *adab* and who wrote much poetry, is not esteemed highly as a historian, but this part of his work possesses some interest, in view of its being contemporary with the events it claims to portray.

For the medieval East two great local histories survive, the *Taʾrīkh Baghdād* of Abū Bakr Aḥmad b. ʿAlī b. Thābit, known almost invariably as al-Khaṭīb al-Baghdādī (the Preacher of Baghdad) who lived from 392/1002 till 463/1071, and the *Taʾrīkh Madīnat Dimashq* (History of the City of Damascus). The first of these in fourteen volumes was printed in Cairo in 1349/1931. The second, the work of Ibn ʿAsākir (499/1106–571/1176), is in course of publication, and three volumes, the first, second and tenth, have already appeared under the editorship of Dr Ṣalāḥ ad-Dīn al-Munajjid.[336] These works, the aim of which is to a great extent biographical, have set a standard in their kind which has never been surpassed, and are still to some extent the models for modern books such as the *Iʿlām an-Nubalāʾ bi-Taʾrīkh Ḥalab ash-Shahbāʾ* (History of the Learned of Aleppo) by Muḥammad Rāghib aṭ-Ṭabbākh.[337]

What may perhaps be called the first secular biography in Islam appeared on Iranian ground, in the shape of al-ʿUtbī's *Kitāb al-Yamīnī*,[338] which gives the history of Maḥmūd of Ghazna, called Yamīn ad-Dawla ('Right Hand of the Empire'), hence of course the title. The author served in the Ghaznawid administration and died in 421/1030. In a later generation the striking career of Ṣalāḥ ad-Dīn, ruler of Egypt from 564/1169 to 589/1193, the chivalrous and successful adversary of the Crusaders, was the subject of books by ʿImād ad-Dīn al-Kātib al-Iṣfahānī, Bahāʾ ad-Dīn Ibn Shaddād and Shihāb ad-Dīn Abū Shāma, of whom the first two were Ṣalāḥ ad-Dīn's contemporaries and Abū Shāma of the next generation.[339] The *genre* was subsequently maintained down to modern times with, among other works, the *Sīrat as-Sulṭān Jalāl ad-Dīn Mankobirtī* (*Mangbartī*), which is the biography of Jalāl ad-Dīn, the Khwārizm Shāh, the brave opponent of Chingiz Khān, written by an-Nasawī, his secretary, in 639/1241.[340]

The autobiography, making its appearance somewhat later, is represented by Usāma b. Munqidh, a Syrian military chief in the days of Ṣalāḥ ad-Dīn's predecessor Nūr ad-Dīn, whose *Kitāb al-Iʿtibār* was first edited by H. Derenbourg (Paris, 1886).[340a] Usāma's dates are 488/1095 to 584/1188. During his long lifetime ʿUmāra of the Yemen, a man of more peaceful tastes, but who was destined to meet a violent death in 569/1175 (apparently for complicity in a political plot against Ṣalāḥ ad-Dīn), also wrote an autobiographical work.[341] Nor should we omit mention of the Zīrid, ʿAbd Allāh b. Buluqqīn, whose *Mudhakkarāt* (Memoirs), edited by the late Professor E. Lévi-Provençal, afford a picture in detail of his policy as a ruler in Granada from about 469/1076 to 483/1090.[342]

The biographical collection is one of the most characteristic types of historical writing in Arabic, and in this class of work perhaps the best known and most generally useful is Ibn Khallikān's *Kitāb Wafayāt al-Aʿyān wa-ʾAnbāʾ Abnāʾ az-Zamān* (Book of the Deaths of the Famous and Information concerning the Sons of the Time),[343] usually referred to simply as the Biographical Dictionary. This has for long been generally available in the four-volume English translation of Baron MacGuckin de Slane,[344] who also produced an Arabic text of a substantial portion of the work.[345] Ibn Khallikān was born in Irbil (Arbela, mod. Arbil, east of Mosul) in 608/1211, lived in Syria and Egypt, where he held important judicial and teaching posts, and died in 681/1282. The Biographical Dictionary appears to have occupied him during the best part of twenty years, from 654/1256 till 672/1274. Already there were numerous works of the kind, often called 'class-books' (*ṭabaqāt*), going back to Ibn Sa'd (see p. 79) and dealing with very diverse types of men, poets, *faqihs*, grammarians, *ṣūfīs*,[346] etc. Half a century earlier the celebrated Yāqūt (*c.* 574/1179–626/1229; cf. p. 171) had completed his so-to-say definitive biographical compilation on literary men, a standard book of reference even today, the *Muʿjam al-Udabā'*, a substantial work in seven printed volumes.[347] But Ibn Khallikān's book had a wider scope than any of these. He purposed to include those who had distinguished themselves in practically all fields of activity with very few exceptions, omitting only the Companions of Muḥammad and the next generation of Muslims (the *Ṭābiʿūn*, or Followers),[348] also the Caliphs, evidently because these classes were sufficiently dealt with elsewhere,[349] as is explicitly stated for the Caliphs. Otherwise, the Biographical Dictionary was to include scholars (mentioned, we notice, in the first place), kings, *amīrs*, *wazīrs*, poets, and in general all who in the past had attained celebrity and were likely to be inquired about, arranged alphabetically. It was also to contain information about the great men of Ibn Khallikān's own age, whom he had himself known, and others. The work as we have it appeared in three volumes. The author's intention was to reissue it in a revised and enlarged edition of eight or ten volumes, but this was never carried out.[350] The Biographical Dictionary is invaluable for students who are familiar with the main lines of Islamic history, but in the case of other readers may induce a feeling of strangeness amounting to bewilderment, as recorded in an essay of E. V. Lucas,[351] so extensive and rich is the material which it contains.

In the next century a yet more extensive work of the same kind appeared. This was *al-Kitāb al-Wāfī bi'l-Wafayāt* (Abundant Book on Dates of Death) by Khalīl b. Aybak aṣ-Ṣafadī (696/1296–764/1363), said to have contained as many as thirty or even fifty volumes, also arranged alphabetically. Though a book of this size was evidently too large ever to become popular, many volumes have survived, scattered among various libraries, as may be seen from Brockelmann.[352] A conspectus of the contents may be most easily gained from studies by G. Gabrieli.[353] A beginning has been made to publish the work.[354]

On the same enormous scale, typical of the time, was the historical composition, or rather compilation, of adh-Dhahabī, an older contemporary of aṣ-Ṣafadī, who lived from 673/1274 till 748/1348. Though well known as the author of important works on Tradition (*Ḥadīth*), which are still serviceable and widely used, the *Mīzān al-Iʿtidāl fī Tarājim* (or *fī Naqd*) *ar-Rijāl* (Balance of Equilibrium in the Biographies (or 'in Criticism') of the Traditionists),[355] and the *Kitāb al-Mushtabih fī Asmāʾ ar-Rijāl*) (On Similar Names among the Traditionists),[356] adh-Dhahabī's principal production was a very extensive *Taʾrīkh al-Islām* (History of Islam), a work undoubtedly of great value, as can be seen from the part which has been published.[357] From this huge work, perhaps originally in twenty or more volumes, of which many survive,[358] either the author himself or others have extracted shorter books, notably the *Tadhkirat al-Ḥuffāẓ* (Biographical Memoir of Qur'ān Experts)[359] and the *Kitāb Duwal al-Islām* (Book of the Dynasties of Islam),[360] also the *Kitāb al-ʿIbar fī Khabar Man Ghabar* (Book of Examples in the Annals of Those Who Have Passed Away).[361] The *Kitāb Duwal al-Islām* and the *Kitāb al-ʿIbar* are not the same book, as is sometimes said. The *Kitāb al-ʿIbar* has a different exordium, is arranged from the beginning according to strict annalistic form, and is usually somewhat more extensive in its notices. Both the *Kitāb Duwal al-Islām* and the *Kitāb al-ʿIbar* are, as they stand, the work of adh-Dhahabī himself, who speaks at the beginning of both in the first person.[362] The main text of both ends in the year 715/1316, which is apparently the year after the completion of the *Taʾrīkh al-Islām* in 714.[363] Ibn Taghrībirdī mentions both works as separate abbreviations of the *Taʾrīkh al-Islām*, made by adh-Dhahabī.[364] They evidently represent shortened versions of the main work produced by him at different times, even for different purposes. The *K. Duwal al-Islām* has a short *Tadhyīl* (Appendix) from 715/1316 to 744/1344,[365] four years before the death of adh-Dhahabī. Like the *Taʾrīkh al-Islām* itself, both abbreviations deal with general history and give short notices of the deaths of famous persons.

The scale of adh-Dhahabī is naturally enough, considering the far longer period with which he deals, often much less than aṭ-Ṭabarī's. Thus, for example, aṭ-Ṭabarī has more than 100 pages[366] of which the single or at least the main subject is Shabīb b. Yazīd al-Khārijī, who rebelled against the Caliph ʿAbd al-Malik in 76/696 and inflicted defeat after defeat on the forces of the central government in this and the following year, till his death by drowning, accidentally or by contrivance, in a canal of the Tigris.

Adh-Dhahabī in the *Ta'rīkh al-Islām* assigns the episode a mere half-dozen pages,[367] and a few lines each in the *Kitāb Duwal al-Islām* and the *Kitāb al-ʿIbar*, i.e. the *Ta'rīkh al-Islām* is more like the *Kāmil* of Ibn al-Athīr in this respect. But, on the other hand, the *Ta'rīkh al-Islām* contains matters not registered by aṭ-Ṭabarī and Ibn al-Athīr, for example the strange case of the Syrian al-Ḥārith b. Saʿīd al-Kadhdhāb (executed in 79/698–9)[368] and the battle of Ṭarāz (Talas) between the Arabs and the Chinese in 133/751, (see pp. 17 and 94), that is, it represents other sources of information, and this being the case, it should no doubt be consulted, as the other works are, when information is looked for on particular points. The charge of 'bias' made against adh-Dhahabī by some of his contemporaries appears to have depended on *odium theologicum*, and the accusation of deliberate misrepresentation of the truth[369] is not proven.

Of special biographies we may mention here one particular class, those of medicals and men of science in general, including philosophers, of which among the earliest was the *Ṭabaqāt al-Aṭibbā' wa'l-Ḥukamā'* (Classes of the Doctors and Wise Men)[370] of Abū Dāwūd Sulaymān b. Ḥassān b. Juljul of Cordova, completed in 377/987.[371] This interesting and useful little book was utilized, with many other works, by Ibn abī Uṣaybiʿa (600/1203–668/1270) for his well-known *Kitāb ʿUyūn al-Anbā' fī Ṭabaqāt al-Aṭibbā'* (Book of the Sources of Information on the Classes of the Doctors), which is the great repository of information on Arabic medicine and the associated fields.[372] Another work of the same general range was the *Kitāb Ikhbār al-ʿUlamā' bi-Akhbār al-Ḥukamā'* (Book of the Informing of the Learned on the Accounts of the Wise Men) of (Ibn) al-Qifṭī (568/1172–646/1248), of which an excerpt has been published, the *Ṭabaqāt al-Ḥukamā'* made by az-Zawzanī in 647/1249.[373] An earlier compilation was the *Ta'rīkh Ḥukamā' al-Islām* (History of the Wise Men of Islam) of Ẓahīr ad-Dīn al-Bayhaqī (493/1100–565/1169–70), the original title of which was *Tatimmat Ṣiwān al-Ḥikma*,[374] i.e. it was written as a Completion of the *Ṣiwān al-Ḥikma* ('Repository of Wisdom') of Abū Sulaymān as-Sijistānī (as-Sijazī) who flourished considerably earlier (*c.* 370/980). The original work, *Ṣiwān al-Ḥikma* also contains biographical and other information about the 'wise men', but in the centre of interest are rather their 'wise sayings' (*ḥikam*, plur. of *ḥikma*).[375]

Returning to the general historians, we find that an important place is taken by (Ibn) Miskawayh, the date of whose birth appears to be unknown but who died at an advanced age in 421/1030. Miskawayh was a high official of the Buwayhid Sulṭāns and a confidant of ʿAḍud ad-Dawla. In view of the exceedingly important part played by ʿAḍud ad-Dawla in the second half of the fourth/tenth century, Miskawayh gained plenty of experience of affairs, and this is reflected in his principal work, the *Kitāb Tajārib al-Umam wa-Taʿāqib al-Himam* (Book of the Experiences of the Nations and the Results of the Endeavours). The first part is largely dependent on aṭ-Ṭabarī,[376] and consequently is of less importance than the later part of the work which comes down to the death of ʿAḍud ad-Dawla in 372/983. From 340/951–2 Miskawayh depends on eye-witnesses, particularly two of his patrons.[377]

The *Tajārib al-Umam* is partially available in the original Arabic and in translation as follows: in facsimile, ed. by L. Caetani, Principe di Teano, vol. i to A.H. 37 (*GMS*, vii, 1, 1909), vol. v, A.H. 284–326 (*GMS*, vii, 5, 1913), vol. vi, AH. 326–69 (*GMS*, vii, 6, 1917); text and translation in *The Eclipse of the ʿAbbasid Caliphate*, London, 1920–1, vols i–iii, Arabic text edited by H. F. Amedroz (A.H. 295–393),[378] vols iv–vi, the same translated into English by D. S. Margoliouth, vol. vii, Preface and Index by Margoliouth. A further portion extending from A.H. 196 to 251 was edited earlier by De Goeje.[379] For the period after aṭ-Ṭabarī, Miskawayh is probably the best source we have, especially for the generation or so from 340/951–2 till 372/983, in defect, that is, of the works of Thābit b. Sinān (to 363/974) and Hilāl aṣ-Ṣābi (to 447/1055), which are mentioned to the exclusion of Miskawayh by al-Qifṭī,[380] as the best authorities after aṭ-Ṭabarī, but have largely disappeared with the passage of time.

According to a contemporary French scholar,[381] Miskawayh in the last part of his history shows not only real talent as a writer but also a remarkable interest in many aspects of life, social, religious, administrative and governmental as well as political, and is capable of lively and sometimes moving narrative. As a sample of Miskawayh's lively style and excellent information we may cite his account of a remarkable event, the capture and occupation of Bardhaʿa by the Russians in 332/943. Bardhaʿa (modern Barda) was then an important Muslim town, reckoned sometimes in Adharbayjān, sometimes in the more northerly province of Arrān, lying a few miles from the river Kur on a tributary stream. The

Russians arrived in Bardhaʿa from the Caspian, which they had reached in boats evidently via the Volga.[382] The narrative in Miskawayh is headed 'Account of the exploits of the Russians and their issue', and begins:[383]

They (the Russians) are a mighty nation with vast frames and great courage. They know not defeat, nor does any of them turn his back till he slay or be slain. It is the practice of the individual among them to carry his armour, while bearing suspended upon his person an artisan's outfit, axe, saw, hammer, and the like. He fights with spear and shield; he wears a sword and has hung upon him a lance and an instrument resembling a poniard. They fight on foot, especially these invaders. For indeed after sailing the sea which washes their country they crossed to a vast river called the Kur, which has its source in the mountains of Adharbaijan and Armenia, and flows into this sea (sc. the Caspian). It is the river of Bardhaʿah, which they compare to the Tigris. When they reached the Kur they were met by Marzuban's[384] officer who served as his governor of Bardhaʿah at the head of three hundred Dailemites[385] and about the same number of Suʿluks[386] and Kurds. He also summoned the people of the place to arms, and was joined by some 5000 volunteers anxious to fight these invaders. They were however under a delusion, not knowing the strength of the Russians, whom they expected to behave like Greeks or Armenians. When they met them in battle not more than an hour elapsed before the Russians made a fierce onslaught which routed the army of Bardhaʿah; the volunteers and the rest of the troops turned their backs with the exception of the Dailemites, who stood their ground and were killed to a man except such of them as were mounted. The Russians then pursued the fugitives to the town, whence every one, soldier or civilian, who had a mount to carry him fled, leaving the town to be entered and seized by the Russians.

I was informed by Abu'l-ʿAbbas Ibn Nudar[387] and a number of careful enquirers how the Russians when they hurried into the town made a proclamation to the following effect to the citizens: There is no dispute between us on the matter of religion; we only desire the sovereignty; it is our duty to treat you well and yours to be loyal to us. The armies however came against them from all sides, only to be routed by the Russians. . . . After a time they issued a proclamation that none of the original inhabitants were to remain in the town after three days from the day of the proclamation. All who had mounts to carry them, their womenfolk and their children left the place. These, however, were a small minority; when the fourth day came the majority were still there; so the Russians put them to the sword, slaughtering countless numbers. After the massacre they bound over 10,000 men and lads with their womenfolk, their wives and their daughters; they proceeded to place the women and children in a fortress within the city called locally Shahristan, where they had taken up their quarters, lodged their troops and entrenched themselves. They then gathered the men into the Public Mosque, set guards at the doors, and bade the men ransom themselves.

There was in the place a Christian clerk of sound judgment, named Ibn Samʿun, who acted as negotiator between the parties, and made an arrangement with the Russians whereby each man should be ransomed for twenty dirhems. The wiser among the Muslims acceded to this arrangement. . . .

When the Muslims found themselves unable to deal with the Russians and Marzuban began to realize the situation, he had recourse to strategy. It so happened that when the Russians had got into Bardhaʿa,[388] they indulged excessively in the fruit of which there are numerous sorts there. This produced an epidemic among them. . . . When their numbers began thereby to be reduced, Marzuban, seeking for a stratagem, bethought him of laying an ambush for them at night. . . . The morning after this scheme had been arranged, Marzuban with his followers, advanced, and the Russians came out to meet them. Their commander was mounted on an ass, and his followers came out and ranged themselves in order of battle. The usual procedure occurred. Marzuban with the Muslims took to flight, and were pursued by the Russians till they had got beyond the place of the ambush. . . .

The followers of Marzuban continued to attack and besiege the Russians till the latter grew weary. The epidemic became severe in addition. When one of them died they buried with him his arms, clothes and equipment, also his wife or some other of his womenfolk, and his slave, if he happened to be attached to him; this being their practice.[389] After their power had come to an end the Muslims disturbed their graves and brought out a number of swords which are in great demand to this day for their sharpness and excellence. When their numbers were reduced, they left by night the fortress in which they had established their quarters, carrying on their backs all they could of their treasure, gems and fine raiment, and burning the rest. They dragged with them such women, boys and girls as they wanted, and made for the Kur, where the ships in which they had issued from their home were in readiness with their crews, and 300 Russians whom they had been supporting with portions of their booty. They embarked and departed, and God saved the Muslims from them.[390]

Miskawayh was also the author of a number of works on philosophy, not distinguished perhaps by great originality but demonstrating the acumen which he brought to bear on governmental and political matters in his history. Among the best known of these is the *Jāwīdān Khirad* (Eternal Wisdom),[391] so called after the first of its six parts, which is said to be the testament to his successors of the legendary Persian king Ūshhanj (Hushang), translated from the 'ancient language', presumably Avestan or Pahlavi, by 'Kanjūr, son of Isfandiyār, vizier of the king of Irān Shahr', into modern Persian and thence into Arabic by al-Ḥasan b. Sahl, brother of al-Faḍl b. Sahl Dhū'r-Riyāsatayn,[392] and completed by Miskawayh.[393] The remaining parts or chapters deal with the *ḥikam* or wise sayings (cf. p. 122), of the Persians, Indians, Arabs, Greeks and Romans and (modern) Muslims.[394] Other works of Miskawayh are the *Kitāb Tahdhīb al-Akhlāq* (Book of the Amendment of Morals) several times printed in Cairo,[395] a *Risāla fī Māhiyyat al-ʿAdl* (Treatise on the Nature of Justice),[396] and the *Kitāb al-Fawz al-Aṣghar* (Book of the Lesser Success).[397]

Before passing on to consider some other general histories the history of Muslim Spain must again briefly hold our attention. We begin with two remarkable works produced in the fourth/tenth century, the *Akhbār Majmūʿa fī Fatḥ al-Andalus* (Collected Notices on the Conquest of al-Andalus), by an unknown author who lived in the notable reign of ʿAbd ar-Raḥmān III an-Nāṣir, founder of the Spanish Caliphate (300/912–350/961), and the *Ta'rīkh Iftitāḥ al-Andalus* (History of the Conquest of al-Andalus) of Ibn al-Qūṭiyya (died 367/977). Both these books have been known in the West at least since the nineteenth century.[398] The author of the *Ta'rīkh Iftitāḥ al-Andalus* is specially interesting as a descendant of the former ruling dynasty in Visigothic Spain before the coming of the Muslims, and the name Ibn al-Qūṭiyya, 'son of the Gothic woman', no doubt refers to Sarah the Goth, a descendant of Witiza, the last member of the dynasty who actually reigned (A.D. 701–710).[399] Ibn al-Qūṭiyya himself was a typical Muslim scholar, and highly regarded for his historical knowledge.[400] Somewhat later we have a whole range of Spanish Muslim historians, from Ibn al-Faraḍī (351/962–403/1012) to Ibn Saʿīd al-Maghribī (died 673/1274), and including al-Ḥumaydī (died 488/1095), Ibn Khāqān (died 529/1134 or 535/1140), Ibn Bassām (died probably 542/1147), Ibn Bashkuwāl (= Pascual) (494/1101–578/1183), aḍ-Ḍabbī (died 599/1202?), and Ibn al-Abbār (595/1199–658/1260). The principal works of some of these have been published in the series founded by Francisco Codera, *Bibliotheca Arabico-Hispana*, from 1882 onwards, and elsewhere.[401] Outstanding among all the Spanish historians is Ibn Ḥayyān, i.e. Abū Marwān Ḥayyān b. Khalaf

b. Ḥusayn (*sic* without the article in his biographers[402]) b. Ḥayyān, mentioned as one of the glories of his country in the famous *Risāla* in praise of Spanish Islam by ash-Shaqundī,[403] whose surviving work shows breadth of treatment and conscientious accuracy as to facts. In mere extent his writings are comparable with the most voluminous historians of the Muslim East—the enormous *Kitāb al-Matīn* (Solid Book),[404] which, according to Ibn Saʿīd in the appendix (*tadhyīl*) to the *Risāla* of Ibn Ḥazm,[405] contained nearly sixty Books (volumes), which were thought at one time to exist in the Zaytūna Mosque in Tunis,[406] and the more convenient but still extensive *Kitāb al-Muqtabis fī Ta'rīkh al-Andalus* (Book of Him Who Seeks Knowledge about the History of al-Andalus) in ten volumes. Some of his historical production has been published[407] (much has been lost), and an idea of the extent of it may be got from the fact that a recently published volume[408] containing more than 200 pages of Arabic text deals only with a few years, 360/970 to 364/974, of the Caliphate of al-Ḥakam II al-Mustanṣir, and these apparently from the shorter *al-Muqtabis*. Ibn Ḥayyān's dates are 377/987–469/1076.

In addition to the foregoing, mention should be made of the *Kitāb al-Muṭrib fī Ashʿār Ahl al-Maghrib* (The Delightful in the Poetry of the People of the West) of Ibn Diḥya Dhū'n-Nasabayn, 'the Man with the Two Genealogies',[409] which though a simple anthology is the source of the only account which we have of the alleged journey of Yaḥyā al-Ghazāl to the court of the 'king of the Norsemen' (see p. 161). Ibn Diḥya was also the author of a *Kitāb an-Nibrās fī Ta'rīkh Banī l-'Abbās*[410] (Book of the Lamp on the History of the ʿAbbāsids), which is quoted by Ibn Khallikān,[411] and contains some curious things, for example a letter to the Caliph al-Ma'mūn from an Indian king Dhmy, whose name is uncertain but who is known to other Muslim sources at about this time.[412] The *Kitāb an-Nibrās* throws no light on the history of al-Andalus.

Mention should be made of one other work dealing with Spanish history, which may, however, belong to a later period, viz. *al-Kitāb al Khazā'inī* (Treasury Book?) cited by al-Maqqarī (see below) for a long continuous account of the conquest of al-Andalus.[413] Also, when speaking of the West of Islam, we cannot altogether omit notice of historians of North Africa of the calibre of ʿAbd al-Wāḥid al-Marrākushī, whose *History of the Almohads* was written in 621/1224,[414] and Ibn ʿIdhārī (late seventh/thirteenth century), whose extensive work *al-Bayān al-Mughrib fī Akhbār Mulūk al-Andalus wa'l-Maghrib* (The Astonishing Explanation of the History of the Kings of Spain and North Africa), though of course a compilation of earlier books, is one of our best sources of information on its subject,[415] *inter alia* for the history of the Party Kings (*Mulūk aṭ-Ṭawā'if*) in Spain.[416] Another important contribution was the *Rawḍ al-Qirṭās*, in full *al-Anīs al-Muṭrib bi-Rawḍ al-Qirṭās fī Akhbār Mulūk al-Maghrib wa-Madīnat Fās* of Ibn Abī Zarʿ, dealing with the history of the Idrīsids, Banū Zanāta, Almoravids, Almohads and Marīnids from 145/762 till 726/1326, of which there is an old French translation by A. Beaumier (Paris, 1860) and a still older Latin edition and translation by C. J. Tornberg (Upsala, 1843–6). The work is usually read in one of several lithographed editions (Fez, various dates), or in the partial modern edition of Muḥammad al-Hāshimī al-Filālī (2 vols., Rabāṭ, 1355/1936).

5. Period of trouble: general and regional histories

But the main course of Muslim history flowed elsewhere, in the East, and for accounts of the gradual breakdown of the ʿAbbāsid Caliphate, the coming of the Crusaders and the Mongol storm, we have to turn to works of more general scope, including some which have already been mentioned. An older contemporary of Ibn Khallikān (see pp. 119–20) was the celebrated Ibn al-Athīr, one of a family of learned brothers, all of whom gained distinction by their writings. The fame of ʿIzz ad-Dīn, nowadays at least, stands highest of the three,[417] as author of the *Kitāb al-Kamīl fī't-Ta'rīkh* (The Perfect in History), which is one of the great productions of Arabic historiography and, with the *Annals* of aṭ-Ṭabarī, one of the best known and most highly valued sources which we possess on Islamic history. This is partly owing to the circumstance that since 1876 we have had an excellent edition of the *Kāmil* by the Danish Orientalist C. J. Tornberg, which has recently been reprinted.[418] The great merits of Ibn al-Athīr's work, apart from its general reliability which has almost always been recognized, are its coverage of many centuries (it comes down to the year 628/1231) and its readability. Unlike aṭ-Ṭabarī's *Annals*, the *Kāmil* presents a continuous text, leaving the authorities for the most part unmentioned, and abandoning altogether the long *isnāds* which are so much a feature of the earlier book. It has been much studied by scholars in the West. Brockelmann made the relationship between the *Kāmil* and the *Annals* the subject of his doctoral dissertation.[419] Sir William Muir, in the preface to his important work on the Caliphate, characterizes Ibn al-Athīr as 'a singularly impartial annalist, who compiled his work from all available sources' and says that he used him as his chief guide after Ṭabarī.[419a] The passages from Ibn al-Athīr dealing with North Africa and Spain were translated into French by E. Fagnan.[420] If one were restricted to a single Arabic historian for the reconstruction of as long a time as possible of the Arab past, one would probably be well advised to opt for Ibn al-Athīr. As Professor Franz Rosenthal, no blind admirer of the *Kāmil*, truly says, it is a remarkable achievement.[421]

A general history of similar type to Ibn al-Athīr's was the *Mir'āt az-Zamān fī Ta'rīkh al-Aʿyān* (Mirror of the Age in the History of Famous Men) of Sibṭ Ibn al-Jawzī, grandson, that is, of Ibn al-Jawzī (died 597/1200), another historian whose fame, however, in this department[422] has been eclipsed by his grandson's. Of the considerable surviving part of Sibṭ Ibn al-Jawzī's work J. R. Jewett published a handsome facsimile of the years 495/1101 to 654/1256 from a manuscript, once the property of Count de Landberg, in Yale University Library,[423] and the same years were long afterwards given an edition, with Jewett's pagination in the margin, by the Dā'irat al-Maʿārif al-ʿUthmāniyya (the well-known Osmania Oriental Publications Bureau of Haidarabad).[424] This part of the work begins with an assault of Ibn Ṣanjīl (Raymond of Saint Gilles),[425] on Ṭarābulus (Tripoli) during the First Crusade, the mobilizing of the Egyptian forces by the famous vizier al-Afḍal and a hairsbreadth escape of Bardawīl (Baldwin of Edessa), and ends with the great floods at Baghdad which necessitated the evacuation of the palace of the Caliph (at that time the unfortunate al-Mustaʿṣim, the last of the ʿAbbāsids, who a year or two later was to be the victim of the Mongol Hūlāgū) and the establishment of the Ayyūbid al-Malik an-Nāṣir Yūsuf in Damascus in very modest circumstances, after having lost his men and money in Egypt.[426]

Sibṭ Ibn al-Jawzī was born in 582/1186 and died in 654/1257, so that we can be sure that these events narrated for 1256 brought his history, the *Mir'āt az-Zamān*, to a close. It was indeed the end of an age, though Sibṭ Ibn al-Jawzī did not live long enough to record the final catastrophe, the fall of Baghdad to the Mongols in 656/1258. His work often presents an interesting narrative, arranged like Ibn al-Athīr's in annalistic form, while at the same time, consonantly with the second part of the title, the sequence of events is interrupted to record the biographies of notables, placed at the end of the annals of the year of their death, as usual also in Ibn al-Athīr's *Kāmil*. Sibṭ Ibn al-Jawzī is of course dependent on numerous authorities, whom he sometimes names. Among his biographies is that of the philosopher Ibn Bājja (Avempace), containing new information derived from a lost *Mukhtār min an-Naẓm wa'n-Nathr* (Choice of Verse and Prose) by Ibn Bashrūn.[427] Sibṭ Ibn al-Jawzī's *Mir'āt az-Zamān* in the author's own hand was seen by Ibn Khallikān in Damascus in no fewer than forty volumes,[428] and was used by him for his Biographical Dictionary (see p. 119), as was also the *Kāmil* of Ibn al-Athīr. There is no question that the *Mir'āt az-Zamān* is an independent work, and as such it is still valuable for Islamic history. On the other hand, in spite of its bulk, which appears to be due principally to the large number of biographies which it carries and the extent to which these are developed, the *Mir'āt az-Zamān* is often deficient in details of political events by comparison with Ibn al-Athīr's *Kāmil*,[429] and it appears also to omit mention of important incidents and episodes which are taken up by Ibn al-Athīr,[430] whose range of interest and information on the whole seems to have extended more widely than Sibṭ Ibn al-Jawzī's.[431] Apart then from the fact that only a relatively small portion of the *Mir'āt az-Zamān* is available, its services are ancillary rather than anything else, but at the same time neither it nor its continuation by al-Yunīnī of Baalbek (al-Ba'labakkī, died 726/1326–7), some of which has also been published by the Osmania Oriental Publications Bureau (Haidarabad, 1954), is to be disregarded. It may be noted that Ibn Khallikān mentions a work of Sibṭ Ibn al-Jawzī which he calls *Kitāb Jawharat az-Zamān fī Tadhkirat as-Sulṭān* (perhaps 'Book of the Jewel of the Age as a Reminder to the Sulṭān'), a copy or extract of which appears to have been in the former Royal Library, Berlin.[432]

With the *Kāmil* of Ibn al-Athīr and the *Mir'āt az-Zamān* of Sibṭ Ibn al-Jawzī we should probably class also three other works of general history produced at about the same time by authors writing in Arabic, two of them Christians: *al-Majmū' al-Mubārak* (Blessed Collection) a world-history by the Egyptian al-Makīn, much used by Ibn Khaldūn in his History,[433] partly edited at Leiden by the celebrated Erpenius as long ago as 1625,[434] partly still unedited, the *Mukhtaṣar ad-Duwal* (Extract of the Dynasties), a translation into Arabic with additions made by Abū'l-Faraj (Bar Hebraeus) (623/1226–688/1289), the son of a baptized Jew, from his *Syriac Chronicle*, published by Pococke at Oxford in 1663,[435] and the *Mukhtaṣar Ta'rīkh al-Bashar* (Extract of the History of Mankind) by Abū'l-Fidā', the ruling prince of Ḥamāt in Syria (672/1273–732–1331), part of which was published by Gagnier also at Oxford in 1723.[436] The last-named work especially continued to attract the attention of scholars,[437] and until the publication in the nineteenth century first of Ibn al-Athīr and then of aṭ-Ṭabarī was the usual recourse of those who wished to learn the facts of Islamic (also pre-Islamic) history, as registered by the native historians.

There is an affinity between all these general histories and the work of Ibn Taghrībirdī (813/1412–874/1469) entitled *An-Nujūm az-Zāhira fī Mulūk Miṣr wa'l-Qāhira* (The Brilliant Stars in the Kings of Miṣr and Cairo), which offers an account of Egypt from the Arab conquest to 872/1468 in seven volumes of annals. The first part of this to the year 365/976 was edited at Leiden by Juynboll and Matthes in 1855–61. Later the study of Ibn Taghrībirdī became a large part of the life-work of W. Popper, who began publishing the remaining years (from 366/976) in 1909,[438] and by 1963 had completed an Arabic text of much of the *Nujūm az-Zāhira* and an English translation, carefully annotated, of the years dealing with the Circassian Mamlūks of Egypt, 784/1382 to 872/1468,[439] where as already mentioned the work ends. Popper also contributed an edition in four volumes of Ibn Taghrībirdī's *Ḥawādith ad-Duhūr* (Happenings of the Times),[440] which, written on a more elaborate scale than the other work, was intended by its author as a continuation of the *Kitāb as-Sulūk* of al-Maqrīzī, whom we shall mention immediately, and, beginning where al-Maqrīzī's book ended, included the years 845/1441 to 874/1469, that is to say it came down rather more than a year further than the *Nujūm az-Zāhira*, till shortly before Ibn Taghrībirdī's death. For the limited period which it covers the *Ḥawādith ad-Duhūr* is obviously a valuable source.

In the same field of regional or, we might say, national history falls the main part of the work of an older contemporary and teacher of Ibn Taghrībirdī having little affinity with the general historians, but who rather sums up and transcends the earlier historians of Egypt already considered (pp. 116 ff). This was the celebrated Maqrīzī (766/1364–845/1442), a man of considerable originality as well as great productivity, to whom we owe most of what is known about medieval Egypt. His principal work, usually called simply *al-Khiṭaṭ* which has already been referred to in this chapter, deals with topography and archaeology as much as history. Its full title is *Kitāb al-Mawāʿiẓ waʾl-Iʿtibār fī Dhikr al-Khiṭaṭ waʾl-Athār* (Book of Exhortations and Consideration, or Mention, of the Settlements and Monuments). It is concerned with Egypt in general and al-Fusṭāṭ and Cairo in particular. The interest in the first settlements of the Muslims in Egypt is even more prominent than in Ibn ʿAbd al-Ḥakam's book already mentioned (p. 117), and it is of course a compilation, as we have already had occasion to illustrate (pp. 111–13). Al-Maqrīzī clearly cast his net widely: it was shown a long time ago by the Hungarian Arabist I. Goldziher that he had, for example, made use of one of the works of the Spaniard Ibn Ḥazm, which were undoubtedly little known in the East.[441] On the other hand, the assertion of an author of the following century, cited by as-Sakhāwī (830/1427–902/1497), that al-Maqrīzī plagiarized for the *Khiṭaṭ* the work of a certain Aḥmad b. ʿAbd Allāh al-Awḥadī by simply adopting his manuscript, remains unconfirmed.[442] The *Khiṭaṭ* remained for a long time available only in a two-volume edition printed at Bulaq in 1270/1853, but there is now a modern edition from a Lebanese press, not critical, but which at least presents something like al-Maqrīzī's original text.[443]

Next in importance perhaps is al-Maqrīzī's *Kitāb as-Sulūk li-Maʿrifat Duwal al-Mulūk* (Book of Entrance to the Knowledge of the Dynasties of the Kings), a history of Egypt from the accession of Salāḥ ad-Dīn in 564/1169, with some introductory remarks on pre-Islamic times, Muḥammad, the so-called Orthodox Caliphs, Umayyads, ʿAbbāsids, Buwayhids and Saljūqs, becoming regular annals from about 568/1172 and ending in 844/1440–1, after which it is continuated by Ibn Taghrībirdī, as already mentioned. It is thus in effect a complete history of two Egyptian dynasties, the Ayyūbids (i.e. Salāḥ ad-Dīn and his successors) and the Baḥri Mamlūks (mostly Turks and Mongols) and a partial history of a third, the Burjī Mamlūks (mostly Circassians). A considerable portion of this was translated into French by Quatremère, and the Arabic text is now available as far as the end of 755/1354 (i.e. well down in the Baḥri Mamlūk period), in a well-printed critical edition by Muḥammad M. Ziyāda.[444]

Al-Maqrīzī says in his introduction to the *Sulūk*[445] that he has already completed two works, the *ʿIqd Jawāhir al-Asfāṭ min Akhbār Madīnat al-Fusṭāṭ* (Necklace of Jewels of the Caskets from the History of the City of al-Fusṭāṭ) and the *Kitāb Ittiʿāẓ al-Ḥunafāʾ bi-Akhbār al-Khulafāʾ* (Book of the Admonition of True Believers on the History of the Caliphs), which between them cover the period from the first conquest of Egypt by the Muslims to the end of Fāṭimid rule. In his present book (the *Sulūk*) he brings the history of Egypt down to his own time, in fact until shortly before his death in 845/1442. We have no means of telling how al-Maqrīzī treated the earlier history of Egypt in the *ʿIqd Jawāhir al-Asfāṭ* which seems to have disappeared, but on the other hand the *Kitāb Ittiʿāẓ al-Ḥunafāʾ* on the Fāṭimids has survived in a single manuscript and been edited more than once.[446] H. Bunz, the first editor, was able to show that the manuscript was in the author's own hand, and it is most unfortunate that this autograph goes down no further than the attack of the Qarmaṭians on Egypt in 363/974.[447] The account of this incident leads to a long excursus on the history of the Qarmaṭians, ending with a letter of the Fāṭimid Muʿizz to their leader al-Aʿṣam (al-Ḥasan b. Aḥmad al-Qarmaṭī) written in 362/973 shortly after the arrival of al-Muʿizz from the West. This letter, which is incomplete in the text,[448] is long and full of interest. At one point the Fāṭimid reproaches the Qarmaṭian leader with conduct during an attack upon Damascus, worthy only of the Banū'l-Aṣfar ('Sons of the Yellow', i.e. Byzantines), Turks and Khazars,[449] i.e. the worst enemies of the Muslims at this time or a little earlier.[450]

In the first part of the *Kitāb Ittiʿāẓ al-Ḥunafāʾ* al-Maqrīzī gives various opinions on the authenticity of the Fāṭimids' descent, which he is known to have favoured, at considerable length, and goes on to deal with the four reigns of al-Mahdī, al-Qāʾim, al-Manṣūr and al-Muʿizz, the last of which is of course incomplete (al-Muʿizz died in 365/975). It is thus in principle, as we have it, a history of the Fāṭimids while they were still in Ifrīqiya (modern Tunisia). It has some interesting sidelights on al-Muʿizz, for example a scene in which he announces to certain *shaykhs* of the Berber tribe of Kutāma his constant occupation with correspondence from all quarters (he claims to reply to everything in his own hand) and advises them to practise monogamy, his skill in foreign languages, Berber, Rūmī (probably Greek), Sūdānī and Ṣaqlabī (the language of the 'Slavonians', perhaps Italian), the opinion of a distinguished ʿAlid who afterwards suffered at his hands, Abū Jaʿfar Muslim al-Ḥusaynī, that to al-Muʿizz none of the Umayyad or ʿAbbāsid Caliphs could be compared. The excursus on the Qarmaṭians, at first supporters of the Fāṭimids, then for a time a cause of sharp alarm to their former allies, has its full share of atrocity stories, cannibalism, the cursing of the Prophet, and the well-authenticated removal of the celebrated Black Stone from the Kaʿba at Mecca. The part played by Kūfa in the Qarmaṭian revolt is more than once referred to.[451]

We have in fact in the fragmentary *Kitāb Ittiʿāẓ al-Ḥunafāʾ* a valuable source on the period, which compares very favourably with the North African Ibn Ḥammād's *Akhbār Mulūk Banī ʿUbayd* (History of the ʿUbaydids, i.e. the name by which the Fāṭimids were sometimes called especially by opponents), a work written two centuries earlier.[452] The *Durra al-Muḍiyya fī Akhbār ad-Dawla al-Fāṭimiyya* (Shining Pearl in the History of the Fāṭimid Dynasty) which is the sixth part of a larger work, *Kanz ad-Durar* (Crown of Pearls), by Ibn ad-Dawādārī completed in 736/1335, is also inferior to al-Maqrīzī's book from some points of view, certainly in regard to style.[453]

Al-Maqrīzī set his hand to another major work on Egyptian history, the *Kitāb al-Muqaffā*,[454] originally planned in eighty volumes, of which only sixteen seem to have been realized. Some part of these will be found in a French translation by Quatremère,[455] and elsewhere. The work contains biographies of famous historical figures, including the Fāṭimid ʿUbayd Allāh al-Mahdī.

But at least as much as his productiveness al-Maqrīzī's versatility marks him out as one of the great Arabic historians. We still have his book on the quarrel between the Umayyads and the Banū Hāshim (i.e. the ʿAlids and ʿAbbāsids), which throws light on members of the respective families, often in their private as well as public capacity.[456] He here speaks of the 'secret' of the passing of the Caliphate after Muḥammad from ʿAlī b. abī Ṭālib: the Caliphate was deliberately left open by Muḥammad to the common people of Quraysh. We have too an interesting turn to the tradition that Abū Bakr stood in a special relation to Muḥammad. The Prophet is made to say simply: 'If I took a friend, it would be Abū Bakr.' The ʿAbbāsids are not spared. The charge of Ibrāhīm the Imām to Abū Muslim includes the appalling words: 'Muḍar (a North Arabian stem) are the enemy near to the house, so slay any you doubt of, and if you can, leave not any in Khurāsān who speaks Arabic.' The conduct of Abū Muslim at Marv, of ʿAbd Allāh b. ʿAlī in Syria, where the Umayyad tombs were desecrated, and of Ibrāhīm b. Yaḥyā at Mosul is set out without mitigating any of the horrors. Al-Manṣūr introduced the obnoxious practice of prostration before the ruler. It is not surprising after all this to find even an ʿAlid regretting the passing of the Umayyads. A lighter note, at least for the modern reader, is struck when he finds al-Maqrīzī inveighing against the baneful effects of permission by another ʿAbbāsid, al-Maʾmūn, for the translation of books on philosophy. The conclusion of the whole matter, according to al-Maqrīzī, after al-Muʿtaṣim's removing the Arabs from the *Dīwān* (the central office of government, especially the treasury) and replacing them by Turks who, according to Muḥammad's admonition, were to be fought, not favoured, was the end of the Arab empire.[457]

Al-Maqrīzī's other works include the *Kitāb Ighāthat al-Umma bi-Kashf al-Ghumma* (Book of Help to the Nation in Disclosing the Distress), which deals with the famines which have occurred in Egypt from the earliest times down to the year 808/1405, the date of composition.[458] The author draws not only on his knowledge of Muslim history but gives several pages on periods of scarcity in more ancient times, derived from the *Kitāb Akhbār Miṣr* (History of Egypt) of the *ustādh* Ibrāhīm b. Waṣīf Shāh. Al-Maqrīzī's limitations in this matter are evident from the praise which he gives to such a book (cf. pp. 110 ff). His own is a great deal better. It has already been pointed out by Muḥammad Enan that in the *Ighāthat al-Umma* al-Maqrīzī was influenced by Ibn Khaldūn, the older man, who was his teacher in Egypt,[459] and this is accepted by the Cairo editors, who also note that the similarity of treatment here and in the *Muqaddima* (Prolegomena) of Ibn Khaldūn extends even to such a purely stylistic matter as the termination of sections by a verse or verses of the Qurʾān.[460] In other works of al-Maqrīzī, e.g. the *Khiṭaṭ*, this is not a notable feature.

The occasion of the composition of the *Ighāthat al-Umma* was the intermittent famine in Egypt between the years 796/1394 and 808/1405, during which his only daughter died, perhaps of plague. Al-Maqrīzī himself was appointed *muḥtasib* (inspector of the markets) in Cairo in 801/1398–9, and as the editors remark his special experience in this post no doubt helped him in dealing with the subject-matter of the book.[461] He does not confine himself simply to giving a historical account of similar visitations in the past, but offers an analysis of the causes of the present situation, which, he says, is due to bad government.[462] According to al-Maqrīzī, not only has the government shown itself careless of the needs of the people but has also failed to understand what ought to be done. Rents are too high and the coinage has been debased. This leads him to give a short account of the history of currency in Islam, which before or afterwards he made the subject of a separate treatise.[463] In all this we seem to have traces of the influence of Ibn Khaldūn on al-Maqrīzī,[464] for clearly he is here concerned with facts of economics and sociology, which few Muslims in the Middle Ages apart from Ibn Khaldūn appreciated and al-Maqrīzī's perception of which was no doubt sharpened by contact with Ibn Khaldūn. Incidentally, we get some idea of his rapidity of work, when we learn that the *Kitāb Ighāthat al-Umma* was put in order and revised in a single night.[465]

Another work of al-Maqrīzī deals with bees. The date of composition and the purpose of the book are not known. The title is *Kitāb Naḥl ʿIbar an-Naḥl* (Book of the Present from the Examples of the Bee),[466] and here al-Maqrīzī appears as a kind of Arab Maeterlinck. He first speaks of the nature and habits of bees and then, true to his prepossessions as a follower of Ibn Khaldūn, goes on to speak of the important products, honey—'the noblest of foods'[467]—and wax, which are derived from them. At the close his overriding historical interest is shown in accounts of famous occasions, at the court of Masʿūd or Maḥmūd of Ghazna, at the marriage of a daughter of Khumārawayh of Egypt to the Caliph al-Muʿtaḍid, etc., when great numbers of wax-candles were used. This whole section raises the question of illumination in public and private in Islam. We have a picture of al-Manṣūr going to the mosque accompanied by an attendant carrying an oil-lamp, or again of the same Caliph reading and writing by the light of a single wax-candle in a candlestick which was removed when he had finished.[468] The Umayyads, al-Maqrīzī tells us, used oil-lamps for illumination and tall wax-candles in processions, and we get the impression that the use of lamps is the older practice, while very extensive employment of candles is an indication of later luxury.

What is perhaps most remarkable in the book, very original in its subject and perhaps unique in Arabic,[469] is that al-Maqrīzī depends scarcely at all on personal observation of bees, but on passages in earlier Arabic literature where bees, honey, honeycomb, etc. are mentioned incidentally, and surprisingly enough, to a great extent also on Aristotle. Aristotle, as is well known, refers frequently to the bee in his zoological treatises, notably the *History of Animals*, and this book, as the editor Jamāl ad-Dīn ash-Shayyāl has shown, is a principal source of al-Maqrīzī's information. The Arabic translation which he used was doubtless that of Ibn al-Biṭrīq, made at the beginning of the ninth century.[470]

Al-Maqrīzī also wrote two works of general history, the *Kitāb Imtāʿ al-Asmāʿ fīmā li'n-Nabi' min al-Anbā' wa'l-Aḥwāl wa'l-Ḥafada wa'l-Matāʿ* (Book of the Delight of the Ears in the Prophet Muḥammad's News and Conditions and Descendants and Household Goods), and the *Kitāb al-Khabar ʿan al-Bashar*, (History of Mankind) also called *Kitāb al-Madkhal* (Book of Introduction), which began with the Creation, dealt with world-geography and the early history of the Arabs and Persians, and was intended as an introduction to the *Kitāb Imtāʿ al-Asmāʿ* just mentioned. Neither of these books seems to have been the object of any special attention, which they would probably repay. The same applies also to his *Durar al-ʿUqūd al-Farīda fī Tarājim al-Aʿyān al-Mufīda* (Pearls of the Precious Necklaces in the Biographies of Important Personages), which dealt with contemporaries.[471] His short works, apart from those which have been mentioned, cover a wide range of subjects.

6. Ibn Khaldūn and his contemporaries. Al-Maqqarī

We thus see al-Maqrīzī as a voluminous writer, even when judged by the standard of Arabic historiography, and also remarkably diverse and original in his range of subject. His predecessor Abū Zayd ʿAbd ar-Rahmān b. Muḥammad b. Khaldūn, born in Tunis 732/1332, who died in Cairo 808/1406, author of the famous *Muqaddima* (Prolegomena), gave evidence in that work of ample originality and diversity of interest, but apart from the *Muqaddima* and the history *Kitāb al-ʿIbar wa-Dīwān al Mubtada' wa'l-Khabar fī ayyām al-ʿArab wa'l-ʿAjam wa'l-Barbar wa-man ʿāṣarahum min dhawī as-Sulṭān al-Akbar* (Book of Examples and the Commenced Dīwān and History of the Days of the Arabs, Persians, Berbers and their Contemporaries who Possessed Sovereign Power), of which in fact the *Muqaddima* was simply the introduction, the first of seven Books, Ibn Khaldūn produced comparatively little beyond the usual school exercises of the time.[472] The *Kitāb al-ʿIbar*, or as we may call it more conveniently, following the example of Professor Franz Rosenthal, the *History* of Ibn Khaldūn, i.e. the six volumes following the *Muqaddima* in the editions, is for the most part like the run of Arabic general histories and certainly less than we might expect from the character of its Prolegomena. Though it has merits of its own, for example its grouping in one place information about each people or dynasty, instead of following the annalistic method, and the use made practically for the first time[473] of the late Latin writer Orosius whose *Historiae adversus Paganos* had been translated into Arabic in the fourth/tenth century,[474] also the valuable north-west African and Berber history in Books vi and vii[475] which for this subject are our principal source, yet the information given in the *Kitāb al-ʿIbar* is in general what we might expect from an eighth/fourteenth century compiler, and Ibn Khaldūn does not attempt, from lack of time or some other reason, to apply the lessons which he has taught in the *Muqaddima*. Most of the faults for which he blamed his predecessors are conspicuous in his own *History*. Nor could it be otherwise, since for the most part he contents himself with abridging them.

Ibn Khaldūn's reputation depends then not on the *History* as such, but on certain parts of it, above all the *Muqaddima* (Book i), also the Berber history (Books vi and vii). His *Autobiography*, in Arabic *at-Taʿrīf biʾbn Khaldūn wa-Riḥlatuhu Gharban wa-Sharqan* (Account of Ibn Khaldūn and his Journey West and East), printed at the end of the History but designed as a separate work,[476] also comes into account here. A critical edition of the *Autobiography* was recently published by Muḥammad aṭ-Ṭanjī (Cairo, 1370/1951), and for the external facts of Ibn Khaldūn's life this is the best source, but for the man as he was and the peculiar quality of his genius the self-revelation in the *Muqaddima* itself is by no means to be minimized.

The *Muqaddima* is extremely interesting, apart from the novelty of its point of view, as a kind of encyclopedia of the knowledge and culture of western Islam at the time it was written, towards the end of the eighth/fourteenth century. The exact year was 779/1377, and Ibn Khaldūn tells us that he completed the work in the remarkably short space of five months, ending in the middle of the Hijra year, i.e. October–November, 1377.[477] He was then in his middle forties. He could already look back on many years of political activity in North Africa and Spain (Fez, Granada,

Bougie, Constantine, Biskra, al-ʿUbbād near Tlemcen) and had already served Marīnid, Naṣrid, Ḥafṣid and ʿAbd al-Wādid rulers—all the principal contenders for power of the place and time. He was temporarily out of politics, having been so since some date after Ramaḍān, 776/March 1375, when he and his family withdrew to a castle (*qaṣr*) at Qalʿat Ibn Salāma in the province of Oran (Algeria), then belonging to a powerful Arab clan, the Awlād ʿArīf.[478] Here the idea of the *Muqaddima* occurred to him, or as he says himself:

I continued there for four years withdrawing myself from all business. I began to compose this book [the 7-volume *History*] while I resided there, and I completed the *Muqaddima*[479] (Prolegomena) of it in that remarkable manner to which I was guided in that solitary place, where showers of words and ideas deluged my mind till the cream of them was churned and their results put together. Afterwards was the return to Tunis, as we shall mention.[480]

In another place[480a] he says,

When you consider our discussion in the section on dynasties and kingship[481] and have given it its due of examination and attention, you will find contained in it an exposition of these expressions and a detailed, exhaustive, clear account of what they involve, with the most complete explanation and the most evident proof and demonstration. It is God who apprised us of it (*aṭlaʿanā Allāh ʿalayhi*), without the teaching of Aristotle[482] or the lessons of the Zoroastrian priests.[483]

Then, having criticized sharply in passing Ibn al-Muqaffaʿ (see p. 46) and Abū Bakr aṭ-Ṭarṭūshī whose *Sirāj al-Mulūk* (Lamp of the Kings) was written in 516/1122,[484] and contrasting their work with his own, he continues:

We ourselves were inspired to this by God. He showed us a science which gives 'the age of its camel' and makes us 'the Juhayna of its information'.[485] If I have exhausted its problems and have distinguished its theories and methods[486] from those of the other arts, favour and guidance are from God. If anything has escaped me in describing it and its problems have been confused with those of another science, then the judicious reader may rectify it, while I have the merit of having traced the way and made the path plain for him. God guides by his light whom he wills.[487]

What is this science which Ibn Khaldūn claims to have discovered? He gives the definition in a few words a little earlier than the last quotation. The subject of the first Book of the *History*, the *Muqaddima*, is as it were an independent science. For it has a subject, viz. the civilization of mankind and human society, and problems, namely to explain the accidents and conditions which attach themselves successively to the essence of society. This is the characteristic of every science, whether depending on authority (*waḍʿī*)[488] or based on reason (*ʿaqlī*).[489]

This is near enough to the modern conception of sociology for Ibn Khaldūn to have a serious claim as the founder of that branch of investigation, and at the least it may be said of him that he was a bold and independent political thinker. His ideas on the subject of what he calls *jāh*, 'status',[490] and on the importance in all political and social affairs of *ʿaṣabiyya*, 'group feeling',[491] have only to be enunciated nowadays to be readily understood and to gain a measure of acceptance, and since the case was evidently different in his own time, there is no reason to suppose that he derived them from any of the authors he quotes. His whole way of looking at things, apart from some indications which he may conceivably have got from al-Masʿūdī (cf. pp. 104–5) and as-Sakkākī,[492] seems strikingly original.

Ibn Khaldūn was undoubtedly a personality *très réaliste*. This is already apparent from his political career, with its remarkable shifting of loyalties (cf. pp. 138–9), and he showed that he conspicuously lacked at least one ingredient in a high character, when he makes a virtue of obsequiousness.[493] His egotism—not vanity, which he seems to nave lacked—is perhaps harmless, and may have passed unnoticed in the environment in which he moved. The readiness with which he everywhere found intrigues directed against himself is a more unpleasant characteristic. These faults are not such as to have impaired his insight into affairs, but his inability to conceive the entry of the higher motives of conduct was from this point of view a serious defect. However open to dissolving analysis they may be, ideas of duty, self-sacrifice, devotion to an ideal going much beyond Ibn Khaldūn's solidarity within the group (*ʿaṣabiyya*), appear time and again as factors in history. Ibn Khaldūn would disregard these. In his view the spiritual world is real enough,[493a] but religion itself (and he expresses himself regularly as the devout Muslim which he doubtless was) is part of the social environment, something given, whose effects though far-reaching can always be estimated. It is the form of political existence.[494] He realizes of course that religious movements are often the causes of shifts of power and of the creation of new political units, as is specially obvious in the history of Islam, but of religion as a motivating force in the individual, determining political action and operating as often without and contrary to the interest of the group as within it, he has much less to say.[495] Yet Muslim history could have offered him the instances of, on the one hand, an ʿUmar b. ʿAbd al-ʿAzīz, and, on the other hand, a figure like the Fāṭimid al-Ḥākim, with many others showing all the gradations between the devotee and the fanatic, whose religious motivation as individuals had far-reaching consequences. In general, the part of the individual is disregarded in Ibn Khaldūn's scheme. It is one of his weaknesses that he has no heroes.

Ibn Khaldūn speaks freely, as we have seen, about being divinely led or inspired to his new sociological view. There is no reason to suppose that he is being disingenuous, and it is the less surprising to find him expressing himself in terms of this kind, recalling no doubt unintentionally the revelation to Muḥammad, when it appears that one of his leading concepts can be derived from the Qur'ān.[496] It is perhaps consonant with this that he disclaims a foreign (Greek or Persian) origin of the new science.[497] On the other hand, it is permissible to attempt to discover the immediate sources of Ibn Khaldūn's thought. Here comparison with one who has often been considered a kindred genius, the Florentine Niccolo Machiavelli (1469–1527), may be instructive. Living during the Italian Renaissance, but somewhat uninfluenced by the main trends of the time (it is doubtful if he learned Greek), Machiavelli, as all the world knows, wrote *Il Principe*, a remarkable work on politics in which a realism with no place for conventional morality was expounded. The book was admired and criticized, then and since. In the seventeenth century some Venetian senators refused to give permission for the publication of a commentary on Tacitus, on the ground that it was the teaching of Tacitus which produced Machiavelli.[498] Machiavelli indeed quotes Tacitus, also Livy, Polybius, Plutarch and Aristotle's *Politics*, perhaps Thucydides from some Latin translation,[499] but it is extremely difficult to say from which of these authors, if from any, he drew the inspiration of *The Prince*. Rather he derived it from his own experience in the world of Renaissance politics, and from his knowledge of an outstanding figure like Cesare Borgia or another formed the ideal ruler of a work nearly always regarded as a masterpiece. Something of the same kind seems to be called for to explain Ibn Khaldūn's masterpiece. It was much more the product of what he had himself seen and felt during his first political period—say twenty or twenty-five years to 776/1375—than from books, al-Masʿūdī and the rest, for all these, taken together—thought over and transmuted in his mind during a prolonged period of leisure—would scarcely have given the *Muqaddima*. Ibn Khaldūn undoubtedly reflected on what he had seen and known in North Africa and in Spain, and by some kind of imaginative or intellectual effort saw his experiences falling together and becoming capable of a better explanation in the light of his new insight.

There are two points which may be made here. The first is that Ibn Khaldūn himself gives some indication of the genesis of his new science in a long and interesting passage—too long to be quoted here—which shows him as looking for a criterion of historical truth more reliable than the traditional one of testing the *isnāds*, or chains of tradition, by which events are traced back, as nearly as possible to an eye-witness, whose account (*matan*), if the *isnād* passes inspection, may then be accepted as giving what actually took place.[500] Ibn Khaldūn is led to the general conclusion that historical narratives are to be tested by their inherent possibility or absurdity from consideration of al-Masʿūdī's story of the Copper (or Bronze) City somewhere in the desert of Sijilmāsa in North Africa.[501] The alleged facts as narrated are absurd, and contradict what is known of the building and planning of cities, where the metals are present in quantities sufficient for the utensils and appurtenances of houses, not to build the whole city therefrom.

There are a great many similar cases. The testing of them depends on knowledge of the natural characteristics of civilization. To apply this knowledge is the best and most reliable way of testing narratives and distinguishing their truth and falsehood, and precedes testing by criticism (lit. justification) of the transmitters. Recourse should be had to the latter process only when it is known that the account in itself is possible. When the account is impossible, there is no advantage in examining it by the method of justifying and rejecting.[502] Ibn Khaldūn states the same thing once again immediately below. The criterion of truth is correspondence—he means, with what actually happens. Therefore it is necessary to examine if the alleged fact is possible. This is more important than and comes before justifying the transmitters.[503] The conclusion follows:

> If this is so, then the rule or criterion in distinguishing truth from falsehood in historical narratives on the basis of possibility and absurdity

is that we should consider the society of mankind which is civilization,[504] and distinguish which conditions belong to [civilization] essentially and in conformity with its nature, and which are accidental and need not be reckoned with, and which cannot possibly happen in it (*lit.* for it). When we have done that, we have a canon or criterion for distinguishing the true from the false, truth from lies, by a demonstrative method which does not admit of doubt. So then when we have heard of any case of the conditions occurring in civilization, we know what we are to judge worthy of acceptance, what worthy of rejection as false. We have thus a true touchstone (*miʿyār*) by which historians may pursue the path[505] of truth and right in what they report. This is the aim of this first book (i.e. the *Muqaddima*) of our work.[506]

Ibn Khaldūn goes on in the passage already quoted (p. 140), 'This is as it were an independent science etc.' It would seem that we here come as close as may be to the origin of what Ibn Khaldūn calls his new science. The first adumbration of the sociological standpoint came to him while searching for a ready method of determining the truth or falsehood of historical material which he found principally in books (he says nothing at this point of reports of contemporary or recent events). We may suppose that as the result of his discovery the *Muqaddima* rapidly expanded from a short introduction, such as an Arabic historian would normally write, to the elaborate treatise which we know, and that the implications of the new point of view, occurring to him and duly recorded for the first time are the deluge of words and ideas of which he speaks elsewhere (cf. p. 139).

The second point which may be stressed is the relative poverty of Ibn Khaldūn's information and the gross errors into which he was led on that account. To give some examples, while he has the merit of having used the Latin historian Orosius in its Arabic translation, Orosius and Ibn Khaldūn's other sources on the history of Greece and Rome, namely the Arabic Josippon[507] and Ibn al-ʿAmīd (al-Makīn) (see p. 130), are not such as to give him a real understanding of the classical past, and it is not surprising that Roman Emperors in the *Muqaddima* (Augustus, Constantine, Nero)[508] are mentioned only in connection with the Christian history. If more were wanted to show Ibn Khaldūn's lack of appreciation of the Roman, as distinct from the Greek civilization, the scientific legacy of which at least he values, considering that it has passed to the Arabs largely through the official action of the ʿAbbāsid Caliph al-Maʾmūm,[509] it may be seen not so much in the absence of the Romans from his enumeration of earlier civilized nations,[510] since the term Rūm, which appears in the lists, applies to the Romans as well as the Byzantines regarded as one nation, as in his extremely exiguous and sketchy references to Latin.[511] For Ibn Khaldūn, integrated and usable knowledge of the history of the Latin West, apart that is from the confused and partly incomprehensible notices[512] which he derives from the authorities already mentioned, did not exist. He speaks, for example, of the Goths and Umayyads having ruled in Spain for 'thousands of years',[513] and quotes Orosius (fourth century A.D.) without comment for the history of the Visigothic kingdom down to A.D. 711.[514] His real information on the Eastern Empire is scarcely more in evidence, and there is no doubt that on this subject he is much less knowledgeable than al-Masʿūdī (c. pp. 105 ff).

Ibn Ḥajar al-ʿAsqalānī, a younger contemporary who knew him in Egypt, where Ibn Khaldūn spent the last period of his life, complains that he was not well acquainted with the annals of the past, particularly of the East.[515] We have already referred to some of his misconceptions, and it is unnecessary to attempt to list them. Something is no doubt due to the imperfect state of his text, of which there is as yet no critical edition, but it is clear that Ibn Khaldūn was not a careful writer.

His best information, for example on the history of the Berbers (see p. 138), concerns the regions where he was most at home, North Africa and Spain, and it is the conditions there which he has in mind in making some of the assertions which strike us as most paradoxical, for example that the duration of a dynasty is three or at most four generations,[516] or that the modest amount of ornament in towns represented by the planting of orange trees, limes, cypresses, etc. is the 'ultimate in sedentary culture',[517] announcing a dangerous state of luxury and in consequence speedy destruction at the hands of a more virile enemy.[518] Such conclusions obviously have no general validity, though the conditions Ibn Khaldūn describes may correspond to the state of things, in North Africa in particular, in the fourteenth century. There is more than a little here which Ibn Khaldūn has in common with Machiavelli, who also generalized from what he observed in his own time and place, and produced 'laws' of political action which may have been appropriate for Renaissance despots (there is no good ground for thinking that even Cesare Borgia acted on Machiavellian principles—perhaps the author of *Il Principe* hoped that he would, or wished that he had), but are no doubt contradicted by the practice of governments at most times. There is therefore not much that one can learn from Machiavelli, except about political conditions in Renaissance Italy, and the same *mutatis mutandis* applies to Ibn Khaldūn (cf. p. 141).

His *History* throws light not so much on the history of the Arab Caliphate—much less on the history of the world—as on his own environment and on himself, a man of ambition and originality in the small, relatively weak states which, by his time, were all that was left of the Arab empire in the West. The age was one of decline (as was also, politically speaking, the age of Machiavelli), favourable to 'realist' views of men and society, such as undoubtedly Ibn Khaldūn held. Human conduct is, he implies, predictable, not to say determined, and is therefore subject to rules or laws, which the man of political insight learns to recognize. The main principle which has to be grasped is that man acts as a member of a group of some kind, and in the light of this, human action in the past history of mankind can be explained. But if the past can be explained, so also the future can be predicted, and if predicted, controlled. This is of the highest importance in a situation where the future, in the light of the immediate past, is ominous, as it was bound to be in the Muslim West in view of the progress of the Christian *Reconquista* of Spain, and though the idea of predicting future events is not perhaps brought directly by Ibn Khaldūn into connection with the new science which he has discovered, it is a subject which evidently interested him and to which he gives much space in the *Muqaddima*.[519]

The practical value of sociology, if sociology is in fact the new science of Ibn Khaldūn, was it seems, probably as much as its theoretical value for reconstructing the past, what delighted him in his discovery. Instead of spending more time at Qalʿat Ibn Salāma working up the remaining books of the History, which were apparently written after the *Muqaddima*[520] and on which he seems to have spent less care than on the latter, Ibn Khaldūn was ready to leave his retreat and resume his political activity. Thereafter he no doubt improved what had already been written with the help of libraries, to be had, as he tells us, only in the larger towns,[521] but was principally engaged with practical tasks till near the end of his life. He went in Dhū'l-Qaʿda, 784/January 1383, to Egypt, and experienced further vicissitudes and adventures, including the well-known episode when like St Paul he was let down from the town wall of Damascus, in order to have an interview with the Mongol prince Tīmūr-i Lang, then with his army in the neighbourhood.[522] He died in Cairo, still in office as Qāḍī, on 25 Ramaḍān, 808/17 March 1406.

The vizier Lisān ad-Dīn Ibn al-Khaṭīb of Granada (713/1313–776/1374), an older contemporary of Ibn Khaldūn, was the author of numerous historical and other works, among the most useful of which is his *Lamḥa al-Badriyya fī'd-Dawla an-Naṣriyya* (Brightness of the Full Moon on the Naṣrid Dynasty),[523] a history of the last phase of Muslim rule in Spain (the Naṣrids, Banū Naṣr or Banū'l-Aḥmar, survived in Granada till 897/1492). Another is the *Kitab Aʿmāl al-Aʿlām fī man Būyiʿa qabl al-Iḥtilām,* which was not restricted by its title (Deeds of the Great in Those to Whom Allegiance was Done before Maturity), but was in fact a somewhat extensive sketch of general Muslim history in three parts dealing respectively with the Muslim East, Spain, and North Africa and Sicily. The third part was scarcely completed, and the whole work may have been written in forty days.[524] The *Aʿmāl al-Aʿlām* was a late work of Lisān ad-Dīn. The date of its composition falls between 774/1372 and 776/1374, when he was an exile at the Marīnid court in Tlemcen. The title was suggested by the age of the Marīnid Sultan, Abū Zayyān Muḥammad, who succeeded at the age of four years in 774/1372. On p. 64 of the edition the practical aim of the book appears, to induce people to take the oath to an infant sovereign. It was evidently written in haste but contains interesting information[525] and some good phrases: the 'torrent of Islam' at the time of the Muslim conquest of Spain and the 'swords of the Arab propaganda'.[526]

Lisān ad-Dīn's most celebrated work was the *Kitāb al-Iḥāṭa fī Ta'rīkh Gharnāṭa* (Book of Comprehensiveness on the History of Granada), a very complete biographical dictionary of the famous men connected with Granada from the earliest days of the Muslim occupation to Lisān ad-Dīn's own time. The manuscripts are still in considerable confusion, or rather the Arabists remain in considerable confusion regarding the manuscripts, and the complete text has never been printed. An edition with the title *Kitāb al-Iḥāṭa fī Akhbār Gharnāṭa*, in two volumes (a third was promised), appeared in Cairo in 1319/1901,[527] but this is obviously neither the complete *Iḥāṭa*, nor is it, apparently, the compendium made shortly after the death of the author, by one Badr ad-Dīn al-Bishtakī, in 793/1391 to be exact, which has survived in some manuscripts.[528] On the other hand, a critical edition has been begun also in Cairo by Muḥammad Enan,[529] and if this can be brought to a successful conclusion, it will certainly be not the least of the services which this scholar has rendered to Arabic studies.

Lisān ad-Dīn left a list of his works, about sixty, in the autobiography which he appended to his *Iḥāṭa*. A number of them exist in manuscript in the Escorial, and have been discussed by P. Melchor M. Antuña.[530] Several of the Escorial group had already been published a long time previously by M. J. Müller[531] when Antuña's series of articles appeared, including the account from Lisān ad-Dīn's *Rayḥānat al-Kuttāb* (Sweet Basil of the Secretaries) of a journey through the eastern provinces of Granada made by the Naṣrid prince Abū'l-Ḥajjāj Yūsuf, who ruled from 733/1333 to 755/1354,[532] and two pieces of more definitely geographical interest, an imaginary contest between towns of Malaga in Spain and Salā (Sale) in Africa,[533] and descriptions in the *maqāma* style (cf. pp. 61 ff) of Jabal al-Fatḥ (Gibraltar) and places in Morocco (Bādis, Qaṣr Kutāma, Uṣaylā, Rabat, Chella, Azammūr, Āsafī, Marrakesh, Aghmāt, Meknes, Sijilmāsa, Taza, etc.).[534] M. J. Müller also published from an Escorial manuscript a remarkable description by Lisān ad-Dīn of the plague at Granada.[535]

A political work of Lisān ad-Dīn is preserved in the Escorial and in al-Maqqarī (see below). This is said to have been dictated in a single night. It is of a somewhat conventional cast, with nothing corresponding to the treatment of politics by Ibn Khaldūn in his *Muqaddima*, and is not even original. Its basis turns out to be a *Kitāb as-Siyāsa li-Aflāṭūn* by the Egyptian Aḥmad b. Yūsuf b. ad-Dāya (fourth/tenth century; cf. above, p. 117), the arrangement of which has been retained by Lisān ad-Dīn, who in fact does little more than reproduce Ibn ad-Dāya's arguments with some modification of his language.[536] The whole piece is reproduced by al-Maqqarī.[537]

Another work of Lisān ad-Dīn with the odd name of *Nufāḍat al-Jirāb fī ʿUlālat al-Ightirāb* (the Shakings of the Bag in the Diversion of Travelling Abroad) is partly autobiographical and affords information about places in North Africa visited by the author. Vol. 2 of three or four volumes has recently been edited by Miss Elizabeth Warburton.[538]

A more ambitious work than any of these, even the great *Kitāb al-Iḥāta*, seems to have been contemplated by Lisān ad-Dīn. In the *Aʿmāl al-Aʿlām* he says:[539]

It is my purpose, if God grants relief from the present straitened circumstances and the return of pleasant times and a clear future (*naṣba*, lit. 'elevation', 'horoscope') to compose a book on history of very substantial length, which will treat the subject exhaustively, to be called *Biḍāʿat al-Muhawwilīn* (?) *fī Asāṭīr al-Awwalīn*,[540] compared with which this book (sc. the *Aʿmāl al-ʿAlām*) will be like a pebble in comparison with the sand and a drop in comparison with floods of rain.

The work was never completed, perhaps not even begun. Lisān ad-Dīn fell out of favour in North Africa, and met his death in prison in Fez.

The process at which he was condemned[541] was based at least in part on certain expressions of his *Kitāb fī 'l-Maḥabba* (Book of Love), the same, that is, as bore the longer title *Rawḍat at-Taʿrīf bi'l-Ḥubb ash-Sharīf* (Garden of Instruction on Chaste Love). What expressions were intended is not stated in the source, but it may be surmised that the point of the indictment was doctrinal rather than moral.[542] For al-Maqqarī writing some centuries later this same work, which he quotes for many pages, is not evidence of delinquency of any kind but rather a proof of the superiority[543] of the man for whom his *Nafḥ aṭ-Ṭib* is above everything else, in the author's intention, the memorial, perhaps also a defence.

This position of al-Maqqarī is somewhat obscured to his Western readers—though it is plain enough from the full title *Nafḥ aṭ-Ṭib min Ghuṣn al-Andalus ar-Raṭīb wa-Dhikr Wazīrihā Lisān ad-Dīn Ibn al-Khaṭīb* (Breath of Perfume from the Fragrant Branch of al-Andalus and an Account of its Vizier Lisān ad-Dīn Ibn al-Khaṭīb)—owing to the circumstance that the Leiden edition contains only the first part of the book, on the history of Muslim Spain from the time of the Conquest, and in consequence the second part, which is almost, if not quite, as long, dealing with Lisān ad-Dīn and his works and subsequent influence goes largely unread.[544] In any case, al-Maqqarī's admiration, reserved for Lisān ad-Dīn, has given us abundant notices of almost everything connected with the latter in the second part of his book, and in the first part a general history of Spain, which is in its way parallel to the *Muqaddima* of Ibn Khaldūn (see pp. 138 ff).

With al-Maqqarī, whose dates fall as late as *c.* 1000/1591–1041/1632, this survey of Arabic historical writing in medieval Islam may well end. His can be styled perhaps a romantic history of al-Andalus. At all events, the motives which led him to write the *Nafḥ aṭ-Ṭib* for the benefit of the men of Damascus, among whom this native of Tlemcen purposed to settle, were different from the motives of the analyst and super-realist Ibn Khaldūn. If al-Maqqarī idealized Lisān ad-Dīn, whose political career bears a strong resemblance to Ibn Khaldūn's own, being marked by peripeties and tergiversations and the same lack of principle, Ibn Khaldūn idealized nobody, not even himself, and is the great, perhaps the only, example of the pragmatic historian among the Arabs. It is the surprising fact that al-Maqqarī, though his abilities were perhaps inferior to Ibn Khaldūn's and his experience of political affairs undoubtedly much less than the other's, in his late compilation has left us greatly more in the way of data for Peninsular history than Ibn Khaldūn, and so also than Lisān ad-Dīn. If we had to make do with the works of one of these writers, as far at least as Spain is concerned, al-Maqqarī would be on the whole a better source of information than either of his distinguished predecessors. For their own times both Ibn Khaldūn and Lisān ad-Dīn are of course superior to al-Maqqarī, and for a large part of the history of Granada we naturally turn to Lisān ad-Dīn. Ibn Khaldūn in the *Muqaddima* as in the *History* proper keeps his readers in mind of the true perspective: the Maghrib and al-Andalus are only a part, and not the most important part, of the great Muslim empire. But for the beginnings of Arab rule in Spain, the duration of the Amīrate, the Spanish Caliphate and the period of the Party Kings (*Mulūk aṭ-Ṭawā'if*) which followed, al-Maqqarī, with his old-fashioned method of citing his authorities, is the most instructive of the three, and of course he alone knew of the end of Muslim rule in Spain (1492). Unless and until the older sources from which he drew become available, and in fact older texts, known and unknown to al-Maqqarī, are slowly accruing, al-Maqqarī will continue to be one of the mainstays of Spanish Muslim history, and this being so, no doubt deserves an honourable place among Arabic historians.

Chapter 4

Geography and travel

1. Greek sources

In classical antiquity the distinction between descriptive and mathematical geography was already made, and we have the great names of Strabo (died after A.D. 21) and Ptolemy (second century A.D.) as the leading representatives of the one branch and the other. Strabo appears to have been completely unknown to the Arabs (though he has much information on Arabia and elsewhere which might have been expected to be of great interest to them). Ptolemy's *Geography*, on the other hand, was early known, having been translated at an unspecified date for the philosopher al-Kindī (died after 256/870)—a poor translation, we are told, and the work was done again a little later by Thābit b. Qurra[1] (died 288/901). It seems certain that the acquisition of Ptolemy's *Geography*, as the most advanced work which had yet been written on the subject, had a direct effect on the progress of the science among the Arabs, and already in the *Kitāb Ṣūrat al-Arḍ* of Muḥammad b. Mūsā al-Khwārizmī (*c.* 780–850) we have an extensive Arabic book on mathematical geography, described by C. A. Nallino as 'an elaboration of Ptolemaic materials made with much independence'.[2] The same kind of date is indicated by the *Kitāb al-Masālik wa'l-Mamālik* of Ibn Khurradādhbih, who mentions in his dedication to an unnamed ʿAbbāsid prince that he had utilized and translated Ptolemy.[3] Ibn Khurradādhbih's book is the first of a series of works on descriptive geography in Arabic which has come down to us. It is usually said that the first draft of the book dates from 232/846–7, after which the author made successive additions, so that a second edition resulted, not completed before 272/885–6. This was the opinion of the Dutch Arabist De Goeje.[4] On the other hand, J. Marquart, an equally eminent authority, thought that there was only one edition of the work, not completed before 272/885–6.[5] In any case, Aḥmad b. aṭ-Ṭayyib as-Sarakhsī, who died in 286/899, wrote a geographical work of the same or similar title, *Kitāb al-Masālik wa'l-Mamālik*.[6] (As-Sarakhsī was the pupil of al-Kindī.) About the same time al-Jayhānī, the *wazīr* of the Sāmānids, composed yet another work with identical title, different from but apparently based upon the *Kitāb al-Masālik wa'l-Mamālik* of Ibn Khurradādhbih.[7] While the latter thus appears to have introduced a new type of book in Arabic with a new title, which continued to be employed much later, he yet speaks in his introductory words, as we saw, of his dependence on Ptolemy. This may be no more than a gesture, and the translation of Ptolemy which Ibn Khurradādhbih says he carried out, but about which we hear nowhere else even in the work itself, must surely have been of very restricted scope and limited circulation.[8]

Another Greek author who appears to have influenced the development of Arabic geography is Marinus of Tyre, an older contemporary or immediate predecessor of Ptolemy, i.e. alive in the second century A.D., on whose work Ptolemy to a great extent based himself in his own book. The work of Marinus is lost in Greek, and an authority on ancient geography has written that 'the very name of the Tyrian geographer would have been unknown to us had it not been for the criticisms and references of his successor Ptolemy'.[9] But this is not at all the case. The *Book of Geography* of Marinus (*Kitāb Jughrāfiya li-Mārīnūs*) was known to al-Mas'ūdī, and hence to us, at the time when he wrote his *Kitāb at-Tanbīh*, in 345/956. The passage in which he mentions the *Geography* of Marinus most distinctly, as a separate work different from Ptolemy's, is interesting and important:

There is much disagreement among the learned of the different nations, both ancient and modern, in regard to the measurements of these seven Climates [i.e. regional belts on the earth's surface parallel to the equator, about which he has just been speaking, representing in an earlier form the later system of parallels of latitude], their extent in length and breadth, the number of hours which the days have in each of them [this was the determining consideration], where each begins and where it ends, and the habitations of the different nations therein, inland and by the sea. We have already given an explanation anent much of this in our previous books. I have seen these Climates represented in various colours in more than one book. The best that I have seen was in the *Book of Geography* by Mārīnūs (the explanation of 'Geography' is *qaṭ' al-arḍ*, 'the crossing of the earth'[10]), and in the map of al-Ma'mūn which was made for him by the joint efforts of a number of the learned men of his time. There were depicted in it the world with its spheres and planets, its land and sea, its inhabited and uninhabited regions, the dwellings of the different nations, the cities, etc. It is more perfect than its predecessors in the *Geographies* of Ptolemy and Mārīnūs, etc.[11]

We shall have to return to this passage, but meantime we note that the geographical work of Marinus appears to have existed in the time of al-Masʿūdī, and to have been seen by him. Immediately previously, on the same page of the *Kitāb at-Tanbīh*, we find another reference to the 'book of Mārīnūs', which is cited for the statement that the extent of the Climates in length is 38,500 *farsakhs* (parasangs) and in breadth 1,775 *farsakhs*, but that this estimate has been rejected by a number of authors of early and late date.[12] I am not aware that this figure is found in the work of Ptolemy, and it at least has the appearance of a direct quotation from Marinus.

Finally, al-Masʿūdī refers to the *Kitāb Jughrāfiyā* with Marinus as author, in his account of the Roman emperors, placing Marinus, however, under Nero (died A.D. 68), which is presumably too early:

In the days of this emperor, as is said, was the learned (*ḥakīm*) Mārīnūs, author of the *Book of Geography* on the form of the earth (*ṣūrat al-arḍ*), its configuration, its seas, its rivers, its inhabited and uninhabited regions. Claudius Ptolemy has mentioned him in (his) *Kitāb Jughrāfiyā*, also about the form and configuration of the earth, and has rejected a number of his assertions.[13]

It may be conjectured that the geographical work of Marinus which al-Masʿūdī saw, and which presumably was in Arabic, was a great rarity, perhaps a unique copy, and that it was subsequently lost. He tells us nothing about the date of the work which he saw, or where he saw it, as he occasionally does in similar cases,[14] but it may, like the other work of the same kind which he mentions, as possessing excellent maps, go back to the previous century and the time of al-Ma'mūn (198/813–218/833), and if so, possibly formed part of the library at the *Bayt* or *Dār al-Ḥikma*[15] ('House of Wisdom'), which appears to have had the special name of *Khizānat al-Ḥikma*. It is very interesting at all events to read in the *Fihrist* that Muḥammad b. Mūsā al-Khwārizmī mentioned above was set apart to the service of the last-named installation (the *Khizāna*).[16]

Quite independently of his connection with the *Bayt al-Ḥikma*,

Muḥammad b. Mūsā al-Khwārizmī is one of the Arabic authors whose work may be considered to have been under some influence from the *Book of Geography* of Marinus. As already indicated, Nallino who had studied the *Ṣūrat al-Arḍ* with great attention came to the conclusion that it was a *rifacimento* or recasting of the geographical work of Ptolemy, or as he says elsewhere in the words already quoted 'an elaboration of Ptolemaic materials', for the geographical coordinates of many places in Muḥammad b. Mūsā al-Khwārizmī's book differ from Ptolemy's. The extreme limits of the island of Thūlī (Ptolemy's Thule), for example, are thus presented by Nallino:

longitude 26° 20′–32° 20′ Ptolemy 29° 0′–31° 40′
latitude 62° 0′–64° 40′ Ptolemy 62° 40′–63° 40′,

who adds that al-Khwārizmī gives new particulars. He knows a city *'tlī* or *'thlī* at 30° 0′, 62° 45′, and describes a river which flows through the island.[17] What is the source of this additional information on Thule? Nallino expresses his surprise at the independence shown by al-Khwārizmī in general 'which perhaps we should not have expected in the times when the Arabs were making their first step in the geographical sciences and when the name of Ptolemy appeared surrounded by an almost miraculous aureole'. Ptolemy would seem at all events to have had some source for his new particulars on Thule. A later investigator of the *Ṣūrat al-Arḍ* of al-Khwārizmī also allows for the possibility of other sources than Ptolemy.[18] It would seem to be at least a reasonable conjecture that al-Khwārizmī knew and used the Arabic version of the *Geography* of Marinus.

Turning now to the *Kitāb al-Masālik wa'l-Mamālik* of Ibn Khurradādhbih, we find that he has a division of the inhabited earth into four parts, called respectively Arūfā, Lūbiya, Ityūfiyā and 'sqūtiyā (first syllable left without the vowel).[19] This is clearly a division into continents (Europe, Libya, Ethiopia and Scythia), and the source is Greek. We recall the familiar listing of the continents as Europe, Asia and Libya (Africa), which is as old as Herodotus. Here Scythia is for Asia, apparently, and Libya remains with Ethiopia as representing Africa. But this is in appearance only, for Scythia which according to Ibn Khurradādhbih includes Armenia, Khurāsān, the Turks and the Khazars is evidently North Asia, and Ethiopia (Tihāma, the Yaman, as-Sind, al-Hind and aṣ-Ṣīn or China) is South Asia. The details are

Muslim, as is clearly shown by the names, but the four-fold division must for the same reason derive from a Greek geographer, and presumably not Ptolemy. Marinus, we know, reports a Roman expedition against the Ethiopians, apparently in the second century A.D., which attained a country called Agisymba, in which the rhinoceros abounded.[20] Marinus knows the name of the commander, Julius Maternus, but not the date, and arrives at the remarkable conclusion that Agisymba was not less than 24,680 *stadia* or 2,468 geographical miles south of the equator.[21] On this basis, it would have been by no means impossible to speak of Ethiopia as being as large as the other known continents, and this is what may have been done by him. The argument is obviously fine-spun and the result conjectural, but in the defect of another source for Ibn Khurradādhbih's Greek names we may provisionally advance the suggestion that he had them from the Arabic version of Marinus, as al-Khwārizmī, about the same time and place, had his additional information on Thule.

2. India and China

Apart from Greek sources for Arabic geography we have to take into account also an Indian element. This is not nearly so prominent as the Greek contribution, but comes rather conspicuously to light in the importance sometimes attached to the Indian town of Ujjayini or Ujjain, still existing in the district of Malwa (Central Provinces). It is designated by Ptolemy as Ozēnē, hence Arabic Uzayn, regularly corrupted to Arīn, and further characterized as *qubbat al-arḍ*, the 'cupola of the earth' or 'world summit'. The idea is explained as follows by the Arabic geographer or encylopaedist Ibn Rusta, writing about 290/903.

It is said that the earth's centre, i.e. the place which is called the cupola or summit, is a city named Udhayn (Uzayn). It is the place where the hours of the day at all seasons do not exceed the hours of the night nor those of the night the day, so that the day is always twelve hours and the night the same. But when you descend from this place which is called the cupola or summit, and take the direction of north or south, the hours of night and day differ, and the difference increases according to the distance from the cupola or summit. We have deliberately kept the explanation here short, because it would take much space to go into it in full.[22]

The above account of Ibn Rusta indicates that the *qubbat al-arḍ* must have been considered to have been on the equator, and this was actually the case. In point of fact Ujjain is approximately 24° 0′ latitude N., as was later registered by al-Bīrūnī (eleventh century A.D.).[23] How then did the early Muslim geographers come to displace the Indian city so seriously? The answer is afforded by the same Bīrūnī. For the Indian men of learning Lanka, the island of Ceylon, is between the two ends of the inhabitable world and without latitude, i.e. on the equator. Longitude for all places east and west is reckoned by them from Lanka, or rather from the imaginary or great circle, which passes through Ujjain and other places connecting Lanka with the semilegendary Mount Meru behind the mountains of Himavant (cf. Himalayas) 'which are covered with everlasting snow, and where the rivers of their country rise'.[24] Lanka for the Indians is the centre of the earth, being equidistant from east and west and from north and south, but the expression *qubbat al-arḍ* is an invention of the Muslims, or at least in employment among them.[25] It is never used by the Indians for Lanka, to which it would evidently apply at least somewhat better than to Ujjayni (Ujjain, Uzayn, Arīn). Therefore the Muslims who use this conception are wrong, and while it is permissible to use the line through Ujjain and Lanka for the beginning of longitude, as the Indians do, it is a serious error of some 'undiscriminating Muslim astronomer' to place Ujjain on the same meridian of 0° with Shabūraqān (Shibarghān) in al-Jūzajān (Gūzgān) which lies west of Balkh and south of the Oxus, many degrees west of the meridian of Ujjain.[26] Al-Bīrūnī implies that it is better to make longitude begin in the 'Islands of the Blest', or Canaries, as Ptolemy but not al-Khwārizmī had done.[27]

It remains to be added that the idea of the 'cupola of the earth' or 'world-summit' has probably to be connected with the ancient Semitic (Babylonian) notion of the 'earth-mountain',[28] perhaps also with that of the 'navel of the earth' among the Greeks. The view that it is Indian, though often repeated, seems to be excluded by al-Bīrūnī's express testimony (cf. above). As regards the form Arīn mentioned above, it seems that, while it is difficult to attest from the Arabic texts, there seems no special ground for supposing that Arin or Arim is the form which the name assumed in passing from Arabic into Latin. There is of course no dearth of medieval Latin authors where Arin or Arim appears. Albertus Magnus, Gerard of Cremona, the Alfonsine Tables and Roger

Bacon are cited for one form or another of the name by Reinaud,[29] and Adelard of Bath, Hermann of Carinthia (Hermannus Dalmata), Raymond of Marseilles and Michael Scot may be added from Professor Haskins.[30] The Arin theory survived much later than any of the authors just cited, passing into the work *Imago Mundi* of Cardinal Peter of Ailly, published in 1410.[31] But perhaps the most remarkable passage where the name occurs is the following from a letter of Christopher Columbus to Queen Isabella of Spain in the course of his third voyage in 1498.[32]

> The Eastern Hemisphere [Columbus calls it the Old Hemisphere] from Cape St Vincent (Spain) to Cattigara [?Hanoi in N. Vietnam], having for centre under the Equator the island of Arin, is spherical. But the other Hemisphere has the form of the lower half of a pear. A hundred leagues west of the Azores the earth rises under the Equator and the temperature freshens. The highest part, i.e. the tail of the pear, is situated near to Trinity Island, near the mouth of the Orinoco.

No doubt therefore as Kramers said, Islamic geographical theory may claim a share in the discovery of the New World.[33]

In the works of the later Arabic geographers the theory of the 'cupola of the earth' has disappeared. The noted traveller Ibn Baṭṭūṭa in the fourteenth century visited the authentic Ujjain in Malwa,[34] but instead of affording us some account of what had formerly been held about this place by earlier Arabic writers and correcting their misapprehensions, he tells us merely the names of two distinguished inhabitants, one of whom curiously enough was a man from the Maghrib, Jamāl ad-Dīn al-Gharnāṭī, so-called from Granada in Spain. Nor apparently is Ibn Baṭṭūṭa's neglect to speak of the 'cupola of the earth' due to the fact that al-Bīrūnī's explanation was by this time too common to mention. He does not refer to al-Bīrūnī in his work, and presumably had never read him. Ibn Baṭṭūṭa's ignorance of his predecessors would also seem to emerge from his account of the Chinese junks seen by him at Calicut,[35] where no indication is given that these vessels had formerly voyaged much further west. There seems to be evidence that in the ninth century or earlier Chinese ships (*as-sufun aṣ-Ṣīniyya, marākib aṣ-Ṣīn*) reached the Persian Gulf.[36]

Though no Muslim man of science appears to have been in the vicinity of Ujjain in the period when the theory of the 'earth-summit' was fashionable, Ceylon was visited and described in the ninth century. Ibn Khurradādhbih, whose work has already been referred to, describes it under the name Sarandīb,[37] as follows:

Sarandīb is 80 *farsakhs* by 80 *farsakhs*. In it is the mountain on which Adam—may Allāh bless him—descended.[38] It is a mountain going up into the sky, seen by those on seafaring ships from a distance of several days. The Brahmans, who are the religious devotees of the Indians, have mentioned that upon this mountain is the footprint of Adam—may Allāh bless him—, sunk in the rock. It is about 70 cubits—the one foot. (They also say that) upon this mountain there is always something like lightning, and that Adam—may Allāh bless him and give him peace—set his other step in the sea and it is at a distance of two or three days from (the first). Upon this mountain and round about it are precious stones of all colours and all kinds, and in its valley are diamonds. Upon the mountain are aloes, pepper, attar of roses and (other) perfumes, and the animals that carry musk and civet. In Sarandīb are cocoa-nuts, and its soil is the emery with which jewels are polished. Its rivers produce rock-crystal, and in the sea round about it men dive for pearls.[39]

This account of Ceylon stands in close relation with the notice given by 'Sulaymān the merchant' in the *Akhbār aṣ-Ṣīn wa'l-Hind*,[40] without it being certain that it is derived from the *Akhbār*.[41] On the other hand, the latter account, i.e. Sulaymān's notice dated to 237/851, reappears almost *verbatim* 300 years later at the head of al-Idrīsī's description of Ceylon in the 8th Section of the 1st Climate.[42]

If this account of Ceylon, which we may call traditional,[43] has the appearance of being legendary rather than factual—al-Masʿūdī, who evidently knew a version resembling that in the *Akhbār*, has omitted all the picturesque details[44]—there is evidence of Arab enterprise still further afield and apparently on a large scale, viz. in China, especially at Canton which is mentioned repeatedly in the *Akhbār* (Khānfū). Fires frequently take place in Khānfū, which is the anchorage for ships and the point of assemblage of the commerce of the Arabs and the people of China.[45] At Khānfū, which is the meeting-place of the merchants, is a Muslim judge appointed by the ruler of the Chinese to decide cases between the Muslims who repair to this region, by the express intention of the king of China. When it is a feast, (the judge) prays with the Muslims, pronounces the sermon (*khuṭba*) and prays for the Sulṭān of the Muslims. The ʿIrāqī merchants accept all his judgments and his actions (which are) according to the truth and according to the contents of the Qur'ān and the laws of Islam.[46] In 758, according to Chinese sources, the Arabs and Persians who had been in force in China since 756, when al-Manṣūr sent a contingent of troops to support the emperor Su Tsung,[47] at

Canton raised a revolt against the Chinese authorities, and burned and looted in the city.[48] Yet for more than a century after this the Muslim merchants and sailing-men of whom Sulaymān is the type, appear to have frequented the port, until the year 264/878 and the rebellion of Yān Shū (Huang Chhao), during which Canton was sacked. Reports of the sack of Canton are in existence both in Chinese and Arabic.[49] Al-Masʿūdī states that the population at this time included Muslims, Christians, Jews and Magians, in addition to native Chinese, and that the number of the foreign groups who perished when Canton fell, either by the sword or by drowning, was estimated at 200,000. He adds that this figure came from the census returns of the Chinese.[50] Since then, till 943 when al-Masʿūdī wrote, events have taken place which have troubled public order and upset the authority of the laws.[51] We are to understand that up to his own time the number of Muslim residents or visitors has been greatly reduced, by comparison with the earlier period.

Yet further afield the Arabic geographers knew of the land of al-Wāqwāq (apparently Japan), mentioned by Ibn Khurradādhbih as producing gold and ebony.[52] At some time, the same name al-Wāqwāq was introduced into geographical writings in Arabic for an African people or region, and some Arabic maps show land stretching from Africa to the Far East under al-Wāqwāq as a common designation. The African Wāqwāq has been identified as Madagascar.[53] As to the name of al-Wāqwāq here, the French Africanist L. Homburger has suggested a derivation from *Khoiqua*, the Hottentots.[54] This of course does not prejudice another derivation for the Far Eastern Wāqwāq, described as follows by Ibn Khurradādhbih:

In the eastern parts of aṣ-Ṣīn (China) is the country of al-Wāqwāq, which is so rich in gold that its people make the chains of their dogs and the neck-rings of their apes from gold, and they bring shirts woven with gold for sale. In al-Wāqwāq is excellent ebony.[55]

Yāqūt, perhaps because of the confusion caused by the two Wāqwāqs, is somewhat scornful of the 'legends' which are told concerning the name.[56] He himself lived in the thirteenth century A.D. in an age when the early commercial enterprise of the Muslim Arabs had ceased altogether, or been directed into different channels. That a real place, if not Japan, perhaps Sumatra, was intended by the early geographers by al-Wāqwāq, is rendered likely by somewhat similar notices of ash-Shīlā (sometimes as-

Sīlā), which without any doubt is Corea, from the name of a dynasty Sin-lo or Silla ruling there in the ninth century and earlier (till 904).[57] Ash-Shīlā, though actually existing, was clearly a place of wonder for the early Muslim travellers, like al-Wāqwāq.

A Buddhist monk from Corea, Hui-Chhao, travelled from China to the 'Five Indias' and beyond in the first half of the eighth century A.D. He also visited Central Asia, and the account which he has left of his journey indicates that he had some knowledge of Persia, Arabia, and even the Byzantine empire.[58] We may thus perhaps speak of Corean knowledge of Muslim lands before any Muslim knowledge of Corea, for our first notice in Arabic, as it appears to be, states:

Towards the sea [i.e. east of the Chinese mainland] are the islands of as-Sīlā [*sic*]. [The inhabitants] are white. They give presents to [or 'exchange presents with'] the ruler of China (*ṣāḥib aṣ-Ṣīn*), and allege that if they did not give him presents [or 'exchange presents with him'] they would have no rain. None of our people has reached [the islands] so as to tell us about them. They have white falcons.[59]

This has at least the appearance of being older than Ibn Khurradādhbih's account; it has been understood since Reinaud's time as meaning that no Arab had hitherto visited Corea.[60] Ibn Khurradādhbih at all events tells us differently.

At the extremity of China, over against Qānṣū,[61] are numerous mountains and numerous kings. It is the country of ash-Shīlā. In it is much gold. The Muslims who enter it settle in it on account of its goodness. It is not known what is beyond it.[62]

In a later section of the book, where he describes 'extraordinary natural characteristics of different countries', Ibn Khurradādhbih repeats his previous information.

The Muslims who enter a country at the extremity of China called ash-Shīlā, wherein is much gold, settle in it on account of its goodness, and never leave it at all.[63]

The latter passage is repeated almost *verbatim* by Ibn Rusta,[64] and al-Masʿūdī has a composite notice of Corea, which presents the idea not explicit in Sulaymān or Ibn Khurradādhbih that the country is visited by strangers from Iraq.[65]

There is thus good evidence of 'Arab navigation in Pacific waters'—the phrase is J. Needham's, with reference to what he has himself called 'the great Chinese–Arab period', i.e. from the eighth to the thirteenth century A.D.[66]—in the early Arabic geographers especially. Much more could be cited. We mention as a curiosity, no doubt connected with Arab commercial activity, the discovery in 1964 in a tomb of the T'ang dynasty (618–906) of three gold *dīnārs* dated in the reigns of three Umayyad Caliphs, ʿAbd al-Malik (702), ʿUmar b. ʿAbd al-ʿAzīz (718) and Marwān II (746). The site of the find was on the outskirts of Sian, the capital of Shensi province in north China.[67]

3. The Arabs and the Atlantic

Having now considered Muslim Arab seafaring in the Pacific, let us turn briefly to what was achieved in the Atlantic. It is sometimes said that the Arab empire at its greatest expansion in Umayyad and early ʿAbbāsid times extended from Spain in the West to China in the East, and in round terms this is the fact, but perhaps the extraordinary outward thrust of the Arabs in the seventh century is conveyed best to the imagination by emphasizing the maritime activity of the same nation at the same time off the Atlantic and Pacific coasts of Eurasia. This was a phenomenon which had scarcely as yet been seen, and pointed forward to the achievements of the great colonial empires of modern Europe.

In the Atlantic the Arabs came to know familiarly the Western seaboard of al-Andalus (the Iberian peninsula) with the important port of al-Ushbūna (Lisbon) on the Tājuh (Tagus), and Muslim ships at least upon occasion operated at Oporto (Burtuqāl).[68] The Atlantic coast of Morocco was also for a considerable distance south familiar. Further afield, the Sea of Burdīl (Bordeaux),[69] that is the Bay of Biscay, was known, certainly by name, probably also from experience, though of this we have perhaps no positive evidence. Of the adjacent islands—the islands lying off the continent of western Europe and Africa in al-Baḥr al-Muḥīṭ (the Circumambient Ocean) otherwise called by such names as Baḥr aẓ-Ẓulmāt (the Sea of Darkness) or al-Baḥr al-Akhḍar (the Green Sea),[70] the British Isles (Jazā'ir Barṭāniya or Barṭīniya—twelve in number according to al-Battānī,[71] were known, with Ankarṭara, Inkiltara, Lanqalṭara (l'Angleterre), Sqūsiya (Scotia) and Īrlanda or Birlanda (Ireland). Whether there was any Arab contact, except perhaps with Ireland, is, however, more than doubtful.[72] Further to the south, the Canaries and the Cape Verde islands or perhaps the Madeira group were also known (*al-Jazā'ir al-Khālidāt*, literally the Eternal Isles, and *Jazā'ir as-Saʿāda* (Isles of Happiness). Either name could stand for the 'Islands of the Blest' mentioned above, but it is not clear at what point the meridians of longitude are taken to begin. Along the northern shores of the European continent, from the English Channel to Flanders and Scandinavia, there is no evidence of Arab shipping, and the fact is unlikely.

Of particular voyages in this region we have a certain amount of somewhat controversial evidence. The visit of a ninth-century Spanish Arab, the courtier and poet Yaḥyā al-Ghazāl ('the Gazelle', so-called apparently for his youthful beauty), to the court of the 'king of the Norsemen' (Majūs) is known to us from a single source, the *Kitāb al-Muṭrib* of Ibn Diḥya[73] (d. 633/1235), an author who lived long after the events he describes and whose authority is not high among his own people.[74] Yaḥyā b. Ḥakam al-Ghazāl, to give him his full name, is a historical character. He was the author of a long poem in the *rajaz* metre on the conquest of al-Andalus by the Muslims, which Ibn Ḥayyān tells us was much appreciated in his day, i.e. in the tenth century A.D.[75] Unfortunately it is now lost. He did service to the recently established Umayyad dynasty in Spain (from A.D. 756) and in or about the year 840 went on an embassy to Constantinople to the court of the emperor Theophilus (829–42) on behalf of the then ruler of Cordova, ʿAbd ar-Raḥmān II.[76] A little later, if Ibn Diḥya is to be relied on, he undertook a similar mission to the court of the 'king of the Norsemen', following upon the great Viking assault on south Spain in 844. We are well enough informed about this event, very characteristic of the times, from other sources,[77] but the narrative of al-Ghazal's journey stands alone, and it is very difficult to determine where in fact the Norsemen whom he is said to have visited may have lived—in Jutland, as used to be thought, or in Ireland. He and his party are represented as sailing from Silves, now in Portugal, and after having passed opposite 'the great promontory which enters the sea, the boundary of al-Andalus in the extreme west, the mountain known as Aluwiya', which appears to be mentioned only here, and has been variously interpreted as Cape St Vincent and Cape Finisterre, but perhaps stands for Alūyā in al-Khwārizmī, Ptolemy's Alouiōn, Albion[78]—in any case, after this they are lost to sight in Atlantic mists till they reappear again at Shant Yaʿqūb (St James of Compostella) and finally reach Cordova by way of Castile and Toledo, after an absence of twenty months. The situation of the court of the 'king of the Norsemen' is also too vague to permit of certain identification—on a large island in the Circumambient Ocean with springing waters and gardens, three days' sail, or 300 miles, from the mainland, having numerous other islands in the vicinity.[79] The people are all Norsemen (Majūs), and they have mostly been converted to Christianity, except in the outlying islands, where there are still pagans. Is this ninth-century Ireland, or somewhere else? Or is it simply fantasy? The account given of the stay of the ambassadors (Yaḥyā al-Ghazāl and another Yaḥyā) is shadowy—a matter of protocol arranged with the king, conversations with the queen, and the recitation of poetry in her honour—all this through an interpreter—but nothing whatever about the business of the mission, which, if the mission actually took place, must surely have been to complain about the Viking raid on al-Andalus in 844 and to secure, if possible, that nothing of the kind should occur again. In point of fact it did; in 245/859 or 860 the Norsemen reappeared in force, first in Galicia, then farther south and on the east coast of Spain.[80] There are one or two points in favour of the authenticity, which have to be omitted here owing to considerations of space, but clearly the narrative cannot be regarded as unexceptionable. It has been accepted as genuine by the majority of scholars who have examined it, though there is no agreement as to where Yaḥyā actually went. It has not at all events been finally shown to be unauthentic, though there are serious doubts, and there meantime we must leave the matter.

On the other hand, there is some evidence that the Spanish Arabs knew of whale- and seal-fisheries in the Atlantic (cf. p. 16). At all events, al-Qazwīnī reports whaling in the vicinity of Ireland (Īrlanda),[81] and seal-skin appears to have been known both at Saraqusṭa (Saragossa) and Cordova.[82] Arab participation in the actual hunting is not, however, specifically stated.

Al-Masʿūdī mentions a young Spanish Muslim of Cordova called Khashkhāsh, who, with other young men of the same place, embarked on an expedition with specially equipped vessels into the Circumambient Ocean (*al-Baḥr al-Muḥīṭ*). He was absent for a time, then returned with rich booty, and his exploit is well known among the Spaniards.[83] It is tempting to connect this story, which al-Masʿūdī alludes to in passing, perhaps indicating that he has referred to it in his lost *Akhbār az-Zamān*, with another concerning a group called the 'Adventurers' (*al-Mugharrirūn*) of Lisbon, who sailed out into the Atlantic at an unspecified date on a voyage of discovery.[84] Starting 'when the east wind begins to blow', they reached after eleven days 'a sea with huge waves and thick clouds, with numerous reefs scarcely illumined by a feeble light'—a description which might fit some northern coast—then, turning south, they ran for twelve days before the wind and came to the 'island of Sheep' (mentioned occasionally elsewhere).[85] After another twelve days they put in at an inhabited island, were made prisoners, but were eventually released and reached the African mainland at Asfī (modern Safī). This has the appearance of an authentic voyage, and is reported as such by al-Idrīsī, who mentions that a street in Lisbon was named after the Adventurers *darb al-Mugharrirūn*. As to dating, the expedition must have taken place before 541/1147 or 543/1148–49, when Lisbon was captured by the Christians, but possibly already in the ninth century.

4. Descriptive geography

Arabic geography continued to be pursued along the lines of the *Ṣūrat al-Arḍ* of al-Khwārizmī (mathematical geography), as in the Geographical Tables of al-Battānī (died 317/929), published by C. A. Nallino,[86] the *Kitāb al-Aṭwāl wa'l-ʿUrūḍ* which served as the basis of the Tables of Abū'l-Fidā',[87] (died 732/1331) and other similar works. In the other department of descriptive geography activity developed at first with some observable dependence on the *Kitāb al-Masālik wa'l-Mamālik* of Ibn Khurradādhbih. Ibn Wāḍiḥ usually known as al-Yaʿqūbī, who is also the author of a valuable work of history,[88] wrote a *Kitāb al-Buldān*, completed in 278/891 towards the end of a long life spent in travels in many parts of the Muslim empire.[89] The purpose of the work was 'to describe the routes leading to the frontiers of the Empire and the territories adjacent to them',[90] i.e. al-Yaʿqūbī's aim, like Ibn Khurradādhbih's, was in the first place practical. Very close to Ibn Khurradādhbih's plan also was Qudāma's eleventh chapter of the fifth book of his *Kitāb al-Kharāj* (Book of the Land-Tax), written apparently a short time after 316/928.[91] The content of the section is geographical and statistical, that is it deals with the routes and revenues of the empire. The author emphasizes the danger from Byzantium.[92] Still more closely connected with Ibn Khurradādhbih's book was the work of the same title (*Kitāb al-Masālik wa'l-Mamālik*) by the Sāmānid *wazīr* al-Jayhānī mentioned above (early fourth/tenth century). Ibn Khurradādhbih's *Kitāb al-Masālik* was apparently the basis of the other, which was in seven books. No copy of al-Jayhānī's book has survived. Ibn al-Faqīh al-Hamadhānī (*flor. c.* 289/902) was the author of another

Kitāb al-Buldān, for which according to Ibn an-Nadīm[93] he 'plundered al-Jayhānī', and showed dependence also upon Ibn Khurradādhbih.[94] Another derivative writer was Ibn Rusta, whose little geographical encyclopaedia *al-Aʿlāq an-Nafīsa* depends heavily on his predecessors (written about 290/903).[95] The *Ḥudūd al-ʿĀlam* of an anonymous author, perhaps Ibn Farīghūn, author of a short encyclopaedia entitled *Jawāmiʿ al-ʿUlūm*,[96] was written in Persian in 372/982, and is known from a single manuscript, discovered in Bukhara last century by the Russian Orientalist A. G. Toumansky. This was edited in 1930 by Barthold,[97] and later Minorsky produced an exemplary commentary on the very difficult text, which appeared with the English translation in 1937.[98] The *Ḥudūd al-ʿĀlam* gives us an impression of the state of geographical knowledge in Khurāsān in the tenth century A.D., and is especially valuable for the lands of the Eastern Caliphate. The author naturally made use of his predecessors who had written in Arabic, among these al-Iṣṭakhrī, 'without doubt the source most systematically utilized', as Minorsky has told us.[99] But with the name of al-Iṣṭakhrī we come to a separate development in Arabic geography, which deserves a paragraph to itself.

Abū Zayd Aḥmad b. Sahl was born about 235/849–50 in the village of Shāmistiyān, near Balkh, from which he took his name al-Balkhī, the son of a schoolmaster. He travelled as a young man to Iraq, met the celebrated al-Kindī and under the latter's influence became, as we are told, enthusiastic for the exact sciences. Towards the end of a long and successful life as a scholar, in 308 or 309 (i.e. A.D. 920 or a little later), he wrote a work *Kitāb al-Ashkāl* or *Ṣuwar al-Aqālīm*, titles which suggest that it was primarily a text accompanying maps of the inhabitable world.[100] The *aqālīm* or climes in question were either the 'Seven Climates' of which mention has already been made above, or the twenty climes enumerated by al-Iṣṭakhrī. This work, now lost, was destined to be very influential. A new and apparently greatly enlarged edition was compiled by the younger writer, al-Iṣṭakhrī, not later than 340/951 but perhaps as early as about 320/932, within the lifetime of al-Balkhī, who died in 322/934. To this work al-Iṣṭakhrī gave the title *Kitāb al-Masālik wa'l-Mamālik*, the old name which had been used by Ibn Khurradādhbih. But apart from the title of his book al-Iṣṭakhrī was not dependent on Ibn Khurradādhbih, and his conception of geography goes much beyond the providing of a guide to the post routes within the empire. We now have a developed description of the lands, furnished by al-Iṣṭakhrī in part from his own travels. How much is due to al-Balkhī is difficult to determine, apart from the maps, which can be assumed to have been his. Some manuscripts of the *Kitāb al-Masālik wa'l-Mamālik* as early as the second half of the tenth century seem to have carried the name of al-Balkhī as author,[101] and in modern times the 'Iṣṭakrī-Balkhī question' has been widely discussed.[102] We have at all events in the work which no doubt rightly goes under the name of al-Iṣṭakhrī a production of the classical Arabic school of geography, the value of which for originality and general accuracy has been generally appreciated since its first appearance. Some time thereafter Abū'l-Qāsim Muḥammad b. Ḥawqal, a native probably of al-Jazīra (Mesopotamia)[103] who had travelled widely and had met al-Iṣṭakhrī (where and when he does not tell us),[104] at his request revised his work. Ibn Ḥawqal's book with the title *Kitāb Ṣūrat al-Arḍ* appears to have been completed in 367/977. Again we have an older title revived, but as in the previous case it is simply a name that is recalled. There is no close relationship between Ibn Ḥawqal's work and the *Ṣūrat al-Arḍ* of al-Khwārizmī mentioned above. The maps were again a feature of the new book. The text is often verbally al-Iṣṭakhrī's, with minor alterations which are not always improvements. But there are important new additions, and Ibn Ḥawqal was a diligent student of the works of the previous Arabic geographers, who undoubtedly knew his subject. His book also stands high in geographical literature in Arabic. As in the case of al-Iṣṭakhrī, not much is known of the personal circumstances of Ibn Ḥawqal. It is possible that he was an agent in the Fāṭimid interest.[105] Finally, we have al-Muqqaddasī, also in the line of al-Balkhī though showing much independence and originality. His book *Aḥsan at-Taqāsīm fī Ma'rifat al-Aqālīm* (The Best of Divisions in the Knowledge of the Climes) was completed in or about 375/985, i.e. his preface is dated in that year.[106] The work marks the final development of the Balkhī school and its author has won the highest praise: 'the greatest geographer of all time' according to Sprenger,[107] and if this has to be discounted somewhat since Sprenger was the first man to make al-Muqaddasī widely known in the West, we none the less find Barthold echoing his words: 'one of the greatest geographers of all time'.[108]

It seems desirable to see a little more closely what the basis of such judgments may be, and for the purpose we may make use of the excellent analysis of al-Muqaddasī's book furnished by J. H. Kramers.[109] After preliminary chapters on general geographical ideas and one in which he gives 'a comprehensive view of the empire of Islam, the geographical arrangement of its different parts and an approximate estimate of the distance from frontier to frontier', al-Muqaddasī proceeds to deal with the different countries separately.

Beginning from the centre of the Muslim empire he describes first Arabia, Iraq and Mesopotamia, then Syria, Egypt, and the Maghrib (North Africa), and finally Spain. He regards all these territories as forming the western half of Islam. The eastern part is subdivided into regions which are for the most part Iranian territory: Transoxiana (W. Turkestan), Khurāsān, North-West Iran (Adharbayjān, Armenia, Transcaucasia), Jibāl (practically ancient Media), Khūzistān (the South-West, ancient Elam or Susiana), Fars (Persis), Kirmān and finally Sind (the valley of the Indus). The desert of central Iran is also treated. Each chapter is generally divided into two parts, the first of which enumerates the different localities and gives good topographical descriptions, especially of the principal towns. The second part lists all sorts of subjects which the author groups under the label of 'particular characteristics'. Here there is a successive examination, for every territory envisaged, of the climate, the population with its good and bad qualities, its composition according to religion, the social groups, the professions, etc., commerce and its products, the products of the soil, the rivers, the mountains, the minerals and mines, the 'curiosities', which include not only the description of archaeological monuments but also all sorts of stories of fantastic character. There is found also in this subdivision an account of the weights and measures, moneys, languages, political climate, fiscal charges falling on the population and on commerce. In conclusion, itineraries are always furnished between the principal places, with distances generally given in days' journeys but sometimes also in *farsakhs*.

There is thus no subject of interest to modern geography which is not treated by al-Muqaddasī. We must here immediately remark that many authors who preceded or followed him also incorporate all these subjects into their works. Al-Muqaddasī, however, is at once the most encyclopaedic and systematic.[110]

A recent study of al-Muqaddasī,[111] while placing him firmly in the line of development through al-Iṣṭakhrī and Ibn Ḥawqal, finds in his book the expression of other tendencies in previous geographical work among the Arabs, and regards the author as the creator of 'total geographical science',[112] well on the way to the 'geographical syntheses', whose representative is al-Idrīsī. It is plain from the observations of the critics that in al-Muqaddasī we have already a fully developed geography with a scientific method, for the most part rigorously carried out, and a technical terminology.[113] To this we may add that alone of the elements of geography in Arabic, the mathematical science inherited from Ptolemy and Marinus is lacking. Al-Muqaddasī, considerable traveller, acute observer and great systematizer as he was, failed to produce a work of the range and general utility of al-Idrīsī's *Kitāb Rujayr*,[114] or even the compilations of Yāqūt and Abū'l-Fidā'.[115] His originality is not in question, but it may be that by omitting, for whatever reason, to make use of such texts as the Arabic translation of Ptolemy and the *Ṣūrat al-Arḍ* of al-Khwārizmī, for which the works of the purely Arabic school were no complete substitute, al-Muqaddasī fell short of producing a work of the widest interest. At most, what he did was to write a masterpiece on the descriptive geography of the lands of Islam.

Mention should also be made of some authors of special reports or memoirs who contributed to geographical knowledge in Arabic. One such was a certain Hārūn b. Yaḥyā who left an important account of Constantinople.[116] Another was Muslim b. Abī Muslim al-Jarmī, one of four or five thousand prisoners ransomed from Greek captivity at the river Lāmis (Lamus in Cilicia) in 231/845. Al-Masʿūdī who gives this information[117] adds that he was an authority on the Byzantines and their neighbours, the Bulgars, Ṣaqāliba, Khazars, etc., and wrote works (*muṣannafāt*) on the Greek emperors and dignitaries and their routes and territories. These works must have perished at an early date, but some use of them was made by Arabic authors interested in such topics, quite possibly by al-Masʿūdī himself,[118] and certainly by Ibn Khurradādhbih.[119]

We have also in Ibn Khurradādhbih the narrative of a journey of Sallām at-Tarjumān (Sallām the Interpreter) to the 'Wall of Gog and Magog', undertaken by him at the request of the Caliph al-Wāthiq (227/842–232/847).[120] Ibn Khurradādhbih states that he had the narrative directly from Sallām, and that Sallām later dictated it to him from a full report which he had drawn up in writing for the Caliph. The Dyke (*sadd*) of Dhū'l-Qarnayn, i.e. Alexander the Great, figured rather prominently in the minds of the Muslims, since it is mentioned in the Qur'ān,[121] where it appears as a barrier built by Alexander against Gog and Magog (i.e. the barbarian peoples of the North), and al-Wāthiq is said to have been apprehensive about whether it still held. Sallām the Interpreter, who dealt with the Caliph's Turkish correspondence and is credited with a knowledge of thirty languages, was indicated to him as the right man to be sent to see what was happening. An expedition of fifty persons was fitted out with money and suitable equipment for a journey into the north—felt and fur garments, and wooden stirrups. Under the leadership of Sallām they proceeded first to the Khazar country north of the Caucasus,[122] and then further afield into Central Asia. We need not attempt to follow their route, which has caused great difficulties to commentators who have attempted to describe it. De Goeje thought that they went as far as the Great Wall of China,[123] for which the length of time spent is perhaps sufficient: sixteen months out and twelve months back[124] via Samarqand and Bukhārā. The identification of the 'Wall of Gog and Magog' with the Great Wall is perhaps possible, and is still mentioned by commentators. A competing suggestion was offered by the Turkish scholar A. Zeki Validi Togan: the destination reached by Sallām and his party was the mountain pass known as the Iron Gate, Talka, north of Kulja in the eastern Tien Shan,[125] and in some ways this is more plausible. Determination of the point perhaps depends on the identification of the town of Īka mentioned in Ibn Khurradādhbih's narrative as three days' journey from the Wall either with Iki-oguz on the Ili river (Zeki Validi) or with Hami much further east, an earlier name of which is given as Igu.[126] The narrative was taken over by subsequent geographers, Ibn Rusta, who finds in it 'confusion and exaggeration',[127] al-Muqaddasī,[128] al-Idrīsī,[129] and others.[130] That some extensive expedition was undertaken by Sallām the Interpreter in al-Wāthiq's Caliphate does not seem open to doubt, since Ibn Khurradādhbih whose expertise in such matters is not questioned, evidently accepted the account as genuine.[131] He does not vouch for details, of course, and some appear to have been added as the story of the adventure passed from one writer to another.[132] The real reason for the expedition may, as J. Marquart suggested, have been rumours reaching the Caliphate of movements of the tribes in Central Asia, where, it appears, the powerful Uigur state had been overthrown shortly before this time (in 840).[133]

We must pass quickly over the journeys of Tamīm b. Baḥr al-Muṭṭawwiʿī and Abū Dulaf Misʿar b. al-Muhalhil. The first of these travelled to the Uigur capital on the Orkhon, Kharabalghasun, from a point east of Ṭarāz (Talas), apparently in the year A.D. 821, and on another occasion from nearly the same starting point to the territory of the Kimaks, a journey of eighty days northwards through the steppes in the general direction of the river Irtish and Siberia.[134] Abū Dulaf, on the other hand, was later (about A.D. 950), and left an account of his travels in two *Risālas* (Letters), the first describing in a confused manner what he claimed to have been his peregrinations in Turkestan, China and India, the second, discovered by A. Zeki Validi Togan in 1922, affording 'an easily recognizable itinerary' in western and northern Iran.[135] Both authors were extensively used by Yāqūt in his geographical dictionary *Muʿjam al-Buldān*, sometimes without acknowledgement, and both have been critically appraised by the late Professor V. Minorsky.

Better known and authenticated is the *faqīh* and traveller Ibn Faḍlān, who accompanied a mission from the Caliph al-Muqtadir to the Volga Bulgars in 309/921, and left a detailed *Riḥla* (travel-narrative) describing his experiences on that memorable journey.[136] Ibn Faḍlān's *Riḥla* like the narratives of Tamīm b. Baḥr and Abū Dulaf, had been used by Yāqūt, but a better text was forthcoming in the Meshed manuscript discovered by Zeki Validi in 1922. There is no question with Ibn Faḍlān of painfully piecing together facts of obscure import or doubtful authenticity, in order to extract from his narrative a credible account of the people and places visited by the traveller. This *Riḥla* stands out clearly in full historical and geographical light, and in the words of the discoverer of the new text it 'takes its place at the head of the works of the Muslim geographers of the ninth–tenth century as one of the most trustworthy sources for the study of the ethnic and cultural relations of the Aral-Caspian region, which bridges the gap between the times of the rule of the pre-Christian Scythians, on the one hand, and of the Mongols of the thirteenth century, on the other, of whom we have better knowledge'.[137] Ibn Faḍlān affords information on the little-known kingdom of the Khazars, on the manners and customs of the Rūs (i.e. pagan Norsemen), including a detailed scene at the burial of one of their chiefs, and on many other matters, which it is difficult or impossible to find elsewhere, and we have in fact in his narrative, in addition to what it gives us on the peoples of the steppe bordering on the Arab Caliphate, not only one of the few notices of what was later called Magna Bulgaria (i.e. Bulgar territory on the Volga and Kama rivers), but also data of importance for the history of the primitive Russian state.

Another journey, also in the lands of the north, though this time in western and central Europe, and almost as important and interesting, was performed by Ibrahīm b. Yaʿqūb at-Ṭarṭūshī, i.e. of Ṭarṭūsha (Tortosa) in north-east Spain in or about A.D. 973, in which year Ibrahīm b. Yaʿqūb appeared at the court of Otto I. This narrative too has had to be pieced together in recent times by scholars, but when reconstructed, it is a text which throws unexpected light on a variety of dark matters.[138]

5. Conclusion

It will thus be seen that when the great geographical compilers in Arabic came to write in the twelfth and thirteenth centuries of our era, there was a rich variety of material on which they could draw and a geographical area wider in many respects than Ptolemy's available for which facts had already been registered. (Nothing has been said here about North Africa, where the Arabic geographers had a conspectus further than their classical predecessors, stretching across the Sahara as far as the Niger and beyond the Sudan to the equatorial regions.) But on the other hand to bring everything together proved impossible. Important works had evidently been lost in the centuries which intervened since the time of their composition. We have already spoken of the Arabic translation of Marinus. The situation is further illustrated by a *Kitāb Jughrāfiyā* or *Jaʿrāfiya*[139] (Book of Geography) of a certain Muḥammad b. abī Bakr az-Zuhrī, who lived *c.* 532/1137–8. This work claims to be derived from a copy made by al-Fazārī from the Geography of al-Ma'mūn, i.e. apparently the text accompanying al-Ma'mūn's map made three centuries earlier, as we saw (p. 152). Az-Zuhrī's book, however, contains personal recollections, for example of a cavern near Granada visited by him, and citations from such works as al-Masʿūdī's *Murūj adh-Dhahab* (written in the tenth century), and is certainly not an exact transcript of al-Ma'mūn's Geography. At most, it contains elements of the latter, which may be taken to have been irretrievably lost, certainly as a unitary work, by the twelfth century. There was also the difficulty of bringing together at one time and place such works as survived. The point is made clear by al-Idrīsī's list of his sources,[140] which, although it contains the titles of several books not at present known, is by no means exhaustive. (Al-Idrīsī was apparently not in a position to consult either al-Iṣṭakhrī or al-Muqaddasī, whose works were of course in existence in his time.) To this must be added the somewhat desultory character of much Arabic geographical writing, and the shortcomings of the copyists. It is, on the whole, little to be wondered at that the final synthesis which would have summed up all the geographical work which had been done in Arabic was never made. What is remarkable rather is that in the last period, i.e. the twelfth and thirteenth centuries, so much was done by Yāqūt, Abū'l-Fidā' and especially al-Idrīsī. The geographical works of the two former are extremely useful and meritorious,[141] but remain compilations, made by men of encyclopaedic knowledge indeed, but whose interests were diversified, as their other works show. Al-Idrīsī, on the other hand, was much more a geographer *pur sang*. His method of ascertaining the facts can be read in his Preface, in which he tells us that he spent fifteen years on his great work.[142] It is interesting to note that like al-Ma'mūn's Geography the 'Book of Roger' was also based on a model of the earth's surface, in al-Idrīsī's case a silver planisphere constructed with the greatest attention to scientific accuracy. The planisphere has perished, melted down, no doubt, in some contingency, in Sicily or elsewhere, but the book remains, shortly to be edited, it is hoped, thanks to Italian enterprise, for the first time on the scale which it deserves. It is certainly a great monument of Arabic and Muslim geography and the measure of al-Idrīsī's achievement can perhaps best be conveyed not by comparing him with his predecessors or contemporaries in the East, but rather by giving him his place simply as a geographer among geographers. Here he stands with Ptolemy, and if again we refrain from pressing the comparison, there is no doubt that, as far as cartography is concerned, the maps of the 'Book of Roger' were superior to anything produced in Europe or in the Muslim East (let him who doubts this last compare Ibn Ḥawqal's Mediterranean[143] with al-Idrīsī's) between Ptolemy and Matthew Paris.

Chapter 5

Arabic philosophy

1. Forerunners

The principal influence on the development of philosophy among the Arabs is generally admitted to have been Greek,[1] though there may have been other strains as well, for example Indian,[2] and the earliest stirrings seem to have come from Alexandria (finally captured by the Muslims in 25/646). There are notices in some detail of Yaḥyā an-Naḥwī (John the Grammarian), identified with Philoponus, as in contact with the Arab leader ʿAmr b. al-ʿĀṣ at the time of the Arab conquest of Egypt.[3] The work of Philoponus as a commentator on Aristotle is well known, and a commentary on the *Kitāb as-Samāʿ aṭ-Ṭabīʿī* (Aristotle's *Physics*) by Yaḥyā an-Naḥwī with a reference in the text to the date of composition as 343 of the era of Diocletian (A.D. 627) is mentioned in the *Fihrist*.[4] This accords well with the older dating of Philoponus, which placed him in the seventh century,[5] but the newer dating makes him considerably earlier (first half of the sixth century),[6] so that the sources may have confused two distinct persons.[7] In any case,[8] there is reason to think that philosophical activity continued at Alexandria down through the sixth century and even later, since the Greek philosophers who took refuge at the Persian court after the closing of the schools of Athens by Justinian in 529 returned to the territory of the Byzantine empire and settled at Alexandria.[9] When therefore we read that the Umayyad prince Khālid b. Yazīd (a minor in A.D. 683), who is often credited with 'philosophical' interests in general as well as his more or less well authenticated alchemical interest, summoned to his presence, presumably to Damascus, 'a number of Greek philosophers who resided in the Egyptian city',[10] the statement has nothing astonishing about it, and we probably have to think of something like a continuous tradition of study and teaching in Alexandria going back to classical times. The existence of a real school seems proved by notices that a relation of Khālid b. Yazīd, ʿUmar b. ʿAbd al-ʿAzīz, when he came to be Caliph in 99/717 as ʿUmar II, 'transferred the instruction from al-Iskandariyya (Alexandria) to Anṭākiya (Antioch), whence later it passed to Ḥarrān in the days of al-Mutawakkil (Caliph 232/847–247/861)'.[11] The context clearly envisages the teaching of philosophy, though elsewhere when ʿUmar is found in contact with a professor at Alexandria, he is a doctor,[12] and what may have been the earliest translation in Islam, published under ʿUmar's auspices, the *Kunnāsh* or 'Pandects' of Aaron the Priest, also an Alexandrian, was a medical work (see pp. 38, 220).

The fact is that we know very little for certain about the beginnings of philosophy in Islam. Some positive affirmations can be made. We can assume that philosophical thinking, or at least the *disposition* to think philosophically, first arose from reflection on the ideas, not necessarily consistent, contained explicitly or implicitly in the Qur'ān, that is it had the same source as the movement of rationalizing theology represented by the Muʿtazila sect, though the Muʿtazila was and remained distinct from the *falāsifa* (plural of *failasūf*),the exponents of *falsafa* (Greek philosophy). Further, we are entitled to think that philosophy first made an impression upon a few highly placed, wealthy individuals, not on the middle and lower orders. The Umayyads Khālid b. Yazīd and ʿUmar b. ʿAbd al-ʿAzīz seem to illustrate this, and it is certain that al-Kindī, presently to be mentioned, the first of the great philosophers in Islam, came of a distinguished family and enjoyed all the advantages of money and social position. A third consideration of the greatest importance is that evidently philosophy had to wait for the translation of the right kind of texts before it could develop. That translation into Arabic began in Umayyad times (i.e. before A.D. 750) is beyond doubt. When the first translation of a philosophical work was made is uncertain. The Qāḍī Ṣāʿid, an eleventh-century author living in Muslim Spain, states that four fundamental works on logic, the *Categories*, *De Interpretatione* and *Analytics* of Aristotle and the *Eisagoge* of Porphyry, were translated by ʿAbd Allāh b. al-Muqaffaʿ (died 142/759) and that according to Ibn al-Muqaffaʿ himself only the first of these had previously been translated.[13] This is so far confirmed by Ibn an-Nadīm in the *Fihrist*, who mentions extracts and compendia (*mukhtaṣarāt wa-jawāmiʿ*) of the *Categories* and *De Interpretatione* by Ibn al-Muqaffaʿ.[14] This would put these translations, presumably from

Pahlavi, far back in time (and of course the previous translation of the *Categories*, if it existed, earlier still). That they were ever made by Ibn al-Muqaffaʿ has been doubted, and it is perhaps better to suppose that they were the work of his son.[15] However this may be, we have a list of translators in the *Fihrist*, headed by 'Iṣṭifan (Stephanus) the Old', who translated books of alchemy, etc. for Khālid b. Yazīd', and 'al-Biṭrīq, who lived in the days of al-Manṣūr and was ordered by him to translate things from the ancient books'.[16] In another list given by Ibn Abī Uṣaybiʿa[17] al-Biṭrīq is preceded by Asṭāth (Eustathius) and Ibn Bakus (Bakūs), but the order is not chronological. Asṭāth translated for al Kindī[18] (born shortly before 185/801), and Ibn Bakus, who corrected earlier translations, was not among the first translators himself.[19] Of the early translators al-Biṭrīq at least is more than simply a name, and his son Abū Zakariyyā' Yaḥyā b. al-Biṭrīq, an associate of al-Ḥasan b. Sahl, the minister of al-Ma'mūn from 196/811 for several years, produced versions of the *Timaeus* of Plato, the *De Coelo* (*Kitāb as-Samā' wa'l-ʿĀlam*) and other works of Aristotle, including a compendium of the *De Anima* (*Jawāmiʿ Kitāb an-Nafs*).[20] Yaḥyā b. al-Biṭrīq is perhaps the first who translated Greek philosophical works in Islam, or at least the first to do so on an extensive scale.[21] Since, however, he is credited with translating only the *Prior Analytics*[22] of the works of Aristotle upon logic, it may well be that other parts of the Organon were already in Arabic.

There is at all events enough evidence to show that by the time of al-Kindī books of Greek philosophy were becoming available in Arabic, and that while he no doubt gave an impulse to translation, he was not the originator of the translation movement. Nor was he a translator himself. This has frequently been said in ancient and modern times, and we have the statement in precise terms in the *Ṭabaqāt al-Umam* of the Qādī Ṣāʿid and elsewhere[23] that al-Kindī was one of the four most proficient translators in Islam.[24] The source of this is Abū Maʿshar al-Balkhī (Albumasar) in his astrological work *Kitāb al-Mudhākarāt*, but as he also speaks of al-Kindī as the Persian translator who translated Greek and Coptic books,[25] he is not to be taken very seriously. Certainly al-Kindī was not a translator in the ordinary sense of the word. His function was rather to diffuse the new knowledge derived from the translated texts among the Arab upper class, so that he might with some reservation be called a popularizer. As a student and teacher, he was above all an interpreter of the texts. But indeed it does not seem profitable to concern ourselves with the exact meaning of Abū Maʿshar's statement, which he appears to have made without any special regard for the facts.

2. Al-Kindī

Khālid b. Yazīd was called by Ibn an-Nadīm the 'scholar of the Marwānids' (*ḥakīm Āl Marwān*).[26] Al-Kindī was the 'philosopher of the Arabs' (*faylasūf al-ʿArab*).[27] Analogy would suggest that the latter expression means the philosopher of Arab race rather than the one who taught the Arabs philosophy, though indeed this claim might also be made for him.[28] As to his name and descent, he was Abū Yūsuf Yaʿqūb b. Isḥāq al-Kindī, with a long line of ancestors going back through al-Ashʿath b. Qays, the adviser of ʿAlī, to Kinda in pre-Islamic times.[29] It was the same stock as had given rise to the famous poet Imruʾ al-Qays, about whom something has already been said, and could be traced back to the legendary Yaʿrub b. Qaḥṭān.[30]

Though al-Kindī the philosopher does not appear to have been descended through the same royal line as Imruʾ al-Qays,[31] he probably belonged to the ruling family of Kinda. His grandfather is said to have held governorships for the Banū Hāshim (i.e. the ʾAbbāsids),[32] and his father had been governor of al-Kūfa. At the time of his father's death, probably towards the end of the Caliphate of Hārūn ar-Rashīd (170/786–193/809),[33] the family was still living at the latter place, but some time afterwards al-Kindī came to al-Baṣra, and then to Baghdad. Since he was already known for his philosophical attainments at the court of al-Maʾmūn (Caliph 198/813–218/833), Abū Rīda thinks that he was born some time before 185/801, the date which had previously been given.[34] We cannot in fact do much better than earlier investigators who put al-Kindī's birth about A.D. 800, for his Arabic biographers, the earliest of whom is Ibn an-Nadīm in the passage already cited from the *Fihrist* of 377/987, have no date of birth and no information about his teachers. The date of al-Kindī's death is also matter for conjecture, but we may take it that Abū Rīda's estimate 'towards the end of 252/866'[35] is not far out.

Al-Kindī served the Caliphs al-Maʾmūn and al-Muʿtaṣim. We hear of him particularly as the instructor of Aḥmad b. al-Muʿtaṣim, the ʿAbbāsid prince who was nearly elected Caliph on the death of al-Muntaṣir in 248/862, when he was the candidate of the Turkish chief Bughā al-Kabīr. In the event his nephew was elected, Aḥmad b. Muḥammad b. al-Muʿtaṣim, a young man who appeared less dangerous to the *de facto* electors. He took the name of al-Mustaʿīn. Aṣ-Ṣūlī (d. 335/946) has a circumstantial story in which he relates that the chiefs were finally swayed by Muḥammad b. Mūsā al-Munajjim who persuaded them not to appoint Aḥmad b. al-Muʿtaṣim, on the ground that he was a man of strong character who had already been passed over twice (at the accessions of al-Mutawakkil and al-Muntaṣir), and would neither favour them nor even allow power to remain in their hands. It was much better to appoint a younger man, he said, and this they in fact did. But the motive, according to aṣ-Ṣūlī's story, for the advice thus to set aside Aḥmad b. al-Muʿtaṣim was really the enmity between Muḥammad and Aḥmad his brother, the sons of Mūsā al-Munajjim,[36] and al-Kindī, and their determination not to see his pupil and friend (*ṣāḥib*) attaining the Caliphate.[37]

The hostility of Muḥammad and Aḥmad, the sons of Mūsā al-Munajjim (with a younger brother al-Ḥasan often called the Banū Mūsā b. Shākir), was no doubt due in part to al-Kindī's Muʿtazilite opinions.[38] On the other hand, the philosopher seems to have been a man of stiff temperament, who displeased others besides the Banū Mūsā in the course of his career. He appears to have had a popular reputation as a miser,[39] and this may have served Abū Maʿshar Jaʿfar b. Muḥammad al-Balkhī, who resented al-Kindī, to stir the commons against him. Abū Maʿshar later completely changed his attitude, and at the age of forty-seven, it is said, gave up the profession of traditionist in which he had held a respectable place, to devote himself, first, in imitation of al-Kindi to the exact sciences, arithmetic (*ḥisāb*) and geometry (*handasa*), and later, since he had no great success in these branches, to judicial astrology (*aḥkām an-nujūm*), in which he became a leading authority.[40] His name was well known to the Latins in the Middle Ages as Albumasar, sometimes Geofar.[41] Al-Bayhaqī reports that there is a difference of opinion in regard to the religion of al-Kindī, some saying that he was a Jew, others that he was a Christian.[42] This probably indicates opposition during his lifetime, no doubt from the narrowly orthodox. (Abū Rīda points out that, on the contrary, al-Kindī appears from his works to have been a good Muslim, zealous for the tenets of his religion and prepared to defend them on rational, philosophical grounds. So far as practice goes, his death is said to have been caused by a scruple against the continued use of wine in treatment of a physical condition.)[43] The most serious attack of the Banū Mūsā on al-Kindī came after the accession of al-Mutawakkil (Caliph 232/847–247/861), who did not share the views of his Muʿtazilite predecessors. We read that the brothers succeeded in complicating his relations with various persons of distinction, especially the Caliph himself, so that al-Mutawakkil had the philosopher scourged, and the Banū Shākir were able to take his books and transfer them to al-Baṣra where they placed them in a special library, called al-Kindiyya. A project of theirs having failed, they fell into disgrace with al-Mutawakkil, but the court astronomer Sind b. ʿAlī undertook to reinstate them in the Caliph's favour if they restored the books of al-Kindī.[44]

We should also notice the critical estimate of al-Kindī which appears in the *Ṭabaqāt al-Umam* of the Qādī Ṣāʿid (tenth century) and in al-Qifṭī (thirteenth century). With al-Kindī's works in their totality the Qāḍī was certainly unacquainted, for he puts their total at somewhat above fifty, whereas in the *Fihrist*, Ibn Abī Uṣaybiʿa and elsewhere we have the titles of over 300.[45] Ṣāʿid complains that in a work on the divine unity entitled *Fam adh-Dhahab* (Golden-Mouth)[46] al-Kindī has adopted the doctrine of Plato concerning the creation of the world outside of time and supports this opinion with ill-based arguments.[47] Al-Kindī's logical works, none of which at present have been recovered, are also subjected to rather severe criticism. They had, we are told, a great success with the public, but are not authoritative. Apart from these writings al-Kindī has other works where he expresses false (*fāsid*) opinions and doctrines far removed from the truth.[48] Al-Qifṭī in the main follows the Qāḍī Ṣāʿid, and repeats his predecessor's charge that al-Kindī had used rhetorical and poetical arguments[49] (Ṣāʿid had said 'sophistical and rhetorical'). On the other hand, Ibn Abī Uṣaybiʿa is ready to defend the philosopher, declaring that the Qāḍī Ṣāʿid appears to have a great prejudice against al-Kindī, and that what he says by way of criticism 'does not lower the science of al-Kindī, and does not discourage people from examining his books (in his own time, he means, i.e. the thirteenth century A.D.) and profiting from them'.[48] Ibn abī Uṣaybiʿa, thinks Abū Rīda, is no doubt right—and we should agree, because people still study al-Kindī with profit—and his modern biographer adds that the Qāḍī Ṣāʿid and al-Qifṭī have a common principle inimical to the philosopher or else they had a limited knowledge or lack of understanding of what he wrote.[49]

Al-Kindī got back his books, with the help, it seems, of Sind b. ʿAlī, but did not recover court favour. He withdrew into retirement, permanently, it would appear. It is perhaps to this period of his life that certain verses of al-Kindī's, no doubt authentic,[52] are to be attributed, not in themselves great poetry, but well expressing the philosophical ideal:

> The followers are exalted above the chiefs,
> So close your eyes or lower them.
> Make small your person and restrain your hands,
> And seat yourself in the interior of your house.
> In the presence of your King seek the heights,
> And enjoy society today in solitude.
> For it is in the hearts of men that wealth is found
> And in our souls that greatness lies.[53]

For a general view of al-Kindī, the most useful works for a long time have probably been those of Flügel[54] and Loth.[55] The first of these is a bio-bibliographical study, representing all or the most of what was known about the philosopher up to the date of publication. The second discusses him primarily as an astrologer, and deals in particular with a *Risāla* (Treatise) of al-Kindī on the subject of the duration of the Arab empire (*Fī Mulk al-ʿArab wa-Kammiyyatihā*), which on astrological principles he calculates will come to an end in 693/1293.[56] (This may be regarded as a remarkably close approximation to 656/1258, when Baghdad was captured by the Mongols of Hūlāgū, and the Arab Caliphate did come to an end.) Another important work published much later, the *Kitāb Kīmiyāʾ al-ʿIṭr waʾt-Taṣʿīdāt* (Book of the Alchemy or Chemistry of Perfume and Distillations), attributed to al-Kindī, at least represents him as actively concerned with chemical experiments.[57] But al-Kindī as a philosopher was scarcely known in the original, in modern times,[58] till the discovery by the German Orientalist Hellmut Ritter in an Istanbul library[59] of a manuscript containing a *Majmūʿ Rasāʾil al-Kindī* (Collection of the Treatises of al-Kindī). The discovery was signalized in 1932,[60] and some subsequent studies were made. It was not, however, till 1950 that a substantial number of philosophical treatises from the collection was published by Abū Rīda in his book already referred to more than once.[61] In his preface (distinct from the introduction already quoted) Abū Rīda mentions the circumstances in which his work was begun. He had the assistance of Fuʾād Firʿawnī Bey of the

Egyptian Ministry of Foreign Affairs in obtaining a photographic copy of the manuscript for al-Azhar. Upon this he commenced to prepare his edition, which must be allowed to mark an epoch in the study of al-Kindī. (There was already another photograph of the Aya Sofia manuscript in Cairo, at the Dār al-Kutub al-Miṣriyya, but this Abū Rīda was unaware of at the time.) The manuscript consisted of two parts. The first contained a collection of treatises, mostly on mathematics, by Thābit b. Qurra (died 288/901). The second part began with a new numeration, and was headed 'Part I of the books and treatises of Yaʿqūb b. Isḥāq al-Kindī, containing sixty works'. Actually the contents included one or two mathematical works by others, for example by Ibn al-Haytham on squaring the circle, and a work by Ibn al-Qūhī. But these are extraneous to the collection of al-Kindī's works, and have been inserted in it. The *rasā'il* of al-Kindī are in an old hand (Kufan *naskhī*) almost without diacritical points. The manuscript is dated by Professor Ritter to the fifth/eleventh century. Apparently it is stated on the manuscript that it belonged to Ibn Sīnā (Avicenna), who died in 428/1037, and that it is in his hand.[62] This does not seem specially likely, and can apply, if at all, presumably only to the *rasā'il* of Thābit b. Qurra, since there are many mistakes in the copy of the works of al-Kindī. Further, there are in fact only twenty-nine, not sixty, *rasā'il* of al-Kindī at present. Of these Abū Rīda has published fourteen *rasā'il* in Part i, and others in Part ii of his book. This constitutes no doubt the greatest single step forward in our knowledge of the 'philosopher of the Arabs' for a long time.

Abū Rīda rightly points out that hitherto it has been impossible to pass beyond the domain of inference or even of conjecture in regard to such questions as the nature of al-Kindī's philosophy and his place in the history of philosophy. He has been regarded differently by different writers, primarily as a scientist or natural philosopher, a physician and mathematical astronomer, a popularizer, or a speculative theologian and Muʿtazilite.[63] The exact orientation and cast of his thought become apparent, or at least much more precise than before, by the study of the recently recovered treatises.[64]

We here give the titles, with comments in some cases, of the treatises following Abū Rīda's order. This is designed to present the purely philosophical *rasā'il* first, considering in this their importance and interconnection of subject, also their appropriateness (*makāna*) to afford a picture of al-Kindī's philosophical view, and does not follow the order of the manuscript.[65]

1. *On the First Philosophy* (metaphysics: knowledge of the First Cause). To the Caliph al-Muʿtaṣim. It contains an impassioned defence against obscurantists,[66] and a prayer of al-Kindī.[67]
2. *On Definitions and Descriptions.* These are taken from the different sciences, and the principle of arrangement is not clear, since the work lacks an introduction.
3. *On the True First Agent and the Second Agent.* The First Agent is God, who alone acts without being acted upon. The Second Agent is created and acted upon by the First Agent, and is therefore Agent only metaphorically (*biʾl-majāz*)—the case of all created things.
4. *Elucidation of the Finitude of the Body of the World.* Uses mathematical axioms, a characteristic of al-Kindī's argumentation.
5. *On the Nature of That Which Cannot Possess Infinity* (e.g. Time and Movement).
6. *On the Unity of God and the Finitude of the Body of the World.*
7. *In Explanation of the Proximate Efficient Cause of Generation and Corruption.* To al-Muʿtaṣim or al-Kindī's pupil, Aḥmad b. al-Muʿtaṣim. After mentioning Aristotle's Four Causes (Material, Formal, Efficient and Final), and explaining that the Ultimate Efficient Cause of all generation and corruption is God (discussed in the treatise, no. 1 above, to which he here refers)[68] al-Kindī goes on to isolate the Proximate Efficient Cause, which he finds in the movements of the heavenly bodies according to natural, divinely appointed law, a conclusion to which he is led, in part, by considering the physical and intellectual differences in the inhabitants of the torrid, temperate and frigid zones of the earth's surface.
8. *In Explanation of the Adoration of the Farthest Body and its Obedience to God.* To Aḥmad b. al-Muʿtaṣim. This was written with reference to a question of his pupil about the meaning of the Qurʾān verse 55, 5/6, and is more obviously religious in character than the previous treatises. Like no. 7, it was composed after the *risāla* on the First Philosophy (no. 1). The principle is laid down at the beginning that the words of the Qurʾān are to be understood by rational standards (*biʾl-maqāyīs al-ʿaqliyya*).[69] Al-Kindī is not explicit, but his development clearly implies that he

understands the Qur'ān verse (*wa'n-najm wa'sh-shajar yasjudāni*) as 'The stars and the trees do obeisance'. This is of some interest, because al-Bayḍāwī and some modern translators[70] instead of 'stars' have '(herbaceous) plants', or something of the kind, for the first word. They are almost certainly wrong, cf. *Sūr.* 22, 18.[71] The *risāla* contains the same ideas as no. 7 on the movements of the heavenly bodies as governed by law and influencing life on earth, and adds the conceptions of the celestial sphere and its contents as in some sense a sentient animal (*ḥayy mumayyiz*), and as the macrocosm compared with man, the microcosm.

9. *On Non-corporeal Essences*, e.g. the soul.
10. and 11. Two short pieces *On the Soul.*
12. *On the Nature of Sleep and Dreams.*
13. *On the Intellect.*
14. *On the Number of the Books of Aristotle and What is Requisite for the Study of Philosophy.*

Abū Rīda's Part ii, though valuable in providing additional texts of al-Kindī in the original Arabic, is of somewhat miscellaneous character,[72] and we need not consider it further here.

What are we to conclude of al-Kindī as a philosopher on the basis of what has already been said, and especially in the light of the new material? His metaphysical interest stands out clear. It is as a metaphysician that al-Kindī meets us in many of the treatises, though elsewhere he appears conspicuously as a man of science. The combination of natural science and metaphysics both developed to a high degree is reminiscent of Aristotle, and quite clearly, as we can see, the influence of Aristotle on his thought has been more potent than Plato, who is mentioned only occasionally in these works.[73] Yet al-Kindī is not dominated by Aristotle's thought or overpowered by his reputation, which he may not indeed have fully realized, assuming him to have been relatively ignorant of the development of Greek philosophy after Aristotle. He appears much more under the influence of orthodox Muslim ideas, based on the Qur'ān. We can be sure that speculation on the eternity of the world, as well as on its infinity, and speculative views in general were not congenial to him. On the other hand, his rationalism is everywhere apparent, and it is the pursuit of the argument on purely intellectual grounds, starting from his Islamic premises, which leads him into opposition to Aristotle, for example on the influence of the heavenly bodies. It appears to be a mistake to look for the origin of al-Kindī's view that the movements of the heavenly bodies affect life on earth in any specific astrological teaching of earlier times. Though he was acquainted with the *Almagest* (translated and commented on for Yaḥya b. Khālid the Barmecide, according to the *Fihrist*,[74] i.e. before the fall of the Barmecides in 187/803) and perhaps other works of Ptolemy,[75] he does not in these philosophical works refer to him or to more esoteric authorities for the so characteristic astrological doctrine of the influence of the stars, which he appears to have reached as affording the most logical cause of terrestrial changes. This is not to say that he concluded independently that generation and corruption were due to changes in the heavens, for we may assume that this was a view generally held from earlier times. Rather he adopted it because, however absurd according to presentday notions, it appeared a reasonable solution, in maintaining which he was prepared to oppose authority, principally Aristotle. This speaks for al-Kindī's independence of mind, not to say originality, in this instance, and in general. Further, we have to consider that al-Kindī's position was to a great extent adopted by his successors, not simply those who like Abū Maʿshar and as-Sarakhsī[76] had come directly under his influence, but by the Arabic philosophers as a whole. These naturally differed on many points, for example, as Ibn Khaldūn, perhaps with a shade of cynicism, notices, Ibn Sīnā (Avicenna), the rich vizier, disbelieved in the practicability of alchemy, whereas al-Fārābī, a poor man, accepted it as feasible.[77] He actually wrote on the subject.[78] But in the general cast of their philosophy the greatest names, that is to say, al-Fārābī and Ibn Sīnā in the East, and in the West Ibn Bājja (Avempace) and Ibn Rushd (Averroes),[79] are seen to have followed the example of al-Kindī in relying on the methodology of Aristotle (logic, etc.), while at the same time striving to maintain the truths of revelation, in its Islamic form, and in attending, to a greater or less degree, to natural phenomena after the Aristotelian manner.[80] Al-Kindī's influence on the subsequent development of philosophy in Islam is not easily to be traced in citations in books. He appears to be ignored by his successor al-Fārābī, not to mention the later masters, though of course he finds a place in all the histories of philosophy.[81] At the same time, we must allow that in the works of al-Kindī we are in the same climate of thought as in the later Arabic philosophers, and it is difficult to avoid concluding not simply that many of the conditions which formed his work have formed theirs, but that in some sense he showed the best or perhaps the only way along which Arabic philosophy, which also of necessity had to be Islamic philosophy, could develop, and was a real innovator, who old-fashioned[82] or not—this was no doubt the reason why he ceased to be much quoted[83]—was at the head of an impressive movement.[84]

One important technical innovation introduced by al-Kindī and subsequently retained by later Arabic philosophers was the use of the *risāla* form for scientific purposes,[85] involving the extension of the meaning of this word from 'message, (written) communication, letter' to something like 'treatise'. On the other hand, while in the second of his works from the *Majmūʿ* mentioned above, *On Definitions and Descriptions*, he often offers succinct and telling equivalents, for example 'form' is that by which the thing is what it is (*aṣ-ṣūra ash-shayʾ alladhī bihi ash-shayʾ huwa mā huwa*),[86] or again 'the state of man, humanity' is life, rationality and death (*al-insāniyya hiya al-ḥayyāt waʾn-nuṭq waʾl-mawt*), 'the state of the angels' is life and rationality (*al-malāʾikiyya al-ḥayyāt waʾn-nuṭq*), 'the state of the animals, animality' is life and death (*al-bahīmiyya hiya al-ḥayyāt waʾl-mawt*),[87] his style in general is not easy and his philosophical vocabulary includes a number of expressions which are far from being readily understood and make great demands upon the reader. He sometimes adopts old words, e.g. *al-ays* (correlative with the common word *laysa*, 'is not') which he uses in the plural *aysāt* for 'existents', and then derives from it *aysiyya*, 'existence', also a verb *yuʾayyisu* meaning 'brings into existence' with the verbal noun *at-taʾyīs* for 'bringing into existence'. So God is *al-muʾayyis*, and al-Kindī can say, for example, that God is *al-muʾayyis al-aysāt ʿan lays*. Similarly he uses, from the pronoun *huwa*, 'he' or 'it', such expressions as *al-huwa*, for the specific existent which is indicated by our saying *huwa*, and *al-huwiyya* for the specific partial existence perceived by sense, as contrasted with *al-ḥaqīqa* and *al-māhiyya*, the 'truth' and 'true nature', which are intellected.[88] Many similar instances could be given of unusual words and expressions in al-Kindī, which were later for the most part dropped. No doubt Arabic philosophical vocabulary in his time is as yet in process of formation, and in this regard it is difficult to determine how far he has moved from the terms as rendered by the earliest translators. It is, however, evident that the use of expressions which non-specialists might consider incorrect and could not readily understand must have lost him readers, as time passed,[89] and there is a great difference between al-Kindī's difficult style and the simple language, for the most part, of al-Fārābī.[90]

3. Al-Fārābī

Al-Fārābī would seem to be first mentioned in the *Kitāb as-Saʿāda waʾl-Isʿād* (Book of Happiness and Causing Happiness) of alʿĀmirī (Abūʾl-Ḥasan Muḥammad b. Abī Dharr), a younger contemporary, who was born and bred in Nīshāpūr and was a pupil of a famous man, Abū Zayd Aḥmad b. Sahl al-Balkhī, already mentioned as a geographer (see p. 164), who was something of a philosopher besides, having been himself a pupil of al-Kindī. Abū Zayd al-Balkhī died in 322/934. The apparent reference to al-Fārābī in al-ʿĀmirī's book may date from about this time, for although al-ʿĀmirī, like his teacher, was longlived and is said to have survived till 381/992, he speaks not of a famous philosopher al-Fārābī, called in later times the 'Second Master' (*al-muʿallim ath-thānī*), second, that is, after Aristotle, but of 'one of the new aspirants to philosophy' or, as Professor Arberry translates 'a modern philosophaster' (*baʿḍ al-ḥadath min al-mutafalsifīn*).[91] There follows a characteristically Alfarabian opinion concerning the division of authority in a state when all the qualities of the ideal ruler are not present in one person. Al-ʿĀmirī insists that this has no meaning, and that there can only be one chief.[92]

Al-Fārābī then was born towards the end of the third/ninth century[93] at a place called Wasīj, two leagues from Fārāb,[94] the capital of a district of the same name on the Syr Daryā (Sayḥūn, Jaxartes). Fārāb in the tenth century was an important place with 70,000 inhabitants.[95] It was later called Utrār, and it was there that Tīmūr died in 807/1405 when about to start his march on China.[96] Al-Fārābī's name, in full Abū Naṣr Muḥammad b. Muḥammad b. Ṭarkhān b. Ūzlāgh al-Fārābī, indicates that he was of Turkish extraction and belonged to a family in which the profession of Islam was recent, his father Muḥammad or perhaps his grandfather having apparently been the first to be converted. The latter's name Ṭarkhān signifies in Turkish a military officer, implying at least in later times feudal privileges and exemptions,[97] so that we may probably consider al-Fārābī's family to have been, if not rich, at least respectable. The same impression is gained from his being said to have accompanied his father, also described as a military officer,[98] to Baghdad, while still young. Whatever schooling he may have had previously, it was to teachers like the Christian Yūḥannā b. Ḥaylān who flourished under the Caliph al-Muʿtaḍid (279/892–289/902) and died in Baghdad in the days of al-Muqtadir (296/908–320/932)[99] that al-Fārābī owed his initiation in philosophy. Addicting himself to hard study—he is said to have read the Arabic translation of the *Physics* of Aristotle forty times—and living simply, then as later in life, al-Fārābī gained an extensive knowledge of Greek philosophy and gradually established a reputation. He is said to have been persuaded to visit Rayy in Persia by aṣ-Ṣaḥib Ibn ʿAbbād, but the story told by al-Bayhaqī (à propos of autograph copies of al-Fārābī's works by himself or his pupil Yaḥyā b. ʿAdī which al-Bayhaqī had seen in a library there) is apocryphal,[100] not so much by reason of its content (al-Fārābī charms a company to sleep by playing upon a lute), as by the date of aṣ-Ṣāhīb Ibn ʿAbbād, who, born probably in 326/938,[101] was young at the time of al-Fārābī's death (see below) and not yet in a position to exercise the patronage for which he was afterwards celebrated. On the other hand, al-Fārābī was late in life welcomed at the court of the Ḥamdānids in Syria, in 330/941–2 according to Ibn Abī Uṣaybiʿa,[102] and later still he paid a visit to Egypt. In Rajab 339/December 950 while travelling between Damascus and Ascalon in Palestine, he and his companions were set upon by robbers. Seeing that there was no escape, al-Fārābī dismounted and fought till he was killed.[103] There is no reason to doubt the account, but it seems less appropriate if the philosopher was then approaching eighty. We should probably bring his birth year nearer to the end of the ninth century than is sometimes done.[104]

Al-Fārābī wrote about alchemy, as we saw (in a highly theoretical manner), and about music.[105] Specially noteworthy is his massive *Kitāb al-Mūsīqā* (*Mūsīqī*) *al-Kabīr*, described as 'the greatest work on Arabic music written by the Arabs from the dawn of Islam to the present day'.[106] The work, dedicated to the *wazīr* Abū Jaʿfar Muḥammad b. al-Qāsim al-Kharkhī or al-Kavajī, begins with a statement of the insufficiency of Greek works on music translated into Arabic, but at the same time shows itself heavily indebted to the Greeks by giving an account of the limits of the civilized world which is clearly the Greek *oikoumenē* adapted to the conditions of the Arab empire in the 10th century (pp. 108–10 of the edition), by reference to the musical theories of Aristoxenus as well as Pythagoras (p. 204) and by listing the Greek musical 'modes', Dorian, Phrygian, Lydian, Mixolydian, etc. (pp. 373–88). Al-Fārābī ends his treatise in characteristic fashion with references to (Aristotle's) *Rhetoric* and *Poetics* (*Kitāb Ṣinā'at al-Balāgha wa-Kitāb ash-Shi'r min kutab al-manṭiq*) and to a *Ṣinā'a Madaniyya* (pp. 1176–88). The work was translated into French by Baron R. d'Erlanger as *Al-Fārābī's Grand Traité de la Musique*, Paris, 1930–35 (vols. i and ii of his *La Musique Arabe*). Al-Fārābī also wrote about other matters which may properly be described as scientific, e.g. empty space or vacuum (*al-khalā'*).[107] Yet it seems quite clear that his interest in natural science was more limited than al-Kindī's, and that he was in the first place and above all a logician and metaphysician. He was likewise interested in ethics and especially in politics, and may indeed be regarded as the founder of political philosophy among the Arabs.[108] These indications of the main lines of his philosophical activity may be illustrated by considering some of his principal works.

He produced a paraphrase of Porphyry's *Eisagoge* and other propaedeutic works on logic,[109] which are contained in an important though not unique manuscript, no. 812 of the Hamidiye collection in Istanbul,[110] and the same manuscript contains also al-Fārābī's paraphrases of the various works belonging to the Organon of Aristotle, with some other pieces. A beginning has been made of the editing of this manuscript with a text and translation of the paraphrase of the *Categories*,[111] and the *Prior Analytics*.[112] Quite a different type of undertaking on the part of al-Fārābī is represented by his full commentary, including the Arabic text, of Aristotle's *De Interpretatione* (*Peri Hermēneias*), which has recently been edited,[113] and it is to be expected that further works of this class will be forthcoming.[114] The question of the date of these works, all obviously intended to further an understanding of the thought of Aristotle, has as yet scarcely been raised, but it would be natural to think of them as having been produced earlier than al-Fārābī's more original works, for which in fact there is evidence that they occupied the later years of the philosopher's life.[115]

Al-Fārābī was also concerned with the physical works of Aristotle and with his metaphysics, the latter of which he treated in a short piece which has been printed more than once, *Maqāla fī Aghrāḍ al-Ḥakīm fī Kull Maqāla fī 'l-Kitāb al-Mawsūm bi'l-*

Ḥurūf, or more simply *Maqāla fī Aghrāḍ Mā ba'd aṭ-Ṭabī'a*, Treatise on the Aims of the Philosopher (Aristotle, sc.) in Each Chapter of the 'Book Designated by Letters' (the *Metaphysics*), Treatise on the Aims of the *Metaphysics*.[116] An important work of al-Fārābī's, the *Kitāb Iḥṣā' al-'Ulūm* (Book of the Classification of Sciences), while from the nature of the subject partially dependent on the Greek (Aristotelian) view of the extent of human knowledge, goes somewhat beyond the Greek encyclopaedia,[117] and may be considered as halfway between the works of al-Fārābī which obviously depend on Arabic translations of Greek and those which are original.[118]

The writings of al-Fārābī which appear to be most original and which in recent times have attracted most attention are the *Kitāb Taḥṣīl as-Sa'āda*[119] (Book of the Attainment of Happiness), the *Kitāb as-Siyāsa al-Madaniyya*[120] (Book of Political Government) and particularly the *Kitāb Arā' Ahl al-Madīna al-Fāḍila*[121] (Book of the Opinions of the People of the Ideal City). To these must now be added the *Kitāb al-Milla al-Fāḍila*, recently edited by Professor Muhsin Mahdi,[122] who has shown its connection with the *Kitāb Iḥsā' al-'Ulūm* already mentioned, and has presented other relevant texts. Here a distinction has to be made. Al-Fārābī adopted at some point the idea of emanation (*fayḍ*) which was no part of the thinking of Aristotle, on whom, with Plato, he principally relied, but rather an idea of the Neoplatonists, perhaps developed from some earlier Oriental notion. This is conspicuous in what may be called al-Fārābī's system, set forth in the *Siyāsa* as we may abbreviate the longer title *Kitāb as-Siyāsa al-Madaniyya* given above, and in the *Madīna Fāḍila* (in full *Kitāb Arā' Ahl al-Madīna al-Fāḍila*, as above), but notably absent from the *Taḥṣīl* (*Kitāb Taḥṣīl as-Sa'āda*). Further, the *Taḥṣīl* is evidently the first part of a composite work, the second and third parts of which are respectively *Falsafat Aflāṭun wa-Ajzā'uhā wa-Marātib Ajzā'ihā min Awwalihā ilā Ākhirihā* (Philosophy of Plato and its Parts and the Order of its Parts from First to Last) usually known as the *De Platonis Philosophia*, from the title of a deservedly popular edition,[123] and the *Falsafat Arisṭūṭālīs wa-Ajzā'uhā* (or *wa-Ajzā' Falsafatihi*)[124] *wa-Marātib Ajzā'ihā wa'l-Mawdi'u 'lladhī minhu 'btada'a wa-ilayhi 'ntahā* (Philosophy of Aristotle and its Parts (var. and the Parts of his Philosophy) and the Order of its Parts and the Position from which he began and with which he ended), shortly *Falsafat Arisṭūṭālīs*.[125] It has been suggested that the

Taḥṣīl represents the most developed stage of the thought of al-Fārābī,[126] in which case it must be dated among his last compositions, and it has even been argued in detail[127] that since the *De Platonis Philosophia* and *Falasafat Arisṭūṭālīs* do not represent the view expressed by al-Fārābī in his *Kitāb al-Jamʿ bayna Raʾyay al-Ḥakīmayn Aflāṭūn al-Ilāhī wa-Arisṭūṭālīs* (Harmony between the Views of the Two Philosophers, the Divine Plato and Aristotle) in which the differences of the two are minimized and Aristotle is shown to be in agreement with Plato and not opposed, in his teaching on the world and the soul, to the dogmas of revelation (creation of the world, personal survival, reward and punishment), as in general maintained by the Arabic philosophers,[128] nor even the view which al-Fārābī expounds in the *Madīna Fadila* and the *Ṣiyāsa*, a distinction is therefore to be drawn between his 'popular and political writings' and his scientific or philosophic' works,[129] the latter being represented as, in addition to the composite *Taḥṣīl—De Platonis Philosophia—Falsafat Arisṭūṭālīs*, his commentaries, especially his large commentaries, of which we have at least one example.[130] It is particularly emphasized that in his real scientific writing in the composite work there is no trace of Neoplatonism (e.g. emanation, grades of existence) nor any mention of the so-called *Theology of Aristotle*,[131] supposedly a work of Aristotle and regarded as such by the Arabic philosophers, but actually a translation of parts of the *Enneads* of Plotinus, which al-Fārābī refers to repeatedly in his *Harmony between the Views of Plato and Aristotle.*

But this whole argument is ill-conceived, and the differences to which it draws attention are to be explained in another and simpler manner. The editors of the *De Platonis Philosophia* have shown that al-Fārābī was here following some Greek source, considered by them to have belonged to a time before the age of the Neoplatonists.[132] There is no need to concern ourselves with asking how many of the Platonic dialogues al-Fārābī had access to,[133] in Arabic translation, at the time. He had what for his immediate purpose was sufficient, a systematic account of the contents of the dialogues by a much older hand, and this is no doubt what he utilized. But if for the Platonic part of the composite work, so also for the Aristotelian part. The *Theology* attributed to Aristotle by the Arabs does not come in the account of Aristotle's philosophy in this third part, not because al-Fārābī no longer accepted it, but because it did not figure in his source. There is the strong probability that the first part also of the composite work, which we have as the *Taḥṣīl*, is similarly ancient, non-Fārābian in origin, with some Arabic and Islamic touches.[134] At the end we have the statement—oddly enough, since the *Taḥṣīl* is supposed to be a 'scientific or philosophic' work, while the opinion is one which should characterize the 'popular and political' writings (see above, p. 188)—'So let it be clear to you that, in what they Plato and Aristotle) presented, their purpose is the same, and that they intended to offer one and the same philosophy.'[135] The alleged discrepancies between the *Taḥṣīl*, on the one hand, and the *Madīna Fāḍila* and the *Siyāsa*, on the other, will have their source in the foreign origin of the first, and there is no need to look in it for a final exposition of al-Fārābī's views, which is difficult in any case in view of what we know of the dates at which some of his last works were written.[136] What immediately strikes the reader is that the *Taḥṣīl*, following Plato and Aristotle in the *Nicomachean Ethics*, discusses the rulers, and then the ideal ruler, at considerable length, and poses the case where a 'follower of opinions found to have good results' (*tābiʿ li-arāʾ mutaʿaqqaba*[137]); may be a substitute for the ideal ruler. Hence, in accordance with what has been said, the *Taḥṣīl* may be the starting-point for questions on the ideal ruler and possible alternatives which evidently greatly exercised al-Fārābī in the *Madīna Fāḍila* and the *Siyāsa*, also in the little work known as the *Fuṣūl al-Madanī*, where in the *fuṣūl* or section form he appears to resume the contents of the others, or perhaps we may say resumed his political philosophy in its final shape.[138] It is characteristic of al-Fārābī that he includes with his investigation of the ideal ruler and the ideal state, an interest which he derives from Plato and Aristotle, a substantial amount of emanationist metaphysics which he gets from the Neoplatonists. This combination is seen at its most developed in the *Madīna Fāḍila* and the *Siyāsa*, whose subject matter is so similar that it seems almost possible that the latter is a working over of the former.[139] In the *Fuṣūl al-Madānī*, on the other hand, Neoplatonism is less prominent.[140]

In what has already been said we have by no means exhausted the list of al-Fārābī's works nor is it necessary that we should. Before leaving him, however, it may be of interest to mention a manuscript, apparently ancient, recently acquired by the British Museum, which contains *inter alia* a commentary by al-Fārābī on the apocryphal *Letter of Zeno*.[141] The manuscript is catalogued as

OPB MSS., 12070, with the English title '*Philosophical Tracts*'. The date on the frontispiece in figures and again in writing is 330/941–2 (no month or day is mentioned), which is of course well within al-Fārābī's lifetime, and this is apparently confirmed by the title of the commentary in Persian (fol. 1a): *Risālat Abū Naṣr Farābī dar Sharḥ Risālat Zīnūn-i Kabīr*, then (fol. 2a): *Risālat ash-Shaikh az-Zāhid Abū* (*sic*) *Naṣr Muḥammad b. Ṭarkhān al-Fārābī aṭāla Allāh baqāhu* (*sic*), i.e. the Letter of the Shaykh . . . al-Fārābī, may God prolong his remaining, and again (fol. 2b): *qāla ash-shaykh al-ajall az-zāhid Abū Naṣr Muḥammad b. Ṭarkhān b. Uzlagh al-Fārābī aṭāla Allāh baqāhu* (*sic*), i.e. said the Shaykh . . . al-Fārābī, may God prolong his remaining. We have here, that is, another text of the commentary on the *Letter of Zeno* which has already been printed in the Haidarabad series, apparently dating from al-Fārābī's own day. What seems remarkable is that this apparently old and therefore authentic text is in many places inferior to the modern printed edition of Haidarabad.[142] How can the text have become corrupt in so short a space of time? It is natural to think that what we have is *a copy* of an ancient manuscript, though we should expect to have an explicit statement of this, if it is so, and such a statement would normally come at the end of the text. Instead of this, the text ends (fol. 43a): *faragha min taʿlīqihi Muḥammad b. ʿAlī b. Drs.wayh* (?) *al-Iṣbahānī sanat thalathīn wa-thalāth miʾa waʾl-ḥamdu liʾllāh ʿalā niʾamihi waʾṣ-ṣalāt ʿalā Muḥammad wa-ālihi aṭ-ṭāhirīn*, i.e. 'Muḥammad b. ʿAli b. Drs.wayh (?) al-Iṣbahānī completed the noting it down (or simply "writing it")[143] in the year 330 (= 941–2), and praise to God for his favours, and blessings upon Muḥammad and his pure family'. Then, on the last page (43b), comes a short *qaṣīda* of consolation in sickness, written as a reminder (*tadhkiratan*), apparently that persons seriously ill often recover, by ʿAlī b. al-Jahm to Muḥammad b. Ibrahīm al-Fārisī, the owner (?) of the book (*ṣāhib al-kitāb*). This notice appears to offer convincing proof that the manuscript—whatever may be its date—was not written in 330/941–2, since ʿAlī b. al-Jahm is presumably the well-known poet[144] of that name, who died in 249/863, well before a commentary of al-Fārābī on the *Letter of Zeno*, contained in the manuscript, as we have seen, can have been written. The poetical piece may be authentic, but cannot belong to this manuscript, as it stands at present, with its repeated indications that al-Fārābī is alive, and that the year is 330/941–2. The suggestion that the commentary on the *Letter of Zeno* is not in fact by al-Fārābī,[145] and may therefore theoretically be earlier, will not help the situation. The circumstances are suspicious, especially in view of the poor text of the commentary which the British Museum manuscript contains, and we may provisionally conclude that it does not date from al-Fārābī's lifetime, nor is it a copy of a manuscript so dating, but is in some sense a compilation. The commentary on the *Letter of Zeno*, if not by al-Fārābī, at all events deals with the metaphysical subjects which he studied in his principal works. It is divided into five sections: (1) proof of the existence of the First Creator; (2) his attributes; (3) the relation of created things to him; (4) doctrine of prophecy; (5) the divine law; (6) life after death. The work has not yet received a critical edition, so far as I am aware, but should no doubt be re-examined in the general context of al-Fārābī's philosophy.

4. Ibn Sīnā

For a little book published in 1950, the well-known Oriental scholar ʿUmar Farrūkh chose as title '*Al-Fārābiyyān*', 'The Two Fārābīs', explained immediately as al-Fārābī and Ibn Sīnā (Avicenna).[146] The term appears not to be ancient and to be a mere *jeu d'esprit*, depending on the circumstance that the League of Arab States in 1949, wishing to commemorate the millenary of Ibn Sīnā in the following year, seems to have confused the date with the date of al-Fārābī's death in 950.[147] Ibn Sīnā actually died in 428/1037, having been born in 370/980, and he has no special connection with al-Fārābī or with his birthplace, beyond the fact that Ibn Sīnā was the next in time of the great Muslim philosophers and like al-Fārābī a native of the East, where his career was spent in the service, not of the Caliphate but of the local dynasties, Sāmānids, Buwayhids, etc.[148] Unlike al-Fārābī, his background if not also his origin was Iranian.

Ibn Sīnā appears to have attracted the attention of the West earlier than either al-Kindī or al-Fārābī, and possibly for that very reason the interest in him most recently seems to have been less than in the two others. I shall here confine my remarks to work which has been done within the last thirty or forty years. Ibn Sīnā's production is very extensive, and since he was a doctor by profession, it is natural to find that his interests extended over a wide range of natural science, as well as philosophy. Of his medical writings, which were numerous, the most influential was the *Canon of Medicine* (*al-Qānūn fī'ṭ-Ṭibb*), used as a textbook in Europe as late as the seventeenth century, and much later in the East. The *Treatise on the Canon of Medicine of Avicenna*, containing a translation of Book 1, by O. Cameron Gruner (London, 1930) is one of the most substantial books of recent times on what is no doubt Ibn Sīnā's most celebrated single work. It seems to have been largely neglected by the present generation.

On the other hand, the writings of a French lady, A. M. Goichon, have contributed substantially to knowledge of his philosophy and metaphysics. Her original and valuable writings on Ibn Sīnā, beginning in 1933 with the translation of one of his shorter works *Introduction à Avicenne, son Épitre des Définitions* (Paris, 1933) include a large *Lexique de la langue philosophique d'Ibn Sīnā* (Paris, 1938, with a supplement *Vocabulaires comparés d'Aristote et d'Ibn Sīnā* (Paris, 1939); *Livre des Directives et remarques* (Paris, 1951), which is a translation of Ibn Sīnā's most important and last philosophical treatise the *Kitāb al-Ishārāt wa't-Tanbīhāt*;[149] *Philosophie d'Avicenne et son Influence en Europe mediévale* (Paris, 1951), a set of lectures given in London in 1940; with other works, and represent a sustained attempt to fathom Ibn Sīnā's thought.

New texts have been published, e.g. a *Majmūʿ* (Collection) at Haidarabad in 1354/1934–5, containing: *Risālat al-Faʿl wa'l-Infiʿāl* (Treatise on Acting and Being Acted Upon); *Risāla fī Dhikr Asbāb ar-Raʿd* (Account of the Causes of Thunder); *Risāla fī Sirr al-Qadr* (Mystery of the Divine Decree); *ar-Risāla al-ʿArshiyya fī 't-Tawḥīd* (The Throne Treatise on the Divine Unity); *Risāla fī 's-Saʿāda* (On Happiness), containing ten proofs that the human soul is a substance (*jawhar*), that it does not admit of corruption, that it is supplied from divine emanation, that the heavenly bodies possess a sentient soul, and treating of the conditions of the sentient soul at its departure—quite in the Alfarabian vein, and showing traces of panpsychism, or the doctrine of a general soul, which appears to have been taken up later by Ibn Bājja (Avempace); *Risāla fī'l-Ḥathth ʿalā' dh-Dhikr* (Exhortation to Make Mention, sc. of God's name); *Risāla fī'l-Mūsīqī* (On Music). This collection formed a welcome addition to the *Tisʿ Rasā'il fī'l-Ḥikma wa'ṭ-Ṭabīʿiyyāt* (Nine Treatises on Philosophy and Natural Science) of Ibn Sīnā (Cairo, 1326/1908), and others in *Traités inédits d'anciens philosophes arabes*, which appeared in 1911.[150] The titles in the latter collection show the same range of interest as we have already met with in Ibn Sīnā's predecessors, and it would not be very surprising to find them under the names of al-Kindī or al-Fārābī.

Other works have appeared, among which may be noted H. Corbin's *Récit de Hayy ibn Yaqzan* (Teheran, 1953), a translation of the Arabic text of this piece by Ibn Sīnā, which had already been edited by Mehren,[151] and of a Persian commentary thereon, which is of importance for the *Ḥayy b. Yaqẓān*, connected with Ibn Sīnā's story but much developed, written by Ibn Ṭufail later (cf. below, pp. 197 f). The *Memorial Avicenne* published by the Institut Françaises d'Archéologie Orientale du Caire contains useful material, for example a new text of the *ʿUyūn al-Ḥikma* (*Fontes Sapientiae*) by ʿAbdurraḥman Badawi,[152] an important work for the philosophy of the time, which the editor (p. vii) compares to the *Sentences* of Peter Lombard among the Latins. Undoubtedly the most important undertaking from the point of view of the text of Ibn Sīnā has been the publication by the Ministry of Public Instruction in Egypt, for the millenary of Ibn Sīnā which elicited several of the volumes already mentioned, of his great encyclopaedic work *as-Shifāʾ*, 'the Cure' sc. of ignorance, or perhaps of souls,[153] known as *Sufficientia* to the Latin Middle Ages, in four main sections, Logic, Physics, Mathematics and Metaphysics. An abridgement made by Ibn Sīnā himself was called *Kitāb an-Najāt*, Book of Deliverance.[154] The *Kitāb ash-Shifāʾ* became legendary. The sections on Physics and Metaphysics are said to have been composed at Hamadhān in twenty days, a feat surely beyond the powers even of Ibn Sīnā, and apparently contradicted by the statement that he used to compose two pages of the work in the early morning, before his official duties began.[155] Muḥammad Tughluq, Sultan of Delhi, long afterwards (he reigned 725/1325–752/1351), is said to have given 200,000 *mithqāls* of gold for a copy made by the famous calligrapher al-Mustaʿṣimī.[156] The publication of the *Shifāʾ* by the Egyptian ministry was an enormous undertaking. Several volumes have appeared, but the work, begun in 1952,[157] has not yet been brought to a completion, so far as one can learn. To these texts may be added a useful account of Ibn Sīnā for the general reader published by Dr Soheil Afnan,[158] and I should not like to pass over in silence a work by a former pupil of mine, the late Dr Ḥammūda Ghurāba, *Ibn Sīnā bayna 'd-Dīn wa'l-Falsafa* (Ibn Sīnā between Religion and Philosophy),[159] the title of which sufficiently indicates its subject.

Ibn Sīnā, though according to his detractors a man of unsound religious views[160] and irregular life (he took no trouble to conceal his love of music and wine, and more than hinted at other excesses) clearly enjoyed in his lifetime and later an extraordinary reputation. He is often referred to as *ar-Ra'īs*, the Prince, that is, of philosophers. His authentic works number, in round figures, something like 100. Many of these are no doubt hastily composed and superficial. It is remarkable, not so much that they are so, as that they came into existence at all. His great books, the *Qānūn* and the *Shifā'*, were both the product of his later years, when the demands upon his time as adviser to rulers and man of affairs were continuous. The intellectual energy of an author who could produce them, in what for most men would have been almost impossible circumstances, cannot but astonish us. In the main he seems to have followed al-Fārābī. It is well known that Ibn Sīnā declared that he had read the *Metaphysics* of Aristotle forty times and failed to understand it till a copy of a work of al-Fārābī explanatory of the subject came into his hands,[161] and this may be taken as a measure of his debt to his predecessor. But there is no doubt that with Ibn Sīnā the Greek sources are handled with more independence and worked more in, if the expression may be used, to the Islamic way of thinking. For example, instead of repeated disquisitions, such as we find in al-Fārābī, on ethics, following Aristotle's doctrine of the mean or on the ideal state and the various kinds of declension therefrom, going back to Plato, Ibn Sīnā, who elsewhere knew to appreciate Plato, in the *Shifā'* at least neglects political philosophy and for Aristotelian ethics seems to have substituted mysticism.[162] This is no more than to say that Islamic philosophy is developing, in the new age after al-Fārābī, not standing still. To his contemporaries at least and to many since his time Ibn Sīnā seemed to be the greatest Islamic philosopher (we cannot easily say Arabic philosopher, since Ibn Sīnā in his origin and attitudes was no Arab, and occasionally wrote in Persian) who had yet appeared.[163]

5. Philosophy in the Muslim West

Thereafter, with the exception of al-Ghazāli (451/1059–505/1111), author of the *Tahāfut al-Falāsifa* (Incoherence of the Philosophers), who was rather a great dogmatic theologian than a philosopher in the strict sense of the term, there are no figures of the first magnitude in the Muslim Orient, and we have to turn to the West, where the influence of al-Fārābī is seen to have been exerted on Ibn Bājja (Avempace), in full Abū Bakr Muḥammad b. Yaḥyā b. aṣ-Ṣā'igh at-Tujībī. Ibn Bājja must rank with the greatest of the Arabic philosophers, though hitherto his work has been less known in the West than that of his compeers. He seems never to have been translated into Latin, unlike the others, in the Middle Ages. On the other hand, we have some remarkable testimonies to his merit, not only from Ibn Khaldūn as already indicated,[164] but also from a learned contemporary Abū'l-Ḥasan 'Alī b. 'Abd al-'Azīz b. al-Imām[165] and from the celebrated Maimonides. The latter's testimony is quite precise. After mentioning the works of al-Fārābī on logic as alone worthy of study, with a somewhat disparaging glance at Ibn Sīnā, Maimonides says that Ibn aṣ-Ṣā'igh (Avempace) was also a great philosopher and all his words and works are 'plain to him that understandeth, and right to them that find knowledge'.[166] It is indeed as if, in the words of a recent investigator, al-Fārābī and Ibn Bājja are the only two Arabic philosophers whom Maimonides mentions with unrestricted praise.[167]

Ibn Bājja was born in or near Saragossa towards the end of the fifth/eleventh century. While still in his twenties, apparently, he served as *wazīr* to Abū Bakr b. Tīfalwīt, the Almoravid governor of Saragossa, which had recently passed out of the hands of the Hūdid dynasty, and was employed by him on an embassy to the former Hūdid ruler, 'Imād ad-Dawla, who forthwith threw him into prison. Escaping after some months, Ibn Bājja for a time led a wandering life in Muslim Spain, at Valencia, where news reached him of the death of Ibn Tīfalwīt (510/1117), and at Shāṭiba (Xativa), where he was again imprisoned on a charge of heresy, it is said,[168] but possibly because he was thought to be implicated in the loss of Saragossa, which had fallen to the Christians in 512/1118. Some time later he reached Seville, where a second wazīrate of twenty years, to the Almoravid Yahyā b. Yūsuf b. Tāshifīn, posited for him by some writers, may have begun. Certainly he was at Seville in 530/1135 in the company of Abū'l-Ḥasan 'Alī b. 'Abd al-'Azīz b. al-Imām above mentioned.[169] He died at Fez in Ramaḍān 533/May 1139, while still described as a young man, allegedly of poison.[170]

The career of Ibn Bājja is not known in detail, and it presents some contradictions as it stands (e.g. his obviously high position and wealth at periods in his life[171] and the dissatisfaction with the world which appears in his principal work, the *Tadbīr al-Mutawaḥḥid*, or Régime of the Solitary,[172] where he seems to despair of the realization on earth of a state worthy of the philosopher, or again the contradiction between his high reputation and apparent unpopularity). In restlessness he appears to exceed Ibn Sīnā, who also had a troubled career, and to have differed much in this and other respects from al-Fārābī, whom, however, in philosophy he evidently took as his master, for he commented at length on al-Fārābī's Aristotelian paraphrases[173] and evidently found in the older man's political ideas the starting point for a similar line of thought in the *Tadbīr al-Mutawaḥḥid*.[174]

Apart from Abū'l-Ḥasan b. al-Imām, we have some information concerning Ibn Bājja from another contemporary, Ibn Ṭufayl, who died at an advanced age in 580/1184 or 581/1185, and appears to have been born at the beginning of the century.[175] Ibn Ṭufayl mentions several of Ibn Bājja's works, notably the *Risāla fī Ittiṣāl al-ʿAql bi'l-Insān*[176] (the Union of the Intellect with Man), from which he quotes various passages[177] and which he evidently valued. This is not a mystical work, as has frequently been supposed, and in no way is to be considered as dealing with the religious union of the soul with the Deity. For Ibn Bājja as for al-Fārābī and the Neo-platonists earlier it is an emanation of Deity only, the 'active intellect' (*al-ʿaql al-faʿʿāl*), with which man may, in favourable circumstances, come into contact in the sublunary sphere, and the union with which he deals is consummated by the intellect (*ʿaql*), not by the soul (*nafs*). Ibn Ṭufayl seems to have found some difficulty, shared by modern readers, in understanding exactly what Ibn Bājja meant as the process by which the union is achieved. This is represented to be an intellectual ascent beginning with the sense impressions through a hierarchy of 'spiritual forms' (*ṣuwar rūḥāniyya*) intellected by the mind with ever greater abstraction till the 'active intellect' is reached. Ibn Ṭufayl complains that a book promised by Ibn Bājja in fuller explanation of the subject was never written.[178] It is possible that the latter's *Kitāb an-Nafs*[179] (Book of the Soul) was the work in question, but on the other hand Ibn Ṭufayl knew the *Kitāb an-Nafs*, which he brackets with the *Tadbīr al-Mutawaḥḥid* as being imperfect. Ibn Bājja, he says, was too much taken up with worldly business and died before he had time to open up the treasury of his knowledge, hence both these works are incomplete.[180] In speaking about Ibn Bājja's promised book on the Union Ibn Ṭufayl had observed that it was never written

either because he was straitened for time, being taken up with his journey to Wahrān (Oran) or else because he was sensible that, if he should undertake to give a description of that state, the nature of such a kind of discourse would unavoidably have put him upon a necessity of speaking some things which would manifestly have reproached his own manner of living, and contradicted those principles which he himself had elsewhere laid down; in which he encourages men to heap up riches, and proposes several ways and means in order to the acquiring them.[181]

In regard to Ibn Bājja's journey to Oran and any work 'in which he encourages men to heap up riches' we seem to have no information elsewhere. The critical tone of Ibn Ṭufayl's remarks is apparent. Yet he, like others, admits Ibn Bājja's abilities, speaking of his 'sharp wit' and 'true notion of things'.[182]

The fact is that Ibn Bājja still remains something of a mystery, the most enigmatic of the great Arabic philosophers, as the least studied and as having left behind the least extensive literary legacy (contained for the most part in two or three unpublished manuscripts), with nothing in Latin except quotations in the Latin Averroes. The impression which he made on his fellow-countrymen is not, however, to be set aside. In the next generation a younger contemporary of Ibn Ṭufayl destined, especially in the Latin West, to achieve the highest reputation, the famous Ibn Rushd (Averroes), was clearly influenced by Ibn Bājja, quoted him, and wrote upon occasion on the same subjects, including the Union of the Intellect with Man.[183] This with the explicit testimonies to his merit which we have already quoted makes the difficulties connected with Ibn Bājja's life and teaching something of a challenge. We know more about Ibn Bājja than we did a generation ago, thanks chiefly to the admirable work of the Spanish Arabist Miguel Asín Palacios, but there is no doubt that as yet what we know is hardly in focus.[184]

Compared with Ibn Bājja, Ibn Ṭufayl, author of the well-known work, *Ḥayy b. Yaqẓān*, usually called a philosophic romance and not impossibly the original of Robinson Crusoe,[185] is an altogether less important, also less interesting, figure. Ibn Ṭufayl was a protégé of the Almohads, as Ibn Bājja of the Almoravids, and the sources mention what may be considered one of his chief services to Arabic philosophy, his introduction of Ibn Rushd to the Almohad court. His book *Ḥayy b. Yaqẓān* is loosely connected with the *Ḥayy b. Yaqẓān* of Ibn Sīnā (see above, p. 193), and represents in the form of an allegory the growth of the human mind from the first stirrings of intelligence to full comprehension of the Cosmos and its Creator, according to the Aristotelian *cum* Neoplatonic philosophy in favour at the time. The subject of the allegory is Ḥayy b. Yaqẓān, 'the Living, son of the Wakeful', who, left alone as an infant on an uninhabited island, is brought up by a gazelle, and gradually by observation and reflection, unaided by any teachers, attains full maturity of mind as an intelligent human being, and assisted by the sage Asāl, penetrates all the complexities and obscurities of philosophy and religion. As a literary piece *Ḥayy b. Yaqẓān* is as perfect of its kind as anything else in Arabic. As philosophy it has been highly praised, though Ibn Ṭufayl does not claim for himself any special originality, and Gauthier is no doubt right in claiming that *Ḥayy b. Yaqẓān* has for its essential object the old question of the accord between religion, in principle Islam, and Greek philosophy.[186] Its relation with the views of Ibn Bājja has yet to be further studied, now that we know these somewhat better at least than formerly.[187]

The position of Ibn Rushd (Averroes) among the Arabic philosophers is exceptional, for though he had some influence and continued to be remembered in the west of Islam and was well known in the Latin West from the time of Michael Scot (thirteenth century), he was too late in time to make an impression on the Muslim East, where the *Tahāfut al-Falāsifa* (Incoherence of the Philosophers) of al-Ghazālī (see p. 194) appears to have dealt philosophy a blow from which it never recovered.[188] Further, among the Latins, during the Middle Ages and the Renaissance down to the most recent times, he was known almost exclusively as the great commentator on Aristotle. Thus Dante speaks of

Averroìs, che'l gran comento feo,[189]

and 'Nature interpreted by Aristotle, Aristotle interpreted by Averroes' was a current formula among the scholastics.[190] Ibn Rushd is also singular in having been treated in masterly fashion by a great scholar and stylist, Renan in his *Averroès et l'Averroïsme*[191] in the second half of the nineteenth century and on that account has become better known to the general reader, or at all events was better known to the general reader of that age, than the other Arabic philosophers. We have already referred to Sohail M. Afnan's *Avicenna* which attempts to do for Ibn Sīnā what Renan did for Ibn Rushd in the fifties of last century, and there are other books, on Ibn Sīnā by Carra de Vaux and on Ibn Rushd by Léon Gauthier, all of which are useful, but have attracted far less attention than Renan's. Beyond this, we have the somewhat ponderous volume by Moritz Steinschneider on al-Fārābī, a massive collection of material but scarcely adapted to any but the most resolute reader.[192] On al-Kindī and Ibn Bājja there is as yet no single volume which can be picked up, read through, and set aside with the feeling that one now knows of its subject about as much as a book on a European philosopher might provide.[193]

Yet in Ibn Rushd's case also there has been a marked advance in our knowledge in recent times, and after the edition of several independent works of his (i.e. not commentaries on Aristotle), by M. J. Müller in 1859,[194] the present century has seen new publications which make possible the appreciation of his philosophy more exactly than before. As we have noted in the case of other Arabic philosophers, the advance in knowledge of Averroes has been due to one or two persons who have concentrated much of their time and attention upon him, and here we may mention especially Father Maurice Bouyges, S.J., and Dr Simon van den Bergh, who from quite different approaches have greatly aided the advance which has been indicated. Bouyges carried on practically single-handed the series *Bibliotheca Arabica Scholasticorum*, published at Beirut, which included elaborate editions of works of Ibn Rushd: the *Tahāfut at-Tahāfut* (Incoherence of the Incoherence) a reply to the *Tahāfut al-Falāsifa* of al-Ghazālī already mentioned (*BAS*, iii, 1930); the *Talkhīṣ Kitāb al-Maqūlāt* ('Middle Commentary' on the *Categories*) (*BAS*, iv, 1932); and the *Tafsīr Mā baʿd at-Tabīʿa* ('Great Commentary' on the *Metaphysics*) (*BAS*, v–vii, 1938–48). This represented a very substantial addition to the Arabic texts of Ibn Rushd which were available for study. If Father Bouyges signalized himself as an editor of Ibn Rushd, Dr Van den Bergh contributed translations and textual criticism of the 'Short Commentary' on the *Metaphysics*,[195] which had already been edited by Quirós as *Kitāb ʿIlm Mā baʿd aṭ-Ṭabīʿat*[196] and by M. al-Qabbānī,[197] and of the *Tahāfut at-Tahāfut* in Bouyges's edition.

Other contributions were to come. *Averroes' Commentary on Plato's Republic* was published in a Hebrew version, the original Arabic being lost, by E. I. J. Rosenthal, who provided an English translation.[198] Helmut Gätje published a commentary on the *Parva Naturalia* of Aristotle,[199] and a beginning was made upon the logical works of Ibn Rushd, long known to exist in a manuscript of the Escorial Library.[200]

What kind of man was it who produced these and many other works, some existing in Arabic or Latin or both, some known to later times only by their titles? Not so very different, in important respects, from his predecessors. The same concern with the ancient Greek philosophers, Plato but above all Aristotle,[201] the same wide-ranging interest to include natural science, practical as well as theoretical (like Ibn Sīnā, Ibn Rushd was a practising doctor), the same concern to accommodate philosophy with Islam. One difference is afforded by the fact that Ibn Rushd as *qāḍī* of Cordova during the latter part of his life held an important position in the Muslim hierarchy, until he lost it, owing, it seems, to complaints against his philosophical views made to the Almohad Abū Yūsuf Yaʿqūb al-Manṣūr. He was thus in a special way a defender of Islam, for none of his famous predecessors was actively concerned with administering the *sharīʿa* (religious law).[202] Consequently we find the more usual interests of the other great Arabic philosophers diversified in the case of Ibn Rushd by a preoccupation with jurisprudence which they did not share, determined for him no doubt by circumstances, perhaps also in part by inherited temperament (his grandfather was a famous jurist).[203]

At all events, Ibn Rushd was born in Cordova in 520/1126, of a wealthy house, and studied theology according to the orthodox Ashʿarī system and law according to the Mālikī rite which was at that time dominant in Muslim Spain. His biographers, says Renan, praise his knowledge of jurisprudence nearly as much as his acquirements in medicine and philosophy. Renan adds that Ibn al-Abbār in particular attaches much more importance to that part of his work than to the Aristotelian writings which have made him so celebrated,[204] and that Ibn Saʿīd put him in the front rank of the canon-lawyers of al-Andalus.[205] It is not impossible that he received lessons from Ibn Bājja, but he does not appear to have invariably spoken of him in terms of very profound respect.[206]

The dates with which we can connect definite incidents in the life of Ibn Rushd are not numerous. He seems to have been at Marrākush (Marrakesh) in 548/1153. At this time he observed the star Suhayl (Canopus), which never, he says, appears above the horizon in al-Andalus, and thus satisfied himself that the earth was round.[207] (This was already well enough known theoretically to the learned of Baghdad in the ninth century, as we may learn from al-Masʿūdī.)[208] Ibn Rushd was then a man of twenty-seven. His introduction to the Almohad ruler (cf. p. 197) took place either on that occasion, or as seems somewhat more likely, in 1168 or 1169. Shortly thereafter he became *qāḍī* of Seville and later of Cordova, the Spanish capital, then successor to Ibn Ṭufayl as medical adviser to the sovereign in Marrakesh (1182), and *qāḍī al-quḍāt* (chief *qāḍī*) of Cordova.[209] In 1184 on the death of Abū Yaʿqūb Yūsuf, his son, the new sovereign Abū Yūsuf Yaʿqūb, maintained Ibn Rushd in his appointments and showed him the most distinguished favour. On the occasion of his expedition to Spain which was to lead to the great Muslim victory over the Christians at Alarcos (al-Arak), in which 146,000 Franks are said to have been killed (591/1195),[210] Abū Yūsuf Yaʿqūb was, it seems, obliged by the necessities of his situation to yield to the demands of enemies of Ibn Rushd and remove him from his judicial post. Orders were given that his books should be burned, and he was forced to remove from Cordova and take up residence at al-Yusāna (Lucena), then inhabited mostly or exclusively by Jews. Other persons whose views were obnoxious were also persecuted at the same time. Ibn Rushd did not escape from rough handling by the crowd, but he survived his exile and after the return of the Almohad Caliph to Africa was restored to favour. The philosopher then retired to Marrakesh at the invitation of Abū Yūsuf, where not long afterwards he died (Ṣafar 595/December 1198) at the age of seventy-two.

6. Epilogue

With Ibn Rushd the movement which had begun 400 years earlier came to an end. For he had no real successors, in the sense of men who, having sharpened their wits by intensive study of the ancients, proceeded, while keeping within the great assumptions of Islam, to try to give a rational account of the universe and spared no effort in the attempt. This could be an enterprise only for individuals confident in the environment both material and spiritual in which they found themselves. By the twelfth century in the East of Islam the time for philosophizing on the great scale was already long past, and after the age of the Almohad Caliphs in the West also the preconditions were lacking. Still to come were two great Maghribī intellectual figures, Ibn al-Khaṭīb (713/1313–776/1374) and his slightly younger contemporary Ibn Khaldūn (732/1322–808/1406). Ibn al-Khaṭīb centuries after his death evoked the enthusiasm of a remarkable writer, not to say man of genius, al-Maqqarī, whose *Nafḥ aṭ-Ṭīb*, written down in 1038/1629 but obviously the product of many years of study, is a magnificent tribute to a great figure who comes to represent in the mind of his biographer the lost heritage of Muslim Spain. Ibn Khaldūn, without doubt a man of genius, in the *Muqaddima* or Prolegomena to his History offers a number of original thoughts on human society and the state, for example the importance of what he calls *ʿaṣabiyya*, or solidarity, in establishing and maintaining the state, the factor of mere size of population (irrespective of human quality) as determining wealth and prosperity, etc., and with reason is often regarded as a forerunner of our present day science of sociology.[211]

Both Ibn al-Khaṭīb and Ibn Khaldūn were orthodox Muslims, and both had made acquaintance at some time, presumably in youth, with the range of the Muslim encyclopaedia, including philosophy, on which indeed Ibn Khaldūn wrote more than one work.[212] In maturer age we find both immersed in politics, with a horizon largely bounded by personal and narrowly local views in the small declining world of Western Islam. Both wrote their autobiographies (the philosophers were too busy, and it was, in any case, unusual for Muslims). The principal motive of their activity seems to have been, more than anything else, as far as we can judge from their works, self-interest and the determination to survive. The development here is different. No doubt both Ibn al-Khaṭīb and Ibn Khaldūn, like others before and since, were placed in circumstances which dictated what they should do, and how they should spend their lives. One thing is certain, that the urge to know which determined the activity of al-Kindī and al-Fārābī and Ibn Rushd has been subordinated to other aims, and neither Ibn al-Khaṭīb nor Ibn Khaldūn, in spite of their intellectual superiority, made any important contribution to philosophy, although in certain of the human sciences, history, politics, sociology, etc. their influence has certainly been felt. Ibn al-Khaṭīb on occasion writes merely to pass sleepless hours.[213] Ibn Khaldūn composes the *Muqaddimah* or Prolegomena to his History into which he casts both the fruits of his rather extensive reading and his realistic appreciation of life. But how seriously does he take this?

Ibn Khaldūn's History which follows the Prolegomena in the same book does not differentiate itself from others by Arabic authors, in spite of the theory, which perhaps he was unable to apply. The effort in any case is not made. Ibn Khaldūn's History in due course appears, and deservedly wins applause, like the writings of Ibn al-Khaṭīb. But clearly the operation of both men is different from that of the philosophers, who will comprehend not only men's actions but also nature, and the ultimate questions about existence, to which revelation gives answers but in a somewhat peremptory and not always consistent form. The later intellectuals, of whom Ibn al-Khaṭīb and Ibn Khaldūn are leading types, in general cease to press the metaphysical enquiry and, perhaps with private reservations, accept Islamic dogma, while, if they continue to interrogate nature, do so in the form of specialist enquiries, without relation to other enquiries or to metaphysics, and similarly compartmentalize what remains of philosophy, i.e. ethics, politics, etc., or they turn aside from abstract investigation altogether to the writing of history, jurisprudence, medicine, and any other remaining branches, judicial astrology, interpretation of dreams, and so on. The great synthesis attempted by the Arabic philosophers, on the lines of Aristotle and Plato, thus breaks down in later times entirely. This surely is not without relation to the splintering and weakening of the Arab state, which proceeded apace after the fourth/tenth century.[214]

Chapter 6

Science and medicine

1. Origins

Among the pagan Arabs in the pre-Islamic period the cultural level was low, though the extent to which this was so should not be exaggerated. These people were not savages. Two professions or types among them represented not so much the scientific interest of which it is still too early to speak, as intellectual culture in general, distinct, that is, from the purely practical ends of life though not of course altogether divorced from these, viz. the *kāhin*, or diviner—the word is akin in form and meaning to Hebrew *kōhēn*, 'priest'—and the *shāʿir*, literally the 'percipient one', or poet. Of the two, if the *shaʿir* was socially the more important in his capacity of mouthpiece of his people and moulder of public opinion within and without the tribe,[1] the *kāhin* as attempting to foresee and even control the future seems to approximate more nearly to the scientific type.

Somewhat later apparently, and perhaps under the influence of foreign cultures, such as Persia, the physician, *ṭabīb*, the 'skilful one', makes his entry on the Arabian scene. The extent to which the early Arab doctor was a scientist may be estimated from what is said by Ibn Khaldūn, whose opinions, though not always right, are usually worth considering. According to Ibn Khaldūn:

> The civilized nomads possess a kind of medicine, based in general on experience restricted to a few cases, which has been inherited from the *shaykhs* and old women of the tribe and may be true to a certain extent. But this does not form a natural system nor correspond to the human temperament. The (ancient) Arabs possessed much of this kind of medicine, and there were among them well-known physicians such as al-Ḥārith b. Kalada and others.[2]

From other sources we learn that al-Ḥārith b. Kalada, who is said to have studied in Persia at the medical school of Jundishāpūr, was a relative of the Prophet and died about A.D. 634.[3]

At the time of the Muslim conquests hordes of Arabians streamed out from the Peninsula into Palestine, Syria and Iraq, Egypt and Persia, all the homes of ancient culture, and after this early period contacts with civilization and science were rapidly multiplied. The seat of the Caliphate was transferred from Arabia first to Iraq, then to Damascus in Syria. In both of these new locales but especially at Damascus, the conquerors, imperceptibly at first, began to acquire the usages of a more civilized life. It is thus not surprising to find the Caliphs and other principal men taking advantage of the scientific knowledge of their new subjects. Muʿāwiya the first Umayyad Caliph (A.D. 661–80) employed the physician Ibn Uthāl, a Christian of Damascus.[4] Tayādhūq, evidently a Greek, served al-Hajjāj, the celebrated governor of Iraq, in the same capacity.[5] The private physician of ʿUmar II was ʿAbd al-Malik b. Abjar al-Kinānī, who according to tradition had previously been head of the yet surviving medical school of Alexandria.[6]

The most remarkable notices of scientific activity under the Umayyads are connected with the grandson of Muʿāwiya, Khālid b. Yazīd. In 684, when Marwān I was elected to the Caliphate by the Umayyads in Syria, Khālid b. Yazīd, at that date about twenty years of age, stood next in the succession. Perhaps he had already begun to devote himself to the studies with which his name was afterwards associated. Ibn an-Nadīm, author of the *Fihrist*, has the following account.

Khālid b. Yazīd b. Muʿāwiya was called the *ḥakīm*, or 'wise man' of the family of Marwān. He was of excellent disposition, and had zeal and love for the sciences. He bethought him of alchemy and ordered a number of Greek philosophers who lived in the city (capital) of Egypt and were fluent in Arabic[7] to translate the books of the (alchemical) art from Greek and Coptic into Arabic. This was the first translation ever made in Islam from one language into another.[8]

Khālid b. Yazīd was destined not to succeed to the Caliphate, being passed over in favour of ʿAbd al-Malik b. Marwān, and the change from being no longer heir apparent (*walī al-ʿahd*) but a simple member of the royal house may have determined the development of his scientific interest. This at all events is what is stated by Ibn an-Nadīm in another passage.

The one who concerned himself with bringing out the books of the ancients on the [alchemical] art was Khālid b. Yazīd b. Muʿāwiya. He was an orator and a poet, eloquent, of steady purpose and good judgement, and the first for whom the books of medicine, astrology [lit. of the stars] and alchemy were translated. He was very generous. It is said that someone once said to him: You spend most of your time in the study of alchemy. Khālid replied: I study it only to enrich my friends and brethren thereby. I desired the Caliphate, and it escaped me. I found no substitute, except to attain to the last knowledge of this art. I do not need that anyone who has known me but for a day, or whom I have known, should stand as a humble petitioner or in fear at the gate of the ruler. It is said also—but God knows best—that the operation of the art was successful for him. He wrote thereon a number of books and treatises, and there is much verse by him on this subject. I have seen about five hundred pages of it. I have seen of his books the *Kitāb al-Ḥarārāt* (Book of the Degrees of Heat), the large and the small *Kitāb aṣ-Ṣaḥīfa* (Book of the Scroll),[9] and the *Kitāb Waṣiyyatihi ilā 'bnihi fī 'ṣ-Ṣanʿa* (Book of the Testament to his Son concerning the (Alchemical) Art).[10]

The *Fihrist* also says that a certain Stephen translated for Khālid b. Yazīd books on the alchemical art and others.[11]

That the books mentioned by the author of the *Fihrist* were extant in his time there is no reason to doubt. Al-Masʿūdī, well-known author of the *Murūj adh-Dhahab* (Meadows of Gold) written about 943, gives three verses of the poetry of Khālid b. Yazīd:

> Take talc with gum ammoniac and with what is found in the streets,
> Add a substance which resembles borax and weigh it without error.
> Then, if you love God, your Lord, you will be the master of nature.[12]

It is probably significant for an early date that here crude forms of the ammoniac ingredient are indicated. Later sal ammoniac was universally used by the alchemists, and the substance was manufactured in various ways. An Arabic proverb well expressed the content of the lines, and could be based on them: 'He who dissolves the talc is independent of all nature.'[13]

According to Ibn Khallikān in the thirteenth century A.D., Khālid b. Yazīd learned alchemy from a Greek monk called Marianus and wrote three treatises on the art, one of which contained an account of what passed between him and Marianus, and how he learned the science and the secret names which his master used.[14] The name Marianus passed into the Latin tradition, and we have as the title of an early printed book *Liber de Compositione Alchemiae quem edidit Morienus Romanus Calid Regi Aegyptiorum* (Book on the Composition of Alchemy which Morienus produced for Calid, i.e. Khalid, king of the Egyptians).[15]

With the above citations from Arabic authors is to be taken another, again from Ibn Khaldūn, where a sharply critical note is struck.

People have often attributed certain alchemical methods and writings to Khālid b. Yazīd b. Muʿāwiya, the stepson of Marwān b. al-Ḥakam. But it is well known and obvious that Khālid was of Arab race and nomadism was nearer to him, so that he was far from the sciences and arts in general. What then had he to do with an art involving strange proceedings and based on the knowledge of the natures and temperaments of many composite bodies, like alchemy? The books of those who investigate such matters as physics and medicine had not yet appeared, nor had [the older books] been translated, unless indeed there was another Khālid b. Yazīd[16] among the people who studied alchemy, of similar name.[17]

What Ibn Khaldūn says here is in contradiction to his view expressed elsewhere that the Arabs had shed the rudeness of bedouin life and were becoming civilized by the time of ʿAbd al-Malik (Caliph from A.D. 685 to 705).[18] It is precisely in those years that the main scientific activity of Khālid b. Yazīd should fall. As an Umayyad prince, he might have enjoyed the best education that Syria could offer, and there is no *a priori* reason why his attention should not have been turned in the direction of Greek science, by some tutor or otherwise. The celebrated St John of Damascus, descended from an old Syrian family and steeped in Greek culture, as a young man is said to have been the intimate companion of Khālid's father, the shortlived Yazīd I.[19] John of Damascus kept his position at court till the Caliphate of Hishām (724–43), so that the two, the future saint and doctor of the Eastern Church and Khālid b. Yazīd, must almost certainly have known each other. Through this and other contacts, it is perfectly feasible that Khālid learned enough to lead him to addict himself to study, and eventually to inaugurate the new scientific trend in Islam which afterwards became so important.

The positive evidence which has already been cited and to

which there may be added the statement of al-Balādhurī (ninth century A.D.) that the introduction of the first real Muslim coinage was due to a suggestion made by Khālid b. Yazīd to ʿAbd al-Malik,[20] is not contemporary, and perhaps not quite consistent. On the other hand, there is no doubt that the intellectual interests attributed to him—medicine, astrology and alchemy—are precisely those aspects of the inheritance of the past which first and most strongly appealed to the Arabs, as the titles of Greek and other books at an early date translated into Arabic show.[21] Further, there is the following curious story, which appears to give us that the practice of alchemy existed in Iraq and was known to the Umayyads as early as the Caliphate of ʿAbd al-Malik, i.e. within the lifetime of Khālid b. Yazīd. The story occurs in the *Kitāb al-Imāma wa'ṣ-Siyāsa* (Book of the Religious and Civil Authority), attributed to Ibn Qutayba, who died in 889,[22] or at least to some contemporary of his. It is related on the authority of Yazīd b. Saʿīd, freedman of Muslim.

Wishing to appoint his brother, Bishr b. Marwān, governor of Iraq, (the Caliph ʿAbd al-Malik) wrote to his brother ʿAbd al-ʿAzīz b. Marwān, who was in Egypt. Bishr was with him in command of the troops, and was at that time a young man. (The Caliph's message ran:) I have appointed your brother Bishr over Basra. Dispatch with him Mūsā b. Nuṣayr[23] to be his *wazīr* and adviser. At the same time, I send you the revenue-roll of Iraq. Hand it to Mūsā, and let him know that he is responsible for any defect and shortcoming. So Bishr left Egypt for Iraq, accompanied by Mūsā b. Nuṣayr, and reached Basra. Here he handed over his seal to Mūsā and withdrew from all business. Mūsā remained thus with Bishr for a season.

Then one of the men of Iraq came before Bishr b. Marwān, and said: In God's name, is it your wish that I give you to drink a drink by which you will not grow old, subject to certain conditions which I shall lay upon you? What are the conditions?, asked Bishr. That you do not allow yourself to be angry, do not mount a horse and have no dealings with women during forty (days and) nights, and do not enter the bath, was the reply. Bishr accepted these conditions, and drank what was offered him, shutting himself up from all men, near and far, and remaining secluded in his palace. He continued so, till news reached him that he had been given the governorship of Kufa, in addition to Basra. At this, his joy and delight could not be contained. He called for a horse to go to Kufa, but the same man appeared, and charged him not to go, and not to stir by the least movement from his place. Bishr would not listen to him. When the man saw his determination, he said: Bear me witness against yourself that you have disobeyed me! Bishr did so, testifying that the man was clear of blame. Then he rode out to Kufa, and had not gone many miles when, having placed his hand upon his beard, lo! it fell away in his hand. Seeing this he turned back to Basra, but he remained not many days till he died. When the news of the death of Bishr reached ʿAbd al-Malik, he sent al-Ḥajjāj b. Yūsuf as governor.[24]

Bishr b. Marwān was in fact succeeded in Iraq by al-Ḥajjāj.[25] The surprising story is repeated by Ibn Qutayba,[26] who mentions that the drink prescribed was *idhrīṭūs* or *adhrīṭūs*, a remedy or prophylactic which I have not been able to identify.[27] It is called the 'great remedy' in IbnʿAsākir's version of the story.[28] While one would not be prepared to vouch for the authenticity, this may serve to carry back the beginnings of alchemy among the Arabs to the period of Khālid b. Yazīd, for he and Bishr b. Marwān were of course contemporaries.

The next important name in this connection is Jābir b. Ḥayyān of Kufa, who is said by the *Fihrist* and later sources to have been a prominent alchemist living in the time of Hārūn al-Rashīd (Caliph 786–809).[29] E. J. Holmyard calculated that Jābir was born *c.* 720 and died about 200/815.[30] This is evidently too late to permit of his identification with the unnamed alchemist in the story of Bishr, but puts the early part of his life still in Umayyad times.

The circumstances of Jābir are wrapped in even deeper obscurity than that surrounding Khālid b. Yazīd, and some people, as early as the *Fihrist*, seem to have doubted his existence. The study of early Arabic alchemy may be said to have been first placed on a solid basis by the Frenchman Berthelot, who in 1893, in conjunction with O. Houdas, published a number of Arabic treatises including six short works attributed to Jābir.[31] Berthelot was specially interested in the medieval Latin works going under the name of Geber. In 1906 he drew attention in the Bibliothèque Nationale to a Latin translation by a certain Magister Renaldus Cremonensis of the so-called 'Seventy Books' of Geber.[32] Berthelot came to the conclusion that a number of Latin works attributed to Geber had nothing to do with Jābir b. Ḥayyān, but were apocryphal, having been composed by Latin authors in the thirteenth century.[33]

Later, a lively discussion developed in regard to Jābir b. Ḥayyān and particularly the authenticity of the existing Arabic works attributed to him, between Holmyard and J. Ruska. Holmyard thought it possible to show that the Latin writings of the Middle Ages ascribed to Geber were translations from Arabic, and that Jābir and Geber were identical. He was convinced that Jābir b. Ḥayyān lived in the eighth century and was the real founder of modern chemistry.[34] Ruska was more sceptical and in particular affirmed with new arguments that the Latin writings of Geber were apocryphal.[35] Yet it was Ruska himself who in 1927 signalized the existence of two manuscripts of the Arabic original of the 'Seventy Books' of Geber,[36] and there is no doubt that the Latin version of this, already mentioned, was made from the Arabic in the twelfth century by the well-known translator Gerard of Cremona (see below).

Since then the principal contribution has been made by Paul Kraus, who in 1935 edited a number of Jābir texts in Arabic for the first time,[37] and in 1945 published at Cairo his great work on Jābir b. Ḥayyān, in which he canvassed the whole Arabic tradition and was able to cite the astonishing number of nearly three thousand works, attributed to Jābir, dealing not merely with alchemy but with practically the whole range of ancient science.[38] In most cases only a title survives, either in the bibliographical lists or as a citation in existing works. Assuming that all had an existence, many of the works corresponding to the titles were probably quite short. Yet whatever qualification is made, the total of nearly three thousand is far too large for the production of a single man. Further, as Kraus pointed out, if all these works are thinkable as the result of one man's work in the eighth century, it would be necessary to review all our ideas about the reception of Greek science in Islam and put the main part of the process earlier by a century than hitherto admitted. This would involve abandoning our most reliable sources and would introduce hopeless confusion in attempting to reconstruct the process. It is in fact quite plain that most of the works ascribed to Jābir b. Ḥayyān in the eighth century cannot be by him.

Kraus assigned the appearance of what he called the Jābirian corpus to the ninth century and later. He maintained that its purpose was as much theological and political as scientific. For, according to him, the exposition of scientific ideas was combined with numerous passages of propaganda, containing unequivocal references to the Ismāʿīlī and Qarmaṭian movement, which was then a danger to orthodox Islam. In these passages the so-called Jābir proclaimed the near advent of an Imām—a religious and political leader—who would supplant the law of Islam and replace the revelation of the Qur'ān by Greek science and philosophy. The occult sciences and notably alchemy were a principal part of this new revelation.[39]

There is no doubt that in the main Kraus's view of the Jābirian corpus is right. As well as internal evidence, he was able to adduce the doubts of contemporaries as to the authenticity of these works, and his case seems in the main proven. They are not authentic. One writing Kraus appeared to except and put in a special category, the so-called *Kitāb ar-Raḥma* (Book of Mercy), dealing with alchemy. The *Fihrist* mentions the opinion that it is the only authentic work of Jābir b. Ḥayyān.[40] Kraus did not admit so much, but he regarded it as the earliest of the corpus, composed in the ninth century and independent of the others.[41] The work survives in numerous Arabic manuscripts, has been edited, and is found also in a medieval Latin translation.[42] The same work was commented on by the famous Rhazes, who is even said to have versified its contents.[43] Here if anywhere, as it seems, we are to look for the genuine Jābir b. Ḥayyān.

It may appear that the title, 'Book of Mercy' is a strange one for a work on alchemy. The explanation is simple. In his prologue to the book the author, apparently Jābir, says:

> I have seen people giving themselves over to the search for the art of (transmuting) gold and silver, in ignorance and without consideration, and I have seen that they are of two classes, the deceivers and the deceived. I am filled with feelings of mercy and compassion (*fa-raḥimtu*) because they waste their money which God has given them and weary their bodies in a fruitless search . . ., and for the deceived, because in addition to their toils they lose also their souls uselessly for but a slight portion of the goods of the present world. . . . I have therefore composed a detailed and clear account which no one of the least intelligence can examine with feelings of anger, the profit of which will be obvious, and which will at once free the reader's mind from ignorance and error and save him from losing his money.[44]

In fact, according to this prologue, the true method of alchemy will now be set forth.

The indication that already there have been many amateurs of alchemy does not seem appropriate for such early times, though in all probability there were some even earlier, as we have seen. The book itself strikes one as a very moderate performance. Here is a specimen of an actual experiment.

> There was in our possession a piece of Magnesian stone, which could raise a weight of 100 drachms of iron. It remained in our possession for

a time, then later we tested it with another piece of iron, which it was unable to raise. We therefore thought that the weight was more than the 100 drachms which it previously could raise, but when we weighed it, we found it less than 80 drachms. For the strength of the magnet had decreased, while the weight of its bulk remained the same.[45]

Jābir is here represented as speaking in the first person, so that this account of demagnetization should be his, in view of what has already been said. No attempt is made to explain what happens when demagnetization takes place. In this respect indeed modern science seems not to have gone a great way further, for while demagnetization used to be regarded, in terms of the molecular theory of magnetism, as due to the closing up of molecular chains in the magnet which were previously open, it is not clear that this was ever more than an assumption, or that recent advances have afforded a complete explanation.[46]

Apart from Khālid b. Yazīd and Jābir b. Ḥayyān there are few names connected with Arabic science in the Umayyad period. Several have already been mentioned at the beginning of this chapter. Another was Tawfīl or Thawfīl ar-Rūmī (Theophilus of Edessa), according to Ibn Khaldūn an astrologer in the days of the Umayyads, who calculated that Islam would endure for the period of a great conjunction, that is the space of time between two great conjunctions, or 960 years. When this time had elapsed, the two superior planets, Saturn and Jupiter, would again be together in the sign of the Scorpion as at the beginning of Islam, but the stars would have a different configuration from what they had then. Consequently, either the practice of Islam would be relaxed or new doctrines of an altogether opposite character would be introduced.[47]

Little is known about Theophilus of Edessa, except that he was chief astrologer to the Caliph al-Mahdī and is said to have translated two books of the *Iliad* into Syriac.[48] Al-Mahdī died in 785. Theophilus is also said to have died in 785, so that he was doubtless alive in Umayyad times, as Ibn Khaldūn states. The theory of conjunctions had a great vogue in the astrology of the Middle Ages, both Arabic and Latin, and if Theophilus of Edessa is in fact the first man to speak about it, his originality would be very great, for this was no part of the astrology of the Greeks. The standard Greek work on the subject, the *Tetrabiblos* or *Quadripartitum* of Ptolemy, does not discuss conjunctions. The prevailing view, endorsed by Nallino, a great expert on Arabic astrology and astronomy, is that the Arabs learned about cycles and planetary conjunctions from the Indians.[49] Thus it would appear that Theophilus was no more than an intermediary. His cycle of 960 years, it is to be noted, is an exact fraction (1/4500) of the Indian cycle called *yuga* of 4,320,000 years. The 'great cycle' of 960 years was still known in Mesopotamia in the twelfth century.[50]

Prominently associated also with the beginnings of Arabic science under the Umayyads was Māsarjawayh or Māsarjīs of Basra. He is mentioned in a variety of sources—apart from the biobibliographical compilations of Ibn Juljul,[51] al-Qifṭī[52] and Ibn Abī Uṣaybiʿa,[53] in the *Firdaws al-Ḥikma* (Paradise of Wisdom) of ʿAlī b. Rabban Ṭabarī (*c.* A.D. 850)[54] and the *Kitāb al-Ḥayawān* (Book of Animals) of his fellow-townsman al-Jāḥiẓ (died 869).[55] He is also frequently referred to by the great botanist and pharmacist Ibn al-Bayṭār, perhaps the greatest the Arabs ever produced, who died in A.D. 1248.[56] Yet in spite of all this Māsarjawayh remains little known. He is passed over with a few words in Sarton's *History of Science*,[57] and the standard work of Brockelmann speaks of him in two places as two different persons.[58]

The fullest notice appears to be in Ibn Abī Uṣaybiʿa.[59] Māsarjawayh professed medicine at Basra, and it was he who translated the book of Aaron the Priest from Syriac into Arabic, as mentioned above (p. 38). Māsarjawayh was a Syriac-speaking Jew. It is he who is referred to in the *Kitāb al-Ḥāwī* or *Continens* of the great Rhazes, also by Haly Abbas (ʿAlī b. al-ʿAbbās al-Majūsī), as 'the Jew'. Ibn Abī Uṣaybiʿa, who mentions this, adds that Māsarjawayh flourished under the Marwānids (i.e. the later Umayyad Caliphs), and made his translation for ʿUmar b. ʿAbd al-ʿAzīz (Caliph 99/717–101/720). He is therefore a possibility for identification as Bishr's alchemical adviser (see pp. 208 f), though there is no confirmation in the sources. Ibn Abī Uṣaybiʿa subjoins one or two anecdotes concerning Māsarjawayh from the latter's contemporary Ayyūb b. al-Ḥakam of Basra, known as al-Kisrawī (and therefore no doubt of Iranian origin). It is clear at least that already Māsarjawayh was thinking in terms of Galen's humoral pathology, since he speaks of the yellow bile (*aṣ-ṣafrā*ʾ) and he even used the Arabicized Greek word *dhūsanṭārayā*, dysentery,[60] for the condition.

Apart from authors' names, we have evidence of astrology in practical connections already in Umayyad times. Thus in 66/686 a South Arabian, Baḥīr b. Raysān al-Ḥimyarī, attempted to prevent two captains of ʿAbd Allāh b. az-Zubayr from proceeding to their posts on the ground that the moon was in her first 'mansion', ill-omened because of its name an-Nāṭiḥ, a word meaning also 'adversity'.[61] Again in 71/690, according to al-Masʿūdī,[62] the Caliph ʿAbd al-Malik had with him a favourite astrologer while campaigning in Iraq. Mention may also be made of an astrological work with the title *'Arḍ Miftāḥ an-Nujūm* (Exposition of the Key to the Stars) in a relatively late manuscript (of 1071/1660), which bears that the work was translated in 125/743. Nallino, accepting this, regards it as, apart from alchemical books, which he would associate with Khālid b. Yazīd, probably the first translation of a Greek book into Arabic, seven years before the end of the Umayyad Caliphate.[63]

2. Under the early ʿAbbāsids

It seems that with the beginning of the ʿAbbāsid age the environment to some extent altered and that the times were now more favourable for the reception and development of natural science and intellectual culture in general. Astrology became ever more popular. If this seems a strange example to take as proof of a developing culture, it may be said that there appears to be a great difference between the decadent astrology of modern times, and even astrology as pursued in late antiquity, and the rising science among the Arabs. It may be going too far to say that astronomy was the ancillary science.[64] Certainly astrology at this time was highly developed. Under the early ʿAbbāsids astrology was not a popular form of astronomy, as it has tended to be before and since that time. Rather astronomy was ardently pursued for the sake of astrology. According to Nallino, 'What really distinguishes the astrology of the Muslim peoples from previous systems, is, apart from its eclecticism, the degree of perfection attained in the mathematical processes. . . . In this regard there is a striking contrast with Greek and Indian astrology which made clumsy calculations and always shrank from an excessive complication of mathematical elements.'[65] Those who have examined good Arabic astrological manuscripts will appreciate what is meant. As examples, those in the Escorial Library of works of ʿUmar b. Farrukhān may be cited. (ʿUmar b. Farrukhān, regarded by Albumasar as one of the four most proficient translators in Islam,[66] died before 815). Such books are not the productions of simpletons or charlatans, but highly elaborated works of a system, which, though based on a set of unproven assumptions, as we now see, cannot properly be described as a vulgar superstition.

Court astrologers were a feature of life under the ʿAbbāsids. It is noteworthy that the foundations of the new ʿAbbāsid capital, Baghdad, were laid at a propitious moment chosen by two of them, Nawbakht al-Fārisī (i.e. the Persian), a friend of the Caliph al-Manṣūr, and the Jew Māshā'llāh.[67] When the plan of the city was traced, in circular form, there were present the same Nawbakht, Ibrāhīm b. Ḥabīb al-Fazārī and perhaps the abovementioned ʿUmar b. Farrukhān.[68] With these names we are already in touch with some of the leading exponents of astrology among the Arabs. Works on the science are ascribed both to Nawbakht and to al-Fazārī,[69] and the latter has the distinction, according to the *Fihrist* and other sources, of being the first Muslim to construct an astrolabe (that is, a plane astrolabe, the simplest means of determining a star's altitude above the horizon) and to write a book about it.[70] The instrument, as such, is of course pre-Arab, and is mentioned by Ptolemy in the *Tetrabiblos* (*Quadripartitum*).[71] Better known perhaps than Nawbakht or al-Fazārī is Māshā'llāh, a Jew from Egypt or possibly India,[72] who wrote a number of books. Several of these survive, in Arabic or translated into Latin, including a work on the plane and spherical astrolabes. This was printed several times in Europe in the sixteenth century.[73]

Māshā'llāh's works contain references to the Greek astrologers Dorotheus of Sidon and Antiochus of Athens,[74] but also strange expressions such as *al-haylāj* and *al-kadkhudā*. These appear in the Latin versions as *alhyleg* and *alcochoden*, and are neither Greek nor Arabic, but Persian, meaning respectively 'mistress' and 'master of the house', astrological terms of uncertain import.[75] Such expressions must have been completely incomprehensible to readers in the time of the Renaissance, and must have contributed to the bad repute in which the so-called *barbaro-Latini*—the Latin writers of the early Middle Ages—were then held. They were not always understood even in the times for which the old translations were made. Richard of Bury (fourteenth century, first half) in his *Philobiblon* speaks of the delightful city of Paris with its pleasant libraries, where one may read Aristotle, Ptolemy and the learned astronomer Gensachar.[76] One will look in vain for Gensachar in the works of reference. He is in fact a figment, but Richard of

Bury is not joking. He has made into a person, Gensachar, a technical term in astrology *geusachar* or *geuzachar*, rendering the Persian *jawzahr*, and meaning in such contexts 'the node of a planet's orbit' (Nallino).[77] The prevalence of similar technical terms coupled with the fact that several of the above-mentioned investigators were themselves Persians shows of course a considerable influence from this quarter on the rise of Arabic astrology.

There also flourished in al-Manṣūr's Caliphate the translator Abū Yaḥyā al-Biṭrīq, to whom is due the first Arabic version of Ptolemy's well-known textbook of astrology, the *Tetrabiblos* (Quadripartitum).[78]

A whole other development is also indicated for the Caliphate of al-Manṣūr in connection with Indian works on mathematics and astronomy or astrology. The following passage comes with slight variations in more than one of the biobibliographical compilations.

> Kanka the Indian was the chief among all the scholars of his nation in times past in knowledge of the stars. We have not [or 'not yet'[79]] heard his date nor any definite information about him, because of the remoteness of his home and the intervening of many lands between us. . . . It is for this reason that the works of the Indians are rare among us and only a fraction of their sciences have reached us. Of the three famous methods of the Indians in astronomy, viz. the method of the Sindhind, the Arjabahad[80] and the Arkand, there has reached us in any detail only the method of the Sindhind, and it is that method which has been adopted by a number of the scholars of Islam. . . . Among the works of Kanka commonly reputed to be his are the *Kitāb an-Namūdār* [it is another technical expression from Persian][81] on the (Length of) Men's Lives, the *Kitāb Asrār al-Mawālīd* (Book of the Secrets of Nativities), the *Kitāb al-Qirānāt al-Kabīr* (Great Book of Conjunctions) and *Kitāb al-Qirānāt aṣ-Ṣaghīr* (Lesser Book of Conjunctions).[82]

It appears that Kanka came to Baghdad with an embassy from Sind in 771 or 773 and was found to be expert in all astronomical operations, particularly in the system of the Indian Brahmagupta, who in 628 had composed a work called *Brāhma-sphuṭa-siddhānta*, 'correct book of astonomy attributed to Brahma', for the Indian ruler Vyāghramukha. Vyāghramukha is the Fayghūr, more commonly Faghfūr, of the Muslim sources, from the first part of the name. Somewhat similarly the *Brāhma-sphuṭa-siddhānta* was abbreviated to *Sindhind*. Al-Manṣūr is said to have requested the Indian visitor to dictate a compendium of the work, and this became the basis of an astronomical table (*zīj*) constructed by al-Fazārī, who has already been mentioned. The work of Brahmagupta in al-Fazārī's version apparently remained standard among the Arabs till the time of al-Ma'mūn, when the method of Ptolemy in the *Almagest* for calculating the stellar movements came to be better known. In the same Caliphate a new *Kitāb as-Sindhind* was composed by Muḥammad b. Mūsā al-Khwārizmī, and the older work was sometimes called the 'Great Sindhind', by way of distinction.[83]

Through the *Sindhind* and the other Indian methods of calculation the doctrine of cycles and conjunctions is already in the Caliphate (754–75) of al-Manṣūr or shortly thereafter part of the system of Arabic astrology. Apart from the two works dealing with conjunctions attributed to Kanka, another on the same subject by Māshā'llāh is mentioned in the *Fihrist*.[84] The *Tetrabiblos* of Ptolemy became available in Arabic about this time, but is not concerned with cycles and conjunctions.

We must now turn to what appears to be another contemporary development. That the interest in alchemy of which we have already spoken in connection with Khālid b. Yazīd was not continuous at the Umayyad court, or at least was not inherited by the ʿAbbāsids when they first came to power (in 750), is indicated by the following story from a geographical work written *c.* 290/902.[85]

Al-Manṣūr sent ʿUmāra b. Ḥamza to the Emperor of the Greeks and wrote threatening him with horse and foot. ʿUmāra said: I came to a place which no one might approach even at a great distance, and there sat till the summons reached me. Then I went on to another point and sat down, till the summons reached me three times. I then entered the imperial palace. I was taken into a hall, and lo! in my path were two lions, on both sides of the way which I must needs pass. I said to myself: I must surely die, but I shall not die weakly! So I took heart, and when I passed between them, they became calm and I went on my way. I entered another hall, and behold! two swords played across my path, and I thought that if so much as a fly passed between them, it would be cut in half. But I said: He who preserved me from the lions will preserve me also from the swords! So I committed my case to God and passed on, and when I came between them, they ceased to play. Then I entered a third hall, where the Emperor was, in a wide pavilion so far away that I could scarcely see him. I had walked towards him about a third of the distance, when I was covered by a red cloud through which I could see nothing. So I remained seated for a time where I was. Then the cloud dispersed, and I rose up and walked on till, at about two-thirds of the distance, a green cloud covered me and obscured my sight. So I sat down, till it passed away. Then I rose up and went towards the Emperor and greeted him through an interpreter, and gave him the message, and handed him the letter, whereupon he made me sit down and questioned me concerning the Caliph and the news of the various countries. At last he gave orders for my lodging and provision and bade me withdraw and return early next morning.

ʿUmāra b. Ḥamza then tells in his somewhat rambling style how he and the Emperor met again. The lions and the swords, he was told, where mechanical devices to impress visitors. The clouds of red and green light were produced by means of precious stones, rubies and emeralds.

When the time of his departure came, ʿUmāra b. Hamza was taken to a heavily guarded tower.

We entered and found a number of sealed chambers. The Emperor ordered the door of one of them to be opened. Within were a number of white bags piled round the chamber. He said: Point to which you will. So I indicated a bag. He gave orders for a small earthenware bottle to be filled from it, and the door was closed. Then another door was opened, into a chamber containing red bags. A similar bottle was filled from the contents of one of the bags, and the chamber was resealed. We went to the palace, where the Emperor called for a smith's bellows and a quantity of copper and lead. First the lead was melted, and a small amount of the white preparation was thrown upon it. When cast in a mould, the result was gleaming silver. Next the copper was melted, and a pinch of the red preparation was thrown upon it. It came out bright gold. Then the Emperor said: Tell your master that this is my wealth. As for the cavalry and footsoldiers, you know that they are more numerous and greater (sc. than his). [ʿUmāra concluded:] I related the incident to al-Manṣūr, and it was this that led him to interest himself in alchemy.

ʿUmāra b. Ḥamza is known to have been a *mawlā* or freedman al-Manṣūr.[86] As to the dating, al-Manṣūr had a diplomatic contact with Byzantium in 139/756–7 after which there was a truce which is said to have lasted for seven years[87], and again at the end of his reign, in 155/772, when the Emperor (Constantine V) requested peace and submitted to the payment of a yearly tribute.[88] This latter is possibly the occasion to which the story refers. The existence of mechanical devices of the type here indicated is well attested for the period, both at Byzantium and at Baghdad. The Arabic term is *ḥiyal* (plural of *ḥīla*) and more than one 'book of mechanical devices' (*kitāb al-ḥiyal*)[89] is known. The projection of red and green light should not have been beyond the powers of Byzantine technicians. We note also in the account an early mention of what the European alchemists referred to much later as the 'changing powder'. It may be admitted that al-Manṣūr can have been led to take an interest in alchemy through hearing accounts of the Byzantine court, but with regard to this narrative, there remains some doubt as to its authenticity.

We have previously mentioned the medical school of Jundishāpūr (p. 205), whose influence earlier was considerable, but which springs into special prominence under the ʿAbbāsids. According to the historian of science Aldo Mieli:

> In 489 the Emperor Zeno closed the school of Edessa, and the persecuted Nestorians took refuge in Nisibis, then under Persian rule, and there reorganized a philosophical and medical school which later, in the first half of the sixth century, was transferred to Jundishāpūr. It was there (where a Zoroastrian school was also established) that the Nestorian school, especially from the point of view of medicine, attained an extraordinary development. The city . . . was a point of union for Greek, Syrian, Persian, Hindu and Jewish scholars and doctors, invited by the sovereigns of Iran and enjoying their protection. This flowering, which lasted many centuries, culminated during the reign of Khusrau Anūshirwān (531–79), during which Jundishāpūr became the principal intellectual centre of the world. The basis of the school was essentially Greek, the Nestorians having brought with them a great quantity of Greek texts with their Syriac translations or epitomes, to which they had specially dedicated themselves. However, they made translations also into other languages (Pahlavi, etc.) and exercised the activity of translators in other places which they reached. It is in this sense that the Nestorians figure among the greatest and most influential transmitters of science in the East, especially of Greek medicine.[90]

This is to put the importance of the school of Jundishāpūr very high, but undoubtedly it played an important part from the beginning in the scientific movement in Islam. Details are hard to come by. Tawfīl ar-Rūmī already mentioned (Theophilus of Edessa) studied at Jundishāpūr. Its existence at the site of present-day Shahabad in south-west Iran, at no great distance from Baghdad, was undoubtedly a contributing cause of the rise of science under the ʿAbbāsids. In 148/765 al-Manṣūr summoned from Jundishāpūr its leading physician, the Nestorian Jurjis b. Bakhtīshūʿ to his new capital.[91] Jurjis founded the fortunes of the Bakhtīshūʿ family, who for several generations were prominent at

Baghdad and elsewhere as physicians to the court and in general as leading members of the medical profession.[92] Yaḥyā b. Māsawayh, another famous doctor,[93] was associated with the Bakhtīshūʿ family, and his father Māsawayh was also from Jundishāpūr. Ḥunayn b. Isḥāq, whose services to science through his translations were as great as any of his contemporaries,[94] though himself from al-Ḥīra, was in turn a pupil of Yaḥyā b. Māsawayh. The sequence serves to connect Jundishāpūr with some of the most enterprising intelligences of the age.

Isḥāq b. Ḥunayn, like his father a great translator, wrote in verse:

> Yāḥyā b. Māsawayh and Aaron before him
> Have books full of usefulness to the people.[95]

Yaḥyā or Yūḥannā (the Christian form of the name) b. Māsawayh, who is thus linked with Aaron, presumably Aaron the Priest, author of the medical *Pandects* (cf. p. 173) represented both the theoretical and the practical interests of medicine in his day, and had a great influence on posterity, especially in the West. It is convenient to call him by his Latin name, strictly the name of his father, Mesue.[96] He was born, of obscure parentage, probably in the last years of the eighth century A.D. His father had come to Baghdad after being employed for many years in the hospital of Jundishāpūr. His mother was a slave-girl from the north, described as a Ṣaqlabiyya (i.e. Slav, but the term had a wider acceptation).[97] On this evidence, Mesue can have had little or no Arab blood, for the father was from the Persian province of Khūzistān. By religion the family were Nestorian. The father prospered in Baghdad, and his son enjoyed a good schooling. He was a good enough Greek scholar to be charged with the translation of the ancient books found at Ankara and ʿAmmūriya (Amorium) during the Muslim raids in Hārūn's Caliphate, but it was in Syriac that he preferred in later life to read medical and philosophical books. As a practising doctor he had great success, and he became a wealthy man and a favourite of the Caliphs. He was evidently an industrious writer, as the titles of nearly fifty works show. A feature of his activity was his *majlis* (assembly), a combination of lecture room and consulting hour at which he met pupils, saw patients, discussed scientific topics and in general put himself at the disposal of the community. A contemporary says that this assembly was the most crowded in Baghdad, being frequented by all classes of men of learning, theologians and philosophers as well as doctors. People came for amusement as well as instruction, for Mesue's repartees, some of which survive, were famous. He maintained something like a small private menagerie, including a she-ape which he proposed to dissect. The Caliph al-Muʿtaṣim sent him another ape, which actually was dissected by Mesue. The result was a book of anatomy, the first of its kind in Islam, which won universal praise at the time.[98]

An interesting work of Mesue, the *Medical Axioms* (*an-Nawādir aṭ-Ṭibbiyya*), was twice translated into Latin in the Middle Ages, first by Constantine Africanus (eleventh century), then by Gerard of Cremona (twelfth century), and printed several times during the Renaissance.[99] The original Arabic appeared to have been lost, but was published by Paul Sbath in 1934.[100]

The *Axioms* include dietetics, pathology, diagnosis, and therapeutics, but anatomy, physiology and surgery are here scarcely touched on. The basis is Galenic, for one way or another Galen was now fairly well known to the Arabs. In pathology, the doctrine of the four humours is adopted—blood, phlegm, yellow and black bile—to which individual temperaments correspond. The doctrine of the four humours is as usual connected with that of the elements, characterized as cold or hot, wet or dry. The four seasons of the year also play a part in the system and must be taken into account in treatment. When the combination of the humours is disturbed, disease is the result. The humours become morbid, and the morbid matter has to be got rid of. Its expulsion is the normal crisis of the disease, after which, under suitable dietetic and other treatment, health is restored. Hence the stress on purgatives and emetics, a feature of all Galenic therapy. Bleeding is also important.

There is a pronounced intellectualist approach to medicine in the work. Axiom 3 lays down that much reading of the books of medical men and study of their methods are to be recommended. Axiom 14 states that illiterate doctors are a menace. According to Axiom 18, we should distrust those who are not interested in the principles of medicine, the philosophical sciences, canons of logic and fundamentals of mathematics. According to the 91st Axiom, the doctor fails who is restricted to experience without what Mesue calls analogy, i.e. the theory of medicine. Yet, like Galen, he does not make exclusive claims for sound theoretical knowledge. His first Axiom is that absolute truth in medicine is unattainable.

It is dangerous for the physician to treat according to the text of books without applying his own judgement. Longstanding habits are not to be altered save where necessary (Axiom 75). He repeatedly urges consideration of the age of the patient and the general state of his health. It is better in general to diet than to administer medicines (Axioms 24, 36, 121). The physician should aim at restoring the sick person to his usual state of health, not to some abstract norm (Axiom 68).

Sometimes he is curiously modern, as in his insistence on psychological medicine (Axioms 13, 32, 72), perhaps because he regards the psychical and animal forces as one (Axiom 22). Heredity is important (Axioms 99 and 100), and character, he seems to say, is inherited (Axiom 113). Certainly there is such a thing as inherited chronic disease (Axiom 23).

There are without exception no references to such drastic remedies as the frightful *ustio Arabica* (branding the head for insanity), applied by European doctors in comparatively recent times, and hardly a trace of superstitious or magical remedies. Sometimes indeed Mesue's statements contain crude errors of fact, as when he says that in the countries below the equator there are two seasons every year.[101] On the whole, the Axioms reflect the same sober intelligence as is evidenced by what Ḥunayn b. Isḥāq says of the kind of translations which Mesue required from him. These were of serious works of Galen, and had to be executed with the greatest possible accuracy.[102]

The contents of this typical work of Mesue show the high level which was rapidly reached among the Arabic doctors, once the scientific movement was fairly started. The complete list of his works, as found in the writings of Paul Sbath and elsewhere, indicates the range which medicine had now taken. The list includes several works on ophthalmology (these have been studied by C. Prüfer and Max Meyerhof),[103] two on migraine and dazzlement, etc.; a work on poisons and their antidotes; and a book on elephantiasis (*Kitāb fī'l-Judhām*), which is noted as the earliest on the subject in Islam.[104]

3. Al-Kindī as a man of science

All this represents a great advance, and it has to be noted that it was accomplished by 243/857, the year of Mesue's death, that is for the most part in the Caliphates of al-Ma'mūn (813–33), al-

Muʿtaṣim (833–42) and al-Wāthiq (842–7). As a patron of the new learning, Mesue received the dedication of a *Risāla fīʾn-Nafs* (Treatise on the Soul), written by his contemporary, the celebrated al-Kindī (*c.* 800–*c.* 867).[105] Of al-Kindī as a philosopher we have spoken elsewhere in this book (pp. 175–184). Here we may treat him more particularly as representative of the scientific movement among the Arabs, now at full flood.

The following account of al-Kindī is given in the *Ṣiwān al-Ḥikma* (Repository of Wisdom) of Abū Sulaymān as-Sijistānī, also called as-Sijazī, in the tenth century A.D.[106] Though short, it is important as offering several facts which seem to be found nowhere else.

Abū Yūsuf Yaʿqūb b. Isḥāq al-Kindī. He was the first among the Muslims to become expert in philosophy and all its parts, and in the exact sciences and everything connected with them, apart from his expertise in the sciences of the Arabs [i.e. those connected with the *Qurʾān*, *Ḥadīth* or Tradition, etc.] and his excellence in the polite accomplishments of grammar, poetry, judicial astrology, medicine, and the various arts and sciences, the knowledge of which is but rarely united in one man. The list of his books exceeds a quire (*dast*) of paper, written on both sides. He was the professor of Aḥmad b. Muḥammad al-Muʿtaṣim, (see p. 175), for whom he composed most of his books. It was to him that he sent the bulk of his *Rasāʾil* [or short treatises (plural of *risāla*)] and his responses to questions. He was the first to introduce this method, which has been followed since his time by succeeding (generations of the) followers of Islam. He was preceded indeed by those whose names became celebrated and who earned distinction in the days of al-Maʾmūn.[107] They, however, were mostly Christians, and their writings followed the old style. Owing to the popularity of his books and treatises, which are in every hand and to be found in every place, I have not searched exhaustively for choice sayings nor attempted to make extracts at random from works like these, but there are a few things which I cannot avoid for the embellishing of my book, and among them what follows.[108]

Abū Sulaymān as-Sijistānī goes on to quote a work of al-Kindī, which is given on pp. 231–33 below.

Among the shorter works of al-Kindī in the *risāla* or epistolary form, which according to what is said above he appears to have been the first to use, is a Treatise on the Efficient Cause of the Flow and Ebb (*Risāla fī ʾlʿIlla al-Fāʿila liʾl-Madd waʾl-Jazr*). In treating the movement of the tides his argument depends on the changes which take place in bodies owing to the rise and fall of temperature. This, he says, can be proved experimentally in various ways. To quote his own words:

> One can also observe by the senses . . . how in consequence of extreme cold air changes into water. To do this, one takes a glass bottle, fills it completely with snow, and closes its end carefully. Then one determines its weight by weighing. One places it in a container of very nearly the same size, which has previously been weighed. On the surface of the bottle the air changes into water, and appears upon it like the drops on large porous pitchers, so that a considerable amount of water gradually collects inside the container. One then weighs the bottle, the water and the container, and finds their weight greater than previously, which proves the change.

Al-Kindī adds: 'Some foolish persons are of opinion that the snow exudes through the glass. This is impossible. There is no process by which water or snow can be made to pass through glass.'[109] Apart from the addition this reads like a modern laboratory experiment.

Very different from al-Kindī's experiment is another, said to have been made shortly before his time. It is given by al-Masʿūdī in an interesting account of the fur trade with northern Europe, in the course of which he mentions particularly the black fox-skins of Burṭās, a country on the middle Volga.[110] These were exported to the south, and were well known in Muslim lands. Following the current theory which attempted to describe all physical objects in terms of the properties of the four 'elements', which we have already noted in the pathology of Mesue, al-Masʿūdī says that the temperament or nature of these furs is hot and dry —extremely hot, as is shown by the bitterness of the animals' flesh. Their hair is hotter than any other fur. Its temperament is like fire, by reason of the predominance in it of heat and dryness. In consequence it is excellent to wear for persons of a humid temperament, and for the old. Al-Masʿūdī does not attempt to show the exact degree of dryness and heat in these fox-skins. Instead he cites with approval the experiment undertaken by the ʿAbbāsid prince al-Mahdī, while at Rayy in al-Jibāl (Media). Al-Mahdī reigned as Caliph from 775 till 785, but apparently the notice refers to an earlier period, when he was at Rayy in his father's lifetime. Wishing to know by experiment which was the hottest, or as we should say warmest fur, he procured a number of bottles, which he filled with water, stopping the mouths with furs of various kinds. It was winter-time and very cold, and there was much snow on the ground. The bottles of water with the furs were left out over night. In the morning al-Mahdī sent for them, and found that all were frozen except the one which had been stopped with black fox-fur. He thus knew, says al-Masʿūdī, that this fur was the hottest and dryest.[111] Evidently there are ways and ways of interrogating nature. If such an experiment took place, it clearly was conducted by people who did not know what they were doing.

Another example of al-Kindī's experimentation from the above-mentioned work on the movement of the tides, as told in his own words, is as follows.

> Aristotle, the philosopher of the Greeks, states[112] that if pointed arrows are shot through the air, the lead with which the points are fastened will melt. We thought this statement defective, since the lead which holds the iron fast will not melt if placed in the fire for the time it takes the arrow to pass through the air. But the air can heat no more strongly than when it becomes fire. [Fire according to the theory envisaged by al-Kindī is air from which the quality of cold has been removed.] Further, the arrow at each moment touches new parts of the air. We tested this view, because we held it to be possible, but in order to carry out an exact experiment. For an account of objects perceived by the sense can only be refuted by a similar account [i.e. one derived from observation], and similarly its correctness is only demonstrated by such an account. We therefore prepared an instrument like an arrow, which instead of a point had a knob of horn. In this we bored holes lengthwise right through, and filled the inside of the holes with fine lead. We then shot it into the air from a powerful bow. The arrow fell to the ground, but there was no longer any lead in it. It is not disproved that the air streamed through these holes so as to exercise a hollowing-out effect, work the lead loose and pull it out, without melting it, because we noticed inside the holes the smell of burnt horn which had come into contact with fire [i.e. fire is caused by the friction of the air, not by the lead melting].[113]

According to the German historian of science E. Wiedemann, whose translation I have modified slightly, it can be experimentally shown and theoretically proved that the change of kinetic energy into heat melts a rifle-bullet, and so perhaps also in certain circumstances in the case of an arrow, and al-Kindī is wrong in ascribing the phenomenon to the friction of the air.[114] However this may be, one is, I think, bound to be impressed by al-Kindī's method. He is not deterred by the authority of Aristotle for whom, incidentally, he had the greatest respect. He bases his criticism on theoretical reasons which are first stated, and he goes on—as if he realized the defectiveness of the theory of the elements which he was of course obliged to use—to try to bring the question directly to the test of experiment. A modern scientist could scarcely be more scrupulous, and he might very well be much more dogmatic about contemporary theory.

The examples given show al-Kindī's recognition of the value of direct observation and his willingness to use experiment, involving in the second case the construction of a special piece of apparatus. His ability to invent and apply an appropriate experiment—unlike al-Mahdī and his scientific advisers according to al-Masʿūdī's story—will scarcely be denied. In dealing with the main problem discussed in this treatise, the cause, or as al-Kindī himself calls it, adhering to the Aristotelian terms, the efficient cause, of the tides he must be admitted to be only moderately successful. To the problem he brought a solution in terms of the circular movement of the planets and their spheres, which heat the air and water below them, while what we naturally look for is some account of the gravitational pull of the moon, in the first place, and of the sun. To speak as al-Kindī did of the flow and ebb as dependent on the planetary spheres strikes us as fantastic. But it may be noted that the great Galileo regarded the theory current today, when adumbrated by Kepler, who before Newton recognized the tendency of the water of the ocean to move toward the centres of the moon and sun, as absurd, and expressed regret that so acute a man should have produced a theory which seemed to reintroduce the occult causes of the older philosophers. No doubt Kepler and Newton were right and al-Kindī was wrong, but his account was at least a rational attempt to deal with a difficult problem, which was perhaps insoluble before the modern development of mathematics.

Another work of al-Kindī is a short treatise with the long title *Risāla fī ʿIllat al-Lawn al-Lāzuwardī alladhī yurā fī'l-jaww fī jihat as-samā' wa-yuẓannu annahu launu's-samā'*, i.e. Treatise on the azure colour which is seen in the air in the direct of the heavens and is thought to be the colour of the heavens; in other words, Why is the sky blue?

The little work on the blue of the sky has been edited very conveniently by O. Spies, in the *Journal of the Royal Asiatic Society of Bombay*, xiii, (1937), pp. 7–19, who points out that no comprehensive treatise dealing with the general theory of colour was written before Aristotle. But the work on the subject by Aristotle seems to contain very little about the theory of the colour of the sky. Professor Spies adds that no authoritative explanation seems to have been offered before Alhazen began his experimental studies on the refraction of light. Alhazen is the incorrect but standard Latinization of the name of Ibn al-Haytham of Basra, a successful and distinguished student of optics who died in A.D. 1038.[115] He seems to have believed that the blue colour of the sky is caused by small particles of dust, and Professor Spies finds that he is 'much below the standard of al-Kindī in this matter'. The author of the article on al-Kindī in the *Encyclopaedia of Islam*[116] mentions that the blue of the sky is explained by him as due to the 'mixture of the darkness of the sky with the light of the atoms of dust, vapour, etc. in the air, illuminated by the light of the sun'. The Arabic text of Professor Spies says nothing explicitly about dust and vapour in the air, but attempts correctly, I believe, according to the best modern opinion, to explain the phenomenon purely in terms of light. The passage in question reads:

> The dark air above us is visible by there being mingled with it from the light of the earth and the light of the stars a colour midway between darkness and light, which is the blue colour. It is evident then that this colour is not the colour of the sky, but merely something which supervenes upon our sight when light and darkness encounter it, like what supervenes upon our sight when we look from behind a transparent coloured terrestrial body at bright objects, as in the sunrise, for we see them with their own colours mingled with the colours of the transparent object, as we find when we look from behind a piece of glass, for we see what is beyond of a colour between that of the glass and that of the object regarded.[117]

This is at the same time the conclusion of the investigation. One would not claim that it is perfectly clear, any more than are the several stages of the argument by which it is reached. Yet it seems that al-Kindī was here on right lines, apparently without guidance from outside and in spite of the confused and impossible views which passed for knowledge even in highly educated circles in his time.

One of al-Kindī's works which has survived in Latin while it has apparently been lost in the original Arabic is his treatise on geometrical optics. Gerard of Cremona's Latin translation of the work was published in 1912 by the Danish scholar A. A. Björnbo and Sebastian Vogl.[118] Al-Kindī's preface gives some indication of his approach to a mathematical subject. He says:

Since we wish to complete the mathematics and set forth therein what the ancients have transmitted to us, and increase that which they began and in which there are for us opportunities of attaining all the goods of the soul, it is necessary for us to speak about optics, universally and demonstratively, according to our capacity, and to take the principles of what we say about optics from nature, because the sight by which individual things are comprehended is one of the senses, in order that it may be declared by us how visible things are comprehended. The geometrical principles which will be the principles of our geometrical observations will be second to the natural principles, though first so far as we are concerned, in order that the principles of our demonstrations may not be as it were unnatural relations. Otherwise what we say would be nonsense, departing from the way of demonstration.

We ask the reader to whom this book of ours may come, if he finds anything which we have not spoken of sufficiently, to be patient and not hasten to think ill of us, till he has understood truly all the previous treatises about the other parts of mathematics—for this book follows them—and to supply what he thinks we have omitted, according to what the men of his age require. The length may be curtailed or expanded for all men of any time and place, and thus be made more agreeable to their wishes. Our wish is to thank those who have helped us by their advice and who agree with our work, and to help whom we can, according to human utility, and not to seek after praise and . . . arrogance.[119]

Al-Kindī's preface seems to envisage a long period of usefulness for his book, and this was in fact accorded to it. Even after the appearance of a famous treatise on optics by Alhazen (see p. 227), al-Kindī's work held its own. It was based on the *Optics* of Euclid in the recension of Theon, and discusses in turn, in twenty-four chapters, how the light rays come in a straight line, the process of sight without a mirror, the process of sight involving mirrors, and influence of distance and angle on the sight, together with optical illusions. According to Vogl, 'Roger Bacon not merely counted al-Kindī one of the masters of perspective but in his own *Perspectiva* and others of his works referred repeatedly to his *Optics*. The influence of al-Kindī's work extended to Leonardo da Vinci, and the book was still referred to in the seventeenth century.'[120] Al-Kindī's works on mathematics, of which this on optics must serve here as an example, were numerous—Flügel in his monograph on al-Kindī gives the titles of more than twenty[121]—and their influence is not to be underestimated.

Al-Kindī, the mathematician and physicist, appears in a new guise in a work called *Kitāb Kīmiyā᾽ al-ʿIṭr wa᾽t-Taṣʿīdāt* (Book of the Chemistry of Perfume and Distillations), signalized by Professor H. Ritter in an Istanbul manuscript[122] and edited in 1948 by Karl Garbers.[123] Garbers, in addition to knowing Arabic, had the advantage of being able to deal with the contents as a trained chemist and pharmacist. He does not attempt to throw light on the circumstances in which the book came to be written. The work, he says in his introduction, will speak for itself and al-Kindī. This is true enough in a sense, but the matter is not quite such plain sailing as the editor suggests.

The *Kitāb Kīmiyā᾽ al-ʿIṭr wa᾽t-Taṣʿīdāt* contains more than 100 recipes for fragrant oils, salves, aromatic waters and substitutes or imitations of costly drugs. It is a systematic treatment of the subject, occupying almost sixty pages of the printed Arabic text (ninety-nine folios in the MS). The editor finds it remarkable that a scholar and philosopher like al-Kindī should apply his knowledge and experience, as appears from a number of short remarks at the end of the recipes, to the imitation and falsification of valuable drugs for commercial purposes, and suggests that his doing so is typical of the East.[124]

It is true that the instructions for preparing these recipes regularly involve the addition of a small amount of an authentic article, such as musk, amber or aloes-wood, to what is often a much larger quantity of some compound. When this has been done, according to the end-remarks, a 'uniformly good' article will be produced, or 'one that will not be refused' or 'one that will be able to deceive experts in the matter of the price'.[125] In one case a note of this kind says that the writer sold, for 30 *dīnārs* in Damascus, imitation musk, which he had previously prepared in Baghdad.[126] Or again, in the heading of one of the recipes, it is stated that the writer got it from a certain Aḥmad b. ʿAlī in Egypt.[127] If the author of these observations is al-Kindī, then undoubtedly al-Kindī used his chemical knowledge to make money by more or less fraudulent means, and, moreover, travelled much more extensively than the biographical notices suggest, in order to do so. There appears to be no other indication that he ever left Iraq.

Further, although a *Treatise on the Chemistry of Perfume* is listed among al-Kindī s works, in the present text he is twice cited by name in such a way as to make it quite certain that, as it stands, the text edited by Garbers is not by al-Kindī. Garbers suggests that the book was written down by a pupil of al-Kindī.[128] He has not pursued the matter further, and, leaving al-Kindī's name on the title-page, is prepared to saddle him with what may be called the other additions. This is not very satisfactory. We can and, I think, should say that al-Kindī did not fabricate expensive drugs and go to Damascus and Egypt to sell them. The remarks at the end of the recipes and apparently also some of the headings are due to a professional drug-seller, who has compiled his book for some ruler (*al-mālik*, otherwise unknown).[129] The compiler may have worked with al-Kindī, as he says, but it is not possible in the circumstances to be certain how many of these 107 recipes are al-Kindī's own.

On the other hand, we have the passages where al-Kindī is cited by name, and there is no reason to think that they are not authentic. One of these states:[130] 'I received the following description, or recipe, from Abū Yūsuf Yaʿqūb b. Isḥāq al-Kindī, and I saw him making it and giving it an addition in my presence.' The writer goes on in the same section to speak of the preparation of a perfume called *ghāliya*, which contained musk, amber and other ingredients. The recipe for the compound, which is to be a substitute for the authentic and expensive *ghāliya*, is too long to quote. It is full of technical names of drugs and apparatus. A second recipe for the production of camphor is shorter.

You take fragments of soft marble such as the turners use—it has a bluish look. Weigh a part, and a part of camphor. Set aside a quarter of the camphor, then pulverize the three-quarters of the camphor with the flakes of marble on a hard marble slab. Next take white gum arabic, which should have been placed in water till it has the consistency of thin honey. Allow it to drop on the powder. Knead together making the mass like camphor ice, (*hijārat al-kāfūr*) and dry carefully. Then place it upon a hair sieve, reversing the sieve. On the sieve, over the camphor, is placed as covering a bottle-end. Then take a brazier with a fire of coals, place camphor therein, and set it under the sieve so that the smoke of the camphor ascends. Let it be saturated with the smoke. Lastly, take the quarter of camphor which you set aside. Rub it between the fingers over the preparation, and mix one with the other. It will turn out as you wish, if God wills. Abū Yūsuf (*sc.* al-Kindī) said to me that he had made this recipe with a substitute for the marble. He used pieces which particularly resembled marble, sparkling with light like the stars (planets), and having the nature of camphor in colour, hardness and smoothness. He thought that it had succeeded very well.[131]

We thus see al-Kindī, in these two examples, as occupied with experiments of considerable elaboration to produce synthetic perfumes, etc. That he engaged personally in the drug trade is more than doubtful. The title of one of his lost works is *A Treatise on the Artificial Production of Foodstuffs without their Elements.*[132] This evidently described the same kind of experiment with a different range of material. There is no likelihood, it seems to me, that the purpose was commercial.[133] If not simply for theoretical purposes, the experiments might have been made, for example, for the relief of famine. There is no real evidence for either work on this point.

In any case, the publication of the *Book of the Chemistry of Perfume and Distillations* is of real importance for understanding al-Kindī. It has been known for a long time that al-Kindī's attitude to alchemy was distinctly hostile. The basis for this is a passage in al-Masʿūdī, according to whom:

> Yaʿqūb b. Isḥāq b. aṣ-Ṣabbāḥ al-Kindī composed a *Risāla* on alchemy in two parts, in which he shows the impossibility of man's rivalling the creative power of nature, and exposes the deceptions and artifices of the adepts of this art. This *Risāla* is entitled *Refutation of the Claim of Those Who Claim the Artificial Fabrication of Gold and Silver.*[134]

The *Risāla* in question comes in the list of al-Kindī's works,[135] along with another of similar title and subject, *Warning against the Deceptions of the Alchemists.*[136] We now see that where alchemy was a matter of producing synthetic perfume or synthetic foods al-Kindī was with the alchemists and himself a noted practitioner. In other words, he appears in effect to have distinguished alchemy, in the sense of exclusive pursuit of transmutation of the baser metals from its more respectable sister chemistry, and, if so, this, considering the time at which he lived, must be regarded as a remarkable achievement.

Leaving aside al-Kindī's work as astrologer which has been adverted to in Chapter 5, we may finally consider him as a medical man, quoting here *in extenso* the *Risāla*, or *Treatise, on Diseases Caused by the Phlegm,*[137] from which insights into al-Kindī's manner as well as his matter can be gained.

> May God surround you with salvation, and establish you in its paths and aid you to attain the truth and enjoy the fruits thereof! You have asked me—may God direct you to all things profitable!—that I should outline to you the disease called *ṣarʿ* (the falling-sickness, epilepsy). The

principal cause here is common to several ailments which differ in regard to the parts affected and strength and weakness. I give you a sketch of this according to what I think sufficient having regard to your scientific standing. And in God is our success, and on Him is our trust.

When the phlegm melts and changes to a bad irritant quality, it goes forth and ascends to the brain from a certain direction, then it sinks down through the principal veins towards the heart, and by its irritant quality it deranges the place of sense, thought and recollection in the brain. It passes through the veins towards the heart, and if the natural heat whose source is the heart is strong enough to dissolve it, it does so, and what happens as a consequence is epilepsy (*ṣarʿ*). For the parts of the brain which we have mentioned, becoming injured, are overcome and cease to function. The disturbance which we see in the (patient's) body is owing to the conflict of the natural (heat) with the affection. When it prevails over it, it attacks and dissolves it. This is the meaning of the foam which is seen at the (patient's) mouth. When this occurs, his recovery is near.

When the excess (of the phlegm) is completely predominant, and the natural (heat) is so weak that it enters the inner part of the heart, the natural heat is extinguished, the moisture of the heart is quenched—its element of blood being killed by the cold—and the patient (lit. 'living creature') dies immediately. This affection is called 'rapid death' or, as is commonly said, 'sudden death'.

If the natural (heat) resists the affection before it reaches the heart and combats it, but is not strong enough to dissolve the excess (of the phlegm), the struggle cannot go on for more than seventy-two hours, or three days and nights, because the natural (heat) is greatly weakened by the continuous flow of the humour during this time. Its strength disappears, and it is overcome. The humour reaches the heart, whose heat is extinguished and its moisture quenched, so that the patient (lit. 'living creature') dies. This affection is called *saqṭa* (apoplexy). The utmost survival of one so affected is these three daily periods, after which he dies.

If the natural (heat) is able to prevent the excess from entering the heart but the natural (heat) in the members of the body is not strong enough to resist it, it directs itself to that part of the body which cannot resist it. If it passes into one side of the body, it deranges it and deranges its actions. This is the affection called *fālij* (hemiplegia). If the natural (heat) is altogether too weak to resist it except in the heart, it deranges the actions of the entire body, but the patient survives. This affection is called *khalʿ al-aʿḍāʾ* (general paralysis). If it directs itself to one or two parts, such as the arm or leg or both legs, in the lower part of the body, or both arms, in the upper part of the body, their actions are rendered useless. What affects the legs is called *iqʿād* (crippling), while what affects the arms is called *ʿasam* (rigidity). Similarly, if it directs itself to the tongue or the muscles of the body, it deranges their action, as happens in the eye, when it is called *shatar* (inversion of the lid), in jaw and eye, when it is called *laqwa* (complete paralysis of the mouth), in the tongue, when it is called *kharas* (dumbness), and so on. The distinction between inversion of the eyelid and paralysis of the mouth is that when it directs itself to the muscles of the lower eyelid, it relaxes them, while in paralysis of the mouth it directs itself to the muscles of both eyelids at once, the upper and the lower, and the nerve of the eye which moves it, or else the muscles of the jaw as well. For this element (phlegm) is an element and humour for all these affections at the same time.

The natural (heat) in the body is like the garrison of a fortress. When the enemy surround it and each man fights for his place, whoever of them weakens in combating his enemy, loses his place to the enemy. So when the excess comes down, the natural (heat) which is in every part except the one part struggles against it. Whichever of the parts shows weakness in combating the enemy is entered by it and finds its place taken and itself deranged, since all the defenders of the natural (heat) are labouring to defend the place where they are, except that weak one which was empty and has lost its position.

The humour (phlegm) is one, though the diseases are different according to the difference of the parts affected and the strength and weakness of the excess. The causes of the difference are connected with the weakness of the natural (heat) in some members of the body compared with others.

(The *Risāla*) is finished. And praise be to God, and God bless His Prophet Muḥammad and his family, and give (them) peace.

The recipient of this is not named, and since the question of diseases caused by the phlegm is dealt with in a purely theoretical manner without reference to treatment, it is not necessary to posit a medical man. These notes, which is all the *Risāla* in this case amounts to, need be no more than the reply to a chance question of al-Kindī's pupil Aḥmad b. al-Muʿtaṣim (see p. 223), or another. The influence of the Galenic humoral theory here prevails, to the exclusion of any other. There is nothing to suggest that al-Kindī was a practising doctor. Rather we have in the short work evidence that his scientific curiosity extended beyond the limits of the restricted theme, as is hinted at in the opening remarks, to the fields of anatomy and pathology.[138] This is no more than might be expected, if we consider the field of interest of the man who among the moderns perhaps most nearly resembles al-Kindī, the great Italian natural scientist and philosopher, Geronimo Cardano.[139]

4. Rhazes (ar-Rāzī)

We may now go on to consider a Muslim physician and man of science called the Galen of the Arabs, who enjoyed the greatest reputation during the Middle Ages and whose celebrity has come down to our own time. He is Abū Bakr Muḥammad b. Zakariyyā' ar-Rāzī, the famous Rhazes (spelt alternatively with z or s). As his name indicates, he was a native of the Persian city of Rayy, where he was born in the third/ninth century.

For knowledge of Rhazes in Europe the date 1766 is of considerable importance. In that year the Londoner John Channing published, for the first time, a work of Rhazes in the original Arabic—an edition, Arabic and Latin, of the *Kitāb fī al-Jadarī wa'l-Ḥaṣba* (On Smallpox and Measles),[140] which had already in 1747 attracted the attention of the celebrated Dr Mead (1673–1754) and which has been described as 'the oldest and most important original work on smallpox and measles'[141] and as 'probably the most concise and most original treatise in Arabic medical literature'.[142] Mead knew no Arabic, but had given a Latin translation with the help of several eighteenth-century Orientalists, Salomon Negri, J. Gagnier and Thomas Hunt. Channing used the same basis as his predecessors, a Leiden manuscript of the Arabic original, which had belonged to the collection of Levinus Warner, and he was now able to produce an elegantly printed if not very correct Arabic text and a readable and clear Latin version. Channing says of his method of translation:

> The version is what is called a literal one. It is close and renders word for word as far as possible, while avoiding incorrect expressions, so that not only Rhazes' sentences but also his way of thinking, words and style are exhibited. Where the genius of the Latin language did not admit this, the Arabic phrase is noted at the bottom of the page. . . . The reader is not to be irritated by Arabic words appearing in the Latin text, as, e.g. Savic, Massahhakownia, Tebashir and a very few others, the explanation of which you will see in the margin. These have not been translated because no Latin word exactly corresponds to their sense, or because the meaning is doubtful.[143]

We do not possess, as it happens, any medieval translation of the work on smallpox and measles with which Channing's may be compared, but it is interesting to observe the learned eighteenth-century translator adopting exactly the same practice of retaining in the text difficult Arabic words as a Gerard of Cremona in the twelfth century (cf. p. 210). Nor are the Latinized Arabic words which Channing cites here noticeably closer to their originals than their medieval counterparts. Savic is for *sawīq*, flour of wheat, barley or vetch, Massahhakownia is *mashaqūniyā*, dross of glass, Tebashir is *ṭabāshīr* (from Sanskrit *tavakshīra*), with Rhazes for the substance called bamboo-manna, but in modern usage the word means 'chalk'.

As a sample of Rhazes on the subject of smallpox and measles we may take the following, not from Mead's or Channing's Latin, but from an English translation made in the nineteenth century by a learned physician and Orientalist, William Alexander Greenhill.[144] Greenhill may well have been the determining influence which turned the youthful Richard Burton while at Oxford in the direction of Arabic.[145]

As soon as the symptoms of smallpox appear, we must take especial care of the eyes, then of the throat and afterwards of the nose, ears and joints, in the way I am about to describe. And besides these parts, sometimes it will be necessary for us to extend our care to the soles of the feet, and the palms of the hands, for occasionally violent pains arise in these parts from the eruption of smallpox in them being difficult on account of the hardness of the skin.

As soon as the symptoms of smallpox appear, drop rose-water into the eyes from time to time, and wash the face with cold water several times in the day, and sprinkle the eyes with the same. For if the disease be favorable and the pustules few in number, you will by this mode of treatment prevent their breaking out in the eyes. This indeed is to be done for greater caution; for when the smallpox is favorable, and the matter of the disease is scanty, it seldom happens that any pustules break out in the eyes. But when you see that the ebullition is vehement and the pustules numerous in the beginning of the eruption, with itching of the eyelids and redness of the whites of the eyes, some places of which are redder than others, in this case pustules will certainly break out there unless very strong measures be adopted; and therefore you should immediately drop into the eyes several times in the day rose-water in which sumach has been macerated. It will be still more efficacious to make a collyrium of galls in rose-water, and drop some of it into the eyes; or to drop into them some of the juice of the pulp of the acid pomegranate, first chewed, or squeezed in a cloth. Then wash the eyelids with the collyrium composed of the red horn poppy, the juice of unripe grapes, rusot, aloe and acacia, of each one part, and a tenth part of saffron; and if you also drop some of this collyrium into the eyes, it will be useful at this time.

But if you see that the matter of the disease is violent, and the eruption very copious, so that you conclude that pustules will certainly break out in the eyes, because you see excessive redness in some parts of the *tunica sclerotica*, with a protuberance of the eye itself; and you find that when you have dropped into it some of the remedies which I have prescribed, it does not altogether remove the redness, but only lessens it for a time, after which it returns more violently than before, or at least continues in the same state as it was before you began this treatment; you must not in this case proceed any longer in this method, but instead of these things and the like, drop into the eyes a little Nabataean caviare[146] (*murri Nabaṭi*), in which there is no vinegar nor any other acid.

The pustules which break out in the *tunica sclerotica* do not injure the vision, but those which come out in the cornea obstruct the sight, and are to be cured, according to the degree of their thickness or thinness, by means of such strongly dissolving medicines as we are about to mention; which indeed are sometimes successful and sometimes not, according as the matter is more or less thick, or the body more or less hard or aged. But if one large pustule breaks out in the *tunica uvea*, then rub *kuḥl* in rose-water and drop it into the eye several times during the day, and put over it a compress and bandage; or else drop into it some of the collyrium above-mentioned, after taking out the saffron and adding one part of haematite, that there may not happen any great prominence. And these things are what ought to be known concerning the eyes in this place.

Care is next to be taken of the throat and mouth, in order that no pustules may break out in them which may distress the patient, or hinder his breathing; for it often happens that in the bad kinds of smallpox obstinate and violent suffocations come on, and when this is the case, there is no hope of the patient's recovery. For which reason, as soon as the symptoms of smallpox begin to appear, the patient should gargle with acid pomegranate juice, or an infusion of sumach, or the inspissated juice of white mulberries, or with some of those things which we have mentioned in the chapter on extinguents; or if nothing is ready at hand, with pure cold water, and that very often, in order that there may be either no eruption at all in the throat and mouth, or that what there is may be but slight. And therefore you should strengthen these parts, in order that they may not be attacked by numerous pustules, giving rise to suffocation; and be quick and diligent in applying this cure, when besides the symptoms of smallpox there is a hoarseness of voice, constriction in breathing and about the fauces, and pain in the throat. And if you see these symptoms to be very violent, then take away blood from the cephalic vein, and that even after the whole eruption is over. And if the patient finds anything in his mouth or throat which hurts him, and there is not much heat there . . . then let him lick by degrees butter mixed with white sugar-candy; but if there be any heat and inflammation there, then give him a linctus of the mucilage of fleawort seed, peeled almonds, and white sugar-candy, thus prepared.[147]

In this long quotation the elaboration and exactness of Rhazes' therapeutic method are clearly shown. This is not in any sense primitive doctoring, rather its opposite, and we may be content to concur with Meyerhof's judgment that Rhazes was 'undoubtedly the greatest physician of the Islamic world and one of the greatest physicians of all time'.[148] At all events, this kind of discussion shows Arabic medicine at its maturest and best, and what Rhazes says here is comparable with anything in Avicenna.

Channing, perhaps even Greenhill, did not know a great deal about the life and circumstances of Rhazes, but a later writer, G. S. A. Ranking, has given a very full account of him, based on Ibn Abī Uṣaybiʿa and Ibn Khallikān.[149] These two authorities, as Ranking remarked, are the bases of all notices of Rhazes up to his time. In 1936, however, Paul Kraus published in Paris the Arabic text of another source enumerating the works of Rhazes which, considering its authorship—it was written by the great scientist al-Bīrūnī—is of great interest and importance.[150] Kraus later published also a volume of philosophical works of Rhazes,[151] including the 'Spiritual Physick', which has been translated by Professor A. J. Arberry,[152] and a kind of philosophical autobiography, but these do not concern us here. Al-Bīrūnī's work is in the form of a *Risāla* to an unnamed correspondent, written after 427/1035–6, probably in the course of the next year, when al-Bīrūnī was already a man of sixty-three.[153]

He begins:

You have mentioned—may you not cease to mention and to be mentioned!—that you desire to know the time of Muḥammad b. Zakariyyāʾ b. Yaḥyā ar-Rāzī and to be informed of the number of his works, with their names, that you may have a guide in searching for them, and (you have mentioned also) that your conviction of the penetration of his genius, the excellence of his understanding and his extraordinary progress in the art have inspired in you a desire to know who it was who first inaugurated and devised the medical art. And though this is a historical investigation, it is not strange that you aspire to know. Isḥāq b. Ḥunayn the translator actually wrote a work on the biographies of the famous Greek physicians, those great men who inaugurated the principles of medicine, and composed the canons and observed them for the benefit of mankind, so that their memory remained in the world for a time, and many sick people were led by the soundness of their intentions and thoughts to profit from visiting the temples built in their name,[154] and to seek health from passing within the precincts and presenting sacrifices therein for relief of great sicknesses, and to obtain success without having recourse to the methods of medicine for healing. Isḥāq added a good number of cases of this kind, though what he says has been spoiled by the copyists and transmitters, some learning without correction, others collecting without study.

You have mentioned that, when you discovered that I followed another method, you directed yourself to me in pursuit of your aim, hoping that your heart would be gladdened by me in the matter of your search, in spite of its little usefulness and small advantage. I admit the correctness of what you thought of me as regards the possibility, and I am writing for you the books of Abū Bakr (i.e. Rhazes) which I have seen, or whose names I happen to have come across in the course of reading these by his drawing attention to them and citing them. Were it not for my regard for you, I would not have done this, in view of the risk of incurring the rancour of his opponents, who may think that I share his views and am one of those who make no difference between what he was led to in his search for truth and what his inclination and excessive zeal brought him to, so that his boldness brought him discredit and he fell not short of hardness of heart in the matter of religion, by his neglect of it and turning aside and heedlessness without being concerned to impute to it evil suggestions and wicked deeds, till he was induced to point to the books of Mani and his followers in his efforts to oppose (lit. ensnare) all religions, including Islam. The justification of what I have said will be found at the end of his *Book on Prophetic Missions*, where with unseemly folly he makes light of the good and the great. In writing this passage, he defiles his heart and tongue and pen with expressions which an intelligent man will have nothing to do with and will pay no heed to, since they will bring him in his efforts in this world nothing but hatred.

We still see those by far his inferiors (*man lā yusawwī li-qadamihi turāban*) saying that Rhazes destroyed people's money and their bodies and their beliefs. This is true as to the first head and to a considerable extent as to the last, so that it is difficult to argue with them as to the second head. For myself, though I am exempt from following him in regard to (the alchemy) with which he destroyed men's money—love of money indeed, where personal independence is concerned, I do not claim to be exempt from—I did not escape the dangers under the last head. For I read a book of his on theology, where he begins by pointing to the books of Mani, and particularly one entitled *Sifr al-Asrār* (Volume of Secrets), the title attracted me, as others are attracted by the white and gold of alchemy, and I was induced by the novelty, or rather the concealment of the truth to seek those secrets from my acquaintances in different countries. My desire was not satisfied for more than forty years, till there reached me in Khwārizm a post from Hamadhān with a chance find of books of Faḍl b. Sahlān[155] . . . among them a collection of Manichean works . . . including letters of Mani and the object of my search, the *Sifr al-Asrār*. I was filled with delight, as a thirsty man at the sight of a mirage, but with grief for the result, for the disappointment which greets him when he comes to it. I found the words of the Qurʾān to be true, where it is said: 'He to whom God hath not given light, hath no light.'[156] Then I took down a short account of the unmitigated nonsense and pure rubbish contained in the book, in order that anyone afflicted with my complaint might study it and be quickly cured, as I was.

This then is the situation of Rhazes. I believe him to have been not a deceiver but a dupe, as he was convinced was the case with those men whom God preserved free from such ideas, and his portion is not diminished in what he aspired to. For actions are according to the intention, and on that day 'He shall be a sufficient reckoner against himself.'[157]

He was born in Rayy on 1st Shaʿbān, 251 (August, 865), and I am not certain as to his circumstances, except that he occupied himself with alchemy. His eye was continually fixed and exposed to serious mischances, for his perseverance with fires and sharp odours affected it, and he had to have recourse to medical treatment. The situation led him to occupy himself with medicine,[158] and then he went on to further matters for which he won only disapproval. He reached in the art (*sc.* of medicine) a high standing, and great kings wanted him and sent for him with all honour. He studied continually and engaged unremittingly in research, placing his lamp in a niche in the wall facing him, leaning his book against it, so that when overcome by sleep, the book fell from his hand and wakened him, that he might return to his studies. It was this, together with his fondness for beans, which affected his sight, till in the end he became blind, being, as the Qurʾān says, 'Blind in the Hereafter'.[159] For a cataract descended upon him at the close of his life. There came to him from Ṭabaristān one who claimed a connection with his pupils to treat him. Rhazes asked him what the treatment was to be, and he told him. Rhazes replied: 'I testify that you are the unique among the couchers of cataract and the most learned of the oculists. But you know that this operation is not free from pain such as the soul loathes, and involves long-drawn-out difficulties such as men find tedious. Perhaps my end is near and my life will not be long, and a man like me finds it hard to choose pain at the end of his days, and vexations in preference to rest.' So the oculist left him, after receiving thanks for his intention and efforts and an adequate reward. Rhazes did not linger long thereafter, but died at Rayy on 5th Shaʿbān, 313 (October, 925), at the age of sixty years, two months and a day. The following are the names of the books of his which I know . . .[160]

Al-Birūnī then details 184 works written by Rhazes, before proceeding to answer his correspondent's further enquiry about the rise of medicine. The number of works here given is considerably fewer than the list in Ibn Abī Uṣaybiʿa, where 232 titles are mentioned, according to Ranking.[161] But al-Bīrūnī knows the dates of his birth and death, as to which Ibn Abī Uṣaybiʿa is very uncertain and offers various alternative accounts. In particular, al-Bīrūnī accepts that the activity of Rhazes may be divided into three main heads, according to the scurrilous judgment already quoted. Rhazes was said to have spoiled men's wealth, their bodies and their beliefs, but whatever the value of his work as alchemist or theologian, there was in al-Bīrūnī's view no question in regard to his greatness as a doctor. The book titles themselves fall into a larger number of categories than the threefold division of his work would suggest, but, as we might expect, his strictly medical works greatly outnumber the others (in al-Bīrūnī 56 titles). There follow works on natural science (35), logic (7), mathematics and astronomy (10), commentaries and synopses (7), philosophy and 'hypotheses' (17), metaphysics (6), theology (14), alchemy (22), infidel works (2) and various (10), altogether 184 works, which even without the additions in Ibn Abī Uṣaybiʿa is evidently an enormous number for one man's lifetime. When we take into consideration the huge size of such a book as the *Kitāb al-Hāwī* or *Continens* of Rhazes, which was collected after his death, the industry and persistence of the man, as well as his genius, come to light.

This is not the place to repeat what can be found in Ranking's paper already alluded to (see n. 149), but it seems worth signalizing the fact that Ranking was able to utilize a Latin version of at least some parts of Ibn Abī Uṣaybiʿa made by Salomon Negri, before the latter's death in 1729. This version is now in the Hunterian Library in Glasgow University, the collection of books dealing with medicine, history of medicine and other matters, which was assembled by the celebrated physician Dr William Hunter and bequeathed by him to the University of Glasgow.

One or two observations by way of supplement to Ranking[162] may throw additional light on Rhazes's work and the circumstances in which it was carried out. No. 40 of Ranking's list is a book by Rhazes entitled *Refutation of al-Kindī in Regard to His Including*

Alchemy in the Category of the Impossible. This work seems to be lost. It is most likely a reply to one or other of the two works of al-Kindī against the alchemists which have already been mentioned (see p. 231). We can in fact point to a series of works by masters of Arabic thought dealing with the question of the possibility of alchemy, including the surviving *Kitāb fī Wujūb Sanāʿat al-Kīmiyāʾ* (Book on the Necessity of Alchemy) of al-Fārābī in which he like Rhazes defended alchemy,[163] and which Ibn Khaldūn no doubt had in mind in the well-known passage of the *Muqaddima* (Prolegomena) where he discusses the subject.[164] It is unfortunate that the work of Rhazes appears to be lost, for, as the production of a practical expert, it is likely to have been at least as important as al-Fārābī's short and quite theoretical treatment.

Two titles of Ranking's list, nos. 49 and 50, are informative, because they show us the well-known belletrist al-Jāḥiẓ (see pp. 47–50) tilting at the philosophers. Al-Jāḥiẓ has in one of his works, besides his representation of al-Kindī, apparently the philosopher (see p. 47), a comic description of an unsuccessful Muslim doctor too long to quote here.[165] We would hardly have guessed that the great man of letters had written proposing, no doubt whimsically, to refute the science or art of medicine. This he must have done, for Rhazes writes a work in reply, no. 49 of Ranking's list. So also al-Jāḥiẓ had written on the superiority of *kalām*, or dialectical theology, over philosophy, and Rhazes took him to task for this in the other work.

No. 51 in Ranking's list shows us Rhazes as author of a work on the classification of diseases, written in the schematic form called *tashjīr*, which was also used in a medical work of Ḥunayn b. Isḥāq[166] and in the little encyclopaedia known as *Jawāmi al-ʿUlūm* (Connections of the Sciences).[167] Evidently for such a subject as classification of diseases the 'arborification', to translate *tashjīr* by its literal English equivalent, was very suitable.

One title (no. 157) perhaps may serve to connect Rhazes with the studies cultivated extensively by al-Fārābī, namely the *Book on the Ideal Life and the Life of the People of the Ideal State.*[168] This is very close to al-Fārābī's *Book of the Views of the People of the Ideal State*[169] and others of his titles. It would be of interest to know what, if any, was the relationship between these works. Unfortunately, like so many others, this work of Rhazes is lost.

Two other titles which may here be noted are a *Book on the Cure of Diseases*—what type is not specified—*in One Hour*, composed for a *wazīr*, Abū'l-Qāsim b. ʿAbd Allāh (no. 213), and a work on the common cold dedicated to Abū Zayd al-Balkhī (see p. 164), under whom Rhazes had studied philosophy. Abū Zayd al-Balkhī was a pupil of al-Kindī, and his relation to Rhazes serves to indicate that the latter stood at only one remove from al-Kindī himself.

The work of Rhazes which was most famous in the Middle Ages was the *Kitāb al-Manṣūrī*, or *Liber ad Almansorem*, a ten-book treatise on the various branches of medicine, dedicated by the author to al-Manṣūr b. Isḥāq b. Khāqān,[170] a governor of Rayy. This was translated into Latin by Gerard of Cremona in the twelfth century. The ninth Book (*Nonus Almansoris*) on the cure of diseases of the organs of the body from head to foot, was the most popular. The *Kitāb al-Ḥāwī* (*Continens*), the great medical book of Rhazes, already mentioned, was given a Latin version at the end of the thirteenth century by the Jew Faraj b. Salīm (Farragut). The Arabic text has never been printed *in extenso* and manuscripts must be extremely scarce. Several volumes of the same manuscript copy, not, however, complete, and additional volumes are to be found in the Escorial.[171] The Bodleian manuscript appears to be fragmentary, but from it there has been printed the section on remarkable cures which had happened within Rhazes' own practice. This is specially referred to by Ibn Abī Uṣaybiʿa, was drawn upon by E. G. Browne in his *Arabian Medicine* and most recently has appeared in the original Arabic in a *tirage-à-part* in the University Library, Cambridge.[172]

5. Decline of Arabic science

Arabic science and medicine after Rhazes were marked by such great names as Ibn Sīnā (Avicenna) (980–1037) and al-Bīrūnī (973–1048), but we cannot here follow the development in detail and must now consider Arabic science in decline. For this purpose a good example is the so-called science of *zāʾiraja*, described in the modern encyclopaedia of Muḥammad Farīd Wajdī as a form of astrology calculated to reveal the future by means of the occult properties of the letters of the alphabet.[173] This, we are told, was a study of great importance among the learned Arabs and had its own *shaykhs* and experts, but it has declined together with the other occult sciences. We cannot judge the truth or falsity of its claims except after learning what it is about and subjecting it to experiment, but unfortunately its principles and explanation and the extent to which it attained its aim are alike unknown, so that to pass judgment on it is futile. So far the article in this twentieth-century encyclopaedia. Ḥājjī Khalīfa, author of the famous *Kashf aẓ-Ẓunūn*, the great eighteenth-century repertory of books in Arabic, Persian and Turkish, also mentions the science of *zā'iraja*, devoting to it a section in his third volume, and listing a number of works on the subject.[174]

The account of *zā'iraja* given in both these encyclopaedias is derived from Ibn Khaldūn, writing in the fourteenth century A.D., who deals with the subject in two passages of his *Muqaddima*. One of these is of great length, amounting to more than twenty pages of Arabic text,[175] so that evidently the matter was regarded by Ibn Khaldūn as interesting and important. Among the artificial methods used to disclose the future, he tells us, by those who claim this to be possible, is the *zā'irajat al-ʿālam* or 'Table of the Universe', the invention of which is attributed to a certain Abū'l-ʿAbbās Aḥmad as-Sabtī, i.e. of Ceuta in Morocco, one of the principal Ṣūfīs of the Muslim West, who flourished under the Almohad Sultan Abū Yūsuf Yaʿqūb al-Manṣūr at the end of the sixth/twelfth century. The construction of this table is remarkably elaborate, and many highly placed persons are in the habit of consulting it, in order to obtain knowledge of the invisible world. It is in the form of a large circle with concentric circles corresponding to the heavenly spheres, the elements, the sublunary world, the spirits, and to various other existents and sciences. The whole is enclosed in a rectangular figure, containing 55 compartments in breadth and 131 compartments in length. Ibn Khaldūn gave a representation of the table, not found in all the editions, but reproduced in Professor Franz Rosenthal's recent translation. There is also an elaborate description in Ibn Khaldūn's text.[176] On one of the sides is a verse ascribed to Mālik b. Wuhayb of Seville, one of the greatest of the diviners (*ahl al-ḥadathān*) in the Maghrib, and this was the operative part of the invention. Not only the *zāʿiraja* of as-Sabtī but other models employed Mālik b. Wuhayb's verse. Ibn Khaldūn names one of these which he had himself seen, attributed to Sahl b. ʿAbd Allāh, apparently the mystic of that name, called at-Tustarī, after a place in Khūzistān. Ḥājji Khalīfa, for his part, mentions the *zā'iraja Khiṭā'iyya* or Chinese *zā'iraja* (Khiṭāy = Cathay) composed by one ʿUmar b. Aḥmad

b. ʿAlī al-Khiṭāʾī, a copy of which is in the Bibliothèque Nationale[177] also a *zāʾiraja Shaibāniyya* and a *zāʾiraja Harawiyya*, i.e. of Herat, without further details.[178]

Now as to the method of manipulating the *zāʾiraja*. Ibn Khaldūn tells us that the question is first written down, decomposed into its letters. The sign of the zodiac which is at that moment in the ascendant is taken, and the degree of its ascendancy is determined. Turning next to the *zāʾiraja*, we select the radius which is thus given, passing along it to the centre of the circle, and then to the circumference opposite the place where the ascendant is indicated. Along the radius are letters and numbers in the *ghubār* character.[179] These are all taken, the numbers being transformed into letters by the process known as *ḥisāb al-jummal* (i.e. representation of the numerals by letters, or vice versa). Sometimes the units are raised to tens or the tens to hundreds and conversely, according to certain rules. The resulting letters are placed aside, with the letters of the question.

The radius third in order from that of the ascendant is taken, and all the letters and figures on it as far as the centre are written down also. The verse of Mālik b. Wuhayb is divided into its constituent letters which are placed aside with the others, the number of degrees of the ascendant, already determined, is multiplied by a new number called the *uss* (foundation) of the sign, which is obtained by calculating the number of degrees between the end of the last sign of the zodiac and the degree of the sign at this time in the ascendant, and the product is multiplied in turn by the *uss al-akbar* and the *dawr al-aṣlī*, further numbers the means of computing which are not given in Ibn Khaldūn's text. This result is applied according to further rules to the compartments of the surrounding rectangular figure, and the emergent letters are placed aside with the others. We now have the final material for the solution. By means of certain operative numbers called *dawr*, letters are selected from the pool. These when placed together give a verse in the same rhyme and metre as the verse of Mālik b. Wuhayb, which is the result of the whole complicated operation. Ibn Khaldūn gives as an example the question, Is *zāʾiraja* an ancient or modern science? The answer elicited, couched in cryptic terms appropriate to an oracle, was: 'Go then! the spirit of holiness has manifested the mystery to Idrīs (Enoch), so that through it he has reached the summit of glory', i.e. *zāʾiraja* was really old.

What are we to make of this? Many people, says Ibn Khaldūn, refuse to admit the reality of the art of *zā'iraja* and in the narrowness of their views regard it as a matter of imagination and fantasy. According to them, the exponents of *zā'iraja* manipulate the letters in such a way as to produce a fraudulent answer. This is not the case, says Ibn Khaldūn. Any one who has seen *zā'iraja* knows that it proceeds according to a fixed system of rules, independent of the operator. Yet it is not true to say, as some do, that the appropriateness of the answers to the questions indicates sufficiently that events will be in conformity with them. This opinion is ill-founded, because one cannot learn the secrets of the invisible world by any artificial means whatever. He goes on to cite a long poem on the working of the *zā'iraja* and to give a detailed account of how the result of asking the age of its invention was reached. Any remaining doubt that we may have here, after all, an experiment in the occult, is set at rest by a description of *zā'iraja* as known in nineteenth-century Egypt given by E. W. Lane in his *Manners and Customs of the Modern Egyptians*. Lane there prints a table of 100 letters so arranged that if, beginning anywhere, every fifth letter is taken, an intelligible sentence will be the result.[180] Thus if, in doubt about an action, a man consulted his *zā'iraja*, he would get such a response as 'Abstain and enjoy peace', or 'Who does it, will do wrong'. The table of 100 letters corresponds, that is, to the final collection of letters elicited in the other case from the concentric circles and the surrounding rectangle. In the Egyptian *zā'iraja* five is the operative number or *dawr*. The example given by Ibn Khaldūn is vastly more complicated, but the principle is evidently the same. The astrological calculation of the ascendant at the beginning of the operation serves to get a start made at some point in the table, which in Lane's example is done by placing a finger at random on any of the hundred squares. It also serves of course to introduce the mysterious influence of the stars. The same purpose of mystification is observable elsewhere in the construction or operation of the table. The whole has been contrived with great ingenuity, but quite plainly it is a toy rather than a scientific instrument of any kind.

That the *zā'irjat al-ʿālam* was the invention of the North African Abū'l-ʿAbbās Aḥmad as-Sabtī in the twelfth century, as Ibn Khaldūn states, there is no reason to doubt. But it had a predecessor, and here, it seems to me, the decline of Arabic science by this date comes to a light in a very striking manner. For the predecessor of the *zāʾirajat al-ʿālam*, and presumably of the others which have been mentioned, though connected with astrology, was of an altogether more scientific character. It is mentioned in Lane's great *Arabic Lexicon* under *zīj*, which word itself means an astronomical or astrological table. *Zāʾija*—without the r—is there given as a four-sided or round scheme made to exhibit the horoscope or places of configuration of the stars at the time of a birth, and it is derived from a Persian word of similar form and meaning, *zāʾicha*. This explanation and derivation is said in the *Lexicon* to come from the *Mafātīḥ al-ʿUlūm* of ar-Rāzī, which may be connected with the *Mafātīḥ al-ʿUlum* of Abū ʿAbd Allāh Muḥammad b. Aḥmad al-Khwārizmī, edited by Van Vloten (Leiden, 1895). The passage can therefore be checked[181] and affords evidence that in the tenth century when the *Mafātīḥ al-ʿUlūm* was written the term *zāʾija* was in use for an astrological chart. In view of the technical skill shown by Arabic astrologers at this period, we can be certain that such charts were sometimes of considerable elaboration and accuracy. In the North African *zāʾiraja* of the twelfth century, on the other hand, while elaboration is present even to excess, the relation with observed fact, characteristic of the best astrology, has disappeared, and what we have is a creation of great ingenuity but no real use whatever.

About the same time as the pseudo-science of *zāʾiraja* was being elaborated in the Muslim West, there lived in Khwārizm (Khiva) Abū Yaʿqūb Yūsuf b. Abī Bakr as-Sakkākī. The name Sakkākī means 'cutler, maker of knives' or 'engraver of dies'. It does not necessarily refer to his original occupation, though the story was current that he 'originally embraced learning because of the honours he saw bestowed on great savants'.[182] As-Sakkākī (555/1160–626/1229) is principally known for a single book, the so-called *Key of the Sciences* (*Miftāḥ al-ʿUlūm*). The popularity of this work was very great, and remained so in parts of the East till modern times. It gained for its author the reputation, which he shares with not a few other scholars whose work was incomprehensible to the uneducated, of being a great magician. It is therefore with some surprise that we learn that his *Key of the Sciences* was primarily a work on rhetoric.

Ibn Khaldūn speaks of as-Sakkākī as an example of those men of talent who discover new subjects of study in the old. The original field of as-Sakkākī's investigation was grammar, but from the matters discussed in various works on grammar, he was able to invent a new science, that of *bayān*, exposition or rhetoric.[183] As-Sakkākī would have no place in an account of Arabic science save for one thing, the circumstance that he called his book, being what it was, *Miftāḥ al-ʿUlūm*. One of the biographical notices[184] describes it as dealing with twelve of the specifically Arabic sciences. This of course means that the natural sciences are not treated at all. The situation was very different at the time when Muḥammad b. Aḥmad al-Khwārizmī wrote his work of similar title *Mafātīḥ al-ʿUlūm* (see p. 246), the purpose of which, in his own words, was to provide 'an introduction to the sciences and a key to most of them, so that whoever having read the book and learned its contents, examines philosophical books (*kutub al-ḥikma*) will be able to go through them and understand what they contain, even if he has not previously given attention to them or studied under experts. I have made it in two sections, the first for the sciences connected with Muslim law and the connected Arabic sciences, the second for the sciences of the non-Arabs, Greeks and others. . . .' The work of al-Khwārizmī was a real encyclopaedia, and so, in spite of its lack of order and other deficiencies, the nearly contemporary *Jawāmiʿ al-ʿUlūm* of Ibn Farighūn already referred to on p. 241 (also written apparently towards the end of the tenth century). By the time of as-Sakkākī the 'sciences of the non-Arabs' have been dropped, and his work in spite of its title restricts itself practically to philological subjects. Even the remarks of a sociological cast, where he shows appreciation of the influence of environment on thought and which have been cited for as-Sakkākī as a precursor in Islam of Ibn Khaldūn, are made in the context of a purely literary discussion.[185]

Coming further down in time, we find that the well-known polygraph as-Suyūṭī assigns a place to anatomy and medicine among the fourteen branches of knowledge which he treats of in his encyclopaedia called *an-Nuqāya*,[186] the Siftings of the Wheat, or, as we might say, the *Marrow*. But the treatment of anatomy in particular is unsatisfactory, and while it is true that he presumably knew more of the subject than he mentions here, since he himself wrote a kind of commentary on his own work which he called *Completion of Knowledge* (*Itmām ad-Dirāya*) *for the Readers of the Marrow*,[187] this is scarcely relevant. The fact is striking that it was evidently worth while in the fifteenth century to produce such a meagre and jejune account and publish it. The interest in this part of the *Marrow* seems as much lexicographical as scientific, to provide names for the parts of the human skeleton, the principal organs, etc., rather than to describe their appearance and function, and in this respect the decline from such a writer as Rhazes does not need to be emphasized. References to the great medical authorities, Arabic as well as Greek, are non-existent in the account of anatomy in the *Marrow*, few and far between in the *Completion*. The situation indeed is not so very unlike that centuries earlier, when Arab grammarians, innocent of Greek science, sat down to compile world lists of the principal parts of the body. The interest in and knowledge of medicine displayed by the physicians of early ʿAbbāsid Caliphate are conspicuously absent in this Egyptian production of the later Middle Ages. This section on anatomy in the *Marrow* is about as far as popularization can go and might have served as a warning to its exponents. But by this time the whole of Muslim science was liable to be treated in this way.

As time passed, alchemy comes to be found in a religious setting. The celebrated Ghazālī (451/1059–505/1111) used the term metaphorically as the title of one of his books dealing with ethics and mysticism, *Kīmiyāʾ as-Saʿāda* (Alchemy of Happiness), but later we find the Ṣūfīs or mystics of Islam actually engaged in alchemical operations. The cases of this which are referred to by the well-known religious writer ash-Shaʿrānī (died 973/1565) are numerous enough to warrant attention. Thus he tells us that the Shaykh Aḥmad b. Sulaymān az-Zāhid, who died about A.H. 820 (i.e. towards A.D. 1420), gained his honourable appellation az-Zāhid (the Ascetic) which he alone of the Egyptian religious had enjoyed in ash-Shaʿrānī's young days, because he refused to touch a quantity of about 5 *qinṭārs* (500–600 lb weight) of gold which he had produced by a successful alchemical operation, and gave orders that the gold should be thrown into the cellar of his mosque, lest he be corrupted by the goods of the present world.[188]

In so far as it passed into the hands of the Ṣūfīs, the change cannot have contributed to the advancement of the practice of alchemy. The following examples taken from ash-Shaʿrānī's largely autobiographical work *Laṭāʾif al-Minan waʾl-Akhlāq* (Pleasant Gifts and Traits of Character)[189] illustrate the extent to which alchemy was actually practised in Ṣūfī circles and at the same time the evident decline from the days when the science occupied the attention of men like al-Kindī and Rhazes. Ash-Shaʿrānī thanks God that from childhood he has given no heed to the words of those who claim to know the science of alchemy or to be able to discover hidden treasures. This is one of God's greatest favours to him, for in this way the money of many poor men and seekers after knowledge has been lost, and not only so but the loss has affected their religious beliefs and their hearts have been perverted, so that they have lost the love of God and His Apostle, the Companions and the Followers. 'My master', he says, 'Abū'l-Baqā' al-Barizī, told me that a certain man cheated him and lost about 30,000 *dīnārs* of his money, in amounts of a few hundred *dīnārs* at a time or more, making concoctions which turned out wrong. The alchemist would then say: "Wait till next time, and it will be right, if God wills." But the concoction was always wrong, till al-Barizī's fortune had all been spent. "I said to him", adds ash-Shaʿrānī, "Where was your understanding?" And he said: "Has he understanding who loves the goods of the present world?" '[190]

Ash-Shaʿrānī tells a number of stories of how respectable Muslims were deceived by impostors, one of whom is described as a master of white magic (*sīmiyā'*), who apparently could project a vision of buried treasure by autosuggestion, and did so in several cases, before absconding with his dupe's money. He then says that his *shaykh* Afḍal ad-Dīn had informed him that the alchemists had had an agreement since the days of Jābir (see pp. 209–12) never to mention the complete process, and always omitted certain essential elements and conditions in their descriptions, while confiding real knowledge to the adepts. What they did say was by way of hints and enigmas and names of drugs not intended to be easily understood. Ash-Shaʿrānī had seen a man who read in a book the following recipe: Take oil of wheat from Upper Egypt, red lead (minium, oxide of lead), egg-shells and nitre. So he brought oil of wheat and mixed it with the red lead, sprinkling over it egg-shells and nitre used to whiten thread. He placed it in a cask and watered it abundantly, stirring it with a piece of wood. 'When I told the Shaykh Afḍal ad-Dīn about this, he began to laugh, laughing so much that the turban nearly fell off his head.'

The same Afḍal ad-Dīn wrote a *Risāla* on alchemy, which ash-Shaʿrānī gives in full.[191] The treatise begins:

I charge all my brethren of the Muslims to be abstinent in the present world and not to listen to the words of the wicked Ṣūfīs who claim to know the science of alchemy. For they are liars, because all the sciences which come to man are . . . by way of revelation. And he who loves the present world is withheld from revelation by a thousand thousand veils. Further, it is characteristic of those who know this science and can perform it correctly that they do not profit in body thereby, but are afflicted with diseases which prevent the enjoyment of the present world. . . . Jābir b. Ḥayyān al-Kūfī al-Azdī, the master of the science of Wisdom (*ʿilm al-ḥikma*), invented the arts of alchemy, the philosopher's stone and the special qualities of the letters *kāf*, *hāʾ*, *yāʾ*, *sīn*, and *ṣād*, and extracted therefrom the cream of his sciences, the chief and pole of which is that round which centres the science of Wisdom and science of the Balance . . . and he spoke sufficiently thereon in the *Book of the Seven* (? *Seventy*),[192] mentioning in this book the principles of the Balance,[193] and in the rest of his books how to operate the art by means of it, grudging this science except to experts. . . . If we were to empower you with the knowledge of the science, we should not permit you to know the operation of it, for the operation was abrogated in the year 940 of the Hijra, as the knowledge of it was abrogated in the year 933 of the Hijra, and it is not permitted to occupy oneself with a science which has been abrogated, etc.

It is in shallows like these that this chapter must end. But we have to remember that it was not always so. The years A.H. 933 and 940 mentioned in the passage just quoted are considerably later than A.D. 1500 (1526 and 1533). By this time the tide had turned, as our chapter has shown. Arabic science in full tide was something very different from the *zāʾiraja*, jejune medical texts and ignorant attempts at alchemy. The impression which we may retain is of Baghdad especially, but also Iraq and Iran, in the ninth and tenth centuries, when something was being done, and people really knew something, not of the degenerate days which followed.

Chapter 7

Some famous women in Islam

A feature of the Islamic system which has constantly struck Western observers with much force is the seclusion of women and the small part which they have seemed to play in the social scene, down almost to the present time. The institutions of the *ḥarīm* and the veil, which appeared at an early date among the Muslims, have often been thought of as imposing a kind of anonymity or even nonentity on one half of the population, and it has been said with some truth that Islam is a masculine society. The ground for the seclusion of women is no doubt to be sought in polygamy, but it would be a mistake to suppose that the influence of women in Islam has been greatly less than in other communities. Their anonymity or nonentity is of course largely a matter of appearance only, and in all kinds of domestic affairs, we can be sure, their influence has been paramount at most times, even if under the religious law, for example in regard to divorce, women have suffered from disabilities which were not present or present to a lesser extent, in Western society, ancient and modern. There has been much talk in the Muslim East of the emancipation of women as an aspect of modernism, but this to a great extent has been concerned with the desirability of securing for the Muslim woman advantages which her Western sister has only come to enjoy comparatively recently. The equality of the sexes is a new idea in the West as in the East. Whatever restrictions hedged in the activity of the average Muslim woman during the Middle Ages, it is certain that these were transcended by individuals, often, it is true, but by no means always, belonging to the higher class of society. Perhaps the best way of establishing this is by examples. The present chapter sets forth in outline some conspicuous lives of women who had real careers in medieval Islam in a variety of fields, who were recognized by their contemporaries for what they achieved, and whose typical activity (for the list is evidently anything but exhaustive) disproves the idea that in Islam the lot of women was necessarily limited to narrow domesticity or ministering to the pleasures of the men.

Any roll of famous women in Islam must surely begin with the contrasting figures of Khadīja and ʿĀ'isha, each of whom has a special place for herself among the numerous wives of the Prophet. Khadīja, the wife of his youth, was a widow a dozen years older than he, rich, respectable, concerned with practical affairs, entirely devoted to the interests of her much younger husband, whose aspirations and prophetic despair and raptures she could perhaps only imperfectly understand.[1] Her merits are conspicuous, and it is no doubt significant that in her lifetime Muḥammad took no other wife. She died in A.D. 619, three years, that is, before the *Hijra* or Flight of the Prophet from Mecca to Medina. ʿĀ'isha, the darling wife of Muḥammad's age, was the daughter of Abū Bakr, his closest friend and the first Caliph.[2] ʿĀ'isha was very young—not more than ten or eleven years—when in 622, shortly after the *Hijra*, she was married to the Prophet, by this time a man of fifty-three. The affection of the Prophet for ʿĀ'isha was related to his affection for Abū Bakr. There is no reason to suppose that Muḥammad ever regretted the choice of ʿĀ'isha, though on occasion the peace of his family was disturbed by her sprightliness and at least once by her lack of discretion, when she was left behind by the Prophet's caravan and returned next morning in the company of a young man.[3] Her hostility to ʿAlī, which afterwards appeared strongly, is said to have dated from this occasion. ʿAlī had deeply offended her, before the innocence of the circumstances had been established, by striking her maid and roughly bidding her tell the truth.[4] Long years afterwards, when ʿAlī eventually became Caliph on the death of ʿUthmān, ʿĀ'isha announced that she would avenge the murdered Caliph and conspired with two of the leading Companions,[5] Ṭalḥa and az-Zubayr, to remove or at least coerce ʿAlī, whose lack of positive support for ʿUthmān had, it was widely thought, encouraged his murderers. (That he was not directly implicated in the crime was certain, then and now.) The result of her conspiracy was the battle of the Camel, fought near Basra in 36/656, and so called because of ʿĀ'isha's presence in a camel-borne litter, round which the fighting was fiercest. Though the loyalist forces who supported ʿAlī were successful, large numbers of Muslims were killed on either side—10,000 according to one estimate, equally divided between the two parties. ʿĀ'isha was treated respectfully by the victors, and after a time spent at Basra in the best house of the town, she retired to Medina and thereafter took no more part in politics. She died in 58/678 at the age of nearly seventy.[6]

Maysūn, wife of Muʿāwiya and mother of his son who later succeeded to the Caliphate as Yazīd I, was another lady of high station in early Islam. She was, however, not a Muslim but a Jacobite Christian, daughter of one Baḥdal of the tribe of Kalb, that is she belonged to the dominant Yamanite (South Arabian) group, the firmest supporters of the Umayyads. She is principally known for a famous poem in which she gave expression to her pining in Damascus and her longing for the desert, in spite of all luxury and enjoyments of the Caliph's palace. The verses have become familiar to English readers in Nicholson's rendering, which begins:

> A tent with rustling breezes cool
> Delights me more than palace high,
> And more the cloak of simple wool
> Than robes in which I learned to sigh.[7]

The last line was anything but complimentary to her husband: 'And a slender, handsome young man of my own people is dearer to me than a heavy peasant with a beard.'[8] This observation, which no doubt well suited Muʿāwiya in his later years when (like ʿAlī in similar circumstances) he had grown fat from comfortable living, was specially opprobrious because the descriptive *ʿilj* ('peasant') was commonly applied to non-Arabs.

In consequence, Maysūn was relegated to the pastures of her tribe, where the young Yazīd grew up familiar with the ways of the Desert. Perhaps the slur of Christianity which was afterwards cast on him[9] derives in part from his boyhood home among the Banū Kalb.

We get a glimpse of Maysūn before her banishment from court, combing her little boy's hair, with Muʿāwiya an interested spectator,[10] and, at greater length, we hear of how she got rid of a rival by a well judged prognostication of the future. Her prophecy, according to the story, came to pass when the husband whom the lady, her rival, subsequently married after divorce from Muʿāwiya, met a violent death.[11]

Approximately contemporary with Maysūn was Laylā al-Akhyaliyya, whose life mirrors yet more vividly the wild Bedouin background to Umayyad times. As her name implies, a descendant of a Desert champion of former times, al-Akhyal, Laylā was related to the poet Majnūn,[12] being connected far back with the same genealogical line of Qays ʿAylān (Qays b. ʿAylān).

The Caliph Muʿāwiya one day, while riding in the Desert, saw a horseman and sent one of his guard to bring him into his presence. The solitary rider, challenged in the name of Muʿāwiya, advanced and let down the veil which the Desert men used, and still use, against the dust and sun. But when his face was disclosed, it was no Bedouin fighting man who had been thus by chance encountered, but the poetess, Laylā al-Akhyaliyya. Having made herself known to the Caliph in verses, Laylā received from him a gift of fifty camels—wealth indeed by the standards of the time. Next the Caliph enquired about her friend, Tawba b. al-Ḥumayyir, also of the same gifted stock, who had made many poems in her praise, but who had been killed in a raid by the Banū Awf b. ʿUqayl. 'Is it true what people say of Tawba?' asked the Caliph. 'Not all people tell the truth,' replied the poetess. 'They are a tree of iniquity, and envy God's favours wherever they are found and wherever they fall. Tawba was open-handed and generous, eloquent, noble and handsome in appearance. He was as I have said, not diverging from the truth.' Muʿāwiya objected, 'But many speak of Tawba as a dissolute rascal. Surely you exaggerate his merits?' 'Not so, Commander of the Faithful,' replied she. 'By God! had you seen and known him, you would have thought that I did not say enough in his praise.' 'How old was he?' asked Muʿāwiya. 'He was in the prime of life and unequalled among his peers, brave as a lion defending its den, yet gentle when gentleness was requisite,' said she. 'What is the most poetical of your verses about him?' enquired Muʿāwiya. 'In all that I have said there are good qualities,' replied the poetess, 'but this I say well,' and she repeated:

> He was musk and honey in the comb. I mingled it
> With a theriac of wine of Maysān[13] which causes trembling.

She later also visited Marwān before his Caliphate, probably when governor of Medina, which he was twice,[14] and defended the memory of Tawba.[15] At another time Laylā appeared in the *majlis* (assembly) of al-Ḥajjāj b. Yusūf, where she was unknown to most of the participants but impressed all by her beauty and eloquence. Al-Ḥajjāj was the well-known Umayyad governor of Iraq for twenty years from 694 until his death in 713, and the company is likely to have been a distinguished one. At the governor's request she recited some of Tawba's verses in her praise. Al-Ḥajjāj, intending a compliment, was moved to ask, 'Was he not disturbed when you unveiled?' 'He never saw me except veiled,' was the reply. 'But once he sent to me to say that he was near us. The people of the tribe observed his messenger, and lay in wait for him. I realized the danger, and when Tawba came, I threw aside my *burquʿ*[16] and unveiled. As I knew he would, he at once retired without a word, save the ordinary greeting.' 'How fine!' said al-Ḥajjāj. 'Have you any request to make of me?' 'Yes,' replied Laylā. 'That you allow me to travel by the post (*barīd*) to Qutayba b. Muslim in Khurāsān.' The request was granted, and Laylā started on her long journey eastward. She met the famous general Qutayba, who was her cousin, and was cordially received by him. After some time in Khurāsān (specific places are not mentioned, but she may have travelled as far as Turkestan, where Qutayba campaigned successfully), while returning to her native Arabia, Layla died and was buried at Sāwah between Rayy and Hamadhān. The year was 89/707 or 708.[17]

Wallāda possessed some of the traits of a great lady, if in other respects she more resembles the typical 'emancipated woman', or even a modern teenager. She was the daughter of the Spanish Umayyad Muḥammad III al-Mustakfī, who was installed in the Caliphate by a Cordovan mob in succession to ʿAbd ar-Raḥmān V al-Mustaẓhir in 414/1024 (17 January), and held power briefly till 416/1025 (26 May). One of her father's first acts was to throw into prison the celebrated Ibn Ḥazm, who had been al-Mustaẓhir's *wazīr* for a short period previously. Equally with the poems of Wallāda and her circle, the famous work of Ibn Ḥazm called *Ṭawq al-Hamāma* (The Necklace of the Dove),[18] written in Shātiba (Jativa) when he had escaped from al-Mustakfī's prison, bears ample testimony not only to the refinement and sophistication but also to the relaxed morals of the Spanish Muslims at this time. There is no evidence that Ibn Ḥazm, who shortly afterwards betook himself to those studies which have given him a place in the history of Muslim thought as well as *belles lettres*, ever met Wallāda, but it seems extremely likely that he knew her by reputation. For Wallāda, we are told,[19] was one of the most celebrated women of her age in al-Andalus. It was a whim of hers to have embroidered on the hem of her dress in letters of gold, standing out for all to see against the brocade of the background, on the right border the verse: 'By Allāh! I am apt for high deeds, and I go my way and wander at will (or "behave proudly")'—and on the left border: 'I yield to my lover the round of my cheek, and I give my kiss to him who desires it'.

This curious idea of writing verses on the fringes of a robe was probably derived from a well-attested practice of placing personal names on the borders of pieces of *ṭirāz* (brocade), of which an example is the name of the Spanish Umayyad Hishām II (366/976–399/1009) embroidered on a fragment from San Esteban de Gormaz, now in the Museum of the Royal Academy of History, Madrid.[20] The practice was in vogue earlier in the Arab East.[21] It is remarkable that we find a similar ornamental use of Arabic characters in Italian painting of the Renaissance. In Fra Lippo Lippi's 'Coronation of the Virgin' in the Uffizi Gallery, Florence, this kind of decoration is employed in a scarf held by angels, on the sleeves of the Virgin and on the borders of the dresses.[22]

Wallāda is famous for the love which she inspired in the poet Ibn Zaydūn (1003–71), for her poetry and wit, and for her literary salons at Cordova. She was evidently completely unconventional by ordinary Muslim standards, but she had a kind heart, and Ibn Bashkuwāl records that she visited an old teacher of his to console him on the death of his father. She never married, and died at Cordova at an advanced age in 484/1091 or 1092.[23]

Earlier than Wallāda, we have a group of distinguished women at the ʿAbbāsid court of Baghdad, who certainly deserve mention. The first of these was al-Khayzurān, mother of Hārūn ar-Rashīd. She belonged originally to the household of a governor of Ṭabaristān, south of the Caspian, and appears to have been of mixed Arab and Iranian extraction. The governor rebelled, and in or about 759 was coerced by al-Manṣūr's son, al-Mahdī, then a young man of about twenty. Al-Mahdī was attracted by the beautiful girl, and took her into his household.[24] In the following years she gave birth to two boys, who were named Mūsā and Hārūn (Moses and Aaron), the elder of whom was destined to become the Caliph al-Hādī. The younger was afterwards the celebrated Hārūn ar-Rashīd of *Arabian Nights* fame. Al-Khayzurān won the permanent affections of al-Mahdī. He gave her her freedom, and when he succeeded to the Caliphate in 158/775, married her in form. Hārūn was his mother's favourite and remained so after the elder brother, Mūsā, was proclaimed his father's heir. Al-Khayzurān was much in her husband's counsels, and acquired influence in politics and a large fortune (her income is stated to have amounted to 160 million *dirhams*).[25] She did what she could to secure the succession of Hārūn, and her influence appears also to have been directed steadily in favour of the Barmakids (Barmecides), one of whom, al-Faḍl b. Yaḥyā, she had herself nursed as a young woman.[26] She was unable in the event to alter the succession. Mūsā succeeded as al-Hādī, his brother wisely refraining from an appeal to force, in a situation in which he might well have proved the victor.

During al-Hādī's brief Caliphate al-Khayzurān was kept strictly apart from state affairs. Her salon hitherto frequented by the most influential courtiers of the day was closed, and she herself was obliged to content herself with the society of the *ḥarīm*. It is not surprising that when al-Hādī died near Mosul in somewhat mysterious circumstances (Rabīʿ I, 170/September 786), rumour was ready to credit the Queen-mother with having had part in contriving his removal from the scene. Thereafter, in the reign of her favourite son Hārūn, al-Khayzurān had to contend with another potent feminine influence—that of his wife Zubayda—and we hear less about her, though she continued to support the Barmakids.[27] She died at Baghdad in the year 790.

As-Sitt Zubayda, as she was afterwards called ('Lady' or 'Empress' Zubayda), married Hārūn as early as 165/781.[28] On the day of Hārūn's succession his son al-Ma'mūn was born of a slave-girl (Rabīʿ I, 170/786) and in the month Shawwāl of the same year Zubayda gave birth to al-Amīn.[29] In contrast to many of the women of the Caliphal palace Zubayda was an Arab by race, being the daughter of Jaʿfar b. Abī Jaʿfar and granddaughter of Abū Jaʿfar al-Manṣūr, the famous ʿAbbāsid Caliph, virtual founder of the ʿAbbāsid dynasty. She was thus Hārūn's cousin as well as his wife, and proved a splendid consort for the man who by common consent was one of the greatest of Caliphs. Her religious devotion and munificence were shown by such works as the hospice at Baghrās,[30] which guarded the Syrian end of the Baylān pass across Jabal al-Lukkām (Mt Amanus). The usefulness of such an institution on the route to the north is obvious, and Zubayda's foundation may have renewed an earlier one established in Umayyad times by Maslama b. ʿAbd al-Malik.[31] In any case, it is said to have been the only hospice of the Muslims in Syria.[32] But it is especially with her endowment of the Ḥajj or annual

Pilgrimage to Mecca and Medina that Zubayda's name is associated. She herself had travelled along the Pilgrim route between Iraq and the Ḥijāz, and knew the hardships which awaited the Faithful both on the long road from Baghdad (estimated variously as over 900 miles and as 180 *farsakhs* or parasangs) and in the sacred cities themselves. Apart from other useful installations, especially at Mecca, she constructed or repaired the Pilgrim road, causing wells to be dug at intervals between Baghdad and Medina, and is even said to have had a wall built to serve as guide to pilgrims across the shifting sands of the Desert.[33] Her piety did not end here; for she is recorded to have had 100 girls to recite the Qur'ān, the portion of each of whom was one-tenth of the sacred book. Apparently the recitation was continuous. The sound of reading was heard from her castle like the humming of bees.[34]

Zubayda was clearly a beauty. Her grandfather al-Manṣūr called her Zubayda ('Little Butter-Pat'), and the nickname remained. She had originally been called Amat al-ʿAzīz (Handmaid of the Almighty)—not an uncommon type of name for women.[35] She was a leader of fashion, and 'was the first to ornament her shoes with precious stones'.[36] At table she would have only vessels of gold or silver, studded with jewels.[37] At the time of the siege and fall of Baghdad (September 813) many of the treasures of its palaces were stolen, and some reached the West. ʿAbd ar-Raḥmān II, the Umayyad ruler of Cordova, is said to have paid 10,000 *dīnārs* for a famous necklace, called 'the Snake' (*ath-Thuʿbān*), which had belonged to Zubayda.[38]

Much less conspicuous in politics than her mother-in-law al-Khayzurān, Zubayda did not give way to blind partisanship for her son al-Amīn, when he and his half-brother were brought into sharp conflict for the Caliphate. When Hārūn died in 193/809 she was at ar-Raqqa on the Euphrates. She was met at al-Anbār by al-Amīn and some of the chief men and led back in state to Baghdad, where she remained during al-Amīn's Caliphate. Her words to one of his generals, when the latter was about to march with an army against al-Ma'mūn, are reported in the *Kitāb al-Fakhrī* and are no doubt characteristic:

O ʿAli (the general was called ʿAlī b. ʿIsā b. Māhān), the Commander of the Faithful [al-Amīn], is my son, the exclusive object of my affection. But for ʿAbd Allāh, [al-Ma'mūn], I have much sympathy on account of the dislike and wrongs which have befallen him. My son, the king, has disputed with his brother over his sovereignty, so recognize

ʿAbd Allāh's rights as a son and as a brother; do not affront him in speech, for you are not his peer; nor treat him roughly as you would treat a slave; nor demean him by fetters or chains; nor refuse him a slave-girl or a servant; nor be overweening to him on the journey, nor treat him badly when travelling; nor mount before him, but hold his stirrup when he mounts, and, if he speaks ill of you, be patient with him.[39]

But al-Ma'mūn was not destined to be captured by the forces of his brother. When his troops had stormed Baghdad and al-Amīn was dead, Zubayda was banished by the local commander and passed with her two grandsons to Mosul. Here her popularity was so great that she had to be recalled. It is pleasant to read that she continued resident in Baghdad under al-Ma'mūn, sharing in the life of her stepson's court till nearly the end of his reign. She lived on till 216/831. It may be added that her brother ʿĪsā b. Jaʿfar was at one time governor of Basra.[40]

A few years before, in 210/826, Zubayda had taken part in a great festivity, the marriage of al-Ma'mūn to the daughter of al-Ḥasan b. Sahl, his intendant of finances or military treasurer,[41] an eighteen year old girl called Būrān. The description of this occasion given by the historians almost passes belief. It is no doubt because of the splendour of her wedding that Būrān is considered deserving of a separate entry by Ibn Khallikān in his great Biographical Dictionary (*Wafayāt al-Aʿyān*).[42] He says that according to some people her original name was Khadīja (like the first wife of the Prophet, already mentioned), but that this is not certain. She was betrothed to al-Ma'mūn at the age of ten. The marriage took place eight years later, and was celebrated by her father with greater magnificence than was seen in any other age. The place of the festivities was al-Ḥasan b. Sahl's camp at Fam aṣ-Ṣilḥ on the Tigris below Baghdad near Wāsiṭ. When the most important guests were assembled—members of the imperial house, generals, secretaries and other prominent persons—Būrān's father, as host, scattered among them balls of musk, in which were found tickets entitling the recipient to estates, slaves and slave-girls, horses and other valuables. Arrangements had been made by which these could be claimed immediately. On his less favoured guests al-Ḥasan b. Sahl showered gold *dīnārs* and silver *dirhams* with bags of musk and balls of ambergris. To all the numerous train in attendance on the Caliph when he arrived, down to the camp-followers, porters, muleteers and sailors, presents were given. During the nineteen days that al-Ma'mūn remained with his new father-in-law no man of all this host paid anything for himself or his riding animal, if he had one. According to Ṭabarī[43] the total amount spent was 50 million *dirhams*, while al-Ma'mūn on departure gave al-Ḥasan b. Sahl 10 million *dirhams* in cash from the revenue of Persia and the neighbourhood of aṣ-Ṣilḥ as a fief.

When al-Ma'mūn went to see his bride, he found her in the company of his sister Ḥamdūna, the Empress Zubayda (see above) and her own grandmother, the latter of whom, as al-Ma'mūn sat down, showered the bride with a thousand pearls from a golden bowl. The pearls were then picked up, and al-Ma'mūn set them in Būrān's lap. 'This is your wedding gift,' he said, 'Ask what you will!' At first the young girl was silent, till prompted by her grandmother: 'Speak to your lord, and ask him for what you will, since he has commanded.' Then Būrān requested the pardon of al-Ma'mūn's uncle, Ibrāhīm b. al-Mahdī, who had rebelled some time before. This being immediately granted, it was followed by a second request, for permission to Zubayda to go on pilgrimage.[44] This also was immediately granted by the bridegroom. Finally Zubayda came forward bearing an heirloom of the Caliphate, though connected with the rival house—the seamless robe of the Umayyads, glittering with pearls, and of immense value and significance, which was then placed upon the bride. The ceremony over, al-Ma'mūn spent the night with Būrān. A great candle of ambergris weighing 40 *manns* (about 80 lb) had been set up and was now lit. There appears to have been another special wonder: a contrivance by which when al-Ma'mūn lay down on a couch, numerous pearls were released from above and fell over his feet, greatly to his surprise. This of course was also due to his rich father-in-law. Al-Ma'mūn, we are told, objected at least to the expense of the ambergris candle.

Next day Ibrāhīm b. al-Mahdī appeared, kissed the Caliph's hand, and recited his poem in praise of al-Ma'mūn's clemency. He was pardoned, and even rewarded. Thus Būrān's first request to her husband was carried out. She was with al-Ma'mūn when he died a few years later in 833, and survived him for more than fifty years till 271/884 or 885. Long afterwards in distant Spain, at the court of the Dhūnnūnids in Toledo, there was another Ma'mūn (Yaḥyā b. Dhī'n-Nūn), who like his more famous namesake ruled over a prosperous people (435/1043–467/1075).

Yaḥyā b. Dhī'n-Nūn gave a circumcision-feast for his son, which became famous in al-Andalus, and of which nothing more superlative could be said, even by the poets, than that it recalled the wedding-feast which al-Ḥasan b. Sahl had once given for his daughter Būrān, when she married the Caliph.[45]

A lady of a different kind from those whom we have so far considered was Rābiʿa al-ʿAdawiyya of Basra, who lived *c.* 99/717–185/801. Others place her death in 135/752, which is probably too early. She was famous in her day and later as a saint, and known as Umm al-Khair, 'Mother of Good'. This is of course the kind of name by which a woman was designated with reference usually to her firstborn. (Zubayda, for example, was often called Umm Jaʿfar.) But it does not appear that Rābiʿa was ever married, and her *kunya*, as this type of name is called, was given to her for her devotion and good deeds. Al-Qushayrī, author of a well-known *Risāla* (Treatise) on Sufism, reports that Rābiʿa used to say in her devotions: 'My God, will you burn in the Fire a heart that loves you?' And there was heard on one occasion a voice which called to her: 'We would not do this. Do not think this evil thought of Us.' This is evidently given as an instance of the lack of presumption.[46] We know from another source of the dread which she had for punishment after death: 'When she heard mention of the Fire, she fainted for a time.'[47]

One day, being with the devout Sufyān ath-Thawri, and hearing him say, 'O the sadness that we bear!', she rebuked him: 'No! Say rather, The little amount of sadness that we bear! If you were truly sad, you would be unable to breathe.'

Her thoughts moved on the themes of death and judgment. Her shroud constantly hung in her place of prayer which was continually wet with her tears—'like stagnant water', says the source.[48] In her later days—she lived to be upwards of eighty—she was like an empty water-skin, and tottered as she walked. Her attendant, another saintly woman, ʿAbda bint abī Shawwāl, from whose account of Rābiʿa many of the details of her life are known,[49] reported that she prayed all night, and at the first light slept briefly in her oratory till dawn, when she arose and could be heard saying in tones of alarm, 'O soul! how long do you slumber! For how long will you be awake? You are like to slumber in a sleep from which there is no waking except at the shout which ushers in the Day of Judgement!' This, we are told, was her ordinary habit and practice till she died.

When the end came, ʿAbda shrouded her in the simple garment (*jubba*) which she had worn in life and in a veil of wool. A year later, she saw Rābiʿa in a dream, wearing a resplendent dress of green brocade and a veil of green silk, than which she had never seen any more beautiful. 'Rābiʿa, what have you done with the garment we shrouded you in and with the woollen veil?' she asked. 'They were removed from upon me, and I received in exchange what you see,' was the reply. 'My shroudings were folded up and sealed, and removed on high that my reward might be perfected thereby on the Day of the Resurrection.' 'It was for this that you worked during your days in the present world,' said ʿAbda. 'What is this compared with what I have seen of the favour of God to his saints?' was the reply. 'How is it with ʿUbayda bint Abī Kilān?' asked the other. Rābiʿa answered, 'Alas! alas! she has outstripped me to the higher grades.' 'How so?' asked her friend, 'when it was you in the people's judgment (i.e. you were more highly esteemed than she).'[50] 'She cared not in what state she found herself in the present world,' replied Rābiʿa. ʿAbda asked, 'How is it with Abū Mālik Daygham?' 'He visits Allāh, when he wishes.' 'How is it with Bishr b. Manṣūr?' 'An excellent man! He has been given more than he hoped for.' 'What must I do to draw near to God?' asked ʿAbda finally. 'See that you make mention of Him continually, and it is like that you will be glad therefor after death.'

Rābiʿa wrote religious verse, of which the following is quoted:

> Truly, I have made Thee my heart's intimate,
> and I leave my body to whoever would sit by me.
> So my body companions with the one by whom I sit,
> but the friend of the heart's core is my Beloved.[51]

Very different again was the Sulṭāna Shajar ad-Durr,[52] the only woman ever to rule as sovereign in the Muslim Middle East. She is sometimes thought of as the founder of the power of the Mamluks of Egypt. Originally, it is said, though on insufficient grounds (see below), she was a slave-girl in the family of al-Mustaʿṣim, the last of the ʿAbbāsid Caliphs of Baghdad. Passing into the possession of al-Malik aṣ-Ṣāliḥ, one of the Ayyūbid Sulṭāns of Egypt, she accompanied her husband to exile at al-Krak (Crac des Chevaliers) in Syria, and bore him a son, Khalīl, called al-Malik al-Manṣūr, who died young.[53] After the death of al-Malik aṣ-Ṣāliḥ, at first acting with Fakhr ad-Dīn Yūsuf, she established control over Egypt, then faced with the Crusade of St Louis (Seventh Crusade), while the heir of al-Malik aṣ-Ṣāliḥ, another son known as al-Muʿaẓẓam Tūrān Shah, was detained in Mesopotamia and Syria. Al-Muʿaẓẓam's adventures were numerous—he was nearly lost in the Desert—, but he survived to return to Egypt, where he was attacked and killed by some of his Mamlūks (648/1250). It is difficult to avoid concluding that his step-mother had contrived his removal, acting through the agency of the Mamlūk Baybars, the first man to offer violence to his master.[54] Shajar ad-Durr and he had been brought together earlier, at the time of the detention of al-Malik aṣ-Ṣāliḥ at Crac des Chevaliers. Baybars survived many vicissitudes to become eventually ruler of Egypt (1260–77).

On the death of al-Muʿaẓẓam the Mamlūk *amīrs* and the leading men in Egypt met in conclave to decide what was to be done, and agreed upon the unprecedented step of appointing Shajar ad-Durr as sovereign (not regent). All diplomas were to go out in her name, with the royal insignia upon them. Command of the army alone was withheld, and reserved to the *amīr* ʿIzz ad-Dīn Aybak. (Her former associate in control of Egypt, Fakhr ad-Dīn, had been killed fighting against the Crusaders.) At the time of her accession, the Egyptians had already defeated the forces of Louis IX of France at the battle of al-Manṣūra a few days before the assassination of al-Muʿaẓẓam in the same month of April 1250. The situation was, if no longer critical, at least bristling with difficulties, for the thousands of prisoners taken in the battle, including the French king himself, had still to be disposed of, and we may be certain that there were rivalry and competing claims among the Mamlūk chiefs. It is in any case remarkable that at this point in their fortunes the chiefs of the Baḥrī Mamluks entrusted the supreme authority to a woman, and the fact that they did so speaks more eloquently than words for her boldness and capacity.

The oath of allegiance was taken to Shajar ad-Durr in the Egyptian camp on 10th Ṣafar 648/14 May 1250, and she thus, to her astonishment, we are told,[55] became ruler of Egypt. Soon all matters were fairly under her control. Decrees and diplomas began to issue from her residence, inscribed 'Mother of Khalīl (son of al-Malik aṣ-Ṣāliḥ, as above)'. The *khuṭba* or Friday sermon in the principal mosques was made in her name, and coinage was struck with the superscription 'al-Mustaʿṣimiyya aṣ-Ṣāliḥiyya Malikat al-Muslimīn (Queen of the Muslims) Wālidat al-Malik al-Manṣūr Khalīl Amīr al-Mu'minīn (Parent of al-Malik al-Manṣūr Khalīl, Commander of the Faithful)'. Preachers prayed for her publicly in similar terms. The reference in her titulature to al-Mustaʿṣim, the last ʿAbbāsid Caliph of Baghdad (soon to be overthrown and his dynasty extinguished by the Mongol Hūlāgū in 1258), has been taken to imply that she was at one time in his *ḥarīm*, and this is perhaps supported by the story that upon her accession al-Mustaʿṣim sent a scathing letter to the *amīrs* of Egypt, saying, 'If you have no man to rule you, tell us, and we shall send you one.'[56] But other sources seem to be silent on the matter, and it may be that mention of al-Mustaʿṣim was a conciliatory gesture: al-Malik aṣ-Ṣāliḥ is said to have left his territory, by a verbal bequest, to the Caliph to do with it as seemed good to him.[57]

The most important question to be resolved was what to do with King Louis. As soon as the Egyptian capital was quiet after the excitement of victory and the subsequent startling events, the *amīr* Ḥusām ad-Dīn was sent to hold conversations with 'al-Malik Rīdāfrans (*roi de France*)', who was then a prisoner in the Qāḍī's house (the *Dār Ibn Luqmān* of several contemporary poems) at the town of al-Manṣūra, on the subject of the restoration of Damietta, then in the hands of the Crusaders. There were repeated meetings and discussions. Finally it was agreed that Damietta should be handed over to the Muslims, and that the King should go free on payment of a ransom of 400,000 *dīnars*. Damietta was duly restored,[58] after an occupation by the Franks during eleven months. Louis rejoined his wife, Margaret of Provence, who had accompanied him on crusade and, having remained at Damietta during the fighting, was also suffered to go free. Ḥusām ad-Dīn is stated to have been sent after the oath of allegiance had been taken to Shajar ad-Durr, who in any case must have known something of these negotiations, and may have contrived them.[59]

After a reign of eighty days opposition in Syria, perhaps also at home, led the queen to abdicate, and the rule passed to ʿIzz ad-Dīn Aybak, whom she had previously married. Her subsequent fortunes were tragic. She interfered in the affairs of state, quarrelled violently with her husband, and in 655/1257 contrived his assassination. Shortly thereafter she was herself attacked and done to death by his mother's slave-girls.

To avoid ending on such a note of violence, we may mention al-Kātiba, 'the Scholar', Shuhda (or Shahda) bint Abī Naṣr

Aḥmad b. al-Faraj b. ʿUmar al-Ibarī, i.e. the needle-maker or needle-seller, a learned lady called also Fakhr an-Nisāʾ (Pride of Women), who flourished in the sixth Hijrī, or twelfth Christian century.[60] She wrote a beautiful hand, lectured to many students, and possessed a fund of excellent traditions, linking the older and more recent generations. This lady was married to her father's former servant or apprentice, who later rose in life until he became the confidant of the Caliph al-Muqtafī (reigned 530/1136–555/1160) and the munificent founder of a *madrasa* for the Shāfiʿīs at Baghdad, having beside it a monastery for Ṣūfīs, both handsomely provided with funds. He was known as Thiqat ad-Dawla Ibn al-Anbārī and died in 549/1154 or 1155. Shuhda survived to the age of ninety, dying in 574/1178 or 1179.

Postscript

In the foregoing pages evidence has been cited to show that a high civilization existed in medieval times in the Middle East, and we have examined some of the main lines along which this Islamic or, as we have called it, Arab civilization developed. We may now look back to see what general conclusions are to be drawn. This is of course a legitimate enquiry, yet there are considerations which need to be taken into account. These are of the same kind as the considerations which have throughout made us chary of general statements and especially value judgments. Where the latter are concerned, the best procedure seems to be to evaluate by an internal standard of comparison, not by matching the achievement and productions of Arab genius with those of other peoples. If comparisons are to be made, it is doubtless more instructive to compare medieval Arab civilization with Byzantium than with classical antiquity or modern Western civilization, provided that this is possible in the present state of our knowledge.

And here we come to what is perhaps the main difficulty, our comparative ignorance of the vast material in manuscript as well as in print to illustrate medieval Arab civilization. Some impression of the extent of this material may be gained from Brockelmann's standard *Geschichte der arabischen Litteratur* or from the more recent work, also in German, of Fuat Sezgin.[1] We are as yet in something like the position of the scholars of the Renaissance about 1500, who had gradually become aware of the total extent of classical literature in Greek and Latin, but had hitherto by no means obtained familiarity with it. Arabic literature is still more extensive, and it is safe to say that no man, at least in the West, has read more than a small part of it. Much indeed is nearly unreadable, in a sense that even minor Greek and Latin authors are not. The supply of antiquated works on law and divinity seems inexhaustible, and there is a good deal of less than mediocre poetry. For the rest, not having canvassed the entire field ourselves, we are dependent in the first place on the estimates of native scholars of Arabic, who have pointed out the highlights. It is of course the case that estimates of

Eastern and Western scholars usually coincide, but simply to echo the judgment of others is not what is wanted. In a wider context than the purely literary the same applies : we lack anything like complete familiarity with the facts—in spite of the efforts of a growing number of scholars—and where this is so, it is normally advisable to defer passing judgment.

Some general statements may, however, be offered. The Arab civilization appears as exceedingly diversified, and most of the concerns of mankind found someone to write about them. There was much literary activity. Attention was at all times paid to poetry, and educated people could nearly always be relied upon to produce a couplet or two of verses, when required. Of the educational process itself we can say at least that elementary schools were to be found in all centres of any size and ensured that a considerable percentage of the population could read and write. Higher education, usually religious in character, was carried on in the mosques, later in a new type of institution for study, the *madrasas*, or in church schools. The tone of society at first perhaps predominantly military, came to be much less so, probably less so than in Europe. As an immediate consequence of the Arab conquest economic conditions in much of the Middle East declined,[2] but thereafter apparently improved, with local exceptions, till the middle of the ʿAbbāsid period. It is impossible to estimate the wealth and prosperity of the Caliphate *vis-à-vis* Byzantium, but it seems reasonable to conclude that the greater area and probably also man-power controlled by the Caliphate in its heyday gave it the advantage also in these respects. On the other hand, it would appear unlikely that ʿAbbāsid Baghdad, a new creation of the eighth century, much less Damascus under the Umayyads, though the capital of a vast empire, actually eclipsed Constantinople. An overriding consideration, however, which makes many generalizations about the Arab empire mere personal opinion, is the absence of archives which, except for such documents as happen to be included in the works of historians or others, are almost totally lacking.

NOTES

[1] *Geschichte des arabischen Schrifttums*, Bd. I, Leiden, 1967.

[2] Cf. E. Ashtor, 'Quelques observations d'un orientaliste sur la thèse de Pirenne', *Jesho*, Vol. XIII, fasc. II, 170-1, 1970.

Notes

Abbreviations

Aghānī, *Kitāb al-Aghānī*
AKM, *Abhandlungen für die Kunde die Morgenlandes*
ʿAl., ʿAbd Allāh
AUB, American University of Beirut
b., *ibn*, i.e., son of
BAS, *Bibliotheca Arabica Scholasticorum*
BGA, *Bibliotheca Geographorum Arabicorum*
BSOAS, Bulletin of the School of Oriental and African Studies, London
EI, *Encyclopaedia of Islam*, *EI*(1) and *EI*(2) for the 1st and 2nd editions respectively
ERE, *Encyclopaedia of Religion and Ethics*
FHA, *Fragmenta Historicorum Arabicorum*
Fihrist. ed. Flügel
GAL, *Geschichte der arabischen Litteratur*
GMS, *Gibb Memorial Series*
HMSO, Her Majesty's Stationery Office
JA, *Journal Asiatique*
JAOS, *Journal of the American Oriental Society*
JNES, *Journal of Near Eastern Studies*
JRAS, *Journal of the Royal Asiatic Society*
K., *Kitāb*
RES, *Répertoire d'Épigraphie Sémitique*
RSO, Rivista degli studi orientali
s.ann., *sub anno*, under the year
Sup., *Supp.*, *Supplementband* to Brockelmann's *Geschichte der arabischen Litteratur*
Sūr., *Sūra*
s.v., *s. voce*, *sub voce*, under the word
s.vv., *sub vocibus*, under the words
ZDMG, *Zeitschrift der Deutschen Morgenländischen Gesellschaft*

1 Palgrave's veracity was impugned at the time and later especially by H. St John Philby, but his book was widely read and remains a lively description of the Arab East of his day.
2 By E. W. Lane (3 vols, 1838–40), John Payne (9 vols, 1884), and Richard Burton (16 vols, 1885–8). Of these only the last two aimed at giving a complete translation of the *Nights*.
3 See e.g. Albert Hourani, *Arabic Thought in the Liberal Age*, 1798–1939, Oxford University Press, 1962.
4 *Report of the Interdepartmental Commission of Enquiry on Oriental, Slavonic, East European and African Studies*, H.M.S.O., 1947.
5 Philip K. Hitti, *History of the Arabs*, London, Macmillan, first published 1937. References in the notes are to the 6th edn.
6 Ibn Qutayba, *K. al-Maʿārif*, ed. F. Wüstenfeld, Göttingen, 1850, 56; Ṭabarī, *Annals*, Leiden 1879–1901 (15 vols), ser. I, vol. iii, pp. 1112–13; Wüstenfeld, *Genealogische Tabellen der Arabischen Stämme und Familien*, Übersichts-Tab. d. Ismâʾilitischen Stämme und Familien.
7 Ibn Qutayba, *op. cit.*, 30.
8 For the Lakhmid kings of al-Ḥīra (near Kufa in Iraq) see R. A. Nicholson, *A Literary History of the Arabs*, Cambridge University Press, 1953, (reprint of 1907 edn), 38 ff.
9 Wüstenfeld, *op. cit.*, Tab. 5; Ibn Qutayba, *op. cit.*, 14.
10 Ṭabarī, I, i, 219
11 Cf. A. Jeffery, *The Foreign Vocabulary of the Qurʾān*, Baroda, 1938, 45.
12 Ibn Qutayba, *op. cit.*, 14.
13 For ethnography e.g. see W. Caskel, *Die Bedeutung der Beduinen in der Geschichte der Araber, Arbeitsgemeinschaft für Forschung des Landes Nordrhein-Westfalen*, viii, Cologne, 1953.
14 Sir W. Muir, *The Life of Moḥammad* (revised by T. H. Weir), Edinburgh, 1912, 189 ff. Special works deal with the subject, e.g. C. C. Torrey, *The Jewish Foundation of Islam*, New York, 1933. On the other hand, Richard Bell, *The Origin of Islam in its Christian Environment*, London, Macmillan, 1926, 67, and W. Montgomery Watt, *Muhammad at Mecca*, Oxford University Press, 1953, 25 ff. and Excursus B, 158 ff.
15 *Iraq and the Persian Gulf, Geographical Handbook Series*, British Naval Intelligence Division, 1944, 117.
16 B. Moritz, *Arabien, Studien zur physikalischen und historischen Geographie des Landes*, Hanover, 1923, 21 ff.
17 Al-Hamdānī, *Ṣifat Jazīrat al-ʿArab*, ed. D. H. Müller, Leiden, 1884, 141, 162.
18 *Seven Pillars of Wisdom*, London, Cape, 1935, 43 (end of chap. 3).
19 *From the Stone Age to Christianity*, New York, Doubleday, 1957, 109.

20 Cf. Hitti, *History of the Arabs*, 6th edn., 41. A dissentient would be the great Arabist E. W. Lane, who thought that 'the most probable derivation (of *ʿArab*) is from the old Hebrew word *ʿērebh*, meaning "a mixed people"' (*Arabic–English Lexicon*, Book i, part v, 1939c).

21 For these F. V. Winnett, *A Study of the Lihyanite and Thamudic Inscriptions*, University of Toronto Press, 1937, is still useful.

21a Albright's dates, *op. cit.*, 291.

22 *La Grèce et Saba. Une nouvelle base pour la chronologie sud-arabe, Mém. Acad. des Inscriptions et Belles Lettres, xv*, Paris, 1955, 90–196; also *Paléographie des Inscriptions sud-arabes, i*, 1956 (*Verhandelingen van de Koninklijke Vlaamse Academie voor Wetenschappen, Letteren en Schone Kunsten van Belgie, Klasse der Letteren, Verhandeling–nr. 26*).

23 For the bilingual of Delos see *RES* 3570; Ch. Clermont-Ganneau, *Inscription bilingue minéo-grecque, Comptes-rendus de l'Acad. des Inscr. et Belles Lettres*, 1908, 546–60; reproduced also in Jawād ʿAlī, *Taʾrīkh al-ʿArab qabl al-Islām*, Baghdad, 1371/1952, i, 381.

24 *Sūr.* 71, 22. See for the deity especially C. A. Nallino, *Il verso di an-Nābighah sul dio Wadd, Rendiconti della Reale Accademia dei Lincei, cl. sc. mor., serie V, vol. xxix, fasc. 11–12*, Rome, 1921, 283–90.

25 Apparently with the same meaning as Greek *Sarakēnoi*, Latin *Saraceni*, cf. Arabic *sharqīyūn*, 'men of the east', from *sharq*, 'east'. The Saracens appear to be first mentioned by Pliny (1st century A.D.). See below, n. 36.

26 Genesis 29:1 (the Jacob story).

27 Cf. Albright, *ibid.*, 251.

28 Cf. pp. 5–6, n. 20.

29 *Odyssey*, IV, 84.

30 *Geography*, XVI, iv, 27 (Loeb edn., vol. vii, 368 ff).

31 *Documents from Old Testament Times*, ed. D. Winton Thomas, London and Edinburgh, 1958, 47.

32 *Ibid.*, 55.

33 *Prometheus*, 420: *Arabias t'areion anthos.*

34 Details of the expedition are given by Strabo, xvi (Loeb edn, vol. vii, 353 ff.).

35 For a date in the second half of the 1st century A.D., E. H. Bunbury, *History of Ancient Geography*, 2nd edn, 1883 (reprint, New York, Dover, 1959), ii, 444–5; M. Cary and E. H. Warmington, *The Ancient Explorers*, Penguin Books, 1963, 98. For a later date, Jacqueline Pirenne, *Le Royaume Sud-Arabe de Qatabân et sa Datation, Bibliothèque du Muséon*, vol. xlvii, Louvain, 1961, 167 ff., especially 193, 201.

36 *Natural History*, VI, xxxii, 157 (Loeb edn, vol. ii, 456). His source was, it seems, the Greek Uranius (1st century B.C.), author of a lost *Arabica* in five books (Jacqueline Pirenne, *Le Royaume Sud-Arabe etc.*, 128). Pliny's form *Araceni* is evidently a tribal name; cf. note 25.

37 Cf. Hitti, *History*, 65.

38 An existing inscription proves, however, that the dam was repaired later *c.* A.D. 542 (Hitti, *History*, 64; Jacqueline Pirenne, *Paléographie*, 142, n. 2).

39 By Werner Caskel, *ZDMG*, ciii, 1953, *28* ff.

40 See A. J. Arberry, *The Seven Odes*, London, Allen & Unwin, 1957, 21 ff, for a discussion of the meaning of *Muʿallaqāt* with a new suggestion: *muʿallaqa* = in suspense, half-divorced, i.e. removed from the *Dīwāns* (collected works) of their authors and kept apart in a separate collection (p. 23).

41 Charles James Lyall, *Ancient Arabian Poetry*, London, Williams and Norgate, 1930, 102–3.

42 This is the usual account. Cf., however, the critical remarks of R. Blachère, *Histoire de la littérature arabe*, Paris, 1952–64, ii, 261–2.

43 *Kitāb al-Aghānī*, ed. Beirut, 1957, ix, 76.

44 He died after A.D. 602.

45 Nicholson, *A Literary History*, 1953, 54.

46 Cf. Watt, *op. cit.*, 38.

47 i.e. 'the City', *sc.* of the Prophet, in English usually Medina.

48 One of two Arab tribes remained Christian till later, e.g. Taghlib.

49 Arabic *Khilāfa*, the office of the Caliph (*Khalīfa*), i.e. the successor or lieutenant of Muḥammad.

50 Cf. Régis Blachère, *Le Coran*, i, *Introduction* (*Islam d'Hier et d'Aujourd'hui*, iii), Paris, 1947, 19.

51 Of translations of the Qur'an in English those of J. M. Rodwell (1861), Marmaduke Pickthall (1930), A. J. Arberry (1955) and N. J. Dawood (1956) are available in recent or current editions.

52 Cited below, p. 44.

53 The complete phrase, cf. Qur'ān, 4, 95/97, usually simply *jihād*, 'holy war'.

54 Cf. M. Hamidullah, *Le Prophète de l'Islam, Études Musulmanes*, vii, Paris, 1958–9, i, 229.

55 The chronology is uncertain. Prof. Hitti (*History*, 156) gives 637 for the entry into al-Madā'in. I have followed Sir John Glubb, *The Great Arab Conquests*, London, Hodder and Stoughton, 1963, 202.

56 Defeat of the Byzantines at ʿAyn Shams (Heliopolis), 640, and fall of the Egyptian Babylon, 641.

57 Cf. Yāqūt, *Muʿjam al-Buldān*, i, 640. This date is also given in *Basrah: its Historical Periods* by ʿAbd al-Qādir Bāsh Aʿyān

al-ʿAbbāsī, Baghdad, 1961 (in Arabic), 14, 17. Ch. Pellat in *EI*(2) i, 1085a gives 17/638.

58 The word is now used = 'tent', but originally apparently was an adaptation of Greek *phossaton* = Latin *fossatum*, and so = 'encampment'.

59 Suyūṭī, *History of the Caliphs*, tr. H. S. Jarrett, Calcutta, 1881, 216.

60 Applied equally to the Trinitarian Christians of Byzantium and to the Dualists of Iran.

61 For the name al-Andalus, which gave trouble to several generations of Arabists, see W. Wycichl, *Al-Andalus*, xvii (1952), 449–50.

62 Cf. Ibn ʿIdhārī, *al-Bayān al-Mughrib*, ed. G. S. Colin and E. Lévi-Provençal, Leiden, 1948–51, ii, 29. Otherwise Ṣakhrat Bilāya, 'Rock of Pelayo', Maqqārī, *Nafḥ aṭ-Ṭīb*, ed. Cairo, 1367/1949 (*sic*), i. 258.

63 Cf. D. M. Dunlop, *History of the Jewish Khazars*, Princeton U. P., 1954, 50–1, 55 ff, 64 ff.

64 Narbonne was assaulted by ʿAbd al-ʿAzīz in 714 or 715, according to an Arabic text cited by F. Codera, *Narbona, Gerona y Barcelona bajo la dominación musulmana, Estudios críticos de Historia árabe española (segunda serie), Colección de Estudios árabes. VIII*, Madrid, 1917, 293, cf. E. Lévi-Provençal, *Histoire de l'Espagne musulmane*, Cairo, 1944, i, 22, and Omar A. Farrukh, *Islam and the Arabs in the Western Mediterranean during the Age of Viceroys of Moslem Spain (711–756 C.E.)*, Beirut, 1959 (in Arabic), 103. Others (IbnʿIdhārī, *al-Bayān*, ii, 29) place the capture (recapture?) of Narbonne in the governorship of ʿUqba b. al-Ḥajjāj (A.H. 116–21), i.e. *after* the battle of Tours (see below). It seems probable that Narbonne first passed into the possession of the Arabs during the governorship of as-Samḥ b. Mālik (100/719–102/721), cf. Omar A. Farrukh, *ibsid.* 115–16, and Hitti, *History*, 499.

65 Lévi-Provencal, *Histoire de l'Espagne musulmane*, i, 6; J. B. Bury, *History of the Later Roman Empire from the death of Theodosius I, to the death of Justinian*, i, 462.

66 i.e. the famous twelfth–thirteenth century geographer of Baghdad. See his *Muʿjam al-Buldān*, i, 190.

67 *Nafḥ at-Tīb*, ed. Cairo 1367/1949 (sic), i, 125.

68 Cf. the remarks of Sir W. Muir, *The Caliphate*, 3rd edn, 408. Ameer Ali (*Short History of the Saracens*, 1889, reprinted Macmillan, London, 1953, p. 151) speaks of the loss of the empire of the world when almost within their grasp by the Arabs at Tours. On the other hand, F. Codera, *op. cit.*, 315, expressed doubts of the importance of the battle. Cf. also Hitti, *History*, 501: 'In reality it decided nothing.'

69 Maqqarī, *Nafḥ at-Ṭīb*, ed. Cairo 1367/1949, i, 219 (ed. Leiden, i,

145), iv, 14 (ii, 9), cf. Codera, *op. cit.*, 300 ff, who suggests Tarascon as the place of the death of as-Samḥ.

69a Ṣakhrat A(w)īnyūn (Maqqārī, *Nafḥ aṭ-Ṭīb*, i. 256) = Rock of Avignon, cf. n. 62, Rock of Pelayo.

70 Maqqarī, i, 220 (i, 145), iv, 15, cf. Codera, *ibid.*, 309 ff, Lévi-Provençal, *Histoire*, 41 ff. The Djambatan *Historical Atlas of the Muslim Peoples* (Amsterdam, 1957), Plate 5 'Muslim Expansion in the West', shows Sens and Langres as the furthest points reached by ʿAnbasa, and gives the year as 721 apparently in error. Langres and Sens are also mentioned by J. Calmette, *L'effondrement d'un empire et la naissance d'une Europe*, 114 (cited Lévi-Provençal, *ibid.*, 42, n. 1), but in 731.

71 Omar A. Farrukh, *op. cit.*, 120, cf. n. 70.

72 Aḍ-Ḍabbī, *Bughyat al-Multamis*, ed. F. Codera and J. Ribera (*Bibliotheca Arabico-Hispana*, iii, Madrid, 1885), 12. As-Samḥ was actually sent out by ʿUmar b. ʿAbd al-ʿAzīz, and was to write to him while governor (Maqqarī, iv, 13–14 = ii, 9).

73 Ibn Ḥayyān, Maqqarī, iv, 14 (= ii, 9).

74 *Op. cit.* n. 64 above, 309–12.

75 *Nafḥ at-Ṭib*, i, 220 (i, 146). (The former text has Rudūna, which is read by the MSS.)

76 *Ibid.*, i, 256 (i, 173).

77 Abū'l Faraj al-Iṣfahānī, *Kitāb al-Aghānī*, ed. Beirut, 1956, vi, 251 (not commented on by the editors).

78 *Nafḥ aṭ-Ṭīb*, i, 190 (i, 125–6). Ibn Bashkuwāl's authority in turn appears to have been Sayf, i.e. Sayf b. ʿUmar at-Tamīmī (died 180/796 under Hārūn ar-Rashīd), for whom see J. Wellhausen, *Prolegomena zur ältesten Geschichte des Islams* (*Skizzen und Vorarbeiten*, vi), 3–7, also ʿA. ad-Dūrī, *Baḥth fī Nash'at ʿIlm at-Taʾrīkh ʿindaʾl-ʿArab* ('Inquiry into the Origin of the Science of History among the Arabs'), (*Nuṣūṣ wa-durūs*, 10), Beirut, 1960, 37, etc.

79 *Nafḥ aṭ-Ṭīb* i, 128. Cf. E. Lévi-Provençal, 'La "Description de l'Espagne" de Rāzī', *Al-Andalus*, xviii (1953), 60, 'Bretagne'.

80 *Nafḥ aṭ-Ṭīb*, i, 130: *muqābil jazīrat Brṭāniya* (vocalization uncertain), i.e. Britain, not Brittany (cf. n. 79) appears to be meant. The same form Brṭāniya occurs *Ḥudūd al-ʿĀlam*, fol. 5a, where Minorsky vocalized Briṭāniya.

81 *Nafḥ aṭ-Ṭīb* i, 184 (i, 121–2). See also Chapter 4, p. 162.

82 *Ibid.*

83 Cf. D. M. Dunlop, 'The British Isles according to Medieval Arabic Authors', *Islamic Quarterly*, iv (1957), 19–20, 22.

84 See the art. mentioned in n. 83.

85 Cf. C. H. Becker in the *Cambridge Medieval History*, ii, 1900, 353–4. The date of the siege of Constantinople by Maslama is now

placed in 717–18 (cf. M. Canard, *Cambridge Medieval History*, iv, Part i, (1966), 698).

86 Cf. D. M. Dunlop, *History of the Jewish Khazars*, Princeton U.P., 1954, 47–87.

87 Yaʿqūbī, *Taʾrīkh*, ed. Beirut, 1379/1960, ii, 289.

88 Ibn al-Athīr, *sub anno*; adh-Dhahabī, *Taʾrīkh al-Islām*, ed. Cairo, 1367/1947, v, 210–11, cf. D. M. Dunlop, 'A New Source of Information on the Battle of Talas or Aṭlakh', *Ural-Altaische Jahrbücher*, xxxvi (1964), 326–30.

89 Ṭabarī, ii, 1275–6, *sub anno* 96.

90 The embassy is confirmed, as J. Wellhausen noted (*Das arabische Reich und sein Sturz*, 2nd edn, 272), by contemporary poems (especially Ṭabarī, II, ii, 1279 ff), but may have been a year or two earlier than 96/715, if the date in the annals of the T'ang dynasty, which record an Arab mission to the Chinese court, is right (there A.D. 713, see E. Bretschneider, *Mediaeval Researches from Eastern Asiatic Sources*, London, 1910, ii, 46 n.).

91 The repeated sieges of Constantinople, to mention only one set of operations, involved the employment of a Muslim fleet. This was at first provided by means of former Byzantine installations and personnel in Syria and Egypt, which were taken over by the conquerors. Cf. Hitti, *History*, 167.

92 See the remarks of Sir John Glubb, *Empire of the Arabs*, London, Hodder and Stoughton, 1963, 151.

93 H. Pirenne, *Mohammed and Charlemagne*, Meridian Books, 1957, 150 ff; *A History of Europe*, Doubleday, 1958, i, 27.

94 Pirenne, *ibid.*

95 See e.g. the work of Samuel Dill, *Roman Society in the Last Centuries of Western Europe*, 2nd edn, 1899, reprinted by Meridian Books, 1958 and subsequently.

96 *The Muqaddimah, An Introduction to History*, trans. F. Rosenthal, London, Routledge, 1958, ii, 22.

97 See below, pp. 38–9. Cf. D. M. Dunlop, *Arabic Science in the West*, Pakistan Historical Society, 1965, 2; Fu'ād Sayyid, *Les générations des médecins et des sages* (*Ṭabaqāt al-Aṭibbāʾ waʾl-Ḥukamāʾ* of Ibn Juljul), Cairo, 1955, 61–2.

98 See the works of H. G. Farmer, *A History of Arabian Music to the Thirteenth Century*, London, Luzac, 1929, *Al-Fārābī's Arabic-Latin Writings on Music* (*Collection of Oriental Writers on Music*, ii), 2nd edn, London, Hinrichsen, 1960.

99 See an example from the theatre in D. M. Dunlop, 'The Nicomachean Ethics in Arabic, Books I–VI', *Oriens*, xv (1962), 31–2.

100 See G. Levi della Vida, 'La traduzione araba delle Storie di Orosio, *Miscellanea G. Galbiati*, (*Fontes Ambrosiani*, xxvii, Milan, Biblio-

teca Ambrosiana), iii (1951), 185–203, reprinted with additions and corrections in *Al-Andalus*, xix (1954), 257–93.

101 Distinctive title of descendants of ʿAlī, Muḥammad's son-in-law, through his eldest son al-Ḥasan.

102 A mountainous region south of the Caspian sea.

103 Arabic *sulṭān*, 'power, authority'.

104 Cf. Ibn at-Ṭiqṭaqā, *Kitāb al-Fakhrī*, 380 (trans. C. E. J. Whitting, 274), cited Hitti, *History*, 469–70.

105 For the Mamlūks see *infra*.

106 Cf. B. Lewis in *EI*(2), i, 786–7, art. ʿAyn Djālūt.

107 Cf. Hitti, *History*, 679–80.

108 The Mamlūks survived as a group down to the nineteenth century, when several hundreds of them were massacred by Muḥammad ʿAlī, the dictator of Egypt (1811).

109 Cf. Hitti, *History*, 489, 705.

110 Abolished March 1924.

Chapter 2: Arabic literature

1 See H. Fleisch, *Introduction a l'étude des langues sémitiques, Initiation à l'Islam*, iv, Paris, 1947, 96, and the refs. there.

2 Professor A. J. Arberry's phrase, *The Seven Odes*, London, Allen and Unwin, 1957, 61.

3 'The Origins of Arabic Poetry', *JRAS*, 1925, 417–49.

4 *Fī'sh-shiʿr al-Jāhilī*, Cairo, 1926, and *Fī'l-adab al-Jāhilī*, Cairo, 1927.

5 First published in *Macmillan's Magazine*, 1872, reprinted in *Essays on Eastern Questions*, London, 1872, 303 ff.

6 The 'mischief' was a ghoul, or his sword.

7 *The Book of the 1001 Nights*, 10 vols, 1885–8, iii, 143n.

8 *Amālī*, ed. Beirut, 4 vols (Maktab Tijārī), i, 156.

9 *EI*(1), art. *ash-Shanfarā*.

10 R. Blachère, *Histoire de la littérature arabe des origines à la fin du XVe siècle de J.-C.*, Paris, 1952–64, i, 106.

11 *Kitāb al-Aghānī*, Beirut, 1960, xxi, 201–18.

12 Nicholson, *Literary History*, 134.

13 Palgrave, *op. cit.*, 336.

14 *Sūr.* 26, 221 ff, following Rodwell's translation.

15 A later *Qaṣidat al-Burda* was written by al-Būṣīrī (d. 694/1294).

16 There are variants in the text here and in the following lines of which I have not taken account.

17 It is said to have been sold to Muʿāwiya, after the death of the poet, for a vast sum, and to have remained in the treasury of the Caliphs until the fall of Baghdad (1258). The *Khirqa-i sherif* or Prophet's mantle was religiously preserved at Istanbul under the Ottoman Turks, still associated with the poem of Kaʿb.

18 *Aghānī*, i, 71. It was also said that he owed the nickname to his height.

19 *Ibid.*, 75.

20 See e.g. J. Pirenne, *Paléographie*, i.

21 Ibn Khallikān, ed. De Slane, Paris, 1838–42 (part i only), 526, cf. Muir, *Life of Moḥammad*, rev. Weir, 230.

22 *Aghānī*, i, 216–17.

23 Ibn Khallikān, i, 526–7.

24 *Aghānī*, i, 227–8.

25 Ibn Khallikān, i, 527. The last line was proverbial in the sense 'the favour you ask is too precious to be granted'.

26 ʿUmar b. Abī Rabīʿa, ed. P. Schwartz, Leipzig, 1902; with commentary in Arabic, M.M. ʿAbd al-Ḥamīd, Cairo, 1380/1960.

27 *Aghānī*, ix, 63–4.

28 *Muʿjam al-Buldān*, ii, 634.

29 Ibn Khallikān, i, 527.

30 *Aghānī*, i, 111–12.

31 *Ibid.*, i, 120.

32 Where they are mentioned as contemporaries (*Sūr.* 28, 38; 40, 38/36).

33 *Aghānī*, i, 151–2.

34 Ṭabarī, II, iii, 1338–40.

35 The name means something like 'Propitious', 'Delightful'. The same *qaṣīda* was many years afterwards, when ʿUmar b. Abī Rabīʿa was an old man, recited by his attendants to the Caliph al-Walīd b. ʿAbd al-Malik at Mecca (*Aghānī*, i, 123).

36 *Kāmil*, ed. Wright, 570–2.

37 See below especially Ibn Ḥazm and Bahā' ad-Dīn Zuhayr.

38 *Aghānī*, xv, 193.

39 Or ʿUbayd. Cf. I. Goldziher, *Muʿammarūn*, 29 ff.

40 *GAL*, i, 64–5, and *Supp.*

41 Ibn Juljul, *Ṭabaqāt al-Aṭibbā' wa'l-Ḥukamā*, ed. Fu'ād Sayyid, Cairo, 1955, 61 ff.

42 *Ibid.*, 61.

42a Possibly the mosque of Carmona (Arabic *Qarmūna*), east of Seville. Ibn Juljul, *loc. cit.*, has *fī masjid al-Qarmūnī*, 'in the mosque of al-Qarmūnī'(?). Ibn Abī Vṣaybiʿa (ed. Müller, i, 163), quoting Ibn Juljul, offers *fī masjid at-Tirmidhī*. Fu'ād Sayyid well points out (*op. cit.*, 62) that ʿĪsā b. Muzāhim, an ancestor of Ibn al-Qūṭiyya (he married Sarah the Goth), was a freedman of ʿUmar II, and that the story of ʿUmar and the Arabic translation was no doubt current in the family.

43 See F. Nau, 'Un Colloque du patriarche Jean avec l'émir des Agaréens', *JA*, 1915, 248–55, cf. Michael Syrus, *Chronique*, ii, 431–2.

44 Ibn Khaldūn (*Muqaddimah*, trans. F. Rosenthal, iii, 229–30) and J. Ruska, *Arabische Alchemisten*, (Heidelberg, 1924), 8 ff, do not take all the evidence into account.
45 Dhahabī, *Ta'rīkh al-Islām* (Cairo, A.H. 1367–9), iii, 246.
46 *Fihrist*, ed. Flügel, 242.
47 *Aghānī*, ix, 318, and xxi, 417.
48 *Jamharat*, ed. Beirut, 1383/1963, 81.
49 Brockelmann, *GAL*, i, 19.
50 Cf. Nicholson, *Literary History*, 130.
51 Cf. *Jamharat*, 5.
52 Ed. de Slane, i, 178.
53 Cf. ʿUmar Farrūkh, *Abū Tammām*, Beirut, 1384/1964, 23.
54 *Aghānī*, xiv, 49, but according to others from Salamya near Ḥimṣ. His *Dīwān* has been edited recently in Beirut by Dr A. Maṭlūb and ʿAl. al-Jabūrī.
55 *Ibid.*, xvi, 303.
56 e.g. J. Wellhausen, *Reste arabischen Heidentums*, 3rd edn, Berlin, 1961, 231.
57 Ibn Khallikān, i, 180, says 'in Egypt', but this was apparently only later.
58 Cf. Ṭabarī, III, i, 1101.
59 Ibn Khallikān, i, 368.
60 Text of this and the following verses in ʿUmar Farrūkh, *Abū Tammām*, 173–4, and Ṭaha Ḥusayn, *Min Ḥadith ash-Shiʿr wa'n-Nathr*, Cairo, n.d. (prologue dated 1936), 106–7.
61 Ibn Khallikān, i, 179. But in the *Dīwān* of Abū Tammām (ed. M. ʿAbduh ʿAzzām, ii, 242) the recipient is said to have been Aḥmad b. al-Muʿtaṣim, see p. 44.
62 *Sūr*. 24, 35 (Bell's translation).
63 Ed. de Slane, i, 179–80.
64 *wa-lammā ukhidhati 'l-qasīda min yadihi lam yajidū fīhā hādhayni 'l-baytayn, ibid.*
65 Ibn Khallikān, 180, 286–7. See also Ibn Diḥya, *Kitāb an-Nibrās fī Ta'rīkh Khulafā' Banī 'l-ʿAbbās*, Baghdad, 1365/1946, 146 ff, and especially 149–50. He affected a haughty style and addressed people only in (classical) Arabic. He sometimes appeared wearing two swords, or mounted and with two spears and a turban or cap in the Bedouin fashion. He claimed to belong to *al-ʿArab al-ʿarbā'u*, the pure or genuine Arabs.
66 Near Baghdad on the Khurāsān road, at present an important place.
67 ʿUmar Farrūkh, *op. cit.*, 35.
68 R. Guest, *Life and Works of Ibn ar-Rumi*, London, 1944, 59.
69 Ed. I. Kratchkovsky, *GMS*, 1935.
69a Var. 'spear'.

70 *Dīwān*, Beirut, 1380/1961, 162–3, first pointed out to me by Professor Charles Issawi.

70a Cf. D. D. Kosambi, *Ancient India*, New York, 1965, 204.

71 Masʿūdī, Ṭabarī, Ibn Qutayba, Firdawsī, etc. See Brockelmann, *GAL* i, 152, and *Sup*. i, 235.

72 Ṣāʿid b. Ṣāʿid, *Ṭabaqāt al-Umam*, ed. Cheikho, 49 (trans. Blachère, 101); *Fih*., 248–9, cf. Brockelmann, *Sup*. i, 235, and see below pp. 173–4.

73 Ed. M. Ghufrānī al-Khurāsānī with an introduction by ʿAbbās Iqbāl, Cairo, ʿĀlam al-Kutub, n.d. (preface dated 1341/1922).

74 Cf. Brockelmann, *Sup*., i, 236, and ʿAbbās Iqbāl (see n. 73), 20–1.

75 Masʿūdī, *Tanbih*, ed. Cairo 1357/1938, 66–7 (trans. Carra de Vaux, 111).

76 Others in Iraq were al-Kūfa, Wāsiṭ and of course Baghdad.

77 Ed. Hārūn, 4 vols., Cairo 1367/1947. Other edns in Brockelmann.

78 Cf. C. Pellat in *EI*(2) ii, art. al-Djāḥiẓ.

79 See the French translation of C. Pellat, Beirut and Paris, 1951, 115 ff.

80 Pellat, *EI*(2) ii, 386b.

81 *Ibid*., 385a.

82 French translation by Maurice Adad in *Arabica*, xiii (1966), 268 ff.

83 Ed. Van Vloten, 86–7.

84 *Ibid*., 97–8.

85 Luqmān of ʿĀd lived during the lifetimes of seven vultures, the last of which was named Lubad. The expression is loosely used to convey longevity.

86 Arabic ʿŪj, who, according to Ṭabarī, survived the Flood though not of Noah's company (I, i, 192), and, it is said (*qīla*), lived 3,000 years (I, i, 501).

87 Ed. Van Vloten, 101, 103, 104.

88 *Ibid*., 105, reading *min* for *am min* (line 4), with the edition of C. Pellat (Damascus, 1955), 31.

89 Cf. *EI*(1) ii, 387a.

90 *Ibid*., 386b. The *Kitāb al-ʿUthmāniyya* was edited by ʿAbd as-Salām M. Hārūn, Cairo, 1374/1955.

91 Ed. J. Finkel, Cairo, 1382/1962.

92 *Ibid*., 10.

93 *Ibid*., 12, cf. 24.

94 *Ibid*., 13–20.

95 Ibn Qutayba, *Kitāb Taʾwīl Mukhtalif al-Ḥadith*, 71–2, cited by Finkel, *op. cit*., 7–8, cf. G. Lecomte, *Traité des divergences du Ḥadith*, Damascus, 1962, 65–7, M. Lecomte renders *tajawwaza* (*Traité des divergences du Ḥadith*, 65) 'il le fait en des termes si exagérés', but cf. E. W. Lane, *Arabic-English Lexicon*, 485a and b.

96 Cited Finkel, *op. cit.*, 2, from the *Ṭabaqāt an-Nuḥāt* of Suyūṭī, 282.
97 Finkel, *op. cit.*, 16.
98 Ed. M. Grünert, Leiden, 1900, 2.
99 Cf. above for this as the title of Aristotle's work on the subject.
100 The title of Aristotle's *Physics*.
101 Ed. Grünert, 3–4.
102 *Ibid.*, 5–6. The expression *ḥadd al-manṭiq* ('definition of logic') appears to be for the *Eisagoge* of Porphyry, cf. Yaʿqūbī, *Taʾrīkh*, ed. Hovtsma, i, 144 (ed. Beirut, 1379/1960, i, 127).
103 Cf. Maqrīzī, *An-Nizāʿ waʾt-Takhāṣum fīmā bayn Banī Umayya wa-Banī Hāshim*, ('The Contention and Quarrel between the Umayyads and the Banū Hāshim'), Leiden, 1888, 63.
104 Nicholson rendered 'Choice Histories' (*Literary History*, 346). M. Lecomte in his work on Ibn Qutayba mentioned below, has (144) '*documents essentiels*'.
105 Ed. De Goeje (*Liber Poësis et Poëtarum*), Leiden, 1904, cf. Gaudefroy-Demombynes, *Introduction au Livre de la Poesie et des Poétes*, Paris, 1947.
106 Ibn Qutayba, *Kitāb al-Maʿārif*, ed. Saroite Okacha, Faculté des Lettres et Sciences Humaines de l'Université de Paris, Cairo, 1960.
107 *Ibn Qutayba, l'homme . . .*, 175–6.
108 *Taʾrīkh Iftitāḥ al-Andalus*, ed. J. Ribera, Madrid, 1926, 105–6 (cf. xxvii–xxix); R. Dozy, *Recherches sur l'historie et la littérature de l'Espagne pendant le moyen age*, 3rd edn, i, 21–40.
109 Cf. *Ibn Qutayba, l'homme . . .*, 176.
110 Institut Français de Damas, 1962.
111 Above pp. 49–50.
112 No. 1 in the series. Thaʿlab's biography is given by Ibn Khallikān, ed. De Slane, i, 42–3; trans., i, 83–4.
113 Verse in the *rajaz* metre, considered distinct from *shiʿr*, poetry proper.
114 *Majālis*, introd., 24.
115 Cf. Kratchkovsky (see n. 116), Preface, p. 24.
116 Ed. V. Guirgass, Leiden, 1888, 'Préface, variantes et index', by I. Kratchkovsky, Leiden, 1912. See below, Chapter 3, p. 88.
117 Kratchkovsky. *op. cit.*, 41.
118 Ed. C. Pellat and M. Ḥamidullah, Haidarabad, 1375/1956.
119 *wa-qad salaba dhālika Ibn Qutayba . . . wa-qad faʿala dhālika fī kathīr min kutub Abī Hanīfa ad-Dīnawarī hādhā* (*Murūj*, iii, 442 = ed. (airo, ii, 217).
120 Cf. Lecomte, *Ibn Qutayba*, 108, 204–5.
121 Cf. E. G. Browne, *Literary History of Persia*, Cambridge U. P., 4 vols, 1902–24, i, 446.
122 Ed. De Slane, i, 406; trans., ii, 130.
123 *Ibid.*, i, 30; trans., i, 60.

124 The words *qibla* and *ṭawāf* suggest the Kaʿba at Mecca and religious adoration.
125 The title Tāj al-Milla, 'Crown of Religion', was conferred on ʿAḍud ad-Dawla in 369/979 by the Caliph aṭ-Ṭāʾiʿ, hence the name of the book, in full *al-Kitāb at-Tājī fī ʾd-Dawla ad-Daylamiyya* (Michael Awad, *Some Lost Fragments of the Kitāb al-Wuzarāʾ of Hilâl al-Ṣâbiʾ*, in Arabic, Baghdad, 1948, 81–2).
126 A famous letter-writer and stylist in his own right (323/935–383/993), for whom see Brockelmann, *GAL* i, 93.
127 *yuhāḍiru*, see Lane, *Lexicon*, 589a.
128 The name is supposed to be Indian (*Lisān al-ʿArab*, s.v.), for rice prepared in a particular way, with milk and melted butter.
129 A political man of the day, often mentioned in Miskawayh, *Tajārib al-Umam* (The Experiences of the Nations), see the Index Volume of D. S. Margoliouth (Oxford, 1921).
130 Ḥamdānid chief, see *ibid.*
131 Buwayhid, cousin of ʿAḍud ad-Dawla.
132 With reference to his titles ʿAḍud ad-Dawla and Tāj al-Milla.
133 *Yatīmat ad-Dahr*, Damascus edn, ii, 2–3.
134 *Fiqh al-Lugha*, ed. Rushayd ad-Daḥdāḥ, Paris, 1861, 4.
135 For al-Mīkālī see Brockelmann, *GAL* i, 286 and *Sup.* i, 503.
136 Leiden, 1867. A new edition and translation by Professor C. E. Bosworth are due to appear shortly.
137 *Laṭāʾif al-Maʿārif*, ed. al-Abyārī and aṣ-Ṣīrafī, preface dated 1379/1960, 8–9.
138 *Ibid.*, 5n.
139 *Ibid.*, 15, 18, cf. *EI*(2), art. Bīmāristān (D. M. Dunlop).
140 Cf. D. Sourdel, *Le Vizirat ʿabbāside* (Damascus, 1959), 371, 389. This was in 296/908, after the failure of the conspiracy in favour of Ibn al-Muʿtazz.
141 *Laṭāʾif*, 22–3.
142 *Ibid.*, 42.
143 *Ibid.*, 86, cf. 227.
144 *Ibid.*, 82–3.
145 *Ibid.*, 141–2.
146 Ṭābari, III, ii, 1319. Both names mean much the same thing 'wearing a *burquʿ*, or woman's veil'.
147 Ṭabarī, III, i, 484 (*anno* 160/776–77).
148 Strictly Abū Muslim also during most of his career was a rebel against Umayyad rule.
149 *Laṭāʾif*, 222.
150 *Ibid.*, 105.
151 *Ibid.*, 144.
152 Cf. the remarks of the editors, *Laṭāʾif*, introd. 24–6.
153 *Laṭāʾif*, 156.

154 *Thimār*, 186.

155 *Laṭā'if*, 218, more distinctly *Thimār*, 431. This important action between the forces of the Caliphate and the Chinese is discussed by D. M. Dunlop, 'A new source of information on the Battle of Talas or Aṭlakh', *Ural-Altaische Jahrbücher*, xxxvi, Fasc. 3–4 (A. Zajączkowski Festschrift), 1964, 326–30.

156 Cf. *Laṭā'if*, 152 ff, and *Thimār*, 13 (the Ḥaram of Mecca); *Laṭā'if*, 155, and *Thimār*, 436 (Medina, apparently from al-Jāḥiẓ) etc.

157 *Histoire des Rois de Perse par . . . ath-Thaʿalibî*, Texte arabe publié et traduit par H. Zotenberg, Paris, Imprimerie Nationale, 1900, reprinted as *Publications de M. H. Asadi*, No. 4, Teheran, 1963.

158 Browne, *Lit. Hist. of Persia*, i, 111.

159 *EI*(1), art. ath-Thaʿālibī, no. 2.

160 *Literary History*, 328.

161 Cf. D. M. Dunlop, '*The Nicomachean Ethics in Arabic*, Books I–VI'. *Oriens*, xv, 1962 (Hellmut Ritter Festschrift), 31–2, cf. 27.

162 Antioch, for example, had a theatre at least from the time of Antiochus the Great (223–187 B.C.), possibly earlier (cf. Sir J. E. Sandys, *History of Classical Scholarship*, 1903–8, reprinted New York, 1964, i, 165). Theatrical performances at Antioch were forbidden after A.D. 520 (*Ancient Antioch*, Glanville Downey, Princeton U.P., 1963, 242). During this whole period theatrical shows must have been frequent if not continuous at Antioch, as the numerous surviving mosaics with scenes from Greek plays suggest. For Seleucia-Ctesiphon (Arabic, Madā'in), the story of Orodes I receiving the news of the defeat of Crassus at Carrhae (Ḥarrān) in 53 B.C., while witnessing a performance of Euripides' *Bacchae*, is well-known (Mommsen, *History of Rome*, iv, 337).

163 Brockelmann, *GAL* ii, 8.

164 See especially his *Geschichte des Schattentheaters im Morgen-und Abendland*, Hanover, 1925.

165 Quoted by Paul E. Kahle, 'The Arabic shadow play in Egypt', *JRAS*, 1940, 21–34, reprinted in his *Opera Minora*, Leiden, 1956, 297–306.

166 *Ibid.*

167 Brockelmann, *GAL*, *Sup*, i, 150.

168 Rhymed prose had a long previous history in Arabic from pre-Islamic times (cf. Nicholson, *Literary History*, 74, 327), and by the tenth century was coming into general use.

169 A ship's company, putting out apparently from Bāb al-Abwāb, is caught in a storm on the Caspian Sea.

170 For Abū Zayd of Sarūj see pp. 62 ff. The other name is evidently artificial, perhaps referring to a tradition of Muḥammad '*Kullukum ḥārith wa-kullukum hammām*' i.e. all men toil and are anxious for

their livelihood (Ibn Khallikān, ed. De Slane, i, 587; trans., ii, 491.

171 Ibn Khallikān, ed. de Slane, i, 56–7.

172 *Ibid.*, i, 586–8; trans., ii, 490–6.

173 Apparently Najm ad-Dīn ʿAbd Allāh, mentioned by Ibn Khallikān as the transmitter of his father's *Maqāmāt*, is the same.

174 So the commentator Muḥammad b. ʿAbd ar-Raḥmān al-Panjadīhī (Yāqūt, *Buldān*, i, 743), cited Steingass, *Assemblies of al Ḥarîri*, ii, Oriental Translation Fund, new series (London, 1898), 163.

175 Ibn Khallikān, ed. de Slane, i, 586; trans., ii, 490.

176 Cf. Baron de Slane, *Les Prolégomènes d'Ibn Khaldoun*, new edn, Paris, 1934, pp. cvii–cix.

177 Ibn Khallikān, ed. de Slane, i, 586. trans., ii, 491–2.

178 Ibn Khallikān, *ibid.*

179 With the title *Maḥbᵉrōth Īthī'ēl*, ed. Isaac Peres, Tel-Aviv, 1950. My colleague Professor Gerson D. Cohen kindly drew my attention to this volume.

180 Cf. n. 174.

181 *The Assemblies of Harîrî*, ed. Steingass (London, 1897).

182 M. Blochet had already catalogued the MS in *Catalogue des Manuscrits arabes des nouvelles acquisitions* (1884–1924), Paris, 1925, 125–6.

183 In his Bibliothèque Nationale *Catalogue* mentioned in the previous note, Blochet gave 'Kouvarriha'.

184 Plate XII, folio 19, recto.

184a Mr Julian Reade pointed this out to me.

185 Ed. L. Pinto, Paris, 1884, and later. See also L. Pinto and A. Destrées, *Commentaire du Molhat al-Irab . . . trad. in extenso pour la première fois*, Tunis, 1911.

186 According to the son of Ibn Ḥazm, quoted by Ibn Bashkuwāl (*Kitāb aṣ-Ṣila*, ed. Codera, ii, 409, no. 888), his father left about 400 volumes in writing containing nearly 80,000 folios. Only a few of these works have been published, among the most recent being *at-Taqrīb li-Ḥadd al-Manṭiq wa'l-Madkhal ilayhi* (cf. above, p. 277, n. 102), ed. by Dr Iḥsān ʿAbbās of the University of Khartoum, Beirut, n.d. (preface dated 1959).

187 English (A. R. Nykl, Paris, 1931 and A. J. Arberry, London, 1953), Russian (A. Salie, 1933), German (M. Weisweiler, 1941, and many subsequent edns), Italian (F. Gabrieli, Bari, 1949), Spanish (E. Garcia Gomez, 1952), together with the French version of L. Bercher (see n. 188).

188 *Le Collier du Pigeon ou de l'Amour et des Amants*, *Bibliothèque Arabe-Française*, viii, Algiers, 1949.

189 *Murūj*, vi, 368–86 = ed. Cairo, iii, 379–84 (this and the other reference are due to Bercher, *op. cit.*, p. xi, who, however, by an oversight gave *Murūj*, iv, 368–86).

190 'En relisant le "Collier de la Colombe" ', *Al-Andalus*, xv (1950), 339.
191 *Ibid.*, 337.
192 Ed. Bercher, 72. Cf. above p. 58.
193 Lévi-Provençal, *Al-Andalus*, xv, 359.
194 Bercher, *op. cit.*, 50.
195 Brockelmann, *GAL*, Sup. i, 693. I do not remember to have seen this stated in any Arabic source.
196 These dates approximately as in E. Wagner, *Abū Nuwās, Eine Studie zur arabischen Literatur der frühen ʿAbbāsidenzeit, Akad. der Wissenschaften u. der Literatur*, Wiesbaden, 1965, 10 ff.
197 Ibn Khallikān, trans. De Slane, iii, 176, cf. *ibid.*, ii, 291 (= text, i, 484).
198 Khalīl Mardam Bey, *Dīwān Ibn ʿUnayn*, Damascus, 1946, 15 ff.
199 Nowadays one speaks of the Ghūṭa of Damascus, which is here meant. Cf. Khalīl Mardam Bey, *op. cit.*, 16.
200 Ibn Khallikān, i, 180–1; trans., i, 353.
201 For details see Brockelmann, ii, 372. My own MS copy of the *Dīwān*, bought at Istanbul in 1938, contains additional pages with the date 1276/1859, but the main part of the MS appears to be not later than the twelfth/eighteenth century.
202 *Dīwān*, 94–5, with the notes there.
203 *Dīwān*, 96.
204 *GAL*, *Sup.* i, 466.
205 *Dīwān* of Bahāʾ ad-Dīn Zuhayr, Munīrī ed., n.d. 72 ff.
206 *Ibid.*, biographical introduction, p. k.
207 *Ibid.*, p. l. Cf. Lane, *Arabic–English Lexicon*, iv, 1317a.
208 E. H. Palmer, *Behā-ed-Din Zoheir*, Cambridge University Press, 1877, ii (translation), 197.
209 Ibn Khallikān, i, 276; trans., i, 542.

Chapter 3: History and historians

1 F. Wüstenfeld, *Die Geschichtschreiber der Araber v. ihre Werke*, Gottingen, 1882, 1–2.
2 Brockelmann, *GAL*, *Sup.* i, 100.
3 Ed. I. Goldziher, *Abhandlungen zur arabischen Philologie*, ii, Leiden, 1899.
4 *Ibid.*, pp. 40–1.
5 Ibn Qutayba, *K. al-Maʿārif*, ed. Wüstenfeld, 233: *wa-qāla qaraʾtu min kutub Allāh ithnayn wa-sabʿīn kitāban.* On the other hand, seventy-two is perhaps a round number, cf. M. Steinschneider on Wahb b. Munabbih in *Die arabische Literatur der Juden*, Frankfurt, 1902, 11.
6 Ibn Qutayba, *ʿUyūn al-Akhbār*, Cairo, Dār al-Kutub, ii, 62, also in *al-ʿIqd al-Farīd*, Cairo, 1321/1907, iii, 287.
7 Al-Ghazālī, *Iḥyā ʿUlūm ad-Dīn*, Cairo edn, 1357/1938, xiv, 196 (2736).

8 *Ibid.*, 179–80 (2719–20).
9 *Ibid.*, xv, 135–6 (2879–80).
10 See the indices in the *Dār al-Kutub* edn.
11 Cf. I. Goldziher, *Muhammedanische Studien*, ii, 166.
12 The origins of the classical Arabic poetry, associated with Imru' al-Qays and his uncle, Muhalhil b. Rabīʿa (see pp. 9, 26), perhaps also point to South Arabia, though poetry is usually said to have arisen in the north of the Peninsula, among the tribes.
13 Ibn Qutayba, *K. al-Maʿārif*, 233.
14 *Sitzungsberichte d. preussischen Akademie zu Berlin*, 1904, xi.
14a The late Professor Joseph Schacht considered the *Kitāb al-Maghāzī* of Mūsā b. ʿUqba as an 'early, if not the earliest work of Muhammadan history' (*Acta Orientalia*, xxi, 300, 1953, quoted Franz Rosenthal, *A History of Muslim Historiography*, 2nd rev. edn, Leiden, 1968, 69, n. 2). See also Dr ʿAbd al-ʿAzīz d-Dūrī, *Baḥth fī Nashʾat ʿIlm at-Taʾrīkh ʿindaʾ l-ʿArab* (Enquiry into the Development of History, or Historical Science, among the Arabs), *Nuṣūṣ wa-Durūs*, 10, Beirut, 1960, 27, with texts of Mūsā b. ʿUqba, 159–65.
15 A. Guillaume, *The Life of Muhammad*, London, 1955.
16 W. M. Watt, *Muhammad at Mecca*, p. xii.
17 Ed. Leiden, i, 1192 ff.
18 Cf. Ibn Saʿd, *Ṭabaqāt*, ed. Sachau, I, i, 137.
19 Muir, *Life of Moḥammad*, Edinburgh, 1912, pp. lxxix–lxxx.
20 In spite of the work of A. J. Wensink (*Concordance et Indices de la Tradition musulmane*, Leiden, 1933 and onwards), begun by him and continued by others, to mention only the most ambitious attempt to place the contents of the *Ḥadīth* literature before Western readers, this literature is, meanwhile at least, not easily disposable for the purposes of history.
21 *Kitāb Tadhkirat al-Ḥuffāz*, ed. Dāʾirat al-Māʿarif al-ʿUthmāniyya, Haidarabad, 1375/1955–1377/1958, i, 348.
22 *History of Muhammad's Campaigns*, Bibliotheca Indica, Calcutta, 1856.
23 London, Oxford University Press, 1966.
24 *Muhammed in Medina, Das ist Vâkidî's Kitâb al-Maghâzî*, Berlin, 1882.
25 *Mīzān al-Iʿtidāl*, Cairo, 1382/1963, iii, 663.
26 *Tadhkirat al-Ḥuffāz*, *loc. cit.*
27 Trans. J. Robson, Lahore, 1960–5.
28 Ed. Wüstenfeld, 258–9 (ed. Okacha, Cairo, 1960, 518). This notice is cited by Ibn Khallikān (ed. de Slane, i, 712) as giving that al-Wāqidī was Qāḍī of the west bank at Baghdad (cf. above), but in fact simply says that the Qāḍī of the west bank conducted his funeral service.

29 See *K. al-Maʿārif*, ed. Okacha, 689 (in his *Fihris Rijāl as-Sanad*).
30 *Tanbīh*, ed. Cairo 1357/1938, 242, trans. Carra de Vaux, *Le Livre de l'Avertissement*, Paris, 1896, 367.
31 *Tadhkirat al-Ḥuffāẓ*, *loc. cit.*
32 *Op. cit.*, 711.
33 *Murūj adh-Dhahab*, ed. Cairo, 1384/1964, iv, 33.
34 Cited Lane, *Lexicon*, 91c.
35 Mentioned by Masʿūdī, *Tanbīh*, ed. Cairo, 221, trans. Carra de Vaux, 338, cf. Goldziher, *Muhammedanische Studien*, ii, 115 ff.
36 Marsden Jones from whom I cull this last observation advances reasons to show that al-Wāqidī was not a Shīʿite, but that his text fell into the hands of the Shīʿa. See his edition of the *K. al-Maghāzī*, i, 16–18.
37 *Die Geschichtschreiber der Araber und ihre Werke*, Göttingen, 1881–2, repr. New York, 1964, 11–12.
38 *Hist. of Muhammad's Campaigns*, 4.
39 He cites *ZDMG*, 1849, 452.
40 *Muhammed in Medina*, 11–12.
41 W. M. Watt, *Muhammad at Mecca*, Oxford U.P., 1953, *Muhammad at Medina*, Oxford U.P., 1956, *Muhammad, Prophet and Statesman*, Oxford U.P., 1961; M. Ḥamīdullāh, *Le Prophète de l'Islam, Sa Vie, son Oeuvre*, Paris, 1378/1959.
42 *Muhammed at Mecca*, p. xii.
43 *Fihrist*, 99.
44 So e.g. Ibn Khallikān, ed. de Slane, i, 710.
45 Cf. Lane, *Lexicon*, 931b.
46 Ibn Khallikān, *loc. cit.*
47 So W. Hoenerbach, 'Waṯīma's Kitāb ar-Ridda aus Ibn Ḥaǧar's Isāba', *Akad. d. Wissens. u.d. Lit. in Mainz, Abh. d. Geistes–u. Sozialwissenschaftl. Kl.*, 1951, nr. 4, 222.
48 Caetani, *Annali dell'Islam*, A.H. 11, Nos. 70 and 71, cited Hoenerbach, *op. cit.*, 220.
49 *Catalogue*, xv, 1042.
50 Ed. Flügel, 98–9.
51 *Geschichte der Eroberung von Mesopotamien und Armenien von Mohammed ben Omar el Wakedi*, Hamburg, 1847.
52 By A. D. Mordtmann, the work mentioned in the previous note.
53 In his *Mémoire sur la conquête de la Syrie*, 1864, cf. also the *Mémoire sur le Fotouh aç-Cham attribué à Abou Ismail al-Baçri* published earlier in the same year.
54 Meaning uncertain. Apparently *as-sāqiṭa* are the same as *al-mutanaṣṣira*, the Christianized Arabs, hence perhaps 'falling away', but *sāqiṭa* in the sense of 'ignoble, of no account, etc.' is usually singular, vid. Lane, *Lexicon*, s.v.
55 Al-Aṣfar is given various genealogies: he is a son of Rūm, son of

Esau, or al-Aṣfar is another name for Rūm (Lane, *Lexicon*, s.v.). Ḥamza al-Iṣfahānī (ed. Gottwaldt, 67) states that the Romans were ruled by kings called the 'sons of Ṣūfar' and that the Israelites identify Ṣūfar (= Sōphar, son of Eliphaz, son of Esau, Gen. 36:11, Septuagint version. I owe the reference to Professor Gerson Cohen) with al-Aṣfar, but that the Romans and the Greeks deny this (?). The original significance of the name was perhaps 'Edomite', hence 'Roman', and the form al-Aṣfar, the Yellow, may be due to popular etymology. The name Banū al-Aṣfar is applied to the Caesars specifically by Ibn Khaldūn, ed. Beirut, 1956–9, ii, 432. The Spanish era, which began thirty-eight years before the usual Christian era and which commemorated the final conquest of Spain by Augustus, was called in Arabic *ta'rīkh aṣ-Ṣufr*, i.e. apparently 'the bronze era' (cf. G. della Vida, *JAOS.* 63 (1943), 183–91), but perhaps rather 'the era of the Romans'.

56 'Rūbīs' possibly represents the latter part of the name of Theodorus, the Byzantine commander at Ajnadayn.

57 *Futūḥ ash-Sha'm*, ed. Cairo, 1335/1916. i, 8–9.

58 Ṭabari, I, iii, 1561–5.

59 *Dīwān*, 182, 6 (cited Brockelmann, *GAL*, *Sup.* i, 208).

60 Hitti (*History*, 201) follows Ṭabarī's date (II, i, 86), cf. Theophanes, ed. De Boor, 351.

61 This was five years before the famous Seven Years' War, during which the Arabs invested the Byzantine capital by land and sea, commonly taken as the second attack.

62 Ṭabarī, II, i, 27.

63 All the material is canvassed in the great work of L. Caetani, *Annali dell' Islam*, 10 vols, Milan, 1905–26.

64 For the title, cf. *Jamharat Ashʿār al-ʿArab* above pp. 40–1, which is of course a different work.

65 Several volumes of the *Kitāb Ansāb al-Ashrāf* have been edited, see pp. 86–7 below.

66 *Le Prophète de l'Islam*, Paris, 1378/1959, 599–602.

67 2nd edn, Berlin, 1897, 3rd edn, Berlin, 1961, 10–64.

68 2nd edn, Cairo, 1343/1924.

69 *Sammlung Orientalischer Arbeiten*, Leipzig, 1941, 8 Heft.

70 Cf. F. Taeschner, *ZDMG.*, Band 87 (Neue Folge, Band 12), 1933, 12, n. 1.

71 Brockelmann, *GAL*, i, 140.

72 Ed. F. Wüstenfeld, *Geschichte und Beschreibung der Stadt Mekka von el Azraki*, Leipzig, 1858.

73 Cf. D. Sourdel, *Le Vizirat ʿAbbāside de 749 à 936*, Damascus, 1959, 23.

74 Ed. ʿAbd as-Salām Muḥammad Hārūn, Cairo, 1365/1946, 2nd edn, 1382/1962.

75 ʿAbd as-Salām M. Hārūn, *op. cit.*, 2nd edn, introd. p. z; *Fihrist*, 93.
76 ʿAbd as-Salām Hārūn, *ibid.*, p.h; *Fihrist*, 93.
77 ʿAbd as-Salām Hārūn, p.w.; *Fihrist*, 99.
78 Ṭabarī, I, vi, 3329.
79 *Waqʿat Ṣiffīn*, 479.
80 Cf. Ṭabarī I, vi, 3341.
81 *Mīzān al-Iʿtidāl*, ii, 315.
82 *Waqʿat Ṣiffīn*, 481.
83 See Theophanes, ed. De Boor, 347 (A.D. 658) and 355 (A.D. 678). The latter passage evidently refers to the so-called precedent of Muʿāwiya mentioned by al-Balādhurī (shortly to be discussed) as followed in similar circumstances by ʿAbd al-Malik, see Hitti's translation (*Origins of the Islamic State*, 247).
84 Cf. Maqrīzī, *Ittiʿāẓ al-Ḥunafāʾ*, ed. Bunz, 141; ed. Cairo, 1367/1948 (*Maktabat al-Maqrīzī aṣ-Ṣaghīra*, 2), 263. The Byzantines are mentioned by al-Muʿizz in 362/973, i.e. some years after the successful Byzantine campaigns in Syria under Nicephorus Phocas and John Tzmisces (Hitti, *History*, 459–60). The Fāṭimid Caliph upbraids the Carmathians for their cruel methods of making war, placing them on a par with the Byzantines and the Turks and Khazars. Cf. below p. 133.
85 *Waqʿat Ṣiffīn*, 481.
86 *Id.*, introd. p.z.
87 Cf. for ʿUmar b. Saʿd, Dhahabī, *Mīzān al-Iʿtidāl*, iii, 199, no. 6118.
88 Brockelmann, *GAL*, *Sup.* i, 215. For an edition of al-Madāʾinī's *Kitāb al-Murdifāt min Quraysh* ('Women of Quraysh who had more than one husband') see ʿAbd as-Salām M. Hārūn, *Nawādir al-Makhṭūṭāt*, i (1370/1951), 57–80.
89 *Murūj adh-Dhahab*, Paris edn, also Cairo, 1384/1964, i, 14.
90 Columbia University Studies in History, etc., New York, 1916–24, the first part of which, by Professor Hitti, has been reissued, Beirut, 1966.
91 Cf. e.g. the beginning of the chapter on Armenia.
92 Balʿamī's work used to be called the 'Persian Ṭabarī' (see p. 91).
93 Some exx. in the accounts of the fighting between the Arabs and Khazars. See Dunlop, *Hist. of the Jewish Khazars* 58 ff.
94 Dunlop, *ibid.*, 58.
95 Ed. S. al-Munajjid, 277.
96 *Al-Arḍ al-Kabīra* for the European continental mass is in more frequent use than *al-Arḍ aṣ-Ṣaghira*, the 'Little Land', apparently for the Byzantine possessions beyond the Bosporus (the text in Ibn Ḥawqal, 191, cf. Wiet's trans. 188, is not altogether clear).
97 Reigned from 232/847 until 247/861.
98 i.e. an official at Sāmarrā. The ʿAbbāsids since the rise of the

Aghlabids in Ifrīqiya no longer sent out governors to North Africa.

99 Cf. *K. al-Kāmil, sub anno* 226 (vi, 518–19).
100 Cf. n. 98.
101 *Fihrist*, 113.
102 Cf. Brockelmann, *GAL*, *Sup*. i, 216.
103 Ṣ. al-Munajjid, ed., *K. Futūḥ al-Buldān*, introd. 15, following C. H. Becker, *EI*, art. al-Balādhurī.
104 'Le Livre des généalogies d'al-Balādhurī', *Bulletin d'études orientales de l'Institut Français de Damas*, xiv (1954), 197–211.
105 W. Ahlwardt, *Anonyme arabische Chronik, Bd. xi, vermutlich das Buch der Verwandschaft der Adligen von elbeladori*, Leipzig, 1883.
106 Nos. 597–8, discovered by C. H. Becker (*EI*, art. al-Balādhurī).
107 *Dhakhā'ir al-ʿArab*, No. 27.
108 *RSO*., vi, 427–507.
109 *Il Califfo Muʿāwiya I secondo il 'Kitâb Ansâb al-Ašrâf'*, Rome, 1938.
110 *Liber Expugnationis Regionum*, Leiden, 1870.
111 *Op. cit*., (see p. 84), introd. 14.
112 i.e. titleless. The first part of the work is lost.
113 *Praefatio* to his edn, p. viii. The work in question, for which see W. Wright, *A Short History of Syriac Literature*, 98, was edited with a German translation by C. Bezold in 1883.
114 Cf. Brockelmann, *GAL* (2), i, 259.
115 Ed. Houtsma, i, 2–89, cf. M. Klamroth, *Der Auszug aus den Evangelien bei dem arabischen Historiker al-Jaʿqūbī, Festschrift z. Einweihung des Wilhelm-Gymnasiums in Hamburg*, 1885.
116 Ed. Houtsma, i, 107–61.
117 *Ibid*., 203–4.
118 Cf. Dunlop, *Hist. of the Jewish Khazars*, 20 ff.
119 Ed. Wüstenfeld, Göttingen, 1850, IV.
120 *K. Akhbār aṭ-Ṭiwāl*, ed. V. Guirgass, Leiden, 1888, 116–47.
121 *Ibid*., 337–65.
122 *Wafayāt al-Aʿyān*, ed. de Slane, i, 640. Cf. a similar remark by Masʿūdī cited below, p. 103.
123 Leiden, 1879–1901 (reprinted Leiden, 1964), including two volumes of Introduction and Notes. A new edition, now in its 8th volume, is in course of publication in Egypt at the Dār al-Maʿārif, and makes use of some new materials, see Vol. i (*Dhakhā'ir al-ʿArab*, 30), 1960, introd. 30.
124 Ṭabarī usually cites the names of men, not books, which of course he used. For his sources, see Jawād ʿAli, 'Mawādd Ta'rīkh aṭ-Ṭabari' *Majallat al-Majmaʿ al-ʿIlmī bi'l-ʿIrāq*, 1.
125 *Jāmiʿ al-Bayān fī Tafsīr (Ta'wīl) al-Qur'ān*, 30 vols, Cairo, 1321/1903, and again in 1322–30/1904–12. A new edition was begun in

Cairo, of which some fifteen volumes have already appeared (Dār al-Maʿārif).

126 It was never completed, cf. Brockelmann, i, 143.

127 Cf. M. Abū'l-Faḍl Ibrāhīm, *Taʾrīkh aṭ-Ṭabarī*, Dār al-Maʿārif, i, introd. 25.

128 Brockelmann, *GAL* (2) i, 143, and *Sup*. The sections of ʿArīb dealing with Africa and Spain, which Ibn ʿIdhārī (see below) incorporated in *al-Bayyān al-Maghrib*, were given by Dozy in his edition of the latter book.

129 Paris, 1867–74, reprinted Paris, 1958.

130 Trans. Zotenberg, i, 46.

131 Zotenberg, i, 557.

132 Cf. Dunlop, *Hist. of the Jewish Khazars*, 58, bibliographical note.

133 'Völkerschaften des Chazarenreiches im neunten Jahrhundert', *Kőrösi Csoma-Archivum*, iii, (1940), 54.

134 Ṭabarī, I, 2663–71 and 2889–94.

135 *Ibid.*, II, 1275 ff.

136 *Ibid.*, III, 1742–2103, especially the final defeat of ʿAlī b. Muḥammad Ṣāḥib az-Zanj (2085–98).

137 For example, the speech of al-Ḥajjāj on his entry into Kufa (II, 863–6). It is perhaps worth observing that the speeches in Ṭabarī are the reports of what actually was said, conformably to his method, and while no doubt for various reasons less reliable than shorthand or mechanically produced versions of a modern political speech, are quite different in character from the rhetorical compositions placed in the mouths of prominent figures by the Greek and Roman historians, and those in later times who followed their example.

138 For example, the famous letter of Ṭāhir b. al-Ḥusayn, the general of al-Maʾmūn, to his son ʿAbd Allāh b. Ṭāhir (III, 1046–61). The letter is also in Ibn Khaldūn (ed. Beirut, 1961, i, 542–54) and in Ibn al-Athīr, ed. Tornberg, vi, 364–77 (*S. anno* 206). Ibn Khaldūn's text in some editions gives that he took it from Ṭabarī (cf. F. Rosenthal, *The Muqaddimah*, i, pp. lxx–lxxi, ii, p. 139n).

139 For example, ii, 835–43 (secretaries of the Caliphs to the time of ar-Rashīd).

140 From the Hijra to A.D. 915, beyond which the *Annals* do not extend, is some 293 years. The Arab Caliphate came to an end in 1258, 343 years after A.D. 915, so that aṭ-Ṭabarī's work strictly covers rather less than half the whole period.

141 Brockelmann, *GAL* i, 143.

142 Cairo, As-Sawy Press, and London, Luzac. Title-page has *Kitāb al-Awraḳ (sic)*.

143 London, 1935.

144 As *Histoire de la Dynastie Abbaside de 322 à 333/933 à 944*, 2 vols, Algiers, 1946, 1950.

145 Cf. the remarks of Brockelmann, *GAL*, *Sup*. i, 219, D. Sourdel, *Le Vizirat ʿAbbāside de 749à 936 (132 à 324 de l'Hégire)*, Damascus, 1959, 10, and M. Canard, *Byzance et les Arabes*, II, ii, Brussels, 1950, 28. Ibn Khallikān says (ed. de Slane, i, 714): *wa-kāna aghlabu funūnihi akhbār an-nās.*

146 Brockelmann, *GAL*, *Sup*. i, 220.

147 C. A. Storey, *Persian Literature, a Bio-bibliographical Survey*, London, 1927–58, i, 208.

148 'Die Nordvölker bei Birūnī', *ZDMG*, 90 (1936), 43, *Ibn Faḍlān's Reisebericht*, *AKM*, xxiv, 3 (1939), 295 ff, 'Völkerschaft des Chazarenreiches im neunten Jahrhundert,' *Kőrösi Csoma-Archivum*, iii (1940), 47.

149 Ibn Khurradādhbih, *BGA*, vi, 154, but cf. *ibid*., 124.

150 *Ibn Faḍlān's Reisebericht*, 296–302 (Arabic text, German trans. and commentary).

151 *Taʾrīkh al-Islām*, ed. Cairo, (1367/1948–1369/1950), v, 298. His authority is given as Khalīfa, i.e. Khalīfa b. Khayyāṭ ash-Shaybānī al-ʿUṣfurī al-Baṣrī, author of a Chronicle (*Taʾrīkh*) now lost, and other works. Cf. F. Wüstenfeld, *Die Geschichtschreiber der Araber*, 19, no. 57 (not in Brockelmann). Khalīfa was important enough to have notices in the *Fihrist* (232) and Ibn Khallikān (ed. de Slane, i, 251–2), and died probably in 240/854.

152 Cf. Dunlop, *Hist. of the Jewish Khazars*, 58n, 78n.

153 Brockelmann, *GAL*, *Sup*. i, 220, who does not mention W. Ouseley, 'Historical Anecdote from the Tarikh Aasim Cufi,' *Oriental Collections*, II, 58 ff ('Uthmān's messenger to the governor of Egypt in 35/655 with an order to execute Muḥammad b. Abī Bakr and others, cf. Ṭabarī, I, 2964–5).

154 Pp. 76ff. It would be natural to compare the texts of some of these works with that of Ibn Aʿtham al-Kūfī.

155 *Ibn Faḍlān's Reisebericht*, 296. The translation (299) gives in error Kawthar b. al-Asad.

156 For the distinction between North and South Arabians, see pp. 3, 18.

157 *Murūj adh-Dhahab*, vi, 84, corresponding to iii, 264 of the Cairo edn.

158 *Ibid*., v, 298–300.

159 See Dunlop, 'A New Source of Information on the Battle of Talas or Aṭlakh', *Ural-Altaische Jahrbücher*, Vol. 36, 1964 (Festchrift Ananiasz Zajaczkowskii), 326–30.

160 H. von Mzik, *Bibliothek arabischen Historiker und Geographen, I*, Leipzig, 1926, p. 85.

161 *Berichte des VII. Internationalen Orientalisten-Congresses*, Vienna,

1889, 1–17, 3 Tafel (plates). Von Kremer published this budget from the *K. al. Wuzarā' wa'l-Kuttāb*, fols. 179b–82b. An English version is in R. Levy, *The Social Structure of Islam* (2), Cambridge Univ. Press, 1957, 316–21.

162 *Denkschriften der kaiserlichen Akademie der Wissenschaften, Phil.-hist. Classe, Band 36*, Vienna, 1888, 283–362, 3 Tafel.

163 The eighth/fourteenth century Persian historian Waṣṣāf, see Von Kremer, *op. cit.*, 305–6. Von Kremer also gave as an appendix (ibid., 345–51) a budget of the expenses of the court of the Caliph al-Muʿtaḍid (279/892–289/902), which has recently been translated by H. Busse, 'Das Hofbudget des (alifen al-Muʿtaḍid billāh', *Der Islam*, Bd. 43 (1967), 11–36. There is another court budget for the same year of al-Muqtadir (306/918–9) in Hilāl aṣ-Ṣābi', *Rusūm Dār al-Khilāfa*, ed. Michael Awad, Baghdad, 1964, 21–7. See also n. 175a.

164 See his *Allgemeine Einfuhraung in die arabischen Papyri.*

165 Muṣṭafā as-Saqā, Ibrahīm al-Abyārī and ʿAbd al-Ḥafīẓ Shiblī.

166 *Le Vizirat ʿAbbāside de 749 à 936 (132 à 324 de l'Hégire)*, 8–9.

167 Cf. D. Sourdel, *Le Vizirat ʿAbbaside*, 4.

168 Ṭabarī's version of the story (III, 626–8) sometimes has the same wording as Jahshiyārī's.

169 Ṭabarī, II, 863 ff, Yaʿqūbī, ii, 326–7, Masʿūdī, *Murūj*, v, 290 ff. Cf. n. 137.

170 *K. al-Wuzarā' wa'l-Kuttāb*, 217–20.

171 Ṭabarī, III, 626.

172 *K. al-Wuzarā' wa'l-Kuttāb*, 190.

173 Cf. Sourdel, *op. cit.*, 148–9.

174 M. Awad, *Aqsām Dā'iʿa min Kitāb Tuḥfat al-Umarā' fī Ta'rīkh al-Wuzarā'* (*Some Lost Fragments of the Kitab al-Wuzarâ' of Hilâl aṣ-Ṣâbi'*) 1948, 23, cf. D. Sourdel, *Le Vizirat ʿAbbaside*, 11.

175 Brockelmann, *GAL*, *Sup*. i, 556.

175a This work of Hilāl aṣ-Ṣābi' contains the budget of al-Muʿtaḍid mentioned in n. 163, which may have been copied from the archives by a treasury official and submitted as a memorandum to al-Muqtadir (cf. Busse, *op. cit.*, 13). In the later edition by ʿAbd as-Sattār A. Farrāj (Cairo, 1958) the budget of al-Muʿtadid appears on pp. 15–27.—It has sometimes been thought that the *K. al-Aʿyan wa'l-Amāthil* of Ḥilāl aṣ-Ṣābi' is the same book as his *K. Tuḥfat al-Umarā' fī Ta'rīkh al-Wuzarā'* (e.g. by Von Kremer, *ibid.*, 284), and this is stated by Brockelmann (*Sup. Bd.* i, 556, who there gives *K. al-Amāthil wā'l-Aʿyān*, the form in Ibn Khallikān, trans. De Slane, iii, 628). But the edd. Michael Awad and ʿAbd as-Sattār Farrāj are no doubt right in regarding them as different books, cf. *EI*(2), iii, 388, art. Hilāl b. al-Muḥassin aṣ-Ṣābi' (D. Sourdel).

176 The *Ta'rīkh* of Hilāl aṣ-Ṣābi' was a continuation of the History of his uncle Thābit b. Sinān, which itself continuated Ṭabarī (cf. pp. 90 f). See for the connection of all these histories an important passage of Ibn al-Qifṭī, *Ta'rīkh al-Ḥukamā'*, ed. Lippert, 110 ff, trans. F. Rosenthal, *History of Muslim Historiography*, Leiden, 1952, 72–3 (2nd rev. edn, Leiden, 1968, 71–3).

177 Ed. Michael Awad, Baghdad, 1383/1964.

178 *Rusūm Dār al-Khilāfa*, 3, 140.

179 *Rusūm*, 143, cf. the editor's introduction, 42.

180 The work *Rusūm Dār al-Khilāfa* has been attributed to Ghars an-Ni'ma, the son of Hilāl aṣ-Ṣābi' (Brockelmann, *GAL* i, (2) 324), but this seems to be a mistake, cf. Michael Awad's introduction, 42.

181 Cf. *Cambridge Medieval History*, iv, pt. i (1966), 723–4. The date there suggested, 979, seems too early. The Muslim historians in general give 375/985, but the 376/986 of Hilāl aṣ-Ṣābi' may be right, if Sclerus was in captivity in Baghdad for seven years (cf. *ibid.*, 177), for Hilāl aṣ-Ṣābi' adds that he was not released till shortly before the death of Ṣamsām ad-Dawla in 388/998.

182 The amount of the revenue is given as 14,829,840 *dīnārs*, which corresponds closely with the figure given for the same year by Waṣṣāf (14,529,286 *dīnārs*), see Von Kremer, *Ueber das Einnahmebudget des Abbasiden-Reiches*, 303. We are expressly told (*Rusūm*, 21) that al-Ḥaramān (Mecca and Medina), the Yemen, Barqa, Shahrzūr, aṣ-Ṣāmaghān (Bāmiyān), Kirmān and Khurāsān were exempted, but there were general complaints of scarcity. Details of great interest are given of the expenditure in this year. One large item was 'for the Turks in the private and public kitchens and establishments outside the Palace', which together with fodder for the horses (*kurā'*), birds (probably for sport) and wild animals (sc. in the Caliph's private menagerie) amounted to 528,840 *dīnārs* over twelve months. The largest single item was the monthly stipend to the Queen-mother Shaghb, a former Greek slave-girl, which with those of the *amīrs*, the inmates of the *ḥarīm* and servants, accounted for 743,196 *dīnārs* yearly. No separate establishment is mentioned for al-Muqtadir, who had been Caliph for ten years and was then about twenty-three years of age.

183 The authority given is Abū'l-Wazīr Ibn Hāni' al-Marwazī identified by M. Awad (*Rusūm*, 28, n. 4) with 'Umar b. Muṭarrif, who was then in charge of the land-tax (*kharāj*) acting under an order from Yaḥyā b. Khālid the Barmecide. The total amounted to 338,910,000 *dirhams* plus 5,830,000 *dīnārs* or rather more, which reckoning 22 *dirhams* to one *dīnār* gives an additional 128,200,000 *dirhams*, or altogether 467,110,000 *dirhams*. This is comparable with the 530,312,000 *dirhams* given by Von Kremer *Ueber das*

Budget der Einnahmen unter der Regierung des Harun alrašid, 12, for some unnamed year in the same Caliphate. It is remarkable that this budget of Von Kremer, which is also that in Ibn Khaldūn (*The Muqqaddimah*, trans. F. Rosenthal, i, 361 ff) is similarly said to have been originally drawn up by Abū'l-Wazīr ʿUmar b. Muṭarrif and submitted to Yaḥyā b. Khālid. In the *Rusūm Dār al-Khilāfa* only the totals are given, so that it is not possible to say whether the discrepant figures are intended for the same year or not.

184 Also in al-Muqaddasī (ed. De Goeje, 182) for Palestine *c.* 375/985 and in al-Bīrūnī *c.* 391/1000 (M. Awad, *Rusūm*, 24n).

185 The main part of the work at least is by him.

186 Cf. G. Moravcsik, *Byzantinoturcica*, Berlin, 1958, i, 381. See J. B. Bury, 'The Ceremonial Book of Constantine Porphyrogennetos', *Eng. Hist. Review*, xxii (1907), for a critical estimate.

187 *De Cerimoniis Aulae Byzantinae*, ii, cc. 44, 45. Cf. J. B. Bury, *op. cit.*, 215.

188 *GAL* i, 143.

189 *Osteuropäische und ostasiatische Streifzüge*, reprinted Darmstadt, 1961, p. xxxv.

190 *Fihrist*, 154.

191 '*ʿinda baʿḍ ahl al-buyūtāt al-musharrafa min al-Furs*'.

192 *Tanbīh*, ed. Cairo of 1357/1938, 92; trans. Carra de Vaux, *Le Livre de l'Avertissement*, 150.

193 Cf. *Murūj adh-Dhahab*, i, 5, Brockelmann, *GAL* i, 144.

194 Brockelmann, *loc. cit.*, more complete in Carra de Vaux, *Le Livre de l'Avertissement et de la Revision*, Paris, 1896, 569–70.

195 *Murūj*, i, 2–4. The full title is *K. Akhbār az-Zamān wa Man Abādahu al-Ḥidthān min al-Umam al-Māḍiya wa-Ajyāl al-Ḥāliya wa'l-Mamālik ad- Dāthira.*

196 *Tanbīh*, 1.

197 Brockelmann, *GAL* (1) i, 145.

198 *Murūj*, i, 4.

199 *Ibid.*, ii, 283.

200 *Tanbīh*, 227, trans. 346.

201 Tabūk lies on the main route between the Hijaz and Syria S.E. of al-ʿAqaba (Elath).

202 *Tanbīh*, 243, trans. 368.

203 *Tanbīh*, 196, trans. 302.

204 *Tanbīh*, 236, trans. 358.

205 *Tanbīh*, 237, trans. 359.

206 Mentioned several times but never quoted in the *K. at-Tanbīh*.

207 *Tanbīh*, 85, trans. 140, cf. *Tanbīh*, 1, trans. 1, *Tanbīh*, 149, trans. 238, *Tanbīh*, 347, trans. 508.

208 *Murūj*, ix, 36.

209 *Tanbīh*, 288: *wulāt al-Andalus wa-siyāsatahum wa-ḥurūbahum maʿa*

man yujāwiruhum min al-Jalāliqa wa'l-Jāsqas? (or *al-Jāsqus*, for *al-Jāsqun*?), *wa'l-Washkunish* (cf. *al-Bashkunish*, Basques) *wa-Qarmānīsh* (cf. Ibn Khaldūn, i, 134) *wa-Ghūṭas* (*-sh*) *wa-ghairihim min al-Ifranjīya barran wa-baḥran*. The forms of some of the names here are very doubtful.

210 Cf. n. 207.

211 *Tanbīh*, 225, trans. 343.

212 Cited by Carra de Vaux, *ibid.*, 343, n. 1.

213 *Murūj*, ix, 34 (Cairo, iv, 385).

214 That of the presiding chiefs at the annual Pilgrimage, *Murūj*, i, 45 and 46.

215 *Tanbīh*, 85, 133, trans. 140, 213.

216 *Murūj*, i, 4, Cf. above p. 100.

217 *Tanbīh*, 133, trans. 213, cf. 124, trans. 199, and especially 149, trans. 238, where the possibility of more than two 'editions' is suggested by the plural (*nusakh*) in the text.

218 *Tanbīh*, 347, trans. 508.

219 P. 87 f, above. Cf. Charles Pellat, *Les Prairies d'Or*, Paris, 1962, i, p. vii.

220 *Streifzäge*, xxxiv. See also below, Muslim b. Abī Muslim al-Jarmī.

221 Cf. the remarks of De Goeje, *BGA* vii, Praef. p. viii (the *History* may have included a notice of A.H. 292).

222 *Murūj*, ii, 18, cf. Dunlop, *Hist. of the Jewish Khazars*, 209.

223 *Murūj*, ii, 59, cf. Dunlop, *ibid.*, 213.

224 *Murūj*, i, 10 ff.

225 P. 84.

226 *Ibid.*, i, 15.

227 *Ibid.*, ii, 70 ff.

228 *Ibid.*, i, 234, cf. J. Sauvaget, *Akhbār aṣ-Ṣīn wa'l-Hind* (*Relation de la Chine et de l'Inde*), Paris, 1948, 2, also Dozy, *Supplément*, ii, 776.

229 *Murūj*, iii, 67 (Cairo, ii, 34). The change from *Bwyrh* of the text (rendered by the trans. Bawireh) to *Bryzh*, Barīzah, is not difficult, cf. Marquart, *Streifzüge*, xxxvi. This is perhaps the only passage in a medieval Arabic author where Paris is mentioned. For a similar instance of corruption of the text cf. *Murūj*, ii, 303 (Cairo, i, 312): Tīzūn for Nīrūn, the Emperor Nero.

230 *Murūj*, iii, 69 ff. (Cairo, ii, 36).

231 For his library estimated at 400,000 volumes, Maqqarī, *Nafḥ*, edn. of Cairo, 1327/1949, i, 371. Cf. also Dozy, *Hist. des Musulmans d'Espagne*, revised ed. by E. Lévi-Provençal. ii, 183 ff.

232 Ibn Khaldūn associates al-Wāqidī with him in making this stricture. Cf. above p. 74 .

233 *Muqaddimah*, i, 8, Beirut edn of 1961, i, 3–4. Ibn Khaldūn here speaks of the 'books' (*kutub*) of al-Masʿūdī, but normally he quotes only the *Murūj adh-Dhahab*. See below.

234 *Muqaddimah*, i, 16; Beirut, i, 13.
235 Numbers 1:46.
236 *Annals*, I, i, 479. Other refs. in Rosenthal, *Muqaddimah*, i, 16n.
237 Rosenthal's translation, *Muqaddimah*, i, 175–6; Beirut, i, 149–50.
238 *Muq.*, i, 219; Beir., i, 188–9.
239 *Muq.*, i, 348; Beir., i, 305.
240 *Muq.*, i, 352; Beir., i, 310.
241 *Muq.*, i, 419; Beir., i, 362.
242 *Muq.*, i, 63; Beir., i, 52.
243 *Muq.*, i, 18, Beir., i, 15, cf. *Tanbīh*, 170, trans. 268.
244 *Tanbīh*, 119–24, trans. 190–9, *Murūj*, ii, 311–23.
245 Nothing is here said of the Church of the Resurrection at Jerusalem, for which see below, p. 107.
246 *Tanbīh*, 124, trans. 199.
247 *Murūj*, ii, 311, 314–16, cf. 313.
248 *Tanbīh*, 120, trans. 192.
249 *Murūj*, ii, 319.
250 *Murūj* gives al-Azdi.
251 *Murūj*, ii, 318.
252 *Tanbīh*, 164, 165, trans. 260, 261.
253 Cf. *Cambridge Medieval History*, i (1964), 8.
254 *Murūj*, ii, 311.
255 *Tanbīh*, 120, trans. 191–2.
256 *Tanbīh*, 122, trans. 194, cf. Marquart, *Streifzüge*, 342–53, Dunlop, *Hist. of the Jewish Khazars*, 209n.
257 *Murūj*, ii, 318.
258 North (? and West) of the Propontis.
259 A description of the ceremony in 675/1277 in Qazwīnī, i, 75. For a lively nineteenth-century account, Hon. Robert Curzon Jun., *Visits to the Monasteries of the Levant* (1834), pt. ii, c. 4.
260 Masʿūdī both here (*Tanbīh*, 124, trans. 198) and in the *Murūj* (ii, 312) says that the Church of Ḥimṣ (= Emesa) was one of the wonders of the world, but this is usually said of the Church of al-Ruha (see following note).
261 The *Tanbīh* (*ibid.*) adds that the four wonders of the world are the Mosque of Damascus, the Manāra or Pharos of Alexandria, the Bridge of Sanja (built by Vespasian, see Le Strange, *Lands of the Eastern Caliphate*, 124, n. 1) near Samosata in al-Jazīra (Mesopotamia), and this church. This leaves out of account the Church of Emesa, which he has just named as one of the wonders of the world, an indication of some dislocation of his text or perhaps of a later addition.
262 Plural of *band*, see Carra de Vaux, *Le Livre de l'Avertissement*, 239.
263 *Tanbīh*, 150–60, trans. 239–55. Masʿūdī describes nine Greek provinces, Anatolia, Opsikion, Thrakesion, Pamphylia, Cappadocia,

Bukellarion, Optimaton, Armeniakon and Paphlagonia, and concludes the section with some information about adjoining countries.

264 *Tanbīh*, 132, trans. 212–13. cf. F. Rosenthal, *Historiography*, 96.

265 Discussions at Baghdad and at Takrīt in 313/925 between al-Masʿūdī and the last-named, Dankhā, are mentioned (*Tanbīh*, 132–3), and evidently were reported in al-Masʿūdī's *Kitāb al-Masāʾil waʾl-ʿIlal fīʾl-Madhāhib waʾl-Milal* (Book of Questions and Causes concerning the Sects and Religions) and *Kitāb Sirr al-Ḥayāt* (Secret of Life), both now lost.

266 *Tanbīh*, 165, trans. 261.

267 *Tanbīh*, 160–6, trans. 255–63.

268 Theoph. Cont., ed. Bonn, 443 (= Bk. vi, 9, p. 275).

269 S. Runciman, *The Emperor Lecapenus and His Reign*, Cambridge, reprinted 1963, 231, *Cambridge Medieval History*, iv, pt. i, 143.

270 In A.D. 925 apparently, cf. Runciman, *ibid.*, 68.

271 He took refuge after his fall in a monastery, Runciman, *ibid.*

272 *Tanbīh*, 165, trans. 261.

273 *Tanbīh*, 97, 118, trans. 158, 189, cf. 112, trans. 180.

274 Cf. Sir W. Smith, *Dict. of Greek and Roman Biography*, s.vv. Ptolemaeus, Theon.

275 *Murūj*, ii, 123.

276 *Tanbīh*, 118, trans. 189. Masʿūdī also mentions the astronomical table (*zīj fīʾn-nujūm*) of Muḥammad b. Mūsā al-Khwārizmī as containing chronological data (*Tanbīh*, 157, trans. 251).

277 For example his references to Marinus, and to Greek philosophy, especially its later Islamic development. See for the former pp. 151 ff here, and for the latter cf. *Al-Masʿūdī Millenary Commemoration Volume*, Aligarh, 1960, S. M. Stern, 'Al-Masʿūdī and the philosopher al-Fārābī', 28–41, and D. M. Dunlop, 'A Source of al-Masʿūdī: the Madīnat al-Fāḍilah of al-Fārābī', 69–71.

278 *Tanbīh*, 97–166, trans. 158–263, compared with *Tanbīh*, 74–97, trans. 122–58.

279 *Murūj*, ii, 105–241 (Persians), 242–355, 421–41 (Greeks and Romans). These pages contain both text and translation, the totals (136 and 133) need to be halved.

280 Mentioned under Ptolemy IV, Alexandros (?), *Tanbīh*, 98–9, trans. 159–61.

281 *Murūj*, iv, 37–40 (ii, 234, Cairo).

282 'Storia dell'astronomia presso gli Arabi nel Medio Evo', in *Raccolta di Scritti*, v, 212; in the original Arabic *ʿIlm al-Falak wa-Taʾ-rīkhuhu ʿindʾ al-ʿArab fīʾl-Qurūn al-Wusṭā*, Rome, 1911–12, 160.

283 Arabic text is printed at Cairo, 1357/1938, the French translation by Carra de Vaux, Paris, 1898.

284 Pp. 104, cf. pp. 131, 132, 152, 183, etc., also *K. al-Qaṣd waʾl-Amam* (see below), 164.

285 *Ibid.*, 105, 109, 111, 116, 150–51, 153, etc.
286 *Ibid.*, 68–78.
287 Cf. D. M. Dunlop, 'An 11th Century Spanish Account of the Northern Nations', *BSOAS*, xv, 1953, 159–61.
288 *Murūj*, iii, 61–78.
289 Brockelmann, *GAL* (2) i, 335.
290 *Al-Mawāʿiz waʾl-Iʿtibār fī(bi-) Dhikr al-Khiṭaṭ waʾl-Athār*, Lebanon (ash-Shiyāh) edn (*al-Khiṭaṭ al-Maqrīzīya*, 3 vols, n.d.), i, 56, cf. *K. Akhbār az-Zamān wa-ʿAjāʾib al-Buldān*, Cairo, 1357/1938, 161.
291 *Khiṭaṭ*, i, 92, cf. *K. Akhbār az-Zamān wa-ʿAjāʾib al-Buldān*, 159.
292 *Khiṭaṭ*, i, 125, cf. *K. Akhbār az-Zamān wa-ʿAjāʾib al-Buldān*, 185. there 'king Badāunus'.
293 *Khiṭaṭ*, i, 31.
294 *K. Akhbār az-Zamān*, 110.
295 *Khiṭaṭ*, i, 69.
296 *Murūj*, ii, 398 ff., cf. Ibn ʿAbd al-Ḥakam, *Futūh Miṣr*, ed. C. C. Torrey, New Haven, 1922 (Leiden, 1920), 26; Yāqūt, *Muʿjam al-Buldān*, ed. Wüstenfeld, i, 262.
297 Ṭabarī, *s. anno.*
298 Ed. Cairo, 138–40.
299 i.e. apparently with reference to the foreknowledge of the ancient Egyptians.
300 *Khiṭaṭ*, i, 201–2.
301 *Kitħb Zkhbār az-Zamān*, 138 (i.e. omitting *al-Maʾmūn ibn*).
302 See n. 296.
303 *Khiṭaṭ*, i, 71.
304 Ed. Paris, ii, 414.
305 Cf. *Khiṭaṭ*, i, 69 (an interpretation of Egyptian writing said to have been made by Dhū'n-Nūn al-Miṣrī, d. 245/859) = *Murūj*, ii, 401; *Khiṭaṭ*, i, 71 (anecdote concerning ʿAbd al-ʿAzīz b. Marwān while governor of Egypt for the Caliph ʿAbd al-Malik b. Marwān, his brother) = *Murūj*, i, 414 ff. *Khiṭat*, i, 67, where Maqrīzī cites 'an aged shaykh, Muḥammad b. al-Masʿūdī' for a minor archaeological find, is evidently different.
306 The *Fihrist* of Ibn an-Nadīm gives the title and author's name of hundreds, or rather thousands, of works no longer extant. The same impression of lost literary treasures is conveyed by the works of Ibn abī Uṣaybiʿa, Ḥājjī Khalīfa, etc.
307 Ed. and trans. J. M. E. Gottwaldt, Leipzig, 1844 and 1848. See also art. Ḥamza al-Iṣfahānī in *EI*(2) (F. Rosenthal).
308 Ed. Gottwaldt, 3–4, trans. 2.
309 *Ibid.*, 5, trans. 3.
310 Cf. *Sūr.* 5, 72–3 (Amīrī, 68–9).

311 Cf. e.g. R. Bell, *The Origin of Islam in its Christian Environment*, London, 1926, 60–1, and *Introduction to the Qur'ān*, Edinburgh, 1953, 13.

312 *Ta'rīkh al-Hind*, ed. Sachau, 10, trans. (*Alberuni's India*, London, 1888, reprinted, S. Chand and Co., New Delhi, 1964), i, 21.

313 *Muhammedanische Studien*, i, 209–13.

314 Ed. Gottwaldt, 8–9, trans. 6–7. He gives the figure eight but names only seven books. See the following note.

315 Ed. Gottwaldt, 16 trans. 11–12. This appears to be Ḥamza's eighth codex. See n. 314.

316 *Ibid.*, 13–14, trans. 16–17. Bahrām b. Mardān Shāh's book has already been mentioned by Ḥamza among the seven or eight codices which he consulted.

317 For the Dulafids see *EI* (2), *s. voce.*

318 The name seems to be either a rendering of some Greek name with similar significance, or indicates servile condition, cf. such servile names as Ṭall (Dew), Khazz (Silk).

319 Ed. Gottwaldt, 70, trans. 52–3.

320 See G. Le Strange, *Lands of the Eastern Caliphate*, 197–8. Al-Karaj was about halfway between Hamadhān and Iṣbahān (Yāqūt, *Mu'jam al-Buldān*, iv, 251).

321 Ed. Gottwaldt, 70, 76, trans. 53, 57–8.

322 Ed. Gottwaldt, 79, trans. 59–60.

322a *Fihrist*, 114, Brockelmann, *GAL*, *Sup.*, i, 225 (J. Schacht) and F. Rosenthal, *A History of Muslim Historiography* (2nd edn), 418, n. 4.

323 Ed. Gottwaldt, 80–1, trans. 61. Cf. *Fihrist*, 23–4. Several other translations by Habīb b. Bahrīz are known, including one of the *Eisagōgē Arithmētikē* of Nicomachus of Gerasa made for Ṭāhir b. al-Ḥusayn, governor of Khurāsān from 205/820 (cf. Steinschneider, *Die arab. Uebersetzungen a. d. Griechischen*, repr. Graz, 1960, 351–2.

324 *Ibid.*, 83–4, trans. 65.

325 Ed. C. C. Torrey, Yale Univ. Press, 1922 reprinted al-Muthanna Library, Baghdad, n.d.

326 It was continued by Yaḥyā al-Anṭākī to 425/1033.

327 For Ibn ad-Dāya see Brockelmann, *GAL Sup.*, i, 229, cf. D. M. Dunlop, *The Fusūl al-Madanī of al-Fārābī*, 6–7.

328 See pp. 161 f.

329 Cf. Dunlop, 'An 11th Century Spanish Account of the Northern Nations', *BSOAS*, xv (1953), 161.

330 i.e. 'the Historian' *par excellence.*

331 There is disagreement on the date of his death. According to Ibn al-Faraḍī, no. 137 (edn of Cairo, 1373/1954, i, 55) it was 12 Rajab, 344.

332 The title appears slightly differently in aḍ-Ḍabbī, ed. Codera and Ribera, no. 330 (p. 140) and in Maqqarī, i, 118.
333 The *Taʾrīkh* of Ibn Ḥabīb or of a pupil of his is perhaps extant in a Bodleian MS, cf. Brockelmann, *GAL* (2), i, 156.
334 Madrid, 1898.
335 Numerous editions mentioned by Brockelmann; a synopsis of the work in Pons Boigues, *Historiadores*, 52–6; and *Analytical Indices* by Muḥammad Shafīʿ, Calcutta, 1935–7.
336 Arab Academy of Damascus, 1373/1954 onwards.
337 Aleppo, 1342–5/1923–6 in 7 volumes.
338 Various editions, and an old English translation by J. Reynolds (from a Persian version), Oriental Translation Fund, 1858.
339 See Brockelmann for the titles and other details.
340 Ed. O. Houdas, with French trans., Paris, 1891 and 1895.
340a English trans. by G. R. Potter, *The Autobiography of Ousama*, London, 1929.
341 *Kitāb an-Nukat al-ʿAṣriyya fī Akhbār al-Wuzarāʾ al-Miṣriyya*, ed. H. Derenbourg, Paris, 2 vols, 1898, 1909.
342 *Dhakhāʾir al-ʿArab*, 18, Cairo, 1955.
343 i.e. contemporaries, see below.
344 4 vols, Paris, 1843–71. The Johnson Reprint Corporation of New York and London produced a facsimile edn in 1961.
345 Paris, 1838–42. (Part i only, the last biography being that of ar-Raḍī Muḥammad b. aṭ-Ṭāhir.) There are various Oriental editions, and one by F. Wüstenfeld, Göttingen, 1835–43.
346 e.g. as-Sulamī, *Kitāb Ṭabaqāt aṣ-Ṣūfiyya*, an early work on its subject (*c*. 387/997), ed. J. Pedersen, Leiden, 1960.
347 Ed. D. S. Margoliouth, *GMS*, 1907–26.
348 According to Wüstenfeld, *Geschichtschreiber d. Araber*, No. 358, before A.H. 50 the biographies of only four persons are given.
349 Ed. de Slane, i, 2.
350 Wüstenfeld, *ibid.*
351 *A Boswell of Baghdad*, London, 1917, 1–98.
352 *GAL*, ii, 32.
353 *Indice alfabetico di tutte le biografie contenute nel Wāfi bi-l-wafayāt di al-Ṣafadi*, *Rendiconti della Reale Accademia dei Lincei*, ser. V, vols xxii, xxiv, xxv.
354 By H. Ritter and S. Dedering, *Bibliotheca Islamica*, 6, a-d, 1931–59.
355 4 vols, Cairo, 1382/1963, ed. ʿA. M. al-Bukhārī.
356 Ed. P. de Jong, Leiden, 1881.
357 5 vols, Cairo, 1367/1948 and following years.
358 See Brockelmann, *GAL* ii, 46–7.
359 Edn 3, revised in 4 vols with index, Haidarabad, 1375/1955–1377/1958.
360 Edn 2, Haidarabad, 2 vols, 1364–5/1945–6.
361 Vol. i, ed. Ṣalāh ad-Dīn al-Munajjid, Kuwayt, 1960.

362 *Wa-qad ṣanafa al-ʿulamāʾ fī sīrat hādhāʾn-nabiʾ al-karīm wa-mabʿathihi wa-aiyāmihi . . . wa-qad dhakartu min dhālika jumlatan wāfiratan fī kitābī al-kabīr al-mulaqqab bi-Taʾrīkh al-Islām* (*K. Duwal al-Islām*, i, 3); *qāla al-ḥāfiẓ al-ʿallāma al-ʿumda Abū ʿAbd Allāh Muḥammad b. Aḥmad b. ʿUthmān b. adh-Dhahabī . . . wa-baʿd fa-hādha taʾrīkh mukhtaṣar ʿalā as-sanawāt adhkuru fīhi mā quddira lī min ashhar al-ḥawādith waʾl-wafayāt* (*K. al-ʿIbar*, 1).
363 Ṣalāḥ ad-Dīn al-Munajjid in introd. of the *Kitāb al-ʿIbar*, p. 6. The work goes down to 700/1300–1.
364 Quoted *Taʾrikh al-Islam*, i, 7.
365 ii, 169–91 in the Haidarabad edn.
366 Ṭabarī II, ii, 884–994.
367 iii, 121–6, 160.
368 See Dunlop, 'Al-Ḥārith b. Saʿīd al-Kadhdhāb, a claimant to prophecy in the Caliphate of ʿAbd al-Malik', *Studies in Islam*, New Delhi, i (Jan. 1964), 12–18.
369 See F. Rosenthal, *Hist. of Muslim Historiography*, 277–80, 303–6 (from the *Iʿlān* of as-Sakhāwī).
370 'Wise Men' (*ḥukamāʾ*) in the sense of 'sages, philosophers'.
371 Ed. Fuʾād Sayyid, Cairo, 1955.
372 Ed. August Müller (Imruʾ al-Qays aṭ-Ṭaḥḥān), Königsberg and Cairo, 1884.
373 Ed. as *Taʾrīkh al-Ḥukamāʾ* by J. Lippert, Leipzig, 1903.
374 Ed. Muḥammad Shafīʿ, Lahore, 1935.
375 Cf. D. M. Dunlop, 'Biographical Material from the Ṣiwān al-Ḥikmah', *JRAS*, 1957, 82–9.
376 See the refs given by Brockelmann, *GAL*, *Sup*. i, 583.
377 Brockelmann, *ibid.*, names Abūʾl Faḍl M. b. al-Ḥusayn b. al-ʿAmīd and Abū Muḥammad al-Muhallabī.
378 Note that Vol. iii contains additions to Miskawayh's *Tajārib al-Umam* by Abū Shujāʿ Rudhrāwarī, i.e. Zahīr ad-Dīn Muḥammad b. al-Ḥusayn al-Hamadhāni (cf. Brockelmann, *GAL* i, 342) and Hilāl b. al-Muḥassin, i.e. Hilāl aṣ-Ṣābiʾ, for whom see above.
379 *FHA*, ii, Leiden, 1871.
380 See the passage already referred to, n. 176.
381 D. Sourdel, *Le Vizirat ʿAbbaside*, i, 25. See now also the appreciation by Dr M. S. Khan in ʿMiskawaih and Arabic Historiography', JAOS, 89 (1969), 710–30.
382 *EI* (2), art. Bardhaʿa.
383 Translated Margoliouth IV (ii), 62–7. The translator's renderings of proper names are here retained.
384 i.e. al-Marzubān b. Muḥammad the Musāfirid (Zambaur, *Manuel de Généalogie et de Chronologie*, 180).
385 Highlanders of Daylam, south of the Caspian.
386 The Arabic word originally means 'poor men, vagrants, thieves'.
387 Not known.
388 Text has Maragha, apparently in error.

389 A detailed account of the burial of a Russian chief on the Volga in 310/922 is given by Ibn Faḍlān (*Riḥla*, ed. A. Zeki Validi Togan, 38 ff, German trans., 88 ff).

390 For Russian expeditions down the Volga to the Caspian, see Dunlop, *Hist. of the Jewish Khazars*, 238 ff.

391 Ed. ʿAbdurrahmān Badawī, Cairo, 1952, with the Arabic title *al-Ḥikma al-Khālida*.

392 For the brothers see pp. 95, 105. The designation Dhū'r-Riyāsatayn' means 'Possessor of the two commands', i.e. military and civil. Thus the same man was both *amīr* and *wazīr* (cf. Sourdel, *op. cit.*, i, 201–2).

393 Ed. Badawi, 3, cf. 375.

394 The last class is defined (ed. Badawi, 285) as 'modern philosophers, scholars and amateurs of science'.

395 A commentary on one of these is the article of M. Arkoun, 'A propos d'une édition récente [that of 1959] du *Kitāb Tahḏīb al-ʾAḫlāq*', *Arabica*, ix, 61–73. A new edition of *Tahdhīb al-Akhlāq* was published by Professor Constantine Zurayk, (American University of Beirut, Centennial Publications, 1966), followed by an English trans. (A.V.B., 1968).

396 Cf. M. S. Khan, *An Unpublished Treatise of Miskawaih on Justice*, Leiden, 1964.

397 The most recent edition listed by Brockelmann is Cairo, 1325/1907.

398 *Akhbār Majmūʿa*, ed. Lafuente y Alcantara, Madrid, 1867; Ibn al-Qūṭiyya, *Taʾrīkh Iftitāḥ al-Andalus*, ed. Madrid, 1868, trans. J. Ribera, Madrid, 1926.

399 Cf. Ibn al-Qūṭiyya, *op. cit.*, 4 ff.

400 See his biographer Ibn al-Faraḍī, ed. F. Codera, no. 1316 (ed. Cairo, 1373/1954, no. 1318).

401 For details see especially Brockelmann, *GAL*.

402 Aḍ-Ḍabbī, ed. Codera, no. 679; Ibn Khallikān, ed. de Slane, i, 245.

403 *Elogio del Islam español*, trans. E. Garcia Gomez, Madrid 1934, 55, Arabic text in Maqqarī, *Nafḥ aṭ-Ṭīb*, ed. Cairo, iv, 182. New edn by Salāḥ ad-Dīn al-Munajjid in *Faḍāʾil al-Andalus wa-Ahlihā*, Beirut, 1387/1968, 29–60.

404 There is some MS authority for *al-Mubīn* (Clear Book), but the more difficult reading is preferable.

405 Maqqarī, *Nafḥ aṭ-Ṭīb*, ed. Cairo, iv, 172 (ed. Leiden, ii, 122).

406 Cf. Brockelmann, *Sup.*, i, 578.

407 Details in Brockelmann, i, 338.

408 Ibn Ḥayyān, *al-Muqtabis fī Akhbār Balad al-Andalus*, ed. ʿAbd ar-Raḥmān ʿAlī al-Ḥajjī, Beirut, 1965.

409 Ed. Muṣṭafā ʿAwwad al-Karīm, Khartoum, 1954. Ibn Diḥya claimed descent from Diḥya al-Kalbī, a famous Companion of Muḥammad and on the maternal side from al-Ḥusayn b. ʿAlī.

410 Ed. ʿAbbās al-ʿAzzāwī, Baghdad, 1365/1946.

411 Ibn Khallikān, trans. de Slane, iv, 126, takes him to task for a genealogical error. Adh-Dhahabī mentions Ibn Diḥya in a long notice in the *Mīzān al-Iʿtidāl* (ed. Cairo, 1382/1963, iii, 186), where he is very severely handled.

412 *Op. cit.*, 50–3. Cf. V. Minorsky, *Ḥudūd alʿAlam*, *GMS*, 1937, 236 ff. The Indian king is mentioned in *Ḥudūd al-ʿĀlam* itself as Dahum (quite distinct in the MS, fol. 14b). He is of course quite different from Dhūbān, the envoy to al-Maʾmūn from the king of Kābulistān about the same time (Miskawayh, *Jāwīdān Khirad*, 19–22).

413 Ed. Leiden, i, 156 ff (ed. Cairo, i, 234 ff).

414 Ed. for the first time by Dozy, Leiden, 1847, reprint Amsterdam, 1968.

415 The first two volumes were also edited by Dozy, Leiden, 1848–51, vol. iii by E. Lévi-Provençal, Paris, 1930, and further portions dealing with the history of the Almoravids and Almohads by Huici Miranda and E. Lévi-Provencal. Details in *EI* (2), art. Ibn ʿIdhārī (J. Bosch-Vílá).

416 Cf. Dunlop, 'Ibn ʿIdhāri's account of the Party Kings'. *Trans. Glasgow Univ. Oriental Soc.*, xvii (1959), 19–28.

417 Majd ad-Dīn, the eldest brother, a traditionist, was born in 544/1149. Ḍiyāʾ ad-Dīn was a philologist and was born in 588/1163. The historian's dates are 555/1160–630/1233.

418 Twelve vols. *plus* index vol., Beirut, 1965–6.

419 *GAL* i, 346.

419a Muir, *The Caliphate* Preface to 2nd edn (3rd edn. p. v).

420 *Histoire de l'Afrique du Nord et de l'Espagne*, 1904 (as 'Ibn al-Athir, Annales du Maghreb et de l'Espagne', *Revue Africaine*, xl–xlv, Algiers, 1896–1901).

421 *Hist. of Muslim Historiography*, 128.

422 Ibn al-Jawzī was an encyclopedic writer especially on religious subjects, see Brockelmann, *GAL* i, 500 ff, and the art. Ibn al-Djawzī in *Enc. Īslam* (2) (H. Laoust).

423 This facsimile was published at Chicago in 1907.

424 Two vols, Haidarabad, 1951–2.

425 The use of *ibn* apparently for *de* is notable.

426 Al-Malik an-Nāṣir was also put to death by Hūlāgū later (Zambaur, *Manuel de Généalogie*, 97n).

427 Ed. Haidarabad, 172–3 (anno 533), where the title of the work is given as *Mukhtār min an-Naẓr* (sic) etc.

428 Ibn Khallikān refers to this autograph several times towards the end of his own work (De Slane's translation, iv, 122 and 244), and appears to have taken notes from it.

429 Cf. *Mirʾāt āz-Zamān* for the year 535 (ed. Haidarabad, i, 176 ff) where a tumult in Baghdad is treated at some length and the only

other political event noticed is the taking of the Syrian fortress of Maṣyāf (Maṣyāth) by the Assassins (a bare mention of a line and a half). Ibn al-Athīr in the *Kāmil* for the same year describes an attack upon Baghdad by officers of the Saljūq Sultan Masʿūd (no doubt the popular excitement mentioned by Sibṭ b. al-Jawzī was connected in some way) and a number of other significant matters.

430 Contrast the accounts of an incident in the career of Ṣalāḥ ad-Dīn (Saladin) given by both writers and reported by Ibn Khallikān (translation of de Slane, iv, 544–5).

431 Cf. the remarks in Sauvaget-Cahen, *Introduction to the History oȷ the Muslim East*, Univ. of California Press, 1965, 154.

432 No. 8781, described in W. Ahlwardt's Catalogue of the Berlin Library, vol. xix. In spite of Ahlwardt's doubts and the hesitations of Brockelmann (*GAL* i, 348) the work seems to be identifiable.

433 Especially in the second volume.

434 *GAL* i, 348.

435 *Ibid.*, i, 349.

436 *Ibid.*, ii, 45.

437 Notably J. Reiske and H. L. Fleischer. The lattter edited and translated the pre-Islamic part, Leipzig, 1831.

438 Details in Brockelmann, *GAL Sup.* ii, 39.

439 *University of California Publications in Semitic Philology*, 1954–63.

440 *University of California Publications in Semitic Philology*, 1930 and subsequently.

441 The work of Ibn Ḥazm is the *Kitāb al-Milal waʾn-Niḥal* (Book of Religions and Sects) otherwise called *Kitāb al-Faṣl fīʾl-Milal waʾl-Ahwāʾ waʾn-Niḥal* (Book of the Distinction in the Religions, Heresies and Sects). See I. Goldziher, *Die Zahiriten*, Leipzig, 1884, reprinted Hildesheim, 1967, 201 ff.

442 See the passage trans. in Rosenthal, *Hist. of Muslim Historiography*, 402 (2nd edn, 479).

443 *Al-Khiṭaṭ al-Maqrīziyya*, 3 vols, ash-Shiyāḥ Lebanon, n.d.

444 Cairo, 1956–8, 6 vols, i, parts 1–3, ii, parts 1–3.

445 Ed. Ziyāda, i, 9.

446 By Hugo Bunz, Leipzig, 1909, and again by Jamāl ad-Dīn ash-Shayyāl, Cairo, 1367/1948.

447 Ed. Bunz, 100 (ed. Shayyāl, 203–4).

448 Cf. De Goeje, *Mémoire sur les Carmathes du Bahrain et les Fatimides*, Leiden, 1886, 189.

449 Ed. Bunz, 141.

450 The Khazars appear to have lost their independence some time after A.D. 965 (cf. Dunlop, *Hist. of the Jewish Khazars*, 241 ff).

451 Ed. Bunz, 61, 65, 99, 112, 113, 122, 127, 129.

452 Ed. and trans. M. Vonderheyden, Algiers and Paris, 1927.

453 Cf. the remarks of the editor Ṣalāḥ ad-Dīn al-Munajjid, *Die*

Chronik des Ibn ad-Dawādārī, sechster Teil, Der Bericht über die Fatimiden, Deutsches Archäologisches Institut Kairo, Quellen zur Geschichte des islamischen Agyptens, I. f, Cairo, 1961, 10.

454 This should mean 'the Rhymed' in ordinary speech of later times at least, but apparently here 'the Subsequent Book', with reference perhaps to the three-fold 'History of Egypt' composed of the *ʿIqd*, the *Ittiʿāẓ* and the *Sulūk*, for which see above.

455 'Mémoires Historiques sur la dynastie des Khalifes Fatimites', *Journal Asiatique*, 1836, 97–142.

456 *Kitāb an-Nizāʿ waʾt-Takhāṣum fīmā bayna Banī Umayya wa-Banī Hāshim*, ed. G. Vos, Leiden, 1888.

457 Ed. Vos, 47–63.

458 Ed. Muḥammad Ziyāda and Jamāl ad-Dīn ash-Shayyāl, Cairo, 1359/1940. The same work was inadvertently named by me *Causes of the Decay of Egypt* in a review of Professor Charles Issawi's '*An Arab Philosophy of History*' (i.e. Ibn Khaldūn's) in the *Philosophical Quarterly*, i (1951), 473.

459 M. A. Enan, *Ibn Khaldun, His life and work*, Lahore, 1946, 73 ff.

460 *Ighāthat al-Umma*, ed. Cairo, introd. page d.

461 *Ibid.*, pp. d–h.

462 *Ibid.*, 4.

463 *Ibid.*, 43–62. The separate treatise was the *Shudhūr al-ʿUqūd fī Dhikr an-Nuqūd*, which has been translated more than once.

464 Cf. n. 459.

465 This seems to be the meaning of the words in the colophon (ed. Cairo, 86) *tayassara lī tartīb hādhiʾl-maqāla wa-tahdhībuha fī layla waḥida*, cf. the closing words of Ibn Khaldūn's *Muqaddima*, ed. Beirut, i, 1169.

466 Ed. J. ash-Shayyāl, Cairo, 1365/1946. The title varies in different MSS.

467 Ed. Cairo, 45.

468 *Ibid.*, 79–80.

469 Cf. the editor's introduction, pp. k–l.

470 Cf. D. M. Dunlop, 'Translations of al-Biṭrīq and Yaḥyā (Yuḥannā) b. al-Biṭrīq', *JRAS*, 1959, 140–50.

471 For details of the existing MSS of these works see Brockelmann, *GAL* ii, 39 ff.

472 For these, see De Slane, *Les Prolégomènes d'Ibn Khaldoun*, reprinted Paris, 1934–8, i, pp. xciv–v and Franz Rosenthal, *The Muqaddimah, An Introduction to History*, London, Routledge, 1958, i, pp. xliv ff.

473 The Arabic Orosius had been utilized by Abū ʿUbayd al-Bakrī (432/1040–487/1094) and by al-Idrīsī (493/1099–560/1166) for his geographical information) cf. G. Levi della Vida, 'La traduzione araba delle storie di Orosio', *Al-Andalus*, xix (1954), 263–4nn, also in *Miscellanea G. Galbiati* (*Fontes Ambrosiani*, xxvii, Milan,

Biblioteca Ambrosiana), iii, 1951, but as yet perhaps, by no historian.

474 Cf. Levi della Vida, *op. cit.*, and Fu'ād Sayyid, *Les Générations des médecins et des sages* (*Ṭabaqāt al-atibbā' wa'l ḥukamā'*) . . . *par . . . Ibn Ğulğul al-Andalusī*, Cairo, 1955, introd., pp. la-lg, and text, p. 2.

475 Translated separately by Baron de Slane, 4 vols, Algiers, 1852, new edition under the direction of P. Casanova, 3 vols, Paris, 1925–34.

476 *Kitāb al-ʿIbar*, ed. Beirut, vii, 793–1224, partially translated by De Slane, *Prolégomènes*, i, pp. xxix ff.

477 Colophon of the *Muqaddima*, *K. al-ʿIbar*, ed. Beirut, i, 1169.

478 *At-Taʿrīf bi'bn Khaldūn*, ed. at-Tanjī, Cairo, 1370/1951, 230.

479 So text. For the form cf. the note, *The Muqaddimah*, i, xxix.

480 *At-Taʿrīf*, 228–9.

480a *Kitāb al-ʿIbar*, i, 65, cf. *Muqaddimah*, i, 82.

481 i.e. *Muqaddimah*, i, 313 ff (*K. al-ʿIbar*, i, 271 ff).

482 Ibn Khaldūn supposed that the *Secretum Secretorum*, in Arabic *Sirr al-Asrār*, was the *Politics* of Aristotle, and refers to it here.

483 These priests (*mawbadhān*) as well as Aristotle have already been mentioned in the context.

484 Trans. M. Alcarcón, *Lámpara de los Principes*, Madrid, 1930.

485 Both these expressions are proverbial for true information, and are usually cited in the forms 'He gave me the age of his camel' and 'Juhayna (a tribe) has the true account'.

486 'Aspects', 'tendances' (de Slane), 'aspects and characteristics' (F. Rosenthal) (*anẓārahu wa-anḥā'ahu*).

487 *Kitāb al-ʿIbar*, i, 66, cf. *Muqaddimah*, i, 83.

488 Or 'conventional', as *waḍʿī* means in the modern language.

489 *K. al-ʿIbar*, i, 62, cf. *Muqaddimah*, i, 77.

490 See especially the chapter *K. al-ʿIbar*, i, 693 ff (*Muqaddimah*, ii, 326 ff).

491 Ibn Khaldūn speaks, e.g., of the *ʿaṣabiyya* of the soldiers of Muʿāwiya being stronger than that of ʿAlī's supporters (*K. al-ʿIbar*, iii, 6). Cf. *ibid.*, i, 358 (*Muqaddimah*, i, 414).

492 Cf. G. E. von Grunebaum, 'As-Sakkâkî on Milieu and Thought', *JAOS*, lxv (1945), 62.

493 *K. al-ʿIbar*, i, 697 ff, (*Muqaddimah*, ii, 330 ff).

493a e.g. *Muqaddimah*, ii, 423.

494 *K. al-ʿIbar*, i, 675 (*Muqaddimah*, ii, 305).

495 Cf., however, *K. al-ʿIbar*, i, 280, (*Muqaddimah*, i, 323 ff), and he appreciates the position of the isolated prophet, Muḥammad or others (*K. al-ʿIbar*, i, 159 ff, *Muqaddimah*, i, 184 ff).

496 Cf. a review of Mazheruddin Siddiqi, *The Qur'ānic Concept of History*, Karachi, 1965, *Muslim World*, April, 1967, 138–9.

497 Cf. a passage already quoted, p. 139.

498 Sir J. E. Sandys, *A History of Classical Scholarship*, New York reprint, 1964, ii, 88.
499 *Ibid.*, 89.
500 Cf. above pp. 89 ff, where the traditional method is discussed.
501 *Murūj adh-Dhahab*, iv, 95 (Cairo edn, ii, 262).
502 *Muqaddimah*, i, 75 ff (*K. al-ʿIbar*, i, 60 ff).
503 *Muqaddimah*, i, 76 (*K. al-ʿIbar*, i, 61).
504 Cf. above (p. 140) 'civilization of mankind and human society'. Ibn Khaldūn is not very careful about terminology: 'society' (*ijtimāʿ*) and 'civilization' (*ʿumrān*) appear to be practically interchangeable terms.
505 The mixed metaphor is already in the text (*miʿyāran saḥīḥan yataḥḥarā bihi al-muʾarrikhūn ṭarīq aṣ-ṣidq*).
506 *Muqaddimah*, i, 77 (*K. al-ʿIbar*, i, 61–2).
507 Ibn Khaldūn's text of Josippon (Ibn Gorion) appears to have been different from that studied by J. Wellhausen in *Der. arabische Josippus, Abhandlungen d. k. Gesellschaft d. Wissenschaften zu Göttingen, Phil.-hist. Kl., Neue Folge*, B. i, no. 4, Berlin, 1897, from a single Paris manuscript (De Slane, no. 1906).
508 *Muqaddimah*, i, 476, 478, 479 (*K. al-ʿIbar*, i, 411–13).
509 *Muqaddimah*, i, 78 (*K. al-ʿIbar*, i, 63).
510 *K. al-ʿIbar*, i, 7, (*Muqaddimah*, i, 12) and i, 146 (*Muqaddimah*, i, 172).
511 One of these (*K. al-ʿIbar*, I, 411, *Muqaddimah*, i, 476) is the statement that the Gospel of Matthew was translated into Latin by John, son of Zebedee, to which Ibn Khaldūn adds that Luke's Gospel was written in Latin originally 'for a Roman dignitary'.
512 Cf. *K. al-ʿIbar*, ii, 404–5, which concludes with the statement that the name of Caesar (Qayṣar) is an Arabicized form of an original Jāshar (*fa-ʿarrabathu al-ʿArab ilā Qayṣar*).
513 *Muqaddimah*, ii, 288 (*K. al-ʿIbar*, i, 658).
514 *K. al-ʿIbar*, ii, 493, first pointed out by G. Levi della Vida, 'La traduzione araba delle storie di Orosio', *Al-Andalus*, xix (1954), 265.
515 Quoted from Ibn Ḥajar's *Rafʿ al-Iṣr* by Enan, *Ibn Khaldun . . .*, 71, cf. F. Rosenthal, *History of Muslim Historiography*, 420, 2nd edn, 498 (from as-Sakhāwī's *Iʿlān biʾt-Tawbīkh*), also *Muqaddimah*, i, p. liv, where Rosenthal discounts the importance of the criticism. But there was something in it. Cf. what Ibn Khaldūn says himself about his lack of information on the conditions of the East and the Oriental nations (*Muqaddimah*, i, 65, *K. al-ʿIbar*, i, 54).
516 *Muqaddimah*, i, 243 ff (*K. al-ʿIbar*, i, 301 ff), cf. *Muq.* i, 279 ff (*K. al-ʿIbar*, i, 240 ff).
517 Professor Rosenthal's phrase, see next note.
518 *Muqaddimah*, ii, 295 (*K. al-ʿIbar*, i, 665).
519 Ibn Khaldūn's interest in *zāʾiraja*—which he explains in great

detail and mentions more than once in his book (*Muq.* i, 238–45= *K. al-ʿIbar*, i, 203–9, and *Muq.* iii, 182–214=*K. al-ʿIbar*, i, 941, foot of page–965) is worth remarking, cf. pp. 243ff,.

520 *At-Taʿrīf biʾbn Khaldūn*, ed. Ṭanjī, 230, is not absolutely clear on the point, but there is general agreement that it was so (De Slane, *Prolégomènes*, i, p. lxviii, Enan, *Ibn Khaldun*, 39, Rosenthal, *Muqaddimah*, i, p. liii).

521 *At-Taʿrīf biʾbn Khaldūn, loc. cit.*

522 See W. Fischel, *Ibn Khaldūn and Tamerlane: their historic meeting in Damascus, A.D. 1401 (A.H. 803)*, Berkeley and Los Angeles, 1952.

523 Ed. Muḥibb ad-Dīn al-Khaṭīb, Cairo, 1347/1928.

524 E. Lévi-Provençal, *Histoire de l'Espagne musulmane extraite du Kitâb Aʿmâl al-Aʿlâm*, Rabat, 1934 (i.e. Part 2 only), ii.

525 E.g. on the Dhūnnūnids (Banū Dhīʾn-Nūn), ed. Lévi-Provençal, 204 ff.

526 *Ibid.*, 3.

527 The editor gives an account of the texts used in the introduction, i, 3 ff.

528 For example, in Cambridge Univ. Library, with the title *Markaz al-Iḥāta bi-Udabāʾ Gharnāṭa*. The run of names here is quite different from that in the printed edition of 1319/1901 (Dr M. C. Lyons kindly collected the names from this MS and sent them to me in Salamanca).

529 Vol. i appeared in 1956 (*Dhakhāʾir al-ʿArab*, no. 17), with a good critical introduction by Dr Enan.

530 'Obras del polígrafo granadino Abenaljatib existentes en la Real Biblioteca del Escorial', *Ciudad de Dios*, cxlvii (1926), nos. 1281–1285.

531 *Beiträge zur Geschichte der westlichen Araber*, Munich, 1866 and 1878, 2 vols, the last published posthumously.

532 *Ibid.*, i, 14–41.

533 Entitled *Mufākhara Mālaqa wa-Salā, ibid.*, i, 1–13.

534 *Ibid.*, i, 45–100. From the same work F. J. Simonet had already published his *Descripción del reino de Granada bajo la dominación de los Naseritas*, Madrid, 1861, new edn, Granada, 1872.

535 *Sitzungsberichte d.k. bayer. Ak. d. W., Phil.-hist. Cl., 6 June 1863*, 1–34.

536 See Dunlop, 'A little-known work on politics by Lisān ad-Dīn b. al-Khaṭīb', *Miscelánea de Estudios arabes y hebraicos*, Universidad de Granada, viii (1959), 47–54.

537 *Nafḥ aṭ-Ṭīb*, ed. Cairo, 1369/1949, ix, 134–49.

538 Doctoral dissertation, Cambridge University, not yet published. The work *Nufāḍat al-Jirāb* is discussed in Muḥammad b. abī Bakr at-Teṭuānī, *Ibn al-Jaṭīb segun sus Libros*, i, 114 ff—in Arabic—Tetouan, 1954.

539 Quoted by Maqqarī, *Nafḥ aṭ-Ṭib*, viii, 325.

540 Text has . . . *fī Asāṭīn*, cf. F. Rosenthal, *Hist. of Muslim Historiography*, 26 ff (2nd edn, 28 ff.).

541 Ibn Khaldūn, *K. al-ʿIbar*, vii, 709, more fully Maqqarī, *Nafḥ aṭ-Ṭib*, vii, 38–9.

542 See a discussion of Lisān ad-Dīn's theory of love in ʿAbd al-ʿAzīz b. ʿAbd Allāh, *La Filosofía y la Moral en Ibn al-Jatīb*, 190–6 —in Arabic—, Tetouan 1372/1953. Note the phrase *aṣ-Ṣūfiyya sādat al-Muslimīn* in the *K. fī'l-Maḥabba* (Maqqarī, *Nafḥ aṭ-Ṭib*, vii, 404).

543 *Ibid.*, viii, 386: *dalāla ʿalā faḍlihi.*

544 In the Egyptian edn, the second part begins at p. 309 of vol. vi. The most recent edition appeared (1968) in Beirut in seven volumes and two volumes of indices; the editor is Iḥsān Abbās.

Chapter 4: Geography and travel

1 *Fihrist*, 268.

2 C. A. Nallino, *Al-Ḫuwârizmî e il suo rifacimento della Geografia di Tolomeo, Memorie della R. Accademia dei Lincei, Classe di scienze morali, storiche e filologiche*, 1894, ser. V, vol. ii, parte 1, 51 = *Raccolta di Scritti editi e inediti*, Rome, 1939–48, v, 528.

3 Ibn Khurradādhbih, ed. De Goeje, *BGA*, vi, 3.

4 *Ibid.*, p. xx.

5 J. Marquart, *Osteuropäische und ostasiatische Streifzüge*, Leipzig, 1903 (repr. Darmstadt, 1961), 390.

6 Masʿūdī, *Tanbīh*, ed. Cairo, 1357/1938, 65, cf. F. Rosenthal, *Aḥmad B. aṭ-Ṭayyib as-Saraḫsî, American Oriental Series*, xxvi, New Haven, 1943, 60 ff.

7 Cf. *EI*(2), ii, 581, col. a, art. *Djughrāfiyā* (S. Maqbul Ahmad).

8 Nallino, *Al-Ḫuwârizmî*, 7 = *Raccolta*, v, 463, thinks that Ibn Khurradādhbih's was a private version, apparently of the whole work.

9 E. H. Bunbury, *Hist. of Ancient Geography*, 2nd edn, 1883 (Dover reprint, 1959), ii, 519.

10 So Barthold in V. Minorsky, *Ḥudūd al-ʿAlam*, 11, n. 6. Barthold suggests (*ibid.*, 11) that this was exceptional, the usual rendering of *jughrāfiyā* in Arabic being *ṣūrat al-arḍ* cf. above.

11 *Tanbīh*, ed. Cairo, 30.

12 *Ibid.*

13 *Ibid.* 110.

14 Al-Masʿūdī mentions (*Tanbīh*, 92–3) that in a Persian nobleman's house at Iṣṭakhr (Persepolis) in 303/917–18 he saw a large work in Arabic dealing with the history of the Persian kings, etc. which had been translated for the Caliph Hishām b. ʿAbd al-Malik in 113/731.

Again, he tells us (*Murūj adh-Dhahab*, iii, 69 ff) that in 336/947 he saw a history of the Franks, composed by a bishop of Gerona eight years previously in 328/939 for the Umayyad prince al-Ḥakam, in al-Fusṭāṭ (Egypt).

15 Usually *Bayt al-Ḥikma* in the Arabic sources, but Nallino (*Raccolta*, v, 463) and De Lacy O'Leary (*How Greek Science Passed to the Arabs*, London, Routledge, 1948, 166) have the other name.

16 *Fihrist*, 274.

17 *Al-Ḫuwārizmī*, 50 = *Raccolta*, v, 526.

18 Hans von Mzik, *Das Kitāb ṣūrat al-arḍ des Abū Ǧaʿfar Muḥammad ibn Mūsā al-Ḫuwārizmī, Bibliothek arabischer Historiker und Geographen*, iii, Leipzig, 1926, xv.

19 Ed. De Goeje, 155.

20 Ptolemy, *Geography*, i, 8 (7), cf. iv, 8.

21 Bunbury, *Hist. of Ancient Geogr.*, ii, 524.

22 Ibn Rusta, ed. De Goeje, *BGA*, vii, 22.

23 Cf. *Alberuni's India*, trans. Sachau, i, 317.

24 *Ibid.*, i, 308.

25 *Ibid.*, 306. Sachau notes (ii, 338): 'If this expression has not been derived from the Indian, the question arises, Who introduced it among the Arabs? Was it Alfazari?'

26 For the Indian theory of longitude, see *Alberuni's India*, trans. Sachau, i, 303 ff (Shabūraqān, 304, 308).

27 *Ibid.*, 304.

28 Cf. J. Oliver Thomson, *History of Ancient Geography*, Cambridge University Press, 1948, 388.

29 Reinaud, *Géographie d'Aboulféda*, i, pp. ccxlii ff.

30 C. H. Haskins, *Studies in the History of Mediaeval Science*, 32, 63, 98, 288.

31 J. H. Kramers in *The Legacy of Islam*, Oxford University Press, 1931, 94.

32 Reinaud, *Géographie*, i, p. ccliii. Cattigara below is from Ptolemy, *Geography*, i, 14, a place in the extreme East, with which may be compared Kangdiz(h) of Iranian legend, built according to Bīrūnī. (Ibid., i, 304) by Kaikā'us or Jam in the most remote East, behind the sea. Cf. Reinaud, *op. cit.*, i, ccxx. It is remarkable that 'Kinkidiz' is still mentioned in the 16th century Ottoman work *Tarih-i Hind-i Gharbī* which deals with America, recently discovered at that time. See the trans. by Thomas D. Goodrich [unpublished], p. 226.

33 J. H. Kramers, 'Geography and Commerce' in *The Legacy of Islam*, 94.

34 *Voyages d'Ibn Batoutah*, ed. Defrémery and Sanguinetti, Paris, *Société Asiatique*, iv, 45–6.

35 *Ibid.*, 91.

36 The Chinese ships loading at Sīrāf on the Gulf are mentioned by the 'merchant Sulaymān' in *Akhbār aṣ-Ṣīn wa'l-Hind* (ed. and trans. J. Sauvaget, Paris, 1948, 7) followed by Ibn al-Faqīh, ed. De Goeje, *BGA*, v, 11. Sulaymān's date is 851. Masʿūdī says that in his time the ships of China no longer come to Sīrāf, etc. as they formerly did (*Murūj adh-Dhahab*, i, 308 (i, 140) = trans. C. Pellat, i, 127, §336).

37 For an explanation of this and other names of Ceylon, see Sir Alexander Cunningham, *The Ancient Geography of India*, reprint of 1963, 469–70.

38 i.e. after his expulsion from Paradise.

39 Ibn Khurradādhbih, 64.

40 *Akhbār*, ed. Sauvaget, 4 = Reinaud, *Relation des Voyages faits par les Arabes et les Persans dans l'Inde et à la Chine, Paris*, 1845, text (*Silsilat at-Tawarīkh*) 6 ff, trans. 5 ff.

41 Cf. Sauvaget, *ibid.*, p. xxiii.

42 Jaubert, i, 71–2.

43 It reappears in Yāqūt, *Buldān*, art. Sarandīb, iii, 83–4, etc.

44 *Murūj*, i, 338 (i, 152) = Pellat, i, 138, §371.

45 Sauvaget, ib. 6 = Reinaud, *ibid.*, 13, trans. 12.

46 Sauvaget, 7 = Reinaud, 14.

47 Cf. J. Needham, *Science and Civilisation in China*, Cambridge University Press, 1954, i, 215.

48 Sauvaget, *ibid.*, p. xxxviii, and the authorities there cited.

49 Needham, *ibid.*, 216.

50 *Murūj*, i, 302 ff (i, 137 ff.) = Pellat, i, 124 ff.

51 *Ibid.*, cf. Abū Zaid as-Sīrāfī, Reinaud, *ibid.*, 62 ff.

52 *BGA*, vi, 70.

53 Cf. Minorsky, *Ḥudud al-ʿĀlam*, 228.

54 Private letter of 23 August 1963.

55 *BGA*, vi, 69.

56 *Buldān*, iv, 936.

57 Minorsky, *Ḥudud alʿĀlam*, 228, n. 2; Koh Byong-ik, 'Korea's contacts with "the Western Regions" in pre-modern times', *Journal of Social Sciences* (published by The Korean Social Sciences Research Society, Seoul), No. 2, March 1958, 56 ff.

58 *Ibid.*, 59. J. Needham, *Science and Civilisation in China*, i, 208.

59 Sauvaget, 27 = Reinaud, 59.

60 Reinaud, *Géographie d'Aboulféda*, i, p. cclvi. The text is *lam yablughhā aḥad min asḥābinā*, which is not unequivocal (translated above 'None of our people has reached' etc.).

61 Some place in Shantung province seems meant. Cf. De Goeje's note, *BGA*, vi, 69.

62 *BGA*, vi, 70.

63 *Ibid.*, 170.

64 *BGA*, vii, 82–3.
65 *Murūj*, i, 346 (i, 155–6) = Pellat, i, 141, §382.
66 *Science and Civilisation in China*, Cambridge University Press, 1954, i, 180, 214.
67 *Antiquity*, Vol. xl, no. 159 (September 1966), 223–24. I owe the reference to Professor Margaret Bancroft of Columbia University.
68 Cf. E. Lévi-Provençal, *Histoire de l'Espagne musulmane*, 1944, i, 441.
69 Reinaud, *Géographie d'Aboulféda*, ii, 42 (text, p. 35).
70 Ibn Khurradādhbih, 230, 231.
71 C. Nallino, *Al-Battānī sive Albatenii Opus Astronomicum*, Milan, 1903, Arabic text, 26; Latin trans. 18.
72 Cf. D. M. Dunlop, 'The British Isles according to medieval Arabic authors', *Islamic Quarterly*, iv (1957), 28.
73 Ed. Muṣṭafa ʿAwwād al-Karīm, Khartoum, 1954, 125 ff., 130 ff. For other refs. see Dunlop, *Islamic Quarterly*, iv, 12, §2.
74 Cf. Dhahabī, *Tadhkirāt al-Ḥuffāz*, ed. Haidarabad, 1955–8, iv, 1420 ff; the same, *Mīzān al-Iʿtidāl*, ed. ʿAlī Muḥammad al-Bajāwī, 1382/1963, iii, 186 ff.
75 Maqqarī, *Nafḥ aṭ-Ṭīb*, ed. Leiden, i, 178.
76 Maqqarī, *Nafḥ*, ed. Cairo, 1367/1949 (*sic*), i, 324, iii, 25 (= ed. Leiden, i, 223, 631). See E. Lévi-Provençal, 'Un échange d'ambassades entre Cordoue et Byzance au ixe siècle', *Byzantion*, xii (1937), 1–24.
77 To the bibliographical information given by Lévi-Provençal, *Histoire*, i, 152, and Dunlop, *Islamic Quarterly*, iv, 12–14, A. Melvinger, *Les premières incursions des Vikings en Occident d'après les sources arabes*, Upsala, 1955, may be added.
78 Cf. Nallino, *Al-Ḫuwârizmî*, 45 = *Raccolta*, v, 520.
79 Text in the edn of Ibn Diḥya by M. ʿA. al-Karīm, as above, 131, with *biḥār* in error for *majār* (plur. of *majrā*), correct in H. Munis (Monès), 'Contribution à l'étude des invasions des Normands en Espagne musulmane etc.', *Bulletin de la Société Royale d'Études Historiques* (*Égypte*), ii, fasc. 31, 1950, 55.
80 Ibn ʿIdhārī, *al-Bayān*, ii, 96 (99), trans. in Dozy, *Recherches*, ii, 279 ff.
81 Qazwīnī, ed. Wüstenfeld, ii, 388; Eng. trans. in Dunlop, 'British Isles', *Islamic Quarterly*, iv, 19–20.
82 Maqqarī, *Nafḥ*, i, 184 (i, 121–2 of Leiden edn), also al-ʿUdhrī, *K. al-Masālik wa'l-Mamālik al-Andalusiyya*, ed. al-Ahwānī, Madrid, 1965, 22 (Saragossa).
83 *Murūj*, i, 258 (i, 119) = trans. Pellat, i, 106. Al-ʿUdhrī (ed. al-Ahwani, 119) mentions that Khashkhāsh al-Bahrī ('the Sailor') died in A.H. 245 fighting against the Norsemen.

84 Idrīsī, trans. Jaubert, ii, 26 ff. Lévi-Provençal suggested the identification of the two expeditions, *Histoire*, iii (1953), 342, n. 1.

85 Idrīsī, tr. Jaubert, ii, 11. Qazwīnī (died 1283) and Dimashqī (died 1327) have an 'island of Sheep', otherwise Jāliṭa in the Mediterranean (? for Māliṭa, Malta), see *Cosmography*, ed. Wüstenfeld, i, 124, where Qazwīnī cites Abū Ḥāmid al-Andalusī. Dimashqī (ed. Mehren, 142) perhaps follows Qazwīnī.

86 *Le tabelle geografiche d'al-Battani*, Turin, 1898, and again *Al-Battānī sive Albatenii Opus Astronomicum*, ii, Milan, 1907, 33–54.

87 Cf. Reinaud, *Géographie d'Aboulféda*, i, p. lxxxix.

88 *Ta'rīkh*, ed. Houtsma, Leiden, 1883, reprinted Beirut, 1379/1960, for which see pp. 87–8.

89 Ed. De Goeje in *BGA*, vii.

90 S. Maqbul Ahmad in *EI*(2), art. *Djughrāfiya*.

91 Ed. De Goeje in *BGA*, vi.

92 *Ibid.*, 252.

93 *Fihrist*, 154.

94 Ed. De Goeje, *BGA*, v (a compendium).

95 Ed. De Goeje, *BGA*, vii.

96 See V. Minorsky, 'Ibn Farīghūn and the Ḥudūd al-ʿĀlam', in *A Locust's Leg, Studies in honour of S. H. Taqizadeh*, ed. W. B. Henning and E. Yarshater, London, Lund Humphries, 1962, 189 ff.

97 Akademiya Nauk, Leningrad, 1930.

98 *GMS*, New Series XI, 1937.

99 *Ḥudūd*, xviii.

100 Cf. *EI*(2), art. al-Balkhī, Abū Zayd (D. M. Dunlop).

101 Cf. Barthold in *Ḥudūd al-ʿĀlam*, 18.

102 De Goeje, 'Die Istakhrī-Balkhī Frage', *ZDMG*, xxv (1871), 42 ff; J. H. Kramers, 'La question Balḫī—Istaḫrī—Ibn Ḥawḳal et l'Atlas de l'Islam', *Acta Orientalia*, x (1932), 9–30; V. Minorsky, 'A false Jayhānī', *BSOAS*, xiii (1949). 93–4.

103 Ibn Ḥawqal is called an-Naṣībī (ed. Kramers, 1) and *at-tājir al-Mawṣilī*, 'the Mosul merchant', by Yāqūt (*Buldān*, i, 375). Others made him a native of Baghdad.

104 Ibn Ḥawqal mentions the meeting at the end of his section on Sind (ed. De Goeje, *BGA*, ii, 236), but does not say that the two men met there, cf. the French translation of J. H. Kramers and G. Wiet (*Ibn Hauqal, Configuration de la Terre*, Collection Unesco d'Oeuvres Représentatives, Série arabe, Beirut and Paris, 1964, i, x and ii, 322 (they met in the Indus valley). The editor of a new edition of al-Iṣṭakhrī, M. G. Abd el Aal el Hini (Cairo, 1961) suggests that they met in Baghdad (p. 9).

105 So Dozy, *Hist. des Musulmans d'Espagne*, rev. edn, Leiden, 1932, ii, 125.

106 Ed. De Goeje, *BGA*, iii, Leiden, 1885. See Minorsky, *Ḥudūd*, p. xix, n. 1.
107 Cited Kramers, 'La littérature géographique classique des Musulmans', *Analecta Orientalia*, i (Leiden, 1954), 181.
108 W. Barthold, *Turkestan*, *GMS*, 11 (Russian edn, St. Petersburg, 1900, 12).
109 Kramers, *Analecta Orientalia*, i, 182–3.
110 Kramers, *loc. cit.*
111 *Aḥsan at-Taqāsīm fī Maʿrifat al-Aqālīm* (La meillure Répartition pour la connaissance des provinces). Traduction partielle, annotée par André Miquel, Institut francais de Damas, Damascus, 1963. The translator's introduction finds the description of the eastern provinces and Palestine '*de très loin*' the richest part of al-Muqaddasī's book (p. xvii) and suggests that he may have been a Shīʿite missionary (*dāʿī*) (p. xx).
112 *Ibid.*, p. xxiv.
113 *Ibid.*, p. xxxii.
114 i.e. 'Book of Roger', so-called for convenience from al-Idrīsī's patron, Roger II of Sicily. The real title was *Nuzhat al-Mushtāq fī'khtirāq al-Āfāq* ('the Delight of Him Who Desires to Traverse the Horizons'). The work was completed in 548/1154.
115 See below, n. 141.
116 In Ibn Rusta (*BGA*, vii), 119 ff. Hārūn b. Yaḥyā's narrative is discussed very fully by J. Marquart, *op. cit.*, 206 ff.
117 *Tanbīh*, Cairo edn of 1357/1938, 162.
118 e.g. in his account of the Byzantine Emperors.
119 *BGA*, vi, 105.
120 *Ibid.*, 162–70.
121 *Sūr.*, xviii, 88 ff.
122 Presumably because the 'Wall' was at an early date identified with the Caucasus. Sallām may have been a Khazar, like Ītākh, one of the important men in al-Wāthiq's Caliphate (Ṭab. III, 1383, cf. D. Sourdel, *Vizirat ʿAbbāside*, i, 264, n. 2).
123 *De muur van Gog en Magog*, *Verslagen en Meded. d.K. Akad. v. Wetenschappen*, *Afd. Letterkunde*, III Reeks, 5 Deel, 1888, 10 ff. (cited J. Marquart, *Streifzüge*, 86, n. 1).
124 Ibn Khurradādhbih, 170 = Idrīsī, tr. Jaubert, ii, 420: 'vingt-huit mois'.
125 'Ibn Faḍlān's Reisebericht', *AKM*, xxiv, 3, 196n.
126 De Goeje (Ibn Khurradādhbih, 164) following F. von Richthofen, *China*, i, 540.
127 *BGA*, vii, 149.
128 *BGA*, iii, 362–5.
129 Jaubert, ii, 416–20.
130 See Qazwīnī, *Kosmographie*, i, 128–9, ii, 401.

131 This is not perhaps sufficiently taken into account by those who have rejected Sallām's narrative. Barthold does not refer to it in his *Turkestan*, and for Minorsky it was 'a wonder-tale interspersed with three or four geographical names' (*Ḥudūd*, 225). A more recent member of the Russian school, M. I. Artamonov (*Istoriya Khazar*, Leningrad, 1962, 306–7) accepts it as genuine. Artamonov (*ibid.*) is presumably in error in giving seven months for the outward journey instead of sixteen (*BGA*, vi, 170).

132 In al-Qazwīnī, *loc. cit.*, for example. Possibly, however, some details come from a more complete text of Ibn Khurradādhbih than has reached us (cf. Barthold in *Ḥudūd*, 13).

133 *Streifzüge*, 90.

134 See especially V. Minorsky, 'Tamīm ibn Baḥr's journey to the Uyghurs', *BSOAS*, xii, 1947–8, 275–305, and *Ḥudūd al-ʿĀlam*, 268–9.

135 *Abū-Dulaf Misʿar ibn Muhalhil's Travels in Iran, Arabic text with an English Translation and Commentary by Prof. V. Minorsky*, Cairo Univ. Press, 1955, 21.

136 See A. Zeki Validi Togan, 'Ibn Faḍlān's Reisebericht', *AKM*, xxiv, 3, 1939 (Arabic text, German translation and full commentary with valuable excursuses); Russian translation with facsimile of the text of the Meshed MS in I. Y. Kratchkovsky, *Puteshestvie Ibn-Fadlana na Volgu*, Akademiyeĭ nauk SSSR, 1939, and A. P. Kovalevsky, *Kniga Ahmeda Ibn-Fadlana o ego puteshestvii na Volgu v 921–922 gg.*, Kharkov, 1956, also with elaborate commentary.

137 'Ibn Faḍlān's Reisebericht', *AKM*, xxiv, 3, Leipzig, 1939, p. xxvii.

138 See G. Jacob, *Ein arabischer Berichterstatter . . . aus dem 10. Jahrhundert*, 3rd edn, Berlin, 1896, for citations of aṭ-Ṭartūshī in al-Qazwīnī, *Cosmography*, from al-ʿUdhrī's *Kitāb al-Masālik wa'l-Mamālik al-Andalusīya* (for the title cf. above). The other main source of citations is the Spanish geographer al-Bakrī (eleventh century A.D.), see T. Kowalski, *Relacja Ibrāhīma ibn Jaʿkūba etc.*, *Monumenta Poloniae Historica, Nova series*, 1 (Cracow, 1946). There is an older edition of the text by Kunik and Rosen, *Izvestiya al-Bekri i drugikh avtorov o Rusi i Slavyanakh*, St Petersburg, 1878. For the identification of aṭ-Ṭartūshī and Ibrāhīm b. Yaʿqūb cf. M. Canard, in *Études d'orientalisme dediées à la mémoire de Lévi-Provençal*, Paris, 1962, ii, 505.

139 The spelling varies, and there are still other forms of the original Greek *gēographia*, which came to mean, perhaps as early as al-Ma'mūn's time, a representation of the earth's surface, *mappa mundi*, i.e. the word meant much the same as *ṣūrat al-arḍ* (cf. above).

140 Jaubert, i, p. xix.

141 i.e. the Geography (*Taqwīm al-Buldān*) of Abū'l-Fidā', completed

721/1321, when he was fifty years old, and the earlier *Muʿjam al-Buldān* of Yāqūt drafted in 1224 and completed in 625/1228.

142 Jaubert, i, p. xx.

143 *Opus Geographicum auctore Ibn Ḥauḳal . . . cui titulus est 'Liber Imaginis Terrae'*, ed. J. H. Kramers, Leiden and Leipzig, 1938, i, facing p. 66.

Chapter 5: Arabic philosophy

1 Directly, or through the media of Syriac and apparently also Pahlavi. For the latter, see below.

2 As there undoubtedly were in Arabic science. Cf. pp. 216 f.

3 *Fihrist*, 254 ff.

4 *Ibid.*, 255.

5 e.g., W. Smith, *Dict. of Greek and Roman Biography*, London, 1844–9, iii, 321a, where his (commentary on the) Physics is dated 10 May, A.D. 617, apparently from the Greek text.

6 *Encyclopedia Britannica*, 1957, s.v. Philoponus, gives 529 for the *De Aeternitate Mundi.*

7 A. Baumstark in his *Commentar zur εἰσαγωγή des Porphyrios, Aristoteles bei den Syrern vom V.–VIII. Jahrhundert*, I (Leipzig, 1900) is specific: 'confundiert mit einem wohl etwas jüngeren Arzte Ioannes aus Alexandreia' (p. 168).

8 For Philoponus in Arabic see further Muhsin Mahdi, 'Alfarabi against Philoponus', *JNES*, xxvi, 4 (October, 1967), 233–60 also Herbert A. Davidson, 'John Philoponus as a source of Medieval Islamic and Jewish Proofs of Creation', *JAOS*, Vol. 89 (1969), 357–91.

9 J. E. Sandys, *A History of Classical Scholarship*, reprinted New York, 1964, i, 375.

10 *Fihrist*, 242. The 'Egyptian city (*madīnat Miṣr*)' is apparently Alexandria.

11 Al-Fārābī, quoted by Ibn Abī Uṣaybiʿa, ii, 135. Al-Masʿūdī also mentions this event, probably from al-Fārābī, in the *Tanbīh* (Cairo edn of 1357/1938, 105).

12 Ibn Juljul, *Ṭabaqāt al-Aṭibbāʾ*, ed. Fuʾād Sayyid (Cairo, 1955), 59. (Of Ibn Abjar we are told that Umar b. ʿAbd al-ʿAzīz *kāna yabʿathu ilayhi bi-māʾihi.*)

13 *Ṭabaqāt al-Umam*, 49, trans. Blachère, 101. Ibn al-Muqaffaʿ has already been mentioned (pp. 46–7).

14 *Fihrist*, 248, 249.

15 Cf. P. Kraus, 'Zu Ibn al-Muqaffaʿ', *Rivista degli Studi Orientali*, xiv, 1933, 1–14; F. Gabrieli, art. Ibn al-Muḳaffaʿ, *EI* (2), iii, 883b.

16 *Fihrist*, 244.

17 Ibn Abī Uṣaybiʿa, i, 188.

18 *Fihrist*, 251.

19 *Ibid.*, 249. His son is said to have died in 1003, M. Steinschneider, *Die arabischen Übersetzungen aus dem Griechischen* (Graz reprint), 1960, p. 57 (95), §30 (54), n. 278.

20 D. M. Dunlop, 'The translations of al-Biṭrīq and Yaḥyā (Yuḥannā) b. al-Biṭrīq,' *JRAS*, 1959, 144–5.

21 R. Walzer (New Light on 'the Arabic translations of Aristotle', *Oriens*, vi, 1953, 99, 127–8) following P. Kraus, *op. cit.*, 3, n. 3, speaks of Theodore Abū Qurra, a pupil of John of Damascus (who died *c.* 750) as having translated the *Prior Analytics* 'probably during the reign of al-Ma'mūn, or even earlier', but the fact is not altogether clear, cf. Dunlop, *JRAS*, 1959, 145, n. 3.

22 ʿA. Badawi, *Manṭiq Aristū* (Cairo, 1948), i, 112, n. 5. Cf. Walzer, *op. cit.*, 116.

23 See Ibn Abī Uṣaybiʿa, i, 207.

24 Text, 37, trans. 81.

25 *K. al-Mudhākarāt fī (Asrār) ʿIlm an-Nujūm*, MS Cambridge 1028 (Gg. 3.19) fol. 7a: *Yaʿqūb b. Iṣhāq at-tarjumān al-Fārisī alladhī kāna yutarjimu kutub al-Yūnān wa'l-Qubṭ.*

26 *Fihrist*, 242.

27 *Ibid.*, 255.

28 Cf. the remarks of Abū Rīda, *Rasā'il al-Kindī al-Falsafiyya*, Cairo, 1369/1950, introd. p. 8.

29 *Fihrist*, *ibid.*

30 *Fihrist*, Ibn Abī Uṣaybiʿa, Ibn Qutayba, *K. al-Maʿārif*, ed. Wüstenfeld, 14. Cf, p. 70.

31 Cf. *K. al-Aghānī*, vii, 62 (ix, 79), where the genealogy of Imru' al-Qays is given in several forms.

32 Ibn Juljul, *Ṭabaqāt al-Aṭibbā'*, 73.

33 Abū Rīda, *op. cit.*, 4, following Muṣṭafā ʿAbd ar-Rāziq, *Faylasūf al-ʿArab wa'l-Muʿallim al-Awwal*, Cairo, 1945.

34 By M. ʿAbd ar-Rāziq, *op. cit.*, 18 ff, cited Abū Rīda, 4.

35 Abū Rīda, 5.

36 Otherwise Mūsā b. Shākir, cf. *Fihrist*, 271.

37 See Ṭabarī, III, iii, 1502.

38 Cf. the discussion of Abū Rīda (*op. cit.*, 27–31).

39 Jāḥiẓ, *Bukhalā'*, ed. Van Vloten, 85 ff, trans. Pellat, 115 ff.

40 *Fihrist*, 277.

41 Cf. D. M. Dunlop, *Arabic Science in the West*, 91.

42 *Tatimmat Ṣiwān al-Ḥikma*, ed. M. Shafīʿ, 25.

43 *Rasā'il*, introd. 16 (*K. al-Mudhākarāt*, Cambridge MS 1028, *loc. cit.*).

44 Ibn Abī Uṣaybiʿa, i, 207.

45 See the excellent bibliography by the Rev. Richard Joseph McCarthy, S. J., Baghdad, 1962.

46 McCarthy, p. 43, no. 250. The work is mentioned with this title

nowhere else, and there is perhaps confusion with the name Chrysostom, also *Fam adh-Dhahab* in Arabic, cf. Paul Sbath, *Al-Fihris* (*Catalogue de Manuscrits Arabes*), Cairo, 1938, i, 27 (182).

47 *Ṭabaqāt al-Umam*, 52, trans. 105–6.

48 *Ibid.*

49 *Ta'rīkh al-Ḥukamā'*, ed. Lippert, 367.

50 Ibn Abī-Uṣaibi'a, i, 208.

51 *Ibid.*, 12.

52 Quoted by Ibn Abī Uṣaybi'a, ash-Shahrazūrī in the *Nuzhat al-Arwāḥ*, and Ibn Nubāta in the *Sarḥ al-'Uyūn* (Abū Rīda, *ibid.*, 7n).

53 I have followed Abū Rīda's text, *ibid.*, pp. 6–7, omitting some verses.

54 *Al Kindî, genannt 'der Philosoph der Araber'*, *AKM*, i, 2, 1857.

55 'Al Kindî als Astrolog', in *Morgenländische Forschungen* (Festschrift H. L. Fleischer), Leipzig, 1875, 261–310.

56 *Ibid.*, 270.

57 Published by Karl Garbers, *AKM*, xxx, Leipzig, 1948 (reprinted 1966).

58 G. Furlani translated his *Risāla fī'n-Nafs wa-Af'ālihā ilā Yuḥannā b. Māsawayh* in 'Una risala di Al-Kindi sull'anima', *Rivista trimest di studii fil. e religiosi*, iii (1922), 50–63.

59 Aya Sofia, 4832.

60 *Archiv Orientální*, iv (1932), 363–72.

61 *Rasā'il al-Kindī*, Part i, 1369/1950, Part ii, 1372/1953, both in Cairo.

62 *Ibid.*, Part i, p. k.

63 *Ibid.*, Part i, p. t.

64 For a preliminary study of this material see R. Walzer, 'New studies on al-Kindī', *Oriens*, x (1957), 203–32, where the importance of Abū Rīda's publication is not perhaps sufficiently stressed.

65 *Rasā'il al-Kindī*, Part i, p. s.

66 *Ibid.*, 103.

67 *Ibid.*, 105.

68 *Ibid.*, 219.

69 *Ibid.*, 244.

70 Sale, Rodwell, Blachère, Dawood.

71 'Hast thou not seen that unto Allah payeth adoration whosoever is in the heavens and whosoever is in the earth, and the sun, and the moon, and the stars, and the hills, and the trees, and the beasts, and many of mankind, etc.?' (Pickthall's trans.), where it is scarcely possible that the word translated 'stars' (*an-nujūm*) is different in meaning from its singular in *Sūr.* 55, 5/6 (*an-najm*).

72 Cf. Abū Rīda, *ibid.*, ii, 1–2.

73 *Ibid.*, i, 274–5.

74 *Fihrist*, 267. According to a notice at the beginning of the Leiden

MS (Or 680) of the *Almagest* in Arabic, the translation was produced by al-Ḥajjāj b. Yūsuf al-Ḥāsib and Sarjūn b. Hiliyā ar-Rūmī for al-Ma'mūn in 212/827–8. This translation appears to have been used by al-Kindī, with modifications, in his *R. fī Ṣināʿat Baṭalmayūs* (*Baṭlamiyūs*) *al-Falakiyya* (F. Rosenthal, 'Al-Kindī and Ptolemy', *Studi Orientalistici in onore di Giorgio Levi della Vida* (Rome, 1956), ii, 439, n. 2). Or did al-Kindī in fact use the earlier translation, of which the other was a revision barely mentioned in the *Fihrist*?

75 It is not altogether clear when the principal work of Ptolemy dealing with astrology as such, the *Tetrabiblos* (*Quadripartitum*) passed into Arabic, cf. M. Steinschneider, *Die arabischen Übersetzungen aus dem Griechischen* (Graz reprint) 1960, p. 207 (199), §115.

76 Cf. F. Rosenthal, *Aḥmad b. aṭ-Ṭayyib as-Saraḫsî*, American Oriental Society, 1943, 17.

77 *Muqaddima*, trans. F. Rosenthal, iii, 280 = Beirut text, 1961, i, 1021.

78 Al-Fārābī's short treatise *Kitāb fī Wujūb Ṣināʿat al-Kīmiyā'* (Book on the Necessity of the Art of Alchemy) was edited from Leiden MS Or 1270 with a Turkish trans. by Aydın Sayılı in *Türk Tarih Kurumu, Belleten*, xv (1951), 65–79. According to al-Masʿūdī, al-Kindī himself denied the possibility of transmutation (*Murūj adh-Dhahab*, ed. Paris, viii, 176 = ed. Cairo, iv, 258). Cf. p. 231.

79 Cf. Ibn Khaldūn, *Muqaddimah*, trans. Rosenthal, iii, 116 = *Kitāb al-ʿIbar* (*Ta'rīkh al-ʿAllāma Ibn Khaldūn*), Beirut edn, 1961, i, 893.

80 Ibn Rushd was perhaps the exception, yet cf. the titles, Renan, *Averroès et l'Averroïsme*, 4th edn, Paris, 1882, 71.

81 Such as the *Ṭabaqāt al-Aṭibbā' wa'l-Ḥukamā'*, *Ṭabaqāt al-Umam*, Ibn Abī Uṣaybiʿa, etc., already quoted.

82 The same point is made by Walzer, *Oriens*, x, 222.

83 He is mentioned respectfully still by Masʿūdī in the fourth/tenth and by Ibn Khaldūn in the eighth/fourteenth century.

84 See also R. J. McCarthy, *At-Taṣānīf al-Mansūba ilā Faylasūf al-ʿArab*, Baghdad, 1382/1962, N. Rescher, *Al-Kindī: an annotated bibliography*, Pittsburgh, 1964, together with the latter, 'Al-Kindī's sketch of Aristotle's Organon', in *Studies in the History of Arabic Logic*, Pittsburgh, 1963, 28–38, reprinted from *The New Scholasticism*, xxxvii (1963), 44–58, and most recently George N. Atiyeh, *Al-Kindī: the Philosopher of the Arabs*, Islamic Research Institute, Rawalpindi, 1966. This last contains the Arabic text of the notice of al-Kindī in the *Muntakhab Ṣiwān al-Ḥikma* of Abū Sulaymān as-Sijistānī, with an English translation by A. S. Bazmee Ansari.

85 As-Sijistānī, *Ṣiwān al-Ḥikma*, MS Köprülü 902, fol. 825

86 *Rasā'il al-Kindī*, i, 166, cf. 267.

87 *Ibid.*, i, 179.

88 *Ibid.*, i, introd., 21. For further discussion of these words see George N. Atiyeh, *Al-Kindī*, 13, and Matti I. Moosa, ʿAl-Kindī's Role in the Transmission of Greek Knowledge to the Arabs', *Journal of the Pakistan Historical Society*, xv (1967), 15–18.

89 *A fortiori*, the Latin translators of al-Kindī (for whom see M. Steinschneider, *Die europäischen Übersetzungen aus dem Arabischen bis Mitte des 17. Jahrhunderts*, reprinted Graz, 1956) must have felt the difficulties of al-Kindī's style. Abū Rīda (introd. 23) remarks on this, and adduces the Latin versions of several of the treatises in his notes.

90 Cf. 'Alfarabi's style is never obscure', Muhsin Mahdi, *Alfarabi's Philosophy of Plato and Aristotle*, New York, 1962, 9.

91 Al-ʿĀmirī, *As-Saʿāda waʾl-Isʿād* (Facsimile of the copy prepared by Mojtaba Minovi), Wiesbaden, 1957–8, 194–5, cf. A. J. Arberry, 'An Arabic treatise on politics', *Islamic Quarterly*, ii (1955), 15–16.

92 The passage has not been traced in any of al-Fārābī's published works, but it can scarcely be by another.

93 The date sometimes given, *c.* 260/874, seems rather too early, cf. the account of his death below.

94 Not Faryāb as given in the *Tatimma* (n. 100 below).

95 Le Strange, *Lands of the Eastern Caliphate*, 485.

96 Le Strange, *ibid.*, 484.

97 Cf. Redhouse, *A Turkish and English Lexicon*, s.v.

98 *Qāʾid jaysh* (Ibn Abī Uṣaybiʿa, ii, 134).

99 Masʿūdī, *Tanbīh*, Cairo, 1357/1938, 105.

100 *Tatimmat Ṣiwān al-Ḥikma*, ed. M. Shafīʿ, Lahore, 1935, 17–19. A similar story is told by Ibn Khallikān (trans. De Slane, iii, 308–9) of a visit of al-Fārābī to the court of Sayf ad-Dawla.

101 Khalīl Mardam Bek, *Aṣ-Ṣāḥib b. ʿAbbād*—in Arabic—Damascus, 1351/1932, 5.

102 Ed. Müller, ii, 138–9.

103 *Tatimma*, 19.

104 Cf. n. 93.

105 See H. G. Farmer, *Al-Fārābī's Arabic–Latin Writings on Music*, *Collection of Oriental Writers on Music*, ii, 1960.

106 See the edition by Ghaṭṭās ʿAbd al-Malik Khashaba and Dr Maḥmūd Aḥmad al-Ḥafnī, Cairo, 1967, 8.

107 Necati Lugal and Aydın Sayılı, 'Farabi's article on vacuum, *Türk Tarih Kurumu Yayınlarından*, xv. Ser.i No. 1, Ankara, 1951.

108 Cf. D. M. Dunlop, *The Fuṣūl al-Madanī* (*Aphorisms of the Statesman*) *of al-Fārābī*, Cambridge Univ. Press, 1961, 5 ff.

109 These have been published by Dunlop with English translations in the *Islamic Quarterly*: 'Al-Fārābī's introductory sections (Fuṣūl) on Logic', ii (1955), 264–82, 'Al-Fārābī's Eisagoge', iii

(1956), 117–38, 'Al-Fārābī's introductory Risāla on Logic', iii, 224–35. See also M. Türker, 'Farabi'nin bazi mantik eserleri', *Ankara Universitesi Dil- ve Tarih-Cografya Fakultesi Dergisi*, xvi (1958), 165 ff.

110 See Ahmad Ateş, 'Farabinin Eserlerinin Bibliyografyası', *Türk Tarih Kurumu, Belleten*, xv (1951), for the contents of this MS. Other similar MSS. are now known (M. Küyel, op. cit. in following note, 9).

111 Dunlop, 'Al-Fārābī's paraphrase of the "Categories" of Aristotle,' *Islamic Quarterly*, iv (1958), 168–97, and v (1959), 21–54. See further Mübahat Küyel 'Fârâbi'n in Peri Hermeneias Muhtasari', *Araştirma*, iv (1966), 1–85.

112 Türker, *op. cit.* An English translation of the text is given by N. Rescher, *Al-Fārābī's Short Commentary on Aristotle's* Prior Analytics, Univ. of Pittsburgh Press, 1963.

113 Wilhelm Kutsch, S. J., and Stanley Marrow, S. J., *Alfarabi's Commentary on Aristotle's Peri Hermēneias, Recherches publiées sous la direction de l'Institut de Lettres Orientales de Beyrouth*, xiii, 1960.

114 R. Walzer, art. *al-Fārābī*, *EI*(2), ii, 780a.

115 Cf. Dunlop, *Fuṣūl al-Madanī*, 10 ff.

116 Ed. Dieterici, *Alfarabi's philosophische Abhandlungen herausgegeben* etc., Leiden, 1890, 34 ff (German trans., the same, *Alfarabi's philosophische Abhandlungen*, Leiden, 1892, 54–60), also in *Rasā'il al-Fārābī*, Haidarabad, Dā'irat al-Ma'ārif al-'Uthmāniyya, 1349/1930.

117 For example, it deals with *kalām*, Muslim speculative theology.

118 Editions by 'Uthmān Amīn, Cairo, and A. Gonzalez Palencia, Madrid–Granada, 1953, who adds his own Spanish and two medieval Latin versions, by Dominicus Grandisalvi and Gerard of Cremona. That of D. Gundisalvi was first published in 1638 by Gulielmus Camerarius Scotus Fintraeus.

119 Ed. of the Dā'irat al-Ma'ārif al-'Uthmāniyya, Haidarabad, 1345/1926–7; English trans., Muhsin Mahdi, *Alfarabi's Philosophy of Plato and Aristotle*, New York, Free Press of Glencoe, 1962, 11–52.

120 Ed. Haidarabad, 1346/1927–8 (*Kitāb as-Siyāsāt* [*sic*] *al-Madaniyya*); German trans. by F. Dieterici (ed. by P. Brönnle), Leiden, 1904.

121 Ed. Dieterici, Leiden, 1895, trans. Dieterici, Leiden, 1900; French trans. by R. P. Jaussen, Youssef Karam and J. Chlala, Cairo, 1949; text edited by Dr N. Nader, Beirut, Catholic Press, 1959; Spanish trans. by M. Alonso *Al-Andalus*, xxvi (1961), 337–88; xxvii, (1962), 181–227. Dr Walzer's long awaited new edn has not yet appeared.

122 *Alfarabi's Book of Religion and Related Texts*, Beirut, 1968. See also the review by Dunlop in *JAOS*, vol. 89 (1969), 798–800.

123 By F. Rosenthal and R. Walzer, London, 1943 (with Latin trans.), English trans., M. Mahdi, *op. cit.*, 51–67.
124 So in the edn of M. Mahdi (see note below).
125 Ed. Muhsin Mahdi, Beirut, 1961; trans., the same, *Alfarabi's Philosophy of Plato and Aristotle*, 71–130.
126 So E. I. J. Rosenthal, 'The Place of Politics in the philosophy of Al-Farabi', *Islamic Culture*, xxix (1955), 157 ff.
127 Muhsin Mahdi, *Alfarabi's Philosophy etc.*, 3–10.
128 Cf. above (al-Kindī).
129 Muhsin Mahdi, *Alfarabi's Philosophy*, 4, cf. 6, 9.
130 See n. 113.
131 Ed. Fr. Dieterici, Leipzig, 1882 (Nachdruck, Amsterdam, 1965).
132 Rosenthal and Walzer, *De Platonis Philosophia*, pp. ix–x, xii ff.
133 Cf. M. Mahdi, *Alfarabi's Philosophy of Plato and Aristotle*, 6.
134 Cf. §§53, 57 and 58 of Mahdi's translation.
135 *Taḥṣīl*, ed. Haidarabad, 47, Mahdi's translation, *Alfarabi's Philosophy of Plato and Aristotle*, 50.
136 Cf. Dunlop, *Fuṣūl al-Madanī*, 10 ff.
137 Taḥṣīl, 38. For the meaning cf. Lane, *Lexicon*, v, 2100a.
138 Cf. Dunlop, *Fuṣūl al-Madanī*, 17.
139 *Ibid.*, 12.
140 The idea of emanation (*fayḍ*) does not appear in this work.
141 See F. Rosenthal, 'Arabische Nachrichten über Zenon den Eleaten', *Orientalia*, n.s., vi (Rome, 1937), 63–4.
142 Cf. the beginning of Faṣl 4 (fol. 5a): *al-faṣl fī'n-nubūwa fī 'n-nafs al-quḍsiyya an-nabawiyya yakūn fī 'l-ibtidā' l-ʿināya* (?)—text has simply *lʿnā* followed by the ductus for *y*, but it may be another letter, then *tā' marbūṭa—fī mabda' nashwihā thumma taqbalu al-fayḍ fī dafʿa wāḥida etc.* This is strictly incomprehensible. The printed Haidarabad text, on the other hand, reads quite easily: *ar-rābiʿ fī'n-nubūwa* (heading). *wa'n-nafs al-qudsiyya an-nabawiyya takūn fī 'btidā' al-ghāya fī 'btidā' nashwihā taqbalu al-fayḍ fī dafʿa wāḥida etc.* (parallels would no doubt establish if *al-ghāya* is to be retained or altered to *al-ʿināya*), i.e. 'Fourth (Section) on Prophecy. The saintly, prophetic soul is at the beginning of . . . in its first ecstasy recipient of the emanation all at once etc.'.
143 Cf. Dozy, *Supplément aux Dictionaires arabes*, ii, 161a.
144 Brockelmann, *GAL*, i, 79.
145 Made by P. Kraus and F. Rosenthal (cf. the latter's *Arab. Nachrichten über Zenon den Eleaten*, 64, n. 1).
146 *Al-Fārābiyyān, al-Fārābī wa-Ibn Sīnā, Dirāsāt Qaṣīra fī 'l-Adab wa 't-Ta'rīkh wa'l-Falsafa*, no. 10, Beirut, 1369/1950.
147 *Ibid.*, 4.
148 For his autobiography continued by a pupil, al-Juzajānī, see Ibn Abī Uṣaybiʿa, ii, 2–9.

149 The Arabic text was edited by J. Forget, Leiden, 1892.

150 2nd edn, Beirut, Imprimerie Catholique. Previously published in the periodical *al-Mashriq*.

151 A. F. Mehren, *Traités mystiques . . . d'Avicenne*, Leiden, 1889.

152 *Memorial Avicenne, V*, Cairo, 1954.

153 The latter suggested by Dr Ibrahim Madkour in his introduction to *Al-Shifā'*, vid. infra, n. 157. Other English renderings 'the Remedy' (Nicholson), 'Book of Healing' (Hitti).

154 Ed. M. Kurd ʿAlī, Cairo, 1938.

155 *Chahār Maqāla*, quoted Browne, *Literary History of Persia*, ii, 97.

156 Browne, *ibid.*, ii, 488.

157 *Al-Shifā', La Logique, I—L'Isagoge* (*al-madkhal*), Publication du Ministère de l'Instruction Publique (Culture Générale), Imprimerie Nationale, Cairo, 1952. This first volume contains a valuable introduction by Ibrahim Madkour.

158 *Avicenna, His Life and Works*, London, George Allen & Unwin, 1958.

159 Cairo, n.d. (introduction written in 1948), pp. 217.

160 Cf. Ibn al-Athīr, *s. ann.* 428, cited Browne, *Lit. Hist. of Persia*, ii, 107n.

161 Ibn Abī Uṣaybiʿa, ii, 3. A similar statement of al-Fārābī is reported, *ibid.*, ii, 136, and Ibn Khallikān, trans. De Slane, iii, 308. Cf. above, p. 185.

162 Cf. Madkour, *ibid.*, 13.

163 A recent reprint by the house of Minerva, Frankfurt am Main, 1961, of a black-letter edition of works of Avicenna in 1508, contains the following titles in Latin: *Logica, Sufficientia, De Coelo et Mundo, De Anima, De Animalibus, De Intelligentiis*, together with Alpharabius, *De Intelligentiis* and *Philosophia Prima*. The exact nature and extent of these works would have to be made out.

164 See n. 79 above.

165 The collector of the works of Ibn Bājja contained in Bodleian MS Pococke 206. See Dunlop, 'Philosophical Predecessors and Contemporaries of Ibn Bājjah', *Islamic Quarterly*, ii (1955), 100 ff. The first passage translated from MS Pococke 206 in this article needs revision, notably *del* (Ibn Bājjah) in line 9. The ref. is to Ibn Ḥazm.

166 Proverbs 8:9. Another version has simply 'All of them are good'. Text in A. Marx, 'Texts by and about Maimonides', *Jewish Quarterly Review*, xxv (1935) 379, cf. Maimonides, *The Guide of the Perplexed*, trans. with an introd. and notes by S. Pines with an introductory essay by L. Strauss, Univ. of Chicago Press, 1963, p. lx.

167 L. V. Berman, 'Ibn Bājjah and Maimonides', Diss. of the Hebrew University, Jerusalem, 1959, p. i.

168 By Ibn Khāqān, *Qalā'id al-ʿIqyān*, section on Ibn Bājjah.
169 MS Pococke 206, fol. 120a.
170 See also *EI*(2), art. Ibn Bādjdja (D. M. Dunlop).
171 See the curious story of Ibn Bājja producing a handful of rubies in the mosque of Granada (Maqqarī, *Nafḥ aṭ-Ṭīb*, Cairo edn, iv, 345).
172 Ed. Don Miguel Asín Palacios, *El Régimen del Solitario*, Madrid—Granada, 1946; ed. Majid Fakhry, *Ibn Bajjah (Avempace), Opera Metaphysica*, Beirut, 1968, 35–96.
173 Ibn Bājja's commentary on al-Fārābī's paraphrases of the *Organon* is to be found in the Escorial MS 612, as yet unedited.
174 Cf. Dunlop, *The Fuṣūl al Madanī of al-Fārābī*, 19, 92.
175 L. Gauthier, *Ibn Thofaïl, sa Vie, ses Oeuvres*, Paris, 1909, 3.
176 Ed. Miguel Asín Palacios, *Al-Andalus*, viii (1943), with Spanish trans.
177 *Philosophus Autodidactus or Hayy b. Yaqzan*, trans. S. Ockley, reprinted by Edward A. van Dyck, Cairo, 1905, 8, 10, 12.
178 *Philosophus Autodidactus*, trans. Ockley, 10.
179 Ed. M. Ṣaghīr Ḥasan al-Maʿṣūmī, Damascus, 1379/1960; English translation by the same, *Pakistan Historical Society Publication, No. 26*, Karachi, 1961.
180 *Philosophus Autodidactus*, trans., Ockley, 12.
181 *Ibid.*, 10.
182 *Ibid.*, 12.
183 Renan, *Averroès et l'Averroïsme*, 4th edn, Paris, 1882, 66–7.
184 For more detail see the *EI* article referred in to n. 170.
185 Ed. and trans. Léon Gauthier, 2nd edn, Beirut, 1936. For Ockley's English translation *Philosophus Autodidactus*, see n. 177.
186 *Ibn Thofaïl, sa Vie*, etc., 89.
187 Mr Madanī Ṣāliḥ, Iraq, has recently made a special study of Ibn Ṭufayl, and the publication of his work should throw new light on this and other matters.
188 Cf. Simon van den Bergh, *Averroes' Tahafut al-Tahafut*, *GMS*, xix, and Unesco Collection of Great Works, Arabic Series, 1954, i, p. xi.
189 *Inferno*, canto iv, 144.
190 Quoted Léon Gauthier, *Ibn Rochd (Averroès)*, Paris, 1948, 15.
191 First edn, Paris, 1852, 4th edn, Paris, 1882.
192 *Al Fârâbî, des arabischen Philosophen, Leben und Schriften, Mem. de l'Ac. Imp. des Sciences de St Pétersburg*, ser. VII, xiii, no. 4, 1869.
193 See now, however, the work of George N. Atiyeh on al-Kindī mentioned in n. 84, which will repay attention.
194 i.e. *Faṣl al-Maqāl fīmā bayn ash-Sharīʿa wa'l-Ḥikma min al-Ittiṣāl* (Decisive Treatise on the Accord of the Religious Law and Philosophy); *Kitāb al-Kashf ʿan Manāhij al-Adilla fī ʿAqā'id al-Milla* (Exposition of the Methods of the Proofs in regard to the

Dogmas of Religion); and *Ḍamīmat al-Mas'ala allatī dhakarahā Abū'l-Walīd fī Faṣl al-Maqāl* (Appendix to the first treatise), ed. as *Philosophie und Theologie von Averroes*, Munich, 1859, German trans. with the same title, Munich, 1875.

195 *Die Epitome der Metaphysik des Averroes*, Leiden, 1924.

196 Carlos Quirós Rodríguez, *Averroes, Compendio de Metafísica*, Madrid, 1919, with Spanish translation.

197 Cairo, n.d. (*c.* 1907).

198 E. I. J. Rosenthal, *Averroes' Commentary on Plato's Republic*, Cambridge U.P., 1956, reissued with corrections 1966.

199 *Die Epitome der Parva Naturalia des Averroes*, I, Wiesbaden, 1961. It may be noted that the Arabic title of the work calls it a *talkhīṣ*, which usually denotes a 'middle commentary'. The usual term for an epitome or paraphrase, i.e. the shortest type of commentary made by Averroes, is *jawāmiʿ*, compendia. For a similar doubt as to whether a work is a middle or short commentary, cf. Rosenthal, *op. cit.*, 9.

200 No. 632 in Derenbourg's catalogue. See Dunlop, 'Averroes (Ibn Rushd) on the modality of propositions', *Islamic Studies*, Karachi, i (1962), 23–34 (Arabic text), translated Nicholas Rescher, *Studies in the History of Arabic Logic*, Univ. of Pittsburgh Press, 1963, 91–105.

201 Cf. his statement that he was unable to obtain a copy of the *Politics* of Aristotle (*Averroes' Commentary on Plato's Republic*, Heb. text, 22 trans. 112). Apparently he regarded the *Republic* of Plato as a second best. Cf. also the Epilogue to his Commentary on the Ethics as given by Jourdain, *Recherches Critiques sur les anciennes traductions latines d'Aristote*, nouvelle edition (reprint, New York, Burt Franklin, 1960) 438–40, and M. Steinschneider, *Die hebraeischen Übersetzungen des Mittelalters* (reprint Graz, 1956), 219 ff.

202 In the story told of Ibn Bājja in the mosque at Granada (see above, n. 171) he is referred to as *al-faqīh*, '(canon-)lawyer'.

203 See Brockelmann, *GAL*, i, 384.

204 Renan, *Averroès*, 13, and text of Ibn al-Abbār, *ibid.*, 435–6.

205 *Averroès, ibid.*, Maqqarī, *Nafḥ aṭ-Ṭīb*, ii, 122 (Leiden), iv, 172 (Cairo, 1368/1949).

206 '*Superfluitas aut ignorantia aut malitia*' attributed to Ibn Bājja in the Epilogue already cited, n. 201.

207 L. Gauthier, *Ibn Rochd*, 5.

208 *Murūj adh-Dhahab*, ed. Paris, i, 182 (ed. Cairo, i, 86) = Pellat, i, 75, §187.

209 This seems the most probable sequence of Ibn Rushd's *cursus honorum*. Authorities give somewhat differing accounts.

210 Maqqarī, *Nafḥ aṭ-Ṭīb*, ed. Cairo, i, 418.

211 See more fully on this, Chapter 3, pp. 139 ff.

212 See De Slane, *Les Prolégomènes d'Ibn Khaldoun*, Paris, 1934, i, p. xciv.

213 Ibn al-Khaṭīb, *Kitāb al-Wizāra wa-Maqāmat as-Siyāsa*, MS Escorial 554, fol. 34b, cf. D. M. Dunlop, 'A little-known work on politics by Lisān al-Dīn b. al-Khaṭīb', *Miscelánea de Estudios Arabes y Hebraicos*, Universidad de Granada, viii, Fasc. 1, 1959, 48. Cf. above, p. 147.

214 Interesting but isolated and evidently not conceived as part of a comprehensive philosophical scheme, are the *Kitāb fī 's-Siyāsa* (Book on Politics) of al-Wazīr al-Kāmil (the Perfect Vizier) Abū'l-Qāsim al-Ḥusayn b. ʿAlī al-Maghribī (ed. Sāmī ad-Dahhān, Damascus, 1367/1948), who died in 418/1027; one or two philosophical works of Ibn Ṭumlūs (died 620/1223), whose *Kitāb al-Madkhal li-Ṣināʿat al-Manṭiq* (Introduction to the Art of Logic) was edited by Miguel Asín Palacios, Madrid, 1916; the *Sulūk al-Mālik fī Tadbīr al-Mamālik* (Ways of the Ruler in the Regulation of Kingdoms) of Shihāb ad-Dīn Aḥmad b. Muḥammad b. Abī'r-Rabīʿ, ed. M. Ṣabrī al-Kurdī, Cairo, A.H. 1339, dating from shortly before the fall of Baghdad in 656/1258. Ibn Ḥazm of Cordova, whose *Ṭawq al-Ḥamāma* has already been discussed in the chapter on Literature, was evidently a man of great intellectual activity (383/993–456/1064). He wrote several philosophical works, including one on logic (cf. above, p. 282 n. 186) and another on the classification of the sciences.

Chapter 6: Science and medicine

1 For the beginnings of Arabic poetry see Chapter 2.

2 Beirut edn, 1961, i, 918. Cf. *Muqaddimah*, iii, 150.

3 According to Ibn Juljul, *Ṭabaqāt al-Aṭibbā'*, ed. Fu'ād Sayyid (Cairo, 1955), 54, he survived considerably later till the Caliphate of Muʿāwiya. For the school of Jundishāpūr see below, pp. 219 f.

4 Ibn Abī Uṣaybiʿa, i, 116–17.

5 *Ibid.*, i, 121–3. Cf. for the name Masʿūdī, *Tanbīh*, 230.

6 Ibn Abī Uṣaybiʿa, i, 116.

7 By Greek philosophers who were fluent in Arabic such men may be meant as ʿAbd al-Malik b. Abjar, mentioned above, who was a convert to Islam (*loc. cit.*, n. 6) and perhaps a freedman (*mawlā*) of the Arab tribe of Kināna.

8 *Fihrist*, 242; cf. above, pp. 172, 175.

9 The translation of *as-Ṣahīfa* is uncertain, as Ruska noted (*Arabische Alchemisten, i, Chālid ibn Jazīd ibn Muʿāwija*, Heidelberg, 1924, 9, n. 2). Possibly *ṣaḥīfa* is the same as *ṣafīḥa* (cf. Lane, *Lexicon*, 1655b), the name given to the planispheric astrolabe, in Latin rendered *asaphaea*, which, however, is said to have been invented only much later by az-Zarqālī, an eleventh-century Spanish astronomer, cf.

J. Millás Vallicrosa, 'Estudios sobre Azarquiel: el tratado de la azafea', *Archeion*, xiv, 1932, 392 ff.

10 *Fihrist*, 354.

11 *Ibid.*, 244. Cf. p. 174.

12 *Murūj adh-Dhahab*, ed. Paris, viii, 176 (Cairo, iv, 258).

13 Quoted e.g. Steingass, *Persian–English Dictionary*, *s.v.* *ṭalq*.

14 *Biographical Dictionary*, ed. de Slane, i, 246 = trans., i, 482.

15 Brockelmann, *GAL*, i, 67; details in Steinschneider, *Die europäischen Übersetzungen aus dem Arabischen*, 69 (§102, c).

16 For a medical man of this name at Cordova see Ibn Abī Uṣaybiʿa, ii, 41.

17 Cf. *Muqaddimah*, iii, 229–30.

18 *Ibid.*, ii, 22.

19 Hitti, *History*, 246.

20 *Futūḥ al-Buldān*, ed. Cairo, 283.

21 The standard work on the subject is M. Steinschneider, *Die arabischen Übersetzungen aus dem Griechischen*, reprinted Graz, 1960.

22 For this work see Chapter 2, p. 52.

23 The future conqueror of Spain.

24 Ed. Cairo, no date, with the title *Taʾrīkh al-Khulafāʾ ar-Rāshidīn wa-Dawlat Banī Umayya*, ii, 55. For al-Ḥajjāj see pp. 254–5.

25 Zambaur, *Manuel de Généalogie et de Chronologie*, 39, 42, places ʿAbd Allāh b. Khālid as governor for a short time, between Bishr b. Marwān and al-Ḥajjāj but see George C. Miles in *Arabica*, ix (1962), 118. According to Dhahabī, *Taʾrīkh al-Islām*, Cairo edn, iii, 142, Bishr died in 75/694, apparently of blood-poisoning.

26 In the authentic *Kitāb al-Maʿārif*, ed. Saroite Okacha, Cairo, 1960, 355; ed. Wüstenfeld, 180.

27 Cf. D. M. Dunlop, *Theodoretus—Adhrīṭūs*, *26th International Congress of Orientalists, Delhi, 1964*, *Summaries of Papers*, 328–9.

28 *Taʾrīkh Dimashq*, edn of 1331, iii, 252.

29 *Fihrist*, 354 ff.

30 *The Works of Geber*, 1928.

31 *La Chimie au Moyen-Age*, Paris, 1893, iii, 126–224.

32 'Archéologie et Histoire des Sciences', *Mém. Acad. des Sciences*, xlix, Paris, 1906, 310–63.

33 Quoted by Kraus, *Jābir ibn Ḥayyān*, *Contribution*, i, p. ix (see n. 38 *infra*).

34 Kraus, op. cit., x.

35 See Kraus, *Jabir*, *ibid.* xi.

36 In *Studien zur Gesch. d. Chemie, Festgabe fuer E. O. von Lippmann*, Berlin, 1927, 38–47.

37 *Jābir ibn Ḥayyān, Essai sur l'histoire des idées scientifiques dans l'Islam*, vol. i, Textes choisis, Paris and Cairo, 1935.

38 *Jābir ibn Ḥayyān, Contribution à l'histoire des idées scientifiques dans l'Islam*, vols i–ii, *Mémoires présentées à l'Institut d'Égypte*, vols 44–5, Cairo, 1942–43.
39 *Jābir*, i, p. xlix.
40 *Fihrist*, 355.
41 *Jābir*, i, pp. lviii, lxv, 8–9.
42 Arabic edition by Berthelot, with French trans. (text 132–60, trans. 163–90), Latin trans. ed. Darmstadter in *Archiv für die Geschichte der Medizin*, 1925.
43 *Fihrist*, 300, l. 26, and Ibn Abī Uṣaybiʿa, i, 320 (quoted Kraus, *Jabīr*, i, pp. lx–lxi), also *Fihrist*, 301, l. 24.
44 Berthelot, *La Chimie au Moyen Age*, iii, Arabic text 132, French trans. 163.
45 Op. cit., text 145, trans. 165–6.
46 Cf. *Encyclopaedia Britannica*, edn of 1967, xiv, 614–15.
47 Beirut edn, i, 599, cf. *Muqaddimah*, ii, 216.
48 Al-Qifṭī, ed. Lippert, 109, H. Suter, *Die Mathematiker und Astronomen der Araber, Abhandlungen z. Geschichte d. mathematischen Wissenschaften*, x (1900), 223; Ibn al-ʿIbrī- (Bar Hebraeus), *Mukhtaṣar ad-Duwal*, ed. the Rev. A. Ṣālhānī, S.J., Beirut, 1958, 24, 127. Hitti, *History*, 6th edn, 311, appears to be in error (corrected in later edns) in saying that the translation was into Arabic.
49 *Raccolta di Scritti*, v (Rome, 1944), 205 ff, also Nallino's article *Sun, Moon and Stars* (*Muhammadan*) in James Hastings (ed.), *Encyclopaedia of Religion and Ethics*, Edinburgh, 1908–26, xii, 95.
50 Cf. Dunlop, 'The Dīwān attributed to Ibn Bājja', *BSOAS*, 1952, 470.
51 Ed. Fu'ād Sayyid, 61.
52 Ed. Lippert, 324–6.
53 Ed. Müller, i, 163–4.
54 Ed. Siddiqi, Berlin, 1928, 380.
55 Ed. ʿAbd as-Salām Hārūn, Cairo 1938–42, iii, 275, 323; iv, 192, etc.
56 Joseph v. Sontheimer, *Grosse Zusammenstellung über die Kräfte der bekannten einfachen Heil- und Nahrungsmittel von Ebn Baithar*, Stuttgart 1840–2, i, 13, 15, 24, 30, etc.; ii, 42, 45, 47, 48, 78, 122, 426, 465, etc.
57 Sarton, i, 478.
58 *GAL*, *Sup.* i, 106 and 417.
59 Ibn Abī Uṣaybiʿa, *loc. cit.*
60 Through Syriac evidently.
61 Ṭabarī, ii, 601–2.
62 *Murūj*, v, 244.
63 *Raccolta*, v, 198–9.
64 Cf. O. Loth, 'Al-Kindī als Astrolog', *Morgenländische Forschungen*, Leipzig, 1875, 264, and Nallino, *ERE*, xii, 91, who says 'In the Hellenistic world astrology flourishes while astronomy

decays; in the Musalmān world of the Middle Ages astrology becomes a potent ally of mathematical and observational astronomy.'
65 *EI*(1), i, 497a, art. Astrology.
66 Ibn Abī Uṣaybiʿa, i, 207. Cf. Chapter 5, p. 174.
67 Yaʿqūbī, *Kitāb al-Buldān*, *BGA* vii, 238, cf. Yāqūt, *Buldān*, i, 684–5, Masʿūdī, *Murūj*, viii, 290.
68 Yaʿqūbī, *K. al-Buldān*, 241.
69 Brockelmann, *GAL*, *Sup.*, i, 391.
70 *Fihrist*, 273.
71 *Tetrabiblos*, iii, 2.
72 Cf. Steinschneider, *Arabische Literatur der Juden*, 15.
73 Steinschneider, *ibid.*, 18.
74 Nallino, *Raccolta*, v, 201, 256.
75 Cf. Bouché-Leclercq, A., *L'astrologie grecque*, 1899, 406–7, n. 2 and 411, n. 1 (*hyleg* is Greek *aphetēs* and *alcochoden* is *oikodespotēs*), cited L. Thorndike, 'Albumasar in Sadan', *Isis*, xlv (1954), 27n.
76 *Philobiblon*, ed. H. Morley, 1888, 44.
77 *Raccolta*, v, 205.
78 *Fihrist*, 273, cf. D. M. Dunlop, 'The translations of al-Biṭrīq etc.', *JRAS*, 1959, 142. The translation made by Ibrahīm b. aṣ-Ṣalt (*Fihrist*, 268) and corrected by Ḥunayn b. Isḥāq was presumably later.
79 Variants in the Arabic are *lammā* and *lam*.
80 Nallino prefers a form in -r ('Argiabhar') found in the text of al-Qifṭī.
81 Steingass, *Pers. Dict. s.v.*, has 'an astronomical device for verifying the exact date of a birth', more accurately Nallino, *ERE*, art. *Sun, Moon and Stars* cited above, 'the method of ascertaining a factitious ascendant of the nativity'.
82 Qifṭī, 265–7; Casiri, *Escurial Catalogue*, i, 426; Ibn Abī Uṣaybiʿa, ii, 32. The original source is the *Kitāb al-Ulūf* of Albumasar, cf. Qifṭī, 265.
83 The whole of this paragraph based on Nallino, *Raccolta*, v. 203–4.
84 *Fihrist*, 273.
85 Ibn al-Faqīh, *K. al-Aʿlāq an-Nafīsa*, *BGA*, v, 137–9.
86 *Fihrist*, 118, calls him *kātib*.
87 Ṭabari, III, i, 125.
88 Ṭabari, *s. anno*. (III, i, 374).
89 So those of the Banū Mūsā b. Shākir (Brockelmann, i, 216) and of al-Jazarī (id., *Sup.* i, 903).
90 A. Mieli, *Panorama General de la Historia de la Ciencia*, II, *La Epoca Medieval, Mundo Islamico y Occidente Cristiano*, Madrid–Buenos Aires, 1946, 7–8.
91 Ibn Abī Uṣaybiʿa, i, 123, there Jurjis b. Jibrīl. Bakhtishūʿ was the family name later.

92 See the biographies in Ibn Abī Uṣaybiʿa, i, 123 ff.
93 *Ibid.*, i, 175 ff. Cf. D. M. Dunlop, 'John Mesue and his work', *Bulletin of the British Society for the Hist. of Science*, i, (Nov. 1952), 213.
94 See e.g. G. Bergsträsser, *Ḥunain ibn Isḥāq über die syrischen u. arabischen Galen-Übersetzungen*, *AKM*, xvii (1925), 2.
95 Ibn Abī Uṣaybiʿa, i, 201.
96 Otherwise Mesue Senior, to distinguish him from a later medical man known to the Latins as Mesue Junior, for whom one may cf. Sarton, *Introduction to the History of Science*. i, 728–9.
97 Cf. Zeki Validi Togan, *Ibn Faḍlān's Reisebericht*, *AKM*, 1939, 295 ff.
98 Ibn Abī Uṣaybiʿa, i, 178.
99 L. Choulant, *Handbuch der Bücherkunde der älteren Medizin*, Leipzig, 1841, reprinted Graz, 1956, 337; more detailed in Steinschneider, *Die europäischen Übersetzungen aus dem Arabischen*, reprinted Graz, 1956, ii, 39.
100 *Les Maximes médicaux de Yohanna Ben Massawaïh*, Cairo, 1934.
101 Axiom 110, perhaps from his Greek source?
102 Bergsträsser, *op. cit.*, p. 8 of Arabic text. Several medieval Arabic translations of works of Galen, not all certainly by Ḥunayn I. Ishāq, have now been edited by Dr M. C. Lyons, Pembroke College, Cambridge, and published by the Berlin Academy (*In Hippocratis De Officina Medici Commentarii*, 1963; *De Partibus Artis Medicativae*, *De Causis Contentivis* and *De Diaeta in Morbis Acutis secundum Hippocratem*, 1969), to which may be added *Galen, On Anatomical Procedures, the Later Books*, ed. M. C. Lyons and B. Towers from a trans. by W. L. H. Duckworth, Cambridge Univ. Press, 1962.
103 'Die Augenheilkunde des Jûhannâ b. Mâsawaih (777–857 n. Chr.)', *Der Islam*, vi, 1916, 217–68.
104 Ibn Abī Uṣaybiʿa, i, 183.
105 *Ibid.*, ii, 214.
106 Cf. D. M. Dunlop, 'Biographical material from the *Siwān al-Ḥikmah*', *JRAS*, 1957, 88.
107 Several of these have already been mentioned.
108 For comments on this notice, see the article already referred to, n. 106.
109 E. Wiedemann, 'Über al-Kindī's Schrift über Ebbe u. Flut', *Annalen der Physik*, lxvii (1922), 380–1. Arabic text in Abū Rīda, *Rasāʾil al-Kindī al-Falsafiyya*, ii, 115.
110 For Burṭās, see Dunlop, *History of the Jewish Khazars*, 83 and index.
111 *Tanbīh*, ed. Cairo, 55–6.

112 Cf. *De Caelo*, ii, c.7 (289a).
113 Wiedemann, *loc. cit.*, 385–6, Arabic text, Abū Rīda, ii, 117–18.
114 Wiedemann, 386, n. 2.
115 See Sarton, *Introduction to the History of Science*, i, 721–3.
116 In *EI*(1). The new edition has not yet reached so far.
117 Abū Rīda, Part ii, 107–8, cf. *Journal of the Royal Asiatic Society of Bombay*, 1937, xiii.
118 *Abh. z. Gesch. d. math. Wiss.*, xxvi, 3 (Leipzig and Berlin, 1912), 3–70.
119 *Loc. cit.*, 3–4.
120 *Ibid.*, 43, 70.
121 *Al-Kindī genannt 'der Philosoph der Araber'*, *AKM*, I, ii (1857), 25–7. For more recent enumerations see the Kindī bibliographies of McCarthy (1962) and Rescher (1964), the latter of which gives information especially on European studies of al-Kindī. The principal original source is *Fihrist*, 256–60.
122 MS Aya Sofya 3594 (H. Ritter and M. Plessner, 'Schriften Jaʿqūb ibn Isḥāq al-Kindī's in Stambuler Bibliotheken', *Archiv Orientální*, iv, 371).
123 *AKM*, xxx, 1948.
124 *Ibid.*, 2.
125 *Ibid.*
126 *Ibid.*, 3.
127 *Ibid.*, cf. 69.
128 *Ibid.*
129 End of paragraph 47 in the text.
130 End of paragraph 33 of text.
131 Paragraph 66.
132 *Risāla fī Ṣanʿat Aṭʿima min ghayr ʿanāṣirihā* (cf. nos. 156 and 143 in Flügel, no. 136 in McCarthy).
133 Al-Kindī had some reputation for fondness for money if al-Jāḥiz, *Kitāb al-Bukhalāʾ* (Book of Misers), actually refers to him, as he appears to do (cf. Chapter 2, p. 47). On the other hand, if al-Jāḥiẓ had known that the victim of his satire traded in fraudulent cosmetics, he would almost certainly have mentioned it.
134 *Murūj*, ed. Paris, viii, 176 (ed. Cairo, iv, 258).
135 Flügel, no. 260, McCarthy, no. 236.
136 Flügel, no. 245, McCarthy, no. 221.
137 Flügel, no. 148, McCarthy, no. 129. Text in art. al-Kindī in the *Ṣiwān al-Ḥikma* of as-Sijistānī, British Museum MS. Or. 9033, fols. 62a–63a, etc.
138 Al-Kindī's interests included also *materia medica*. See Martin Levey, *The Medical Formulary or Aqrābādhīn of al-Kindī, translated with a study of its materia medica*, Univ. of Wisconsin Press, 1966.

139 Cardano's judgment of al-Kindī as one of the greatest geniuses in recorded history cited by Brockelmann, *GAL, Sup.* i, 372, is well known.

140 Channing, ed. *Rhazes de Variolis et Morbillis*, London, 1766.

141 D. Campbell, *Arabian Medicine*, London, 1926, i, 69, cf. Choulant, *op. cit.*, 341.

142 Amin A. Khairallah, *Outline of Arabic Contributions to Medicine and the Allied Sciences*, Beirut, 1946, 110.

143 Channing, *op. cit.*, p. vii.

144 *A Treatise on the Small-Pox and Measles*, London, Sydenham Society, 1848.

145 See G. M. Stisted, *The True Life of Capt. Sir Richard F. Burton*, London, 1896, 16, and 18 (Burton met the Spanish Arabist Pascual de Gayangos at Dr Greenhill's)

146 *Sic*, cf. Garbers, *Kitāb Kīmiyāʾ al-ʿIṭr waʾt-Taʿṣīdāt*, 282.

147 Greenhill's translation, ch. 7, p. 51, slightly modified.

148 Meyerhof, *Legacy of Islam*, London, 1931, 323.

149 *Proceedings of the XVII Int. Congress of Medicine*, 1913 (Section 23, 237–68).

150 *L'Épître de Bērūnī* (*Risālat al-Bīrūnī fī Fihrist Kutub Muḥammad b. Zakariyyāʾ ar-Rāzī*) Paris, 1936.

151 *Abi Bakr Mohammadi filii Zachariae Raghensis* (*Razis*) *Opera Philosophica fragmentaque quae supersunt collegit et edidit Paulus Kraus, Universitatis Fouadi I Litterarum Facultatis Publicationum fasc.* XXII *Pars Prior*, Cairo, 1939. The Arabic text of the *Spiritual Physick* is on pp. 15–96.

152 London, John Murray, 1950.

153 *L'Épître de Bērūnī*, 29–30.

154 With reference to the cult of Aesculapius and the Asclepiadae.

155 It seems unlikely that al-Faḍl b. Sahl, the famous vizier of al-Maʾmūn (assassinated in 202/818), is intended here.

156 *Sūr.* 24, 40.

157 Cf. *Sūr.* 17, 14/15.

158 Ibn Abī Uṣaybiʿa (i, 309) quoting the *Kitāb fīʾl-Bīmāristānāt* (Book on Hospitals) of Abū Saʿīd Manṣūr b. ʿĪsā, called Zāhid al-ʿUlamāʾ, gives another account.

159 *Sūr.* 17, 72/74.

160 *Épître*, 1–6.

161 *Op. cit.* (see n. 149).

162 See also above, the information from al-Bīrūnī in Kraus's book.

163 Leiden MS. Or. 1270. Cf. Chapter 5, n. 78.

164 Ed. Beirut, i, 1014 = *Muqaddima*, trans. Rosenthal, iii, 272, 280.

165 *Livre des Avares*, trans. Charles Pellat, Paris, 1951, 147–8.

166 Brockelmann, *GAL*, i, 205.

167 D. M. Dunlop, 'The Ǧawāmiʿ al-ʿUlūm of Ibn Fariġūn', in *Zeki*

Velidi Togan'a Armağan, Istanbul 1950–5, 348–53; V. Minorsky, 'Ibn Farīghūn and the *Ḥudūd al-ʿĀlam*,' in *A Locust's Leg*, Lund Humphries, 1962, 189–96.

168 Ibn Abī Uṣaybiʿa, i, 320. (*Kitāb as-Sīra al-Fāḍila wa-Sīrat Ahl al-Madīna al-Fāḍila*).

169 *Kitāb Arāʾ Ahl al-Madīna al-Fāḍila.*

170 Ibn Abī Uṣaybiʿa, i, 310 and index.

171 H. P. J. Renaud, *Les Manuscrits arabes de l'Escurial*, Paris, 1941, nos. 806 ff.

172 There numbered 9828. b. 20.

173 Muḥammad Farīd Wajdī, *Dāʾirat Maʿārif al-Qarn al-ʿIshrīn*, iv, 515.

174 Nos. 6784–6788, pp. 530–3.

175 Ed. Beirut, i, 941–65. The other passage is i, 202–9.

176 See the trans. of Rosenthal, iii, 182 ff, also i, 238 ff. The table is found in vol. iii between pp. 204 and 205.

177 No. 4230.

178 *Kashf aẓ-Ẓunūn*, iii, 532–3.

179 The *ghubār* numbers, i.e. the Arabic numerals 1–9, without zero.

180 *Manners and Customs of the Modern Egyptians*, edn, of 1890, 239.

181 Ed. Van Vloten, 1895, p. 219, with *zāʾish ay al-mawlid* apparently 'increase, i.e. bringing forth' for *zaʾicha.*

182 G. von Grunebaum, *Medieval Islam*, Chicago, 1946, 245, citing Krenkow *EI*(1), iv, 480.

183 *Muqaddimah*, iii, 286.

184 As-Suyūṭī, *Bughyat al-Wuʿāt*, Cairo, 1326–1909, 425.

185 Cf. G. von Grunebaum, 'As-Sakkâkî—on milieu and thought, *JAOS*, lxv (1945), 62.

186 Bombay, 1309/1891.

187 Accompanies *an-Nuqāya* in the Bombay edn of 1891.

188 *Aṭ-Ṭabaqāt al-Kubrā*, Egyptian edn, n.d. (*c.* 1935), ii, 76.

189 2 vols, Cairo, 1311/1894.

190 *Laṭāʾif*, i, 53–4.

191 *Laṭāʾif*, i, 56–7.

192 Cf. above, p. 209.

193 Cf. P. Kraus, *Jābir ibn Ḥayyān, ii, Mém. Inst. Égypte*, Vol. 45, Cairo, 1942, 187 ff.

Chapter 7: Some famous women in Islam

1 On the other hand, Sprenger thought that, but for Khadīja, Muhammad would never have been a prophet (cited by Sir William Muir, *Life of Moḥammed*, rev. T. H. Weir, Edinburgh, 1912, 106n).

2 Arabic, *Khalīfa*, 'successor' or 'lieutenant' of Muḥammad.

3 His name was Ṣafwān b. al-Muʿaṭṭal as-Sulamī (Ṭabarī, I, iii, 1520).
4 According to ʿĀʾisha's account (Ṭabarī, *ibid.*, 1523).
5 Muir, *Caliphate*, 3rd edn, 265.
6 Ibn Qutayba, *K. al-Maʿārif*, ed. Saroite Okasha, Cairo, 1960, 134; ed. Wüstenfeld, 66.
7 Nicholson, *A Literary History of the Arabs*, 1953, 195.
8 Text in Noeldeke, *Delectus Veterum Carminum Arabicorum*, Berlin, 1933 (Nachdruck), 25.
9 Cf. Masʿūdī, *Tanbīh*, Cairo, 1357/1938, 264.
10 *K. al-Aghānī*, Beirut, 1959, xvii, 142.
11 Ṭabarī, II, i, 204–5, fuller in *K. al-Aghānī*, xvi, 11.
12 Majnūn was enamoured of a different girl, Laylā al-ʿĀmiriyya, sometimes said to have been his cousin.
13 A region with a town or village of the same name between Basra and (the later) Wāsiṭ in Iraq.
14 Ibn Qutayba, ed. Saroite Okasha, Cairo, 1960, 353; ed. Wüstenfeld, 179.
15 She married eventually a certain Ṣiwār b. ʿAwfāʾ al-Qushayrī (Brockelmann, *GAL*, *Sup*. i, 93).
16 See a description in E. W. Lane, *Modern Egyptians*, ch. 1, of the *burquʿ*, or lady's long face-veil, still in use in the nineteenth century.
17 Al-Ḥusrī, *Zahr al-Ādāb*, ed. Z. Mubārak, iv, 77; Brockelmann, *GAL*, i, 61.
18 See above pp. 65 f. Text and trans. by L. Bercher, *Le Collier du Pigeon*, Algiers, 1949.
19 Maqqarī, *Nafḥ aṭ-Ṭīb*, edn of Cairo, v, 336 (= Leiden edn, ii, 563).
20 See the plate in E. Lévi-Provençal, *Histoire de l'Espagne musulmane*, iii, Paris, 1953, 304, also the same, *Inscriptions arabes d'Espagne*, Leiden and Paris, 1931, 192, no. 211.
21 Cf. Dominique Sourdel, *Le vizirat ʿabbaside de 749 à 936*, Damascus, 1959, 187.
22 Sir T. Arnold and A. Guillaume, *The Legacy of Islam*, Oxford University Press, 1931, 154 and plate there.
23 For Wallāda, see Maqqarī, *Nafḥ aṭ-Ṭīb*, Cairo, 1367/1949 (*sic*), v, 336 ff = Leiden edn, ii, 563 ff, Ibn Bashkuwāl, *K. aṣ-Ṣila*, ed. Codera, no. 1418 (ii, 632), also R. O. Besthorn, *Ibn Zaiduni vitam etc.*, Copenhagen, 1889, 7 ff.
24 Other accounts of the origin of al-Khayzurān are given by Muir, *Caliphate*, 465, and ʿAbd al-Jabbār al-Jaumard, *Hārūn al-Rashīd*, Beirut, 1956, 55. Ṭabarī (III, i, 599) says she was from Jurash, a district of al-Yaman.
25 Hitti, *History*, 304, citing Masʿūdī, *Murūj*, vi, 289.
26 Ṭabarī, III, i, 599.

27 H. St J. Philby, *Harun al-Rashid*, London, 1933, 113.
28 Ibn Khallikān, ed. De Slane, i, 272 trans., i, 533.
29 Both names of the children are of course proleptic, belonging to their Caliphates. Al-Ma'mūn was ʿAbd Allāh, al-Amīn Muḥammad.
30 In classical antiquity Pagrae.
31 Cf. al-Balādhurī, *K. Futūḥ al-Buldān*, ed. Ṣalāḥ ad-Dīn al-Munajjid, Cairo, 1956, 176, §399.
32 Ibn Ḥawqal, *K. Ṣūrat al-Arḍ*, trans. J. H. Kramers and G. Wiet, Beirut and Paris, 1964, 182.
33 Sir R. Burton, *Pilgrimage to al-Madinah and Meccah*, ch. 24, *ad init*.
34 Ibn Khallikān, ed. De Slane, i, 271.
35 A daughter of Muʿāwiya was called Amat Rabb al-Mashāriq, 'Handmaid of the Lord of East and West', and there were women called Amat Allāh, Amat al-Karīm, Amat al-Wāḥid, etc.
36 Hitti, *History*, 302.
37 Hitti, *ibid.*; S. F. Mahmud, *A Short History of Islam*, Karachi, 1960, 109.
38 E. Lévi-Provençal, *Histoire de l'Espagne musulmane*, Cairo, 1944, 185, cf. Ibn al-Khaṭīb, *K. Aʿmāl al-Aʿlām*, ed. Lévi-Provençal, Rabat, 1934, 21.
39 *Al-Fakhrī*, trans. C. E. J. Whitting, 213.
40 Ibn al-Abbār, *Iʿtāb al-Kuttāb*, Damascus, 1380/1961, 129.
41 Never apparently called *wazīr* (D. Sourdel, *Vizirat ʿAbbāside*, 216).
42 Ed. De Slane i, 136–8, trans., i, 268–72. The story told by Ibn ʿAbn Rabbihi (d. 328/939) at the end of *al-ʿIqd al-Farīd* (ed. Ahmad Amīn and others, Cairo, 1949–50, v, 456 ff.) that al-Ma'mūn met Būrān first in a street adventure in Baghdad is discussed by Ibn Khaldūn, *Muqaddimah*, i, 39–40 (= Beirut ed., i, 31–2) and rightly rejected by him.
43 Cited Ibn Khallikān, ed. De Slane, i, 137; cf., Tabarī, III, ii, 1083, who says that the entertainment lasted seventeen days (confusion of seven and nine is common in the MSS).
44 Presumably she had visited Medina and Mecca earlier in the lifetime of Hārūn, cf. Ṭabarī, III, i, 629. The obstacle now was evidently expense. For her endowment of the Pilgrimage, see above.
45 Cf. Maqqarī, *Nafḥ aṭ-Ṭīb*, Cairo edn, i, 415.
46 Ibn Khallikān, ed. De Slane, i, 263, trans., i, 515 ('Consume with fire, O God . . .').
47 Shaʿrānī, *aṭ-Ṭabaqāt al-Kubrā*, Cairo edn, n.d., i, 56.
48 *Ibid.*
49 Ibn Khallikān, ed. De Slane, i, 264.
50 Some thought on the contrary that ʿUbayda bint Abī Kilāb was superior to Rābiʿa (Shaʿrānī, *ibid.*, 57).

51 For Rābiʿa see especially Margaret Smith, *Rābiʿa the Mystic and her Fellow-Saints in Islam*, Cambridge University Press, 1928.

52 Meaning Spray of Pearls'.

53 Maqrīzī, *Sulūk*, Cairo, 1957, I, 299, 342.

54 *Ibid.*, 359.

55 *Ibid.*, 362.

56 Hitti, *History*, 671, citing Suyūṭī, *Ḥusn al-Muḥāḍara*, ii, 39.

57 Maqrīzī, *Sulūk*, i, 342. See the discussion, *ibid.*, 362n.

58 On 3 Ṣafar 648, or 6 May 1250 according to the usual account (W. B. Stevenson, *The Crusaders in the East*, Cambridge, 1907, 329).

59 Cf. Maqrīzī, *ibid.*, 362. The difficulty is that the oath of allegiance to Shajar ad-Durr seems to have been taken a week later (10th Ṣafar).

60 See Ibn Khallikān, ed. De Slane, i, 318–19; trans. i, 625–6.

Index

Principal references are given in *italics*

Index

Index

Bᵉnē Qedhem, 7
Berbers, 23, 87
Bercher, Léon, 65
Bergsträsser, G., 329 n. 94
Berman, L. V., 322 n. 167
Berlin, Academy, 329 n. 102; Royal Library, 130, Catalogue by W. Ahlwardt, 303 n. 432
Bezold, C., 288 n. 113
Bible, 7; translated into Arabic, 20; Septuagint version of, 71
Biblical, history, 87, 91, 102; legends, 70; quotations, 3–7, 63, 322 n. 166
Bibliotheca Arabica Scholasticorum, 199
Bibliotheca Arabico-Hispana, 126
Bibliothèque Nationale, 64, 244
Bilqīs, 6, 7
bīmāristān, 280 n. 139. *See also* hospital
Binyon, Laurence, 64
biographical collections, 119 ff
Biographical Dictionary of Ibn Khallikān, 119 f
biography, of Muḥammad, 72 ff; secular, 118
al-Bīrūnī, 115, 155, 237 ff, 242; *History of India* (*Ta'rīkh al-Hind*), 21, 298 n. 312; *Chronology of Ancient Nations*, 21; *Risàla* on the works of Rhazes, quoted, 237–9
Bishr b. Manṣūr, 262
Bishr b. Marwān, 208
biṭrīq, 36
al-Biṭrīq, 174, 216
Björnbo, A. A., Danish scholar, 227
Blachère, Régis, 29; *Histoire de la littérature arabe*, 271 n. 42
Black Mountain, 59. *See also* Amanus
blacks, 47, 49; of Iraq, 92. *See also* Zanj
Blochet, E., 64, 282 n. 182
blue of the sky, 226–7
Boigues, Pons, *see* Pons Boigues
Book of Roger, 313 n. 114
Book of the Seven (Seventy ?), 250
borax, 206
Bordeaux, attacked by ʿAbd ar-Raḥmān al-Ghāfiqī, 15; Sea of, 160
Borgia, Cesare, 141
Bostra (Buṣra), era of, 26
Bosworth, C. E., 280 n. 136
botany, 54
Bouché-Leclerq, 328 n. 75
Bouyges, Father Maurice, S.J., 199
Brahmagupta, 216
Brāhma-sphuṭa-siddhānta, 216
branding, 224
breastplates, 57
Bretschneider, E., 274 n. 90
Britain, 1, 16
British, 2; mandate, 2; Museum, 189 f; Isles according to Arabic authors, 273 n. 83
Brittany, 273 n. 80
Brṭāniya, 273 n. 80
brocade, 256, 262
Brockelmann, C., 29, 51, 128–9, 213; notices al-Jahshiyārī only briefly, 95; high opinion of al-Masʿūdī, 99; *Geschichte der arabischen Litteratur*, 59, 266
Bronze City, *see* Copper City
'bronze era', 286 n. 55
Browne, E. G., *A Literary History of Persia*, 279 n. 121; *Arabian Medicine*, 242
Bughā al-Kabīr, 176
Bughyat al-Wuʿāt, 332 n. 184
budgets, 95, 98, 290 nn. 182–3
Buddhists, 114
al-Buḥturī, 21, 45; criticized Ibn Abī Ṭāhir Ṭayfūr, 81
Bukhārā, 168
Bulaq, 132
Bulgaria, Magna, 170
Bulgars, 19, 106, 107, 110, 167
Bunbury, E. H., 270 n. 35, 308 n. 9
bunūd, 107
Bunz, Hugo, 133
Būrān, 259 ff
Burdīl, *see* Bordeaux
bureaucrats, 60
Burjān, 106, 110. *See also* Bulgars
Burjī Mamlūks, 24, 132
burlesque, 48
burquʿ, 255, 280 n. 146
al-Burquʿī, 58
Burṭās, 224
Burton, Sir Richard, 1, 28, 235, 269 n. 2
Burtuqāl, 160
Bury, J. B., 272 n. 65, 293 n. 187
al-Būṣīrī, 275 n. 15
Busr b. Abī Arṭāt, alleged expedition to Constantinople, 79
Busse, H., 291 n. 163
Buwayhid(s), 45, 55, 191; dynasty, 21; Sulṭāns, 123
Byblos, 5
Byzantine(s), Africa, 13; empire, 19, Masʿūdī's description of, 107; first contact with the Arabs, 13; astrologers, 43; defeated by the Arabs, 13; prisoners, 36
Byzantium, contest of the Arabs with, in E. Mediterranean, 18; limited power of, in Mediterranean, 19; truce with, 83; degree of civilization achieved, 99, cf. 267; mechanical devices at, 217–18; fall of, an epoch-making event, 24. *See also* Constantinople

Index

al-Hamadhānī, *see* Zahīr ad-Dīn Muḥammad b. al-Ḥusayn, Ibn al-Faqīh
Haman, 36
ḥamāsa, 41
Ḥamāsa, of Abū Tammām, 29, 41, 43; of al-Buḥturī, 45
Ḥamāt, 131
al-Hamdānī, *Ṣifat Jazīrat al-ʿArab*, 269 n. 17
Ḥamdānids, 46, 58, 185
Ḥamdūna, 260
Hami, 168
Ḥamīdullāh, Dr Muḥammad, 75, 80, 86; *Le Prophète de l'Islam*, 271 n. 54, 285 n. 41
Ḥammād ar-Rāwiya, 41
Ḥamza al-Iṣfahānī, 114 ff
handasa, 176
al-Ḥaramān, 292 n. 182
ḥarīm, 251, 257
al-Ḥarīrī, 21, 61 ff; *Maqāmāt* of, a classic among Arabic authors, 61; his son Najm ad-Dīn ʿAbd Allāh, 282 n. 173, cf. 62 (Abū'l-Qāsim ʿAbd Allāh); *K. Ghurrat al-Ghawwāṣ fī Awhām al-Khawāṣṣ*, 65; *Mulḥat al-Iʿrāb*, 63, 65
al-Ḥārith, king of al-Ḥīra, 26
al-Ḥārith b. Hammām, narrator in the *Maqāmāt* of al-Ḥarīrī, 61; an artificial name, 281 n. 170
al-Ḥārith b. Kalada, 204
al-Ḥārith b. Saʿīd al-Kadhdhāb, 122
al-Ḥarīzī, Spanish Jewish author, 63
Haroun Alraschid, 2. *See also* Hārūn ar-Rashīd
Ḥarrān, 281 n. 162; schools at, 173
Hārūn, ʿAbd as-Salām Muḥammad, 53, 278 nn. 77, 90, 286 n. 74, 287 n. 88
Hārūn ar-Rashīd, ʿAbbāsid Caliph, 110; revenue under, 98. *See also* Haroun Alraschid
al-Ḥasan b. Aḥmad al-Qarmaṭī, 133
al-Ḥasan b. ʿAlī, descendants of, called ash-Sharīf, 275 n. 101
al-Ḥasan b. Sahl, minister, 57, 105, 174, 259 ff; said to have translated *Jāwīdān Khirad* into Arabic, 126
Hāshimids, 86. *See also* Banū Hāshim
Haskins, C. H., *Studies in the History of Medieval Science*, 309 n. 30
Ḥassān b. Thābit, poet of Muḥammad, 30
Ḥātim, 43
Ḥawādīth ad-Duhūr, 131
Ḥawrān, 26
al-haylāj, 215
al-Haytham b. ʿAdī, 80
Ḥayy b. Yaqẓān of Ibn Sīnā, 193; of Ibn Ṭufayl, 197 f
Heber the Kenite, 63
Hebrew, language, 4, 5, 7; University of Jerusalem, 86
Heidelberg, 277 n. 44
Helena, mother of Constantine, 105, 107
Heliopolis, *see* ʿAyn Shams
Helpers, 78
hemiplegia, 232
Henning, W. B., 312 n. 96
Heraclius, 77 f
Herat, 68, 93; *zā'iraja* of, 244
Hermann of Carinthia, 156 (= Hermannus Dalmata)
Hermes, 48; sent to the Nile source, 111
Hermopolis, 110
Herodotus, 7
hijā', 42
Ḥijāz, 32, 35
Hijra, 11, 252; era, 11
ḥikam, 122, 126
Hilāl aṣ-Ṣābi', his lost History, 97; *Rusūm Dār al-Khilāfa*, 97 ff
ḥilm, 71
Himavant mountains, 155
Himerius, Greek admiral, 98
Ḥims, 42, 295 n. 260
Ḥimyar, 6, 32, 38, 71
Ḥimyarite inscriptions, 6
Hinds, G. M., 94
Hippocrates, 87; mentioned by al-Jāḥiẓ, 50
al-Ḥīra, 3, 8, 26, 72, 220
ḥisāb, 176
ḥisāb al-jummal, 244
Hishām b. ʿAbd al-Malik, Umayyad Caliph, 21, 98, 207; translation made for, 308 n. 14
Hishām b. Muḥammad al-Kalbī, 80
Histories (*Historiae adversus Paganos*) of Orosius translated, 20, 138
history, beginnings of, among the Arabs, 70 ff, cf. 38; pre-Islamic, 88, 102, 131; local, 80, 116, 118
History of the Almohads, 127
History of Islam of adh-Dhahabī, 94
Hitti, Professor Philip K., 79, 84; *History of the Arabs*, 3, 269 n. 5, 270 n. 20, 272 n. 68
ḥiyal, 218
Hoenerbach, W., 285 n. 47
Homburger, L., 158
honey, 136
Honeyman, Professor A. M., x
hospital, first in Islam, 57; Book on Hospitals (*K. fī'l-Bīmāristānāt*), 331 n. 158
Houdas, O., 299 n. 340
Hourani, Albert, *Arabic Thought in the Liberal Age, 1798–1935*, 269 n. 3
Houtsma, M. Th., 87
Hūdid dynasty, 195
al-Ḥudaybiyya, 74
Ḥudūd al-ʿĀlam, 164, 273 n. 80
Hui-Chhao, Buddhist monk, 159
Ḥujr b. al-Ḥārith, 26

Ibn Muzayn, 117
Ibn al-Muqaffaʿ, 40, 46 f; works of Aristotle translated by him or by his son, 46, 173 f
Ibn al-Muʿtazz, 45, 280 n. 140; *Kitāb al-Badiʿ* of, 45
Ibn an-Nadīm, author of the *Fihrist*, 74, 164, 175, 205, 297 n. 306
Ibn al-Qūhī, 179
Ibn Qutayba, 29, *50 ff*, 71, 88; antipathy to Greek philosophy, 51; charged with plagiarism by al-Masʿūdī, 54; on al-Jāḥiẓ, 49 f; *K. al-Adab al-Kātib*, 51; *K. al-Maʿārif*, 52, 74, 269 n. 6, 279 n. 106, 283 n. 5; *K. ash-Shiʿr wa'sh-Shuʿarā'*, 29, 52; *ʿUyūn al-Akhbār*, 51, 71, 283 n. 6; *K. Ta'wīl Mukhtalif al-Ḥadīth*, 53, 278 n. 95; *K. al-Imāma wa's-Siyāsa* (attributed to Ibn Qutayba), 52
Ibn al-Qūṭiyya, 39, 52, 126
Ibn ar-Rūmī, 45
Ibn Rushd 23; influenced by Ibn Bājja (Avempace), 197; logical works of, 200; *Tahāfut at-Tahāfut*, 199; *Talkhīṣ Kitāb al-Maqūlāt*, *ibid.*; *Tafsīr Mā Baʿd aṭ-Ṭabīʿa*, *ibid.*; *Faṣl al-Maqāl fīmā bayn ash-Sharīʿa wa'l-Ḥikma min al-Ittiṣāl*, 323 n. 194; *K. al-Kashf ʿan Manāhij al-Adilla fī ʿAqā'id al-Milla*, *ibid.*; *Damīmat al-Mas'ala allatī Dhakarahā Abū'l-Walīd* etc., *ibid.* *See also* Averroes
Ibn Rusta, 154, 168
Ibn Saʿd, 73, 75, 79; *Ṭabaqāt*, 284 n. 18. *See also Kitāb aṭ-Ṭabaqāt al-Kabīr*
Ibn Saʿīd al-Maghribī, 126; 200; his appendix to Ibn Ḥazm's *Risāla*, 127
Ibn aṣ-Ṣā'igh, 195. *See also* Ibn Bājja
Ibn Samʿun, 125
Ibn Ṣanjīl, 129
Ibn Shaddād, 119
Ibn Sīnā, 191 ff, 196; one of the four greatest philosophers of Islam, 182; called *ar-Ra'īs*, the Prince, 194; al-Kindī manuscript said to have belonged to, 179; as man of science and doctor, 242; disbelieved in the practicability of alchemy, 182; millenary of, 191; *Al-Qānūn fī'ṭ-Ṭibb* (Canon of Medicine), 192, 194; *K. al-Ishārāt wa't-Tanbīhāt*, 192; *Majmūʿ* (Collection of short treatises), *ibid.*; *Tisʿ Rasā'il* (Nine Treatises), *ibid.*; *ʿUyūn al-Ḥikma*, 193; *Ḥayy b. Yaqẓān*, 193, 198; *ash-Shifā'*, 193, 194; *K. an-Najāt*, 193
Ibn Sīnā bayn ad-Dīn wa'l-Falsafa by Dr Ḥ. Ghurāba, 193
Ibn Taghrībirdī, 121, 131
Ibn aṭ-Ṭiqṭaqā, *K. al-Fakhrī*, 275 n. 104
Ibn Ṭufayl, 196; *197 f*; introduced Ibn Rushd to the Almohad court, 197–8; his work *Hayy b. Yaqẓān*, 198
Ibn Ṭumlūs, 325 n. 214
Ibn ʿUnayn, poet, 66 ff
Ibn Uthāl, 205
Ibn Wāḍiḥ, 163. *See also* al-Yaʿqūbī
Ibn Zaydūn, Spanish poet, 256
Ibrāhīm b. Ḥabīb al-Fazārī, 215. *See also* al-Fazārī
Ibrāhīm the Imām, charge to Abū Muslim, 134
Ibrāhīm b. al-Mahdī, 260
Ibrāhīm b. Waṣīf Shāh, 111, 135
Ibrāhīm b. Yaḥyā, 135
Ibrāhīm b. Yaʿqūb aṭ-Ṭartūshī, 170, 314 n. 138
ʿId al-Fiṭr, 64
ideal ruler, state, 189
idhrīṭūs, see *adhrīṭūs*
Idrīs (Enoch), 244
al-Idrīsī, 21, 167, 168, *171*
Idrīsid dynasty, 23, 128
Ifranja, 16. *See also* France
Ifrīqiya, 16, 21, 117, 133; often corresponds to the former Roman province of Africa, modern Tunisia, 96
Igu, *see* Hami
Ihyā' ʿUlūm ad-Dīn, 71
Īka, town, 168
Iki-oguz, 168
Iʿlām an-Nubalā' fī Ta'rīkh Ḥalab ash-Shahbā', 118
Ili river, 168
Iliad, books of, translated into Syriac, 212
Īliyā' (= Jerusalem), 77
ʿilj, 253
ʿilm al-hikma, 250
ʿilm ar-rijāl, 90
ʿImād ad-Dawla, Hūdid, 195
ʿImād ad-Dīn al-Kātib al-Iṣfahānī, 119
Imago Mundi, 156
Imām al-Maghāzī, 72
Imāmiyya, religious sect, 74
Imru' al-Qays, early Arab poet, 8 ff, 26 ff, 30, 32, 175; his *Muʿallaqa* quoted, 9, 27; *Dīwān* of, 27
Imru' al-Qays b. ʿAmr, 26
Imru' al-Qays b. Humām, *or* b. Khidhām, 27
Imru' al-Qays aṭ-Ṭaḥḥān, 300 n. 372 (= August Müller)
India, 7, 17; Abū Dulaf in,
Indian, books, 20; blade, Muḥammad likened to, 31; Ocean, 103; Mirror of Princes, 46
Indians, 40, 114
Inkiltara (= England), 160
Institut Français d'Archéologie Orientale du Caire, 193

Index

Index

women, seclusion of, 251; emancipation of, 251, cf. 255
wonders of the world, four, 295 n. 261
world summit, 154
Wright, W., 288 n. 113
Wüstenfeld, F., 52, 72, 75, 88, 95, 299 n. 345; *Die Geschichtschreiber der Araber und ihre Werke*, 283 n. 1; *Geschichte und Beschreibung der Stadt Mekka von el-Azraki*, 286 n. 72; *Genealogische Tabellen der arabischen Stämme und Familien*, 269 n. 6
Wycichl, W., 272 n. 61

Xativa, 195

Yaḥyā b. ʿAdī, pupil of al-Fārābī, 185
Yaḥyā al-Anṭākī, 298 n. 326
Yaḥyā b. Dhī'n-Nūn al-Ma'mūn, 260–1
Yaḥyā al-Ghazāl, 117, 127, *161 ff*
Yaḥyā b. Ḥakam al-Ghazāl, 161. *See also* Yaḥyā al-Ghazāl
Yaḥyā b. Khālid the Barmecide, 182, 292 n. 183
Yaḥyā b. Māsawayh, *see* Yūḥannā b. Māsawayh
Yaḥyā an-Naḥwī, 172
Yaḥyā b. Yūsuf b. Tāshifīn, 195
Yājūj, 110
Yale University Library, 129
al-Yamāma, 76
Yaman, al-Yaman, 9, 70, 76. *See also* Yemen
Yamīn ad-Dawla, *see* Maḥmūd of Ghazna
Yaqṭān, 3
Yaʿqūb al-Fasawī, historian, 94
Yaʿqūb b. Isḥāq al-Kindī, 105. *See also* al-Kindī
Yaʿqūb b. Zakariyyā' al-Kaskarī, 108
al-Yaʿqūbī, 87 f, 103; History (*Ta'rīkh*), 87 f, 103, 274 n. 87, 279 n. 102; *Kitāb al-Buldān*, 103, 163
Yāqūt, 35, 80, 120, 167, 169, 171; *Muʿjam al-Buldān*, 169, 272 n. 66; *Muʿjam al-Udabā'*, 120
Yarmūk, battle of the, 13
Yarshater, E., 312 n. 96
Yaʿrub b. Qaḥṭān, 3, 175
Yathrib, old name of Medina, 11
Yatīmat ad-Dahr fī Maḥāsin Ahl al-ʿAṣr, 55
Yazīd b. Muʿāwiya (Yazīd I), Umayyad Caliph, 13, 86, 207, 253; attacked Constantinople, 79
Yazdagird, last Sāsānid, 17, 88
Yemen, 8, 10, 32, 37
Yūḥannā b. Ḥaylān, 185
Yūḥannā b. Masawayh, *see* Mesue Senior
Yumn, 116
al-Yunīnī, 130
al-Yusāna, *see* Lucena

az-Zābaj, 99
zabarjad, 112
Zabibe, Arabian queen, 7
Zahīr ad-Dīn Muḥammad b. al-Ḥusayn al-Hamadhānī, 300 n. 378
Zahr al-Ādāb of al-Ḥusrī, 333 n. 17
zā'iraja, so-called science of, 242 ff; *zā'irajat al-ʿālam*, 243, 246; *z. Harawiyya*, 244; *z. Khiṭā'iyya*, 243; *z.* Shaybāniyya, 244; origin and derivation of the name, 245 f
Zanāta, 128
Zanj, of Iraq, 92; country of, (East Africa), 99
az-Zarqālī, 325 n. 9
Zaydiyya, Shīʿite group, 50
Zaytūna Mosque, Tunis, 127
Zedekiah, 116
zij, 246 (= astronomical table); *Zij* of Theon of Alexandria, 109, of Muḥammad b. Mūsā al-Khwārizmī, 296 n. 276, of al-Fazārī, 216
Zīrids, 23, 119
Ziyāda, Muḥammad M. 132, 304 n. 458
zoo-men, 98
Zotenberg, H., 59, 91
Zubayda, 58, 257 f
az-Zubayr b. al-ʿAwwām, 13, 72
Zuhayr, author of one of the *Muʿallaqāt*, 30
Zuhayr, Bahā' ad-Dīn, 68 f
az-Zuhrī, author of the *K. Jughrāfiyā*, 170
Zurayk, Professor Constantine, 301 n. 395